OXFORD CLASSICAL MONOGRAPHS

Published under the supervision of a Committee of the
Faculty of Literae Humaniores in the University of Oxford

The aim of the Oxford Classical Monograph series (which replaces the Oxford Classical and Philosophical Monographs) is to publish books based on the best theses on Greek and Latin literature, ancient history, and ancient philosophy examined by the Faculty Board of Literae Humaniores.

The *Andromache*
and Euripidean Tragedy

WILLIAM ALLAN

OXFORD
UNIVERSITY PRESS

OXFORD
UNIVERSITY PRESS

Great Clarendon Street, Oxford OX3 6DP

Oxford University Press is a department of the University of Oxford.
It furthers the University's objective of excellence in research, scholarship,
and education by publishing worldwide in

Oxford New York

Athens Auckland Bangkok Bogotá Buenos Aires Calcutta
Cape Town Chennai Dar es Salaam Delhi Florence Hong Kong Istanbul
Karachi Kuala Lumpur Madrid Melbourne Mexico City Mumbai
Nairobi Paris São Paulo Singapore Taipei Tokyo Toronto Warsaw

with associated companies in Berlin Ibadan

Oxford is a registered trade mark of Oxford University Press
in the UK and in certain other countries

Published in the United States
by Oxford University Press Inc., New York

© William Allan 2000

The moral rights of the author have been asserted
Database right Oxford University Press (maker)

First published 2000

British Library Cataloguing in Publication Data

Data available

Library of Congress Cataloging in Publication Data

Allan, William.
The Andromache and Euripidean tragedy / William Allan.
p. cm.—(Oxford classical monographs)
Includes bibliographical references (p.) and index.
1. Euripides. Andromache. 2. Andromache (Legendary character) in literature.
3. Women and literature—Greece. 4. Tragedy. I. Title. II. Series.
PA3973.A63 A45 2000
882'.01—dc21   99-054337
ISBN 0-19-815297-3

1 3 5 7 9 10 8 6 4 2

Typeset in Imprint
by Joshua Associates Ltd., Oxford
Printed in Great Britain
on acid-free paper by
Biddles Ltd., Guildford & King's Lynn

To the Memory of Rachel Allan

PREFACE

The *Andromache* has been called a strange play, a problem play, a political pamphlet, a *Haßgesang*. The present work studies this play, in the recent age so little loved, from various angles. I hope to draw attention to the neglected artistry of a very impressive and interesting text. The study has wider aspirations too: I relate a reading of the individual work to the discussion of Euripides' theatrical imagination in general. The play is examined closely: for itself, and in the context of other plays, and in that of the cultural and literary background. As a consequence, we may hope for some illumination on the interconnected cosmos, as it were, of one Euripidean creation, and on the larger interconnected cosmos of his *œuvre* as a whole. *ita res* (or so one may hope) *accendent lumina rebus*.

It is a pleasure to record some obligations incurred in the course of my research. The support of the Scottish Education Department made it possible for me to study Classics at the University of Edinburgh and to pursue graduate studies in Oxford. A Theodor Heuss Fellowship from the Alexander von Humboldt-Stiftung allowed me to complete the thesis, on which this book is based, at the Institut für Klassische Philologie in Munich. Particular thanks are due to my research supervisor, Professor Gregory Hutchinson, who, with remarkable patience and great learning, improved the thought, matter and form of the thesis in innumerable ways. My examiners, Dr Edith Hall and Dr Judith Mossman, provided much helpful criticism and encouragement, and Professor Oliver Taplin made invaluable comments on Chapter 5. Professor Jasper Griffin advised me on the development of the thesis into a book; his remarkable knowledge of Greek literature and his sensitivity to matters of style led to numerous improvements. My thanks go also to the staff of the Oxford University Press for their help in producing the book, especially Hilary O'Shea,

Georga Godwin, and Nigel Hope. Finally, I would like to pay tribute to my classics teachers, Mr David W. Potter and Mr †Charles S. Wallace, and to my tutor, Mr J. Gordon Howie, for their inspirational teaching and generous scholarship. I am deeply grateful to all of them.

W. R. A.

Oxford
January 1999

CONTENTS

ABBREVIATIONS

Tragic fragments are referred to in accordance with the *Tragicorum Graecorum Fragmenta* (= *TrGF* i–v), ed. B. Snell, R. Kannicht, and S. Radt (Göttingen, 1971–). Thus R refers to Radt's editions of Aeschylus and Sophocles (vols. iii and iv respectively). Note that K refers to the numbering in the forthcoming *TrGF* v (Euripides), ed. R. Kannicht. Where these numbers were unavailable, the numbering of Nauck² is used (= A. Nauck, *Tragicorum Graecorum Fragmenta*, 2nd edn. with *Supplementum* by B. Snell (Hildesheim, 1964)). Occasionally, reference is also made to Austin (= *Nova Fragmenta Euripidea in Papyris Reperta*, ed. C. Austin (Berlin, 1968)).

A&A	*Antike und Abendland*
AJP	*American Journal of Philology*
AM	*Athenische Mitteilungen*
ARV²	J. D. Beazley, *Attic Red-Figure Vase-Painters* (2nd edn., Oxford, 1963)
AW	*Antike Welt*
BICS	*Bulletin of the Institute of Classical Studies*
CA	*Classical Antiquity*
CAH², vol. v	*The Cambridge Ancient History, Volume V*, ed. D. M. Lewis, J. Boardman, J. K. Davies, and M. Ostwald (2nd edn., Cambridge, 1992)
CJ	*Classical Journal*
CPh	*Classical Philology*
CQ	*Classical Quarterly*
CR	*Classical Review*
DK	H. Diels and W. Kranz, *Die Fragmente der Vorsokratiker* (6th edn., Berlin, 1951–2)
EGF	M. Davies, *Epicorum Graecorum Fragmenta* (Göttingen, 1988) (= D)
FGrH	F. Jacoby, *Fragmente der griechischen Historiker* (Berlin, 1923–58)
G&R	*Greece and Rome*

GRBS	Greek, Roman and Byzantine Studies
HA	J. W. von Goethe, *Schriften zur Kunst und Literatur*, Hamburger Ausgabe vol. 12 (Munich, 1981)
HSCP	*Harvard Studies in Classical Philology*
ICS	*Illinois Classical Studies*
JHS	*Journal of Hellenic Studies*
LEC	*Les études classiques*
LSJ	H. G. Liddell and R. Scott, *A Greek–English Lexicon* (9th edn. rev. H. Stuart-Jones, Oxford, 1940; Suppl. 1968, 1996)
KA	R. Kassel and C. Austin, *Poetae Comici Graeci* (Berlin, 1983–)
LIMC	*Lexicon Iconographicum Mythologiae Classicae* (Zurich, 1981–97)
Mnem.	*Mnemosyne*
MW	R. Merkelbach and M. L. West (eds.), *Hesiodi Fragmenta Selecta* (3rd edn., Oxford, 1990)
*OCD*³	*Oxford Classical Dictionary* (3rd edn., ed. S. Hornblower and A. Spawforth, Oxford, 1996)
OCT	Oxford Classical Text
PCPS	*Proceedings of the Cambridge Philological Society*
PLLS	*Papers of the Leeds International Latin Seminar*
PMG	D. L. Page, *Poetae Melici Graeci* (Oxford, 1962)
PMGF	M. Davies, *Poetarum Melicorum Graecorum Fragmenta* (Oxford, 1991–) (= D)
QUCC	*Quaderni urbinati di cultura classica*
RE	*Real-Encyclopädie der klassischen Altertumswissenschaft* (Stuttgart, 1894–)
REG	*Revue des études grecques*
RhM	*Rheinisches Museum*
SIFC	*Studi italiani di filologia classica*
TAPA	*Transactions of the American Philological Association*
Voigt	E.-M. Voigt, *Sappho et Alcaeus* (Amsterdam, 1971)

W   M. L. West, *Iambi et Elegi Graeci*, i² (Oxford,
                     1989), ii² (Oxford, 1992)
WS   *Wiener Studien*
YCS   *Yale Classical Studies*

Introduction

Nessun maggior dolore
che ricordarsi del tempo felice
nella miseria.

Dante, *Inferno*, v. 121–3

Francesca da Rimini's words might well be applied to the experience of Andromache after the fall of Troy, shadowed by her happy past, and forced to endure the miserable and humiliating life of a slave and concubine in Greece. Euripides' *Andromache* is a rich, moving tragedy which expands the story of the Trojan captive in new and interesting ways. The relative critical neglect of the play is as unfortunate as it is puzzling.[1] The present work attempts to contribute both to an appreciation of the play in its own right, and to a wider understanding of the variety and quality of Euripides' tragedies.[2]

Increasingly, recent scholarship has produced substantial treatments of single plays.[3] This seems a promising way to make progress. Among other gains, it offers an opportunity to test, and to escape, some long-standing commonplaces about Euripidean tragedy. It often makes sense to treat Greek tragedy as a coherent body of literature, but we should not lose sight of the plurality and particularity of the surviving texts. There are family resemblances, as it were, between the various plays, but each represents a distinct dramatic essay. It is important,

---

[1] Neglect, indeed, may be too mild a word. The play has continually met with strong negative criticism, starting perhaps as early as the second hypothesis: τὸ δὲ δρᾶμα τῶν δευτέρων. For the debate on the meaning of this phrase (second-rate, second-prize quality, etc.), see Stevens (1971) 27–8. It is to be hoped that the *Andromache* will be better appreciated; cf. Wittgenstein (1984) 471 'The works of the great masters are suns which rise and set around us. Thus the time will return for every great work which is now set.'

[2] I shall normally cite from Diggle's OCT, noting difficulties or uncertainties where appropriate. The tragedies are referred to as a rule without authors' names (unless this is necessary to avoid confusion).

[3] For example, McDermott (1989) on the *Medea*, Goff (1990) on the *Hippolytus*, Croally (1994) on the *Troades*, Mossman (1995) on the *Hecuba*.

particularly with such a great writer, to get to grips with individual works. Concentrated study is especially desirable for the relatively neglected plays, because discussion of Euripides still tends very much to revolve around certain familiar plays and scenes. I shall seek to show that the *Andromache* is no less valuable than more celebrated plays for the exploration of fundamental aspects of Euripides' theatre.

The critical literature on the *Andromache* is frequently negative. Standard views of the play see it as, among other things, disjointed, melodramatic, and spoiled by anti-Spartan politicking. Of the play's structure, for example, Steidle has observed: 'In recent scholarship the unity of the play has been either totally denied or recognized only with considerable reservations.'[4] As to the atmosphere and effect of the *Andromache*, Page wrote: 'The play was probably very popular in the fourth and third centuries, being very exciting, a story of adventure and romance, sometimes almost melodramatic.'[5] Kitto, from another perspective, is even more dismissive of the play's tragic credentials: 'We might more correctly call it a political pamphlet which has the air of a tragedy'.[6]

Such widely shared views will be shown to rest on very questionable general assumptions.[7] Even for the appreciation of a particular tragedy, we need to conduct the study against the background of wider discussion: against an inquiry into what constitutes dramatic unity, rhetorical relevance, the 'tragic', and so forth. This study looks at the play from different perspectives, under the headings of various widely debated topics. This seemed more helpful for the larger consideration of Euripides than a long analysis of the play scene by scene. Discussion of the wider issues is concentrated at the start of each chapter, but it is also handled at other stages

---

[4] Steidle (1968) 118.

[5] Page (1934) 66.

[6] Kitto (1961) 236. For a bibliography of political interpretations of the play, see Tigerstedt (1965) 417 n. 92. Tragedy is now widely read as a subverter of *polis* discoure. But Friedrich (1996) 263–8 well expresses the hazards of allowing (p. 268) 'the big deconstructive machine of interpretative free-play to take over'. Nevertheless, recent work on the social and religious aspects of the dramatic festivals has enriched our appreciation of the civic context of tragedy.

[7] As we shall see, the play was more highly esteemed in earlier centuries.

where necessary. These remarks are prefatory to the close analysis of the *Andromache* which forms the heart of each chapter. Nevertheless, I hope that the union of detailed consideration with a view of larger issues will illuminate the general from the particular.

Euripides' plays, then, deserve careful, individual attention. I proceed on the assumption that the play will respond to detailed analysis. The successive chapters offer together a close reading of the *Andromache*, but always keeping in view the larger issues and the whole of Euripides' *œuvre*.

I
Myth

διὸ καὶ ὁ φιλόμυθος φιλόσοφός πώς ἐστιν. ὁ γὰρ μῦθος συγκεῖται ἐκ
θαυμασίων.

Thus the myth-lover is in a sense a philosopher. For myths consist of
wonders.

Aristotle *Met.* A, 982[b]18

Les œuvres antiques revivent, sous des jours divers, et en fonction
d'actualités diverses.

Jacqueline de Romilly[1]

One (still) very influential paradigm of Euripides' relation to
tragic myth runs as follows: encountering a fixed body of
traditional heroic tales, he exposed their intellectual absurdity
and hollow morality, and so heralded the end of tragedy as a
viable form of mythical discourse. The picture of Euripides as an
'Alexandrian before his time'[2] is widespread, but as this chapter
aspires to indicate, it cannot do justice to the multiplicity, or to
the seriousness, of his handling of the traditional story-patterns
of tragic myth. Consideration of some very basic aspects of the
nature and uses of myth will make it clear why the conception of
Euripides the debunking iconoclast cannot be right. Firstly, the
picture of a static body of myths, which Euripides subsequently
disturbs, is deeply unsatisfactory: the notion of myths as free-
standing cultural icons is an influential archetype, but quite
false. In reality myths are essentially protean both in form and in
meaning. The absence of an orthodox form of any myth underlies their suitability for literary adaptation.[3]

---

[1] de Romilly (1995) 42.
[2] Winnington-Ingram (1969) 132 with n. 37. McDermott (1991) 132 speaks
of Euripides' 'proto-Alexandrian literary sophistication', but while we may
accept that Euripides' self-consciousness about the use of myths is greater
than that of Aeschylus or Sophocles, this does not imply that his aim is to
expose their fictionality.
[3] Cf. Herington (1985) 66 on the myths as offering 'patterns of narrative . . .

This chapter surveys the extant literary sources for the myths appropriated by Euripides in the *Andromache*, and considers how and to what purpose his treatment differs from that of his predecessors. No one version of any myth could be called canonical or supremely authoritative. Genre mattered a great deal. The performance conventions of tragedy exerted different constraints from epic, choral lyric, or private story-telling.[4] Like all his contemporaries, Euripides will have come into contact with traditional tales, but it was part of his role as a tragedian to take what he had absorbed and adapt it to his dramatic purpose. We observe a poet skilfully exploiting the open-endedness and plasticity of myth with the aim of shaping original and engaging representations of human action.[5]

This emerges forcefully from the plays themselves. Consider, for example, Amphitryon's opening speech in the *Heracles*: Τίς τὸν Διὸς σύλλεκτρον οὐκ οἶδεν βροτῶν, | Ἀργεῖον Ἀμφιτρύων᾽ . . .; ('Who does not know of Argive Amphitryon, who shared Alcmene's bed with Zeus. . .?', 1 ff.). He begins with a long list of proper names, recalling his family's glorious past (1–12), and goes on to relate the misfortunes that have befallen him and his son, Heracles (13–25). But at line 26 he

in a repertoire of stories'. Yet their use in literature does not prevent myths from being adapted or invented for other ends, including political ones (consider, for example, Athenian adaptations of the myths concerning Theseus). Our emphasis on the aesthetic and literary qualities of myth is not incompatible with the structuralist/semiotic insight that myths are tied historically to specific cultures and their value systems. Cf. Barthes (1972) 110: 'Ancient or not, mythology can only have an historical foundation, for myth is a type of speech chosen by history: it cannot possibly evolve from the "nature" of things.' McDermott (1991) 123 and Goff (1990) 92 bring out the fluidity of the tradition and the multiple purposes to which a single myth can be put. The idea is important for such questions as: how do the variant stories concerning the figures of the *Andromache* fit with the idea of myths as repositories of truth? Or in what way is the myth's 'meaning' separable from the individual text?

[4] As an additional indication of the malleability of myth, one need only consider the conjunction of the three tragedies with the performance of a satyr play, where the dignity of heroic myth is sent up by a chorus of ithyphallic satyrs.

[5] Cf. Burkert (1987) 77: 'Without a need for consistency, but rather with an affection for details, myth communicates living experience.'

introduces a new feature to the myth, the usurper Lycus.[6] Thus his opening words, 'Who does not know of Amphitryon?', suggest a familiar myth, but this impression is subsequently complicated by the novel addition: he is saying, in other words, 'You, the audience, may know my story, but you have never heard this λόγος ("version") before!' Amphitryon's list of great ancestors implies that these are famous folk who are worth listening to, while his speech as a whole announces that *this* story about them is *new*. The appeal to fame and novelty is programmatic for plays like this, including the *Andromache*.

In Greek tragedy the literary, generic, and expressive purposes of the myths are always to the fore. There is often a tension between the heroic world of myth and the contemporary relevance of the action; this is part of the complex relationship between the fictional world of the play and that of the audience.[7] Euripides exploits this 'tug' for his own expressive ends. His plays are too complex to be analysed solely in terms of 'demythologization', or to be seen as using (and simultaneously exposing) a mythological veneer. Greek literature since Homer was dominated by the presumption that the proper subject of serious poetry is myth.[8] Euripides stands in the centre of this tradition, while at the same time working in a genre 'which decisively affected the course of Greek mythological narration'.[9] The skilful adaptation of myth is part of each play's exploration of themes and its construction of significant content. While other versions of a myth are relevant, Euripides' aim is not primarily polemical or meta-dramatic. The *Andromache* is a play whose dramatic resourcefulness in the combination of traditional, and in the creation of new, mythic material has been gravely undervalued. Both aspects of the playwright's use of myth are fundamental to the creative

[6] Bond (1981) xxviii remarks: 'The elaborate introduction of Lycus . . . points clearly to Euripidean invention.'

[7] In tragedy, as opposed to comedy, what is being presented as happening on stage is in the past, and usually the very remote past. Friedrich (1996) 275 is eloquent on the way tragedy ponders civic discourse 'by translating its inherent tensions into dramatic conflicts in the medium of heroic myth'.

[8] Cf. Gale (1994) 129: 'the idea of an entirely non-mythological poem was virtually alien to classical literature.' Nevertheless, Parmenides and Empedocles, for example, show how very different poems could in fact be.

[9] Buxton (1994) 31–2.

shaping of the plot. The interaction of inherited myth and fictional freedom powers creative originality.[10]

The treatment of myth plays such an important role in our perception of Greek tragedy, as well as in our understanding of the constitution of the Greek *Weltbild*, that it is hardly surprising that many strong claims have been made for its broader cultural significance.[11] But what are we to understand by the term 'myth'? This foundational question is notoriously problematic, and has generated a scholarly debate which has destroyed forests.[12] A broad working definition has been formulated by Burkert: 'myth is a traditional tale with secondary, partial reference to something of collective importance'.[13] More pertinently to our discussion of tragedy, the same scholar has suggested how such a cultural amalgam may be used as a tool of world-description through *narrative*: 'Myth is applied narrative. It describes a meaningful, supra-individual, collectively important reality.'[14] Importantly, myths were ubiquitous,

[10] Cf. Kermode (1966) 39. Zeitlin's (1980: 52) opposition of myth ('the relatively closed and predetermined form') to fiction ('marked by a receptivity to experimentation and change') is to impose modern notions on a fundamentally different Greek tradition. Sorum (1995) 372 claims misleadingly that in the *Andromache* Euripides is 'simply filling the lacunae within existing narratives'. Graf (1993) 152 ff. speculates that the increase in written texts in the fifth century caused the myths 'to lose their almost limitless capacity for adaptation'. However, he has no secure evidence for this. Fifth-century Athens was not a 'book-dominated culture': see Thomas (1994), esp. p. 37.

[11] A brief sample: Knox (1979) 23: 'It [tragic myth] was a vision of the past shaped by the selective adaptation of the oral tradition to forms symbolic of the permanencies in human nature and the human condition.' Segal (1986) 23: 'The function of myth is to mediate fundamental contradictions in human existence, man's relation to man in society, and man's relation to nature in the external world.' Nagy (1990) 8 goes further: 'From the standpoint of the given society that it articulates, myth *is* the primary reality.' There are some good remarks on the 'timelessness' of myth in Steiner (1967) 199–200 and Havel (1986) 158. As Griffin (1998) 59 notes, many myths relate to 'primitive and universal taboos and anxieties'; cf. Burkert (1996) ch. 3.

[12] For a brief summary of theories, ancient and modern, see Dowden (1992) 22–38 and Graf (1993) 9–56.

[13] Burkert (1979c) 23. With regard to the 'collectivist Golden Age' view of Greece, Feeney (1998) 60–63 has rightly stressed the diversity and pluralism of Greek society (above all in the innovating archaic period, when many of the mythical story-patterns took shape). In this context to picture Euripides as the destroyer of a monolithic mythical tradition seems quite false.

[14] Burkert (1979b) 29.

a staple of education, and an essential aspect of religious worship and civilized life. The pervasiveness and wide diffusion of myth, from tragic competitions to vase-painting, mean that we must reckon with 'a wide spectrum of different kinds of story and discourse' which are all, despite their manifold provenance, 'evidence for how the Greeks talked about the world'.[15] Tragic myth is thus only one part of 'the perpetual reshaping of mythology, that process without beginning or end'.[16] Understanding of Greek myth has improved remarkably in the past two centuries.[17] It is now generally recognized that myths are more than quaint fictions, that they form a complex interlocking network of events whose value as interpretations of experience, and not just as objects of creative beauty or sources of entertainment, is very high.

Before turning in detail to the constitution of myth in the *Andromache*, it will be helpful to touch on the reception and criticism of myth in Greek literature before Euripides. The divine myths of Homer and Hesiod, for example, were attacked for their immorality by Xenophanes (DK 21 frr. 11–16). The attempts of Pherecydes and Hellanicus among others to systematize and rationalize the myths point to a science of *mythopoiia* well before Hellenistic times.[18] The tendency to collect and order heroic and cosmogonic myth is seen as early as Hesiod's *Theogony* and *Catalogue of Women*. Herodotus occasionally questions the veracity of the mythic tradition,[19] as when he posits two Heracles, one mortal, one divine, on the basis (allegedly) of information from the Egyptian priests of Memphis and his own subsequent research in Phoenicia and Thasos (2. 43. 4 ff.; cf. 3. 122 on the legend of Minos).[20] The

---

[15] Bowie (1993) 7. On the profusion and adaptability of myth, cf. Fuqua (1976) 94 and Pozzi and Wickersham (1991) 6–10. The complexity of life demands a flexible use of myth if poetry is to capture it at all: see Schaper (1968) 94–5. [16] Parker (1996) 86.

[17] Burkert (1979a) skilfully relates the treatment of mythology to wider cultural debates since the early nineteenth century.

[18] Socrates playfully criticizes such attempts at rationalization, Pl. *Phdr.* 229c–230a. Consider also the *Tragoidoumena* of the fourth-century Asclepiades of Tragilus (*FGrH* 12); and, of course, *c*.525, Theagenes (DK 8) (allegory) and, *c*.500, Hecataeus (*FGrH* 1 F 1, 19, 26, etc.) (rationalization).

[19] See Pelliccia (1992) 81 ff.

[20] However, Herodotus' criticisms of the poets did not prevent Thucydides

fictionality of *mythoi* was criticized by both historians and philosophers, who set against it their own avowed interest in plausibility, consistency, and truth.[21] It has been argued that in tragedy the 'truthfulness' of myth is generally not an issue,[22] as if extraneous scepticism would jeopardize the emotional and intellectual impact of the drama. However, numerous passages attest creative engagement with this very issue: the chorus of the *Medea*, for example, reject *man*-made myths (*Med.* 410–30), Amphitryon and Lycus argue over Heracles' status as an archer and hero (*Her.* 151–64, 174–203), while the aetiology of the name of the Areopagus is contested in the *Eumenides* (Aesch. *Eum.* 685–90).[23]

Poets and their public were well aware of the distancing and elevating effect of myth. We can see a tendency to relate historical figures to the world of myth in Simonides' elegy on the battle of Plataea (fr. 11 W), where the treatment of the Persian Wars draws on that of the Trojan.[24] So patterns of mythical description influence the commemoration of historical events: this is most evident in epinician lyric[25] and in vase-painting, where battles against the Persians are modelled on scenes of mythical struggle, for example against Amazons and Centaurs.

from impugning his acceptance of τὸ μυθῶδες ('the fantastic', Thuc. 1. 21. 1; cf. 1. 22. 4).

[21] On Plato's ambivalent attitude to myth, see Rutherford (1995) 171 ff. Veyne (1988) 17 argues too indiscriminately that in Greek mythology 'the distinction between fiction and reality had yet to be made and the legendary element was serenely accepted.'

[22] See Stinton (1990) ch. 14. Cf. Sim. fr. 598 *PMG*: τὸ δοκεῖν καὶ τὰν ἀλάθειαν βιᾶται ('appearance compels even truth').

[23] The plausibility of the Judgement of Paris is the theme of a particularly disconcerting speech by Hecuba (*Tro.* 969 ff.).

[24] See Parsons (1992) 32–3; Boedeker and Sider (1996), esp. p. 223 on the sack of Troy as a 'paradigm for recent events'; and Hall (1996a) 7–9 on Aesch. *Pers.* Herington (1985) 129 examines the uniqueness of the Persian Wars in this respect: 'this historical episode *alone* seems to have been accepted almost instantaneously into the corpus of inherited myth'. Cf. Phrynichus' *Capture of Miletus* (by the Persians in 494, *TrGF* 1, 3 T 2) and *Persians* (about their defeat in 480–479, *TrGF* 1, 3 T 1); also relevant is Choerilus' late fifth-century historical epic *Persica*.

[25] Cf. Richardson (1992) 228: 'For Pindar and Bacchylides past and present are inseparable, and the present only has meaning in the light of the past. It is not really possible in these poets to separate history from mythology.'

A few words are necessary too on the subject of innovation in myth. The pre-Euripidean sources are fragmentary; we cannot hope to recover all the variant forms of any given myth. So we can never be certain that Euripides is actually inventing a new version. Yet this is not of fundamental importance, since we are more interested in the peculiar effects of Euripides' deployment of the myths. Our response to the uniqueness of the *Helen* is not diminished by our knowledge of Stesichorus,[26] nor that of the *Andromache* by Sophocles' *Hermione*. (We might indeed be inclined to think that the existence of previous versions will allow us to appreciate better the originality of Euripides' treatment. But the absence of such evidence does not entail devaluation of our response to the extant work.) The transformation of inherited story-patterns into the plots of tragedy is a complex act, a creative response to an established literary tradition.[27] Nevertheless, it is hard to believe that a new tragedy will not have sought to illuminate traditional material from unfamiliar perspectives, if not actually introducing innovations of varying magnitude.[28] Because one cannot conclusively prove innovation,[29] the central issues for us will be the coherence of the mythic material within the world of the heroic fiction, and its contribution to the overall shape and meaning of the play.

Euripides' attitude to myth is often called intellectual (and this is usually intended as a criticism). Before turning to the specific example of the *Andromache*, it is important to consider

[26] On the relation between the two, see Austin (1994) ch. 4, Kannicht (1969) i. 26–41.

[27] Mossman (1995) 19 remarks that 'the process remains to a large extent mysterious'. Easterling (1993) 567 makes a good point (correcting Zeitlin (1980) 53, who exaggerates the peculiarity of the *Orestes*): 'intertextual reference is a major feature of all the Greek tragedy we know, and not a symptom of *fin-de-siècle* fatigue'.

[28] This was indeed almost a competitive necessity; cf. Burian (1997) 185: 'The very fact that the same material was dramatised again and again must have encouraged the impulse to vary and reshape so as to outmanoeuvre expectation.' The idea of a myth's 'standard features' is well discussed by Stinton (1990) 464.

[29] By contrast with Homer and Sophocles (*Od.* 11. 271–80 (Epikaste) ~ *OT fin.*, *Ant.* 53–4), Euripides has Jocasta live on to remonstrate with her sons in the *Phoenissae*, a version which we now know to have been used by Stesichorus (fr. 222(b) *PMGF*).

the extent of Euripides' innovation *vis-à-vis* Aeschylus and
Sophocles, since the radicalism of Euripides is sometimes
exaggerated.[30] The transformation of the Erinyes in the
Eumenides is strikingly new. Sophocles' decision to make
Lemnos a desert island, and not populated as in Aeschylus
and Euripides (cf. Dio Chrys. *Or.* 52), accentuates Philoctetes'
marginalization from human contact and heroic society. A
reasonable case can even be made for the invention of hero-
cult in the *Oedipus Coloneus*;[31] yet it is not emphasized in the
way that one would expect from Euripides. We can imagine
the pressure to handle stock myths differently from his two
great predecessors (one of whom was still a rival). But
Euripides shows not merely a desire for novelty. He allows
us to see that he was influenced by sophistic criticism and
revision of myths to a greater extent than Aeschylus and
Sophocles. And, as the *Andromache* illustrates, he recasts
mythical data with especial zest.[32] But rather than viewing
him as pointing out logical improbabilities and giving the
myths a modern stamp of sophistication, as Gorgias did in
his reworking of the *Helen* and *Palamedes* stories, it is important to seek for the dramatic justification and effect of Euripides' (sometimes self-conscious) alterations.

For it is vital to bear in mind that the tragedians' skill in
inventing, adapting, and reshaping myths is part of a well-
exampled tradition in Greek poetry.[33] The outspoken mythical
revisionism of Pindar is striking in its overt moralizing: σὲ δ'
ἀντία προτέρων φθέγξομαι ('Pelops, I shall tell your story in

---

[30] Graf (1993) 5 makes a common but dubious link: 'Euripides, who
deviated farthest from the tradition, also gained the fewest victories.'

[31] Kearns (1989) 50 ff., 208–9 doubts this.

[32] We must imagine, for example, an *Oedipus* in which the hero does not
blind himself, but is blinded by servants: ἡμεῖς δὲ Πολύβου παῖδ' ἐρείσαντες
πέδωι | ἐξομματοῦμεν καὶ διόλλυμεν κόρας ('We dragged Polybus' son to the
ground and blinded him, destroying his eyes', fr. 84 Austin). We can only
guess as to the manifold differences in dramatic tone and psychological impact
between this version and Sophocles'. Euripides' *Antigone* probably ended
with Antigone and Haemon being saved from death by Dionysus: see
Xanthakis-Karamanos (1986) 109.

[33] On Homer's adaptations and inventions, cf. Rutherford (1996) 6–7 with
n. 16. Edmunds (1997) considers Homer's myths in specific relation to the
tradition of oral storytelling (pp. 420, 440), and notes how his characters
themselves invent new versions of myths (p. 428).

opposition to those before', *Ol.* 1. 36).[34] He is free even to question the inaccuracy introduced by Homer's excessive effectiveness on his audience: thus in speaking of Odysseus' renown, he declares,

ἐγὼ δὲ πλέον' ἔλπομαι
λόγον 'Οδυσσέος ἢ πάθαν
διὰ τὸν ἁδυεπῆ γενέσθ' "Ομηρον·
. . . σοφία
δὲ κλέπτει παράγοισα μύθοις.
Nem. 7. 20–3[35]

I even think that through Homer's sweet poetry Odysseus' reputation is greater than his experience merits. . . . Poetic skill uses myths to deceive.

The χάρις of poetry (cf. *O.* 1. 30–1, *N.* 4. 7–9) authenticates the complex embellishments and revisions and makes the incredible credible.[36] Pindar chooses his myth with particular care:[37] the atmosphere and impact of the ode is deeply affected by it. Often he uses a story derived from the native tradition of the victor's city. The selection of such material lends the moral illustration particular authority. The deployment of myth in tragedy is both subtler and more ambiguous. The moral dilemmas of the epic heroes still power the tragic dramas of fifth-century Athens. But epic values are scrutinized, modified, or rejected from the different perspective of the fifth century. Rather than efface or excise the moral ambiguities implicit in the narratives of heroic myth, the tragedians put them at the centre of their representation of the heroic world. By running these complex and unsettling heroic myths 'through the filter of the democratic *polis*',[38] tragedy challenges the dominant values of its time.

As was mentioned above, our knowledge of the mythical

[34] See Stinton (1990) 244–7; Hutchinson (1988) 12–13 notes Pindar's playfulness but stresses his magnificence.

[35] On the interaction of poetry and truth in the archaic period, cf. Pratt (1993) 11–17.

[36] Feeney (1991) 16 ff. is eloquent on the complexity of Pindaric 'truth'. Cf. Detienne (1981) 96 ff. on Pindar's selection (and invention) of morally acceptable *mythoi*.

[37] The point is made by Willcock (1995) 13.

[38] Buxton (1994) 32.

material available to the tragic poets is severely depleted by the fragmentary preservation of the poetry of the epic cycle and lyric period. But in the case of the *Andromache* (all of whose main characters, excepting Hermione, are major figures of the epic tradition) we possess enough information regarding the central myths and their variations to observe Euripides' flexible, eclectic approach to this material. Neoptolemus is the pivotal figure of the myths underlying the *Andromache*, but appears in the play only as a corpse. This has triggered a great deal of concern about the unity of the play which will be considered in Chapter 2. The few references to him in Homeric epic are supplemented by the Cyclic poems, where he takes a more prominent role in the latter stages of fighting at Troy and in the return to peaceful life in Greece, symbolized by his marriage to Hermione (*Od.* 4. 3–9).[39] In the *Andromache* Euripides takes the epic motif of restored domestic normality and explores the troubled consequences of the marriage in post-war Greece.

The *Andromache* reveals a contrast between concubinage abroad and at home. At the end of the embassy of *Iliad* Book 9, as Achilles and Patroclus go to bed, each of them has a companion from Scyros: 'Achilles feels no need to sleep alone in the absence of Briseis.'[40] On the plain of Troy, where the wives of the Greeks are far away, the use of captive women can cause no marital friction. The *Andromache* depicts the consequences for Achilles' son of exercising such concubinage back in Greece. The play's reflections on legitimacy are enriched by the mythical background to Neoptolemus' own birth. In one version Achilles landed at Scyros during a storm and married the princess Deidameia, who later gave birth to Neoptolemus (*Cypria* 32. 50–2 D; we hear he is being brought up on Scyros at *Il.* 19. 326–33).[41] The Cyclic poems in their extant form do not mention any violence by Achilles. However,

[39] For the Myrmidons' safe return to Greece, see *Od.* 3. 188–9.

[40] Griffin (1995) on 9. 663.

[41] Hermione's contempt for Neoptolemus' island birthplace illuminates her own obsession with wealth and 'true' Greekness (209–12). *Cypria* fr. incert. loc. 4 D relates a very unHomeric version in which Achilles begets Neoptolemus while hiding among the girls of Scyros. Accius' tragedy *Neoptolemus* told how Phoenix brought Neoptolemus from Scyros to Troy, despite Deidameia's unwillingness: cf. Dangel (1995) 145–8, 307–9.

Il. 9. 667–8 report Achilles' capture of Scyros and suggest
Neoptolemus' mother was a captive. This very origin offers
significant connections and contrasts with the situation in
Andromache. In the epic tradition 'Achilles' son is not thought
to suffer any social disadvantage from his father's failure to
marry his mother.'[42] In the *Andromache*, by contrast, Euripides
focuses on the precarious status of a captive-woman's child,
here Neoptolemus' own son.

Andromache herself was of course a familiar figure in the
mythical complex surrounding the Trojan War and one particularly suited to Euripides' exploration of the displacement
and degradation of the defeated in the aftermath of war.[43] From
her first appearance in the *Iliad* (6. 398 ff.), Andromache is one
of the epic's most poignant symbols of the loss inflicted by war,
and her role defines the contrast between the spheres of war
and peace, men and women.[44] The minor role of Andromache
in post-Homeric epic leaves Euripides considerable scope for
innovation.[45] He takes up features of her epic role, but
pointedly elaborates their impact by setting Andromache
herself in conflict with enemy Greeks, both male and female,
and in a domestic context which magnifies both her own
heroism and the pettiness of her persecutors.[46] Strikingly,

---

[42] West *et al.* (1988) 193 on *Od.* 4. 5.

[43] Cf. Segal (1971a) 55: 'With her maternal and conjugal tenderness, her
rich feminine emotionality, her intelligence and sharp-sighted realism quickened by intense involvement, she is the bearer of the suffering of all the
women in the war, and perhaps of all women in all war.' On Andromache's
fertile *Rezeption* in poetry, drama, painting, and especially opera, see Reid
(1993) 102–4 and de Romilly (1995), ch. 2. Racine's *Andromaque* (1667) took
over as the formative force on subsequent work inspired by the legend.
Ambrose Philips wrote a close adaptation of Racine's play, *The Distrest
Mother* (1712), which emphasized 'extremes of pathos, violence, and madness'
(Bevis (1988) 144); it enjoyed great success (with help from favourable reviews
in *The Spectator*: see Boas (1953) 125–9) and remained in the repertoire
throughout the eighteenth century. Racine's version underlies, most recently,
Craig Raine's *1953*, first produced in London in 1995. Mossman (1995) 13 n.
26 correctly points out Racine's (non-Euripidean) emphasis on the 'romantic
possibilities of the story'.   [44] See Arthur (1981), Griffin (1995) 42–3.

[45] Cf. *LIMC* I I s.v. Andromache (Touchefeu-Meynier, p. 767) 'The
sufferings of Andromache in Greece are scarcely represented in art.'

[46] The touching humanity of the domestic scene in *Iliad* 6, with its
insistence on Hector's heroism, points the contrast; cf. de Romilly (1995)
29–32.

Euripides has recast the Homeric picture of the intimate devotion of Hector and Andromache, when he makes Andromache recall her own self-sacrifice in suckling Hector's bastards (222–7).[47] The remark, too often isolated from its rhetorical context (which is discussed in Chapter 4 below), is neither 'a mark of realism'[48] nor intended to frustrate our sympathy for Andromache.[49] This would be ruinous of the scene's effect, which is to contrast the character of the two women and their rival conceptions of feminine virtue. Andromache's apostrophe of Hector (σε . . . σοῖς . . . σοι, 223–5), and the unepic novelty of her thought, combine to enforce her claim to excellence: καὶ ταῦτα δρῶσα τῆι ἀρετῆι προσηγόμην | πόσιν ('By doing this I secured my husband's love with my loyalty', 226–7).

The scholia to *Andr.* 24 indicate that the bearing of children by Andromache to Neoptolemus was part of the epic tradition; but while some sources mention as many as three sons and a daughter,[50] Euripides has for poignant dramatic effect chosen to make 'Molossus' the only offspring of their union: ὃς δ' ἔστι παῖς μοι μόνος ('who is my only son', 47). The change heightens the threat made by the jealous and barren Hermione to the child's safety; it also deliberately echoes the motif of the single son, which is very much part of Andromache's grief in her Iliadic laments (e.g. *Il.* 6. 476–81, 22. 484–507, 24. 732–8; cf. *Od.* 16. 118–20). The death and murder of the young mark key points in the myths surrounding the Trojan War. The sparing

---

[47] Whitman (1974) 124 exaggerates: 'Nowhere in Euripides is the diminution of heroic stature so complete and wholesale'; but this is connected to his overall opinion of the play, which is far from enthusiastic: cf. 123 'the play as it stands is not myth at all . . . it is a domestic triangle, quite on the low mimetic level . . . perhaps the least elevated work that has come down to us.' Hellanicus of Lesbos mentions Hectoridae (*FGrH* 4 F 31), a tradition perhaps drawn on here. (On the relative chronology of Euripides and Hellanicus see *FGrH* 323a and Jacoby (1956) 263 ff. The work in question, the *Troica*, seems undatable.) The theme of bastard sons is presumably prompted partly at least by Priam's many *nothoi* (cf. *Il.* 24. 248–51, 253–64, 5. 472–6). But the idea is here 'unpacked' in typically Euripidean fashion (cf. the theme of brother–sister incest in the *Aeolus*).

[48] Kamerbeek (1943) 58.

[49] Cf. Michelini (1987) 92–3, who thinks the audience 'may be tempted to agree with Hermione that barbarians are queer folk'.

[50] Cf. Nilsson (1951) 107. For Andromache's later children by Helenus and

of Paris lies at the war's remotest origin: the chorus of the *Andromache* lament Hecuba's failure to kill her son, fated to be μεγάλαν Πριάμου πόλεως λώβαν ('great ruin of Priam's city', 298). At the war's end there is the sacrifice of Polyxena (cf. *Hec.* 521 ff., where her killer is Neoptolemus) and the murder of Astyanax (again, in some versions, attributed to Neoptolemus: *Il. Parv.* frr. 20–1 D). The threat to Andromache's second son repeats the pattern of Greek violence against Trojans; but the killing of a potentially dangerous enemy (a revenge theme bogusly reiterated by Menelaus: 515–22) is now complicated by the child's mixed parentage.

Before considering the full extent of Euripides' adaptations and innovations in *Andromache*, we might pause to consider Sophocles' handling of an earlier episode in the myth: the conflict in the betrothing of Hermione.[51] Little of his *Hermione* survives: two citations, one of a line, one of a single word (*TrGF* iv. 192–3), but Eustathius gives us the plot (Eust. Od. 1479, 19 (*TrGF* iv. 192)): Σοφοκλῆς δέ, φασίν, ἐν Ἑρμιόνηι ἱστορεῖ ἐν Τροίαι ὄντος ἔτι Μενελάου ἐκδοθῆναι τὴν Ἑρμιόνην ὑπὸ τοῦ Τυνδάρεω τῶι Ὀρέστηι, εἶτα ὕστερον ἀφαιρεθεῖσαν αὐτοῦ ἐκδοθῆναι τῶι Νεοπτολέμωι κατὰ τὴν ἐν Τροίαι ὑπόσχεσιν. αὐτοῦ δὲ Πυθοῖ ἀναιρεθέντος ὑπὸ Μαχαιρέως, ὅτε τὸν Ἀπόλλω τινύμενος τὸν τοῦ πατρὸς ἐξεδίκει φόνον, ἀποκαταστῆναι αὖθις αὐτὴν τῶι Ὀρέστηι· ἐξ ὧν γενέσθαι τὸν Τισαμενόν, φερωνύμως οὕτω κληθέντα παρὰ τὴν μετὰ μένους τίσιν, ἐπεὶ ὁ πατὴρ Ὀρέστης ἐτίσατο τοὺς φονεῖς τοῦ Ἀγαμέμνονος.[52] Comparison with Euripides brings out the

Pergamus (recorded in Pausanias), see *RE* s.v. 'Andromache' (vol. 1, cols. 2151–2).

[51] Friedrich (1953) 52 confidently asserts, though with little argument, the precedence of *Hermione*; a more convincing case is made by Stephanopoulos (1980) 62–6.

[52] 'Sophocles, it is said, in his *Hermione* tells of how, while Menelaus was still at Troy, Hermione was betrothed to Orestes by Tyndareus. Later she was taken from him and betrothed to Neoptolemus in accordance with the promise made at Troy. But Neoptolemus was killed in Delphi by Machaireus, when he was chastizing Apollo and demanding an apology for the death of his father, and Hermione was restored to Orestes. They begat Tisamenus, so called after the violent punishment which his father meted out to the killers of Agamemnon.' Sutton (1984) 57–61 looks for evidence of Sophocles' play in Pacuvius' *Hermiona*, which is set in Delphi (as was perhaps Sophocles'). In it Neoptolemus comes to ask about Hermione's barrenness (a motif known elsewhere in the fifth century: Pherecydes *FGrH* 3 F 64a), while Orestes

distinctive contours of his tragedy. In Sophocles, according to Eustathius, during Menelaus' absence at Troy, Tyndareus betrothes Hermione to Orestes. However, her father has promised Hermione to Neoptolemus at Troy, and on his return to Sparta fulfils the promise (cf. *Od.* 4. 6–7). By contrast with Sophocles, Euripides stresses the duplicitous role of Menelaus. He, not Tyndareus, promised Hermione to Orestes and later reneged on his undertaking (966–70). Addressing Hermione, Orestes specifically blames the breakdown of trust on σοῦ πατρὸς κάκηι ('your father's treachery', 967).[53]

The plays' explanations of Neoptolemus' arrival in Delphi are significantly different. Sophocles depicts Neoptolemus seeking restitution for his father's death, while in the *Andromache* this visit lies in the past, and Neoptolemus' new purpose is to apologize and to negotiate a reconciliation. This second visit, as we shall see, is likely to be a Euripidean innovation, whose effect is to rehabilitate Neoptolemus. The most notable thing about the *Hermione*, however, is the scope of the play. There is no exploitation of Andromache or Peleus. It is a distinctive, and very likely original, feature of Euripides' play that it combines the stories of Hermione and Andromache, wife and concubine. This indeed is the crucial conception in Euripides, and it is foregrounded by the absence

comes pursued by his mother's Furies. There is an angry confrontation between the two heroes. Orestes complains he has been unjustly robbed of Hermione, and accuses Neoptolemus of coveting Menelaus' Spartan kingship: see D'Anna (1967) 97–107, 208–12. Gentili (1979) 33 even claims extensive *contaminatio* from the *Andromache*, but the surviving fragments of Pacuvius' play are too meagre to support this. Pacuvius may well have drawn on sources more extensive than Sophocles and Euripides. Of Livius Andronicus' *Hermiona* only one line survives (in which Andromache addresses, Anchialus (or Amphialus?), her son by Neoptolemus) and we know next to nothing about its plot; cf. Fraenkel (1931) 602.

[53] The scholiast on *Andr.* 32 states that Philocles and Theognis (before *Andr.*?; *TrGF* i. 24 F 2, 28 F 2) presented Hermione as already betrothed by Tyndareus to Orestes, and pregnant by him, before being given by Menelaus to Neoptolemus. Euripides avoids such detail since it would reflect badly on Neoptolemus as well as Menelaus. So too with the feature in Ovid, *Her.* 8, which may stem from Sophocles' play (cf. Σ on *Od.* 4. 4), where Neoptolemus seizes Hermione by force. The scholia on *Andr.* 53 record a version in which Menelaus decides to marry Hermione to Orestes after all (hence breaking the agreement before Troy) and himself kills Neoptolemus.

of Neoptolemus, another significant difference from the *Hermione*. Seeing the unrealized dramatic potential of their jealous confrontation, Euripides has coupled this with the more familiar rivalry of Orestes and Neoptolemus for Hermione. (In Sophocles' play, Hermione is returned to Orestes and bears him a son, Tisamenus.)[54] Euripides can thus stage his central *agon* between two women (arguing over a man) instead of two men (fighting for a woman), a feature with novel dramatic possibilities.[55] Hermione's failure and calamity link her rescue by Orestes to the death of Neoptolemus, which collapses both triangles and allows the poet to give his plot a tragic end in the grief and desolation of Peleus.

The tragic effect of the *Andromache* works through a novel meshing of disparate personal fortunes, each with their origins in the disruption of war: Andromache's loss of Hector and deportation as a slave; Hermione's barrenness and enforced marriage; Orestes' tainted history as a matricide, itself a distant

---

[54] Tisamenus was later dethroned by the Heracleidae: cf. *TGrF* iii. 192 f., Apollod. 2. 8. 2–3, Strabo 8. 7. 1. The marriage of Hermione and Orestes, and the union of Sparta and Argos, is unsuccessful, in contrast to the flourishing dynasty vouchsafed the descendants of Andromache and Neoptolemus by Thetis (1243 ff.). Calame (1987) 174–5 explains this in terms of deviant inheritance (a recurring idea in *Andr.*): 'Orestes becomes heir to the Argive power as well as the Spartan; but this concentration, coinciding with an alliance between doubly parallel cousins, is by definition doomed to failure.'

[55] The 'catfight' over a man is a remarkable feature, which some ancient critics disliked, presumably thinking it sordid and disruptive of tragic dignity. Their disdain prompted one exceptionally sensitive scholiast to protest, stressing the play's seriousness: οἱ φαύλως ὑπομνηματισάμενοι ἐγκαλοῦσι τῶι Εὐριπίδηι φάσκοντες ἐπὶ τραγικοῖς προσώποις κωμωιδίαν αὐτὸν διατεθεῖσθαι. γυναικῶν τε γὰρ ὑπονοίας κατ' ἀλλήλων καὶ ζήλους καὶ λοιδορίας καὶ ἄλλα ὅσα εἰς κωμωιδίαν συντελεῖ, ἐνταῦθα ἀπαξάπαντα τοῦτο τὸ δρᾶμα περιειληφέναι. ἀγνοοῦσιν· ὅσα εἰς τραγωιδίαν συντελεῖ, ταῦτα περιέχει ἐν τέλει, τὸν θάνατον τοῦ Νεοπτολέμου καὶ τὸν θρῆνον Πηλέως, ἅπερ ἐστὶ τραγικά (Σ on *Andr.* 32). ('Inferior commentators reproach Euripides, alleging that he has settled comedy upon tragic characters. For women's suspicions about one another and their jealousies and insults and other things which make up comedy, all of these things are contained in this play. They are wrong. For as to what contributes to tragedy, this is included at the end, the death of Neoptolemus and the grief of Peleus, which are truly tragic.') In Propertius 4. 8. 51 ff. Cynthia attacks one of the poet's new girlfriends at a party, scratching her rival's cheeks with her nails: *spectaculum capta nec minus urbe fuit* ('the scene was as horrific as the sack of a city', 56); cf. Hubbard (1974) 152–6 for the poet's play with epic motifs.

repercussion of Iphigenia's sacrifice at Aulis; and Neoptolemus' death, which is motivated on both human and divine levels, as the result both of a disastrous marriage and of Apollo's harsh vengeance. Under the aspect of Greek tragic myth as 'a web of interlocking family histories',[56] Euripides develops this feature with particular ingenuity, and articulates with great pathos and intensity the repercussions of war for the family life of three separate households.[57]

The action of the *Andromache* takes place when the ashes of Troy are long cold and the chief Homeric heroes slain, yet in a tumultuous sequel we are presented with the post-war sufferings of Andromache, Neoptolemus and Orestes, as Euripides characteristically proves that no epic closure is final.[58] The past is constantly evoked by the characters, above all by Andromache. Her opening monologue contrasts her former, familiar condition (as wife of Hector) with her present (and mythically unexplored) slavery in Phthia. Her new predicament mirrors her past in cruel and exacting reverse: she is still under attack by the house of Atreus (embodied on the female side by Hermione in place of Helen); her new son has a Greek father but his life is still imperilled by Greeks; she is now a slave, but is addressed as mistress (cf. 56–9). Most remarkably, the story of the Trojan War has come full circle: it started in the remote mythical past with a marriage in Phthia (between Peleus and Thetis) and has returned to a second disastrous union, with the principal victim seeking sanctuary at Thetis' shrine.

The central role played by Andromache in the play shows Euripides expanding her marginal role in post-Homeric epic.[59] She focuses the themes of nobility and family affection, and acts as a foil for Hermione's jealous immaturity and Menelaus' brutal treachery. The novel combination of wife and slave in one action leads to a jealous murder-plot and culminates in the intervention of Peleus. His involvement in

[56] Knox (1979) 21.

[57] Phillippo (1995) 371 well notes in the play 'elements of individuality interacting with kinship ties to produce volatile combinations'.

[58] Not just a tragedian's discovery: the *Iliad* and the *Odyssey* already exploit the concept of a narrative end which does not end the heroes' stories. On Homer's importance to tragedy, cf. *TrGF* 3, T 112a–b.

[59] Racine writes in the second preface to *Andromaque* of the heroine's capacity to arouse pity; cf. Hawcroft (1992) 175–6.

the Neoptolemus–Hermione story is not attested before this. Peleus, the noble Phthian, furthers the denunciation of Spartan mores, paralleling Andromache's role as the noble barbarian.

The changes effected in the portrayal of Menelaus in tragedy, and especially by Euripides, are striking.[60] In epic the inferiority of Menelaus to Hector in battle is explicit (*Il.* 7. 104–5):

> ἔνθα κέ τοι, Μενέλαε, φάνη βιότοιο τελευτὴ
> Ἕκτορος ἐν παλάμῃσιν, ἐπεὶ πολὺ φέρτερος ἦεν.

Then, Menelaus, the end of your life would have appeared at the hands of Hector, since he was by far the stronger man.

Andromache's claim in her *agon* with Menelaus is a forceful rhetorical expansion of the *Iliad* (456–7):[61]

> πόσις θ᾽ ὁ κλεινός, ὅς σε πολλάκις δορὶ
> ναύτην ἔθηκεν ἀντὶ χερσαίου κακόν.

And my glorious husband [was killed], who often with his spear drove you from land to become a cowardly sailor.

Like her description of her suckling of Hector's bastards (222–5), this is a striking addition to, or rather disruption of, the epic scene. The first innovation emphasized Hermione's excessive jealousy, while Andromache's claim that Menelaus *often* sought refuge at sea underlines his unheroic cowardice. He is only impressive when his opponent is a woman: ἐς γυναῖκα γοργὸς ὁπλίτης ('a dashing warrior against a woman', 458).[62] His

---

[60] Cf. Fraenkel (1950), ii. 70 on *Ag.* 115: 'by Aeschylus' time, we may be sure, if not before, [Menelaus] was regarded by popular opinion as δειλός ["cowardly"] or, at any rate, as poorer in spirit [than Agamemnon]'.

[61] In Book 17 Apollo (in mortal form) urges Hector to avenge the death of a comrade, recently killed by Menelaus. The god forces Hector to act by representing Menelaus as a μαλθακὸς αἰχμητής ('feeble warrior', *Il.* 17. 588), of whom it would be shameful to be afraid. Here it is Apollo who speaks to rhetorical effect.

[62] I translate γοργός here as 'dashing'/'brilliant' rather than 'terrible' (*pace* Stevens (1971) 229), though the two ideas are related: cf. Mastronarde (1994) 189 on *Phoen.* 129: 'brightness of glance is associated with ability to inspire terror in γοργός'. The phrase is repeated at 1123, but there used sincerely by the messenger in praise of Neoptolemus. Cf. *Or.* 754 where Menelaus is ἐν γυναιξὶ δ᾽ ἄλκιμος ('only tough among women').

independence is shattered by the sight of Helen's naked breast (627–31).[63]

The Homeric portrayal of a sensitive hero, acutely aware of how he has been insulted, and of his own responsibility for the death of Patroclus,[64] is drained by Euripides of all tragic consciousness. He is reduced to a deceiver (προύτεινα παιδὸς θάνατον, 'I used your son's death as a bait', 427) and glib chauvinist (βάρβαροι δ' ὄντες γένος | Ἕλλησιν ἄρξουσ᾽;, 'Shall born foreigners rule Greeks?', 665–6), whose sense of honour has shrunk to a selfish relativism, which itself undermines his own epic achievements at Troy (368–9):

> εὖ δ' ἴσθ᾽, ὅτου τις τυγχάνει χρείαν ἔχων,
> τοῦτ᾽ ἔσθ᾽ ἑκάστωι μεῖζον ἢ Τροίαν ἑλεῖν.

But make no mistake, gaining what he happens to desire is for each man a more important goal than the capture of Troy.

The degeneracy of Menelaus and his unworthy reputation are condemned out of his own mouth and by his two opponents, Andromache (οὐκ ἀξιῶ | οὔτ᾽ οὖν σὲ Τροίας οὔτε σοῦ Τροίαν ἔτι, 'In my opinion, you are not deserving of Troy, nor Troy of you', 328–9) and Peleus (ὡς καὶ σὺ σός τ᾽ ἀδελφὸς ἐξωγκωμένοι | Τροίαι κάθησθε τῆι τ᾽ ἐκεῖ στρατηγίαι, | μόχθοισιν ἄλλων καὶ πόνοις ἐπηρμένοι, 'Just like you and your brother, sitting back puffed up over Troy and your generalship there, though it was other men's efforts and hardships which exalted you', 703–5). Peleus' own claim regarding Menelaus' conduct at Troy is an even more arresting departure from the epic account, where Menelaus takes an active part in the fighting and at a key turning point in the poem is wounded by Pandarus (616–18; cf. *Il.* 4. 127–47):[65]

---

[63] Cf. *Il. Parv.* fr. 19, Ibycus fr. 296 *PMGF*, *Or.* 742, 1287.

[64] Cf. *Il.* 17. 91–3: ὤ μοι ἐγών, εἰ μέν κε λίπω κάτα τεύχεα καλὰ | Πάτροκλόν θ᾽, ὅς κεῖται ἐμῆς ἕνεκ᾽ ἐνθάδε τιμῆς, | μή τίς μοι Δαναῶν νεμεσήσεται, ὅς κεν ἴδηται ('Alas, if I leave behind this beautiful armour and the body of Patroclus, who lies here dead because of my honour, I fear that any Danaan who sees it will reproach me').

[65] The *Iliad* passage is marked by direct address: οὐδὲ σέθεν, Μενέλαε, θεοὶ μάκαρες λελάθοντο | ἀθάνατοι ('And you, Menelaus, the blessed gods, the immortals, did not forget you', 4. 127 f.) and by 'one of the most striking and unusual of Iliadic similes' (Kirk (1985) 345 on *Il.* 4. 141–7; it compares the blood on Menelaus' legs to a crimson dye that stains ivory). Peleus' charge

ὃς οὐδὲ τρωθεὶς ἦλθες ἐκ Τροίας μόνος,
κάλλιστα τεύχη δ᾽ ἐν καλοῖσι σάγμασιν
ὅμοι᾽ ἐκεῖσε δεῦρό τ᾽ ἤγαγες πάλιν.

You alone returned from Troy unwounded, and as for the very fine
weapons you took there in their fine coverings, you brought them
back in the same condition.

This is an aged Peleus, but one still retaining vestiges of the
vigorous hero of lyric.[66] The tragedy takes us from the
rejuvenated defender of Andromache and her son to the
bereaved and lonely old man familiar from epic.[67] In the last
book of the *Iliad* Achilles weeps for his father as well as for
Patroclus (αὐτὰρ Ἀχιλλεὺς κλαῖεν ἑὸν πατέρ᾽, ἄλλοτε δ᾽ αὖτε |
Πάτροκλον, 'And Achilles wept for his own father, and then
again for Patroclus', 24. 511–12), since the old man ἕνα παῖδα
τέκεν παναώριον ('fathered a single son doomed to an untimely
end', 24. 540).[68] The death of Neoptolemus in the *Andromache*
redoubles his grief, διπλῶν τέκνων μ᾽ ἐστέρησε Φοῖβος ('Phoebus
has deprived me of both my offspring!', 1212), and allows
Euripides to develop the theme of Peleus' tragic suffering—
αἰὼν δ᾽ ἀσφαλὴς | οὐκ ἔγεντ᾽ οὔτ᾽ Αἰακίδαι παρὰ Πηλεῖ ('Nor did
even Peleus, the son of Aeacus, enjoy a life free of suffering',
Pind. *Pyth*. 3. 86–7). The messenger's detailed, vivid, and
Homerically tinged description of Neoptolemus' heroism
intensifies the pain of Peleus' loss. His son and grandson are

recalls his son's insults against Agamemnon: οἰνοβαρές, κυνὸς ὄμματ᾽ ἔχων,
κραδίην δ᾽ ἐλάφοιο ('You drunk, with a dog's shameless eyes and a deer's
cowardly heart', *Il*. 1. 225–8).

[66] E.g. Pind. *Pyth*. 3, *Nem*. 3–5, Alcaeus 42 Voigt; cf. March (1987) 3: 'to
the Greeks this old man would have been almost an afterthought, for to them
Peleus' significance lay in the heroic deeds of his youth and in his glorious
marriage to Thetis.' The darker side of Peleus' history is only glanced at by
Pindar, *Nem* 5. 13–18: he is reluctant to mention the murder of Phocus;
Menelaus has no such scruples (*Andr*. 685–7).

[67] Contrast the rejuvenation of Iolaus in *Hcld*.

[68] At *Il*. 24. 488–9 Priam likens himself to Peleus, harassed by people
around his home and without protection, and in *Od*. 11. 494–503 Achilles'
ghost fears such a dishonourable fate for his father. At *Tro*. 1123 ff. Euripides
has Neoptolemus depart in haste from Troy with Andromache in order to
help Peleus, who has been expelled by Acastus (so too perhaps in Sophocles'
Peleus, *TrGF* iv. 390–2). In *Andromache* the pattern of Neoptolemus' rescue
of Peleus is reversed: Peleus alone defeats the interfering Menelaus and
rescues Neoptolemus' son.

dead, the Aeacid line defunct: πῶς δ᾽ οἴχεταί μοι παῖς μόνου παιδὸς μόνος; ('How did he perish, my only son's only son?', 1083), οἰχόμεθ᾽· οὐκέτι μοι γένος, οὐ τέκνα λείπεται οἴκοις ('We are finished, no family of mine, no children are left in my house!', 1177–8).[69] The rescue of Neoptolemus' body by his men repeats a familiar Homeric archetype, and the messenger's words stress the epic theme of the importance of proper burial rites performed by one's kin (1158–60):[70]

> ἡμεῖς δ᾽ ἀναρπάσαντες ὡς τάχος χεροῖν
> κομίζομέν νίν σοι κατοιμῶξαι γόοις
> κλαῦσαί τε, πρέσβυ, γῆς τε κοσμῆσαι τάφωι.

We quickly picked him up and brought him here for you to mourn, sir, to cry laments and weep for him, before burying him fittingly in the earth.

The rescue of the corpse of Achilles' son ensures its visible presence, offering a poignant, physical focus for the grief of Peleus.[71]

The surprise entry of Orestes adds another layer of complexity to the Neoptolemus–Hermione story. The myth of the matricide, Orestes' defining experience, is mentioned almost proudly by the killer himself (999–1001):[72]

---

[69] Father and son are linked in heroism: Neoptolemus' Τρωικὸν πήδημα ('Trojan leap', 1139) recalls his father's leap from ship to Trojan shore. (Borthwick (1967) 18 f. argues for Neoptolemus' own leap from the Trojan horse, but his evidence is late.)

[70] The brutal response of Achilles in *Il.* 22. 260–72, rejecting the proposal of Hector that the corpse of the defeated should be returned to his family, is the ultimate expression of the breakdown of civilized norms under the pressures of revenge.

[71] Peleus inters his grandson but could not properly mourn the body of his son far off in the Troad, as Achilles' consolation of Priam suggests, *Il.* 24. 518–51—a pathetic contrast with the successful supplication of Priam for Hector's body.

[72] Contrast *IT* 924 ff., where the darker side of the matricide is suppressed; we are to concentrate on the excitement of the escape plot, but even here Orestes' order to keep silent about his past is unsettling (σιγῶμεν αὐτά 925, 'Let's not talk about that'; σιγῶ 927, 'I won't mention it again'). Euripides' ingenious use of myth and its flexibility are evident in Iphigenia's plan, which puts the matricide to beneficial use (*IT* 1033 ff.). She will tell Thoas that Orestes has killed his mother and requires purification. What is presented as a fabrication is in fact horribly true!

ὁ μητροφόντης δ', ἦν δορυξένων ἐμῶν
μείνωσιν ὅρκοι Πυθικὴν ἀνὰ χθόνα,
δείξω γαμεῖν σφε μηδέν' ὧν ἐχρῆν ἐμέ.

I, the mother-killer, provided the oaths of my allies in the Pythian
land hold fast, will teach him not to marry a woman meant for me!

His character here is akin to the near-neurotically suspicious
figure of later legend, but far more purposeful than in Euripides' *Electra* or *Orestes*.[73] He must first reconnoitre the
situation and so claims to be just passing by on the way to
Dodona to consult the oracle of Zeus (885–6). This trip is
probably another, albeit minor, Euripidean innovation (cf. Σ
885 Δίδυμος δέ φησι ψευδῆ ταῦτα εἶναι καὶ ἄπιστα, 'Didymus says
that this is false and untrustworthy'). Orestes' remarks at
959 ff. reveal his prior knowledge of the σύγχυσιν δόμων ('uphea-
val in the house', 959), and make it clear that his avowed
ignorance of the situation was sheer pretence (887–8, 901,
907).[74] So Orestes is far from being the clean-cut rescuing
hero: like Menelaus, and unlike Peleus, he operates by deceit.
In addition, he is motivated largely by jealousy and revenge,
both to abduct Hermione and to punish Neoptolemus' insults
regarding the matricide (977–8). A third plot (in both senses) is
underway: the first, against Andromache, was openly and
ruthlessly prosecuted but finally repelled; the second, against
Hermione, was largely imaginary, but necessary to tie the
action of Andromache's crisis to Neoptolemus' death; while
the third is directed against an unwitting victim. As Kamerbeek well expresses it: 'in the *Andromache* we are dealing
with—as often in Euripides—an experiment; one could call it
"intrigue tragedy"'.[75] Deception (and in Menelaus and Hermione's case, self-deception) is rife, as Euripides exposes the
moral shallowness of characters who dissimulate, or are blind
to, their real motives.[76] The ethical contrast throws the heroism

---

[73] On the figure of the mad Orestes, see Pease (1967) on Verg. *Aen.* 4. 471
scaenis agitatus Orestes ('Orestes driven in flight across the stage'). Paus. 2. 29. 9
records a tradition that Pylades plotted the murder of Neoptolemus.

[74] Hawcroft (1992) 83–91 analyses Oreste's rhetorical manipulation of
Hermione and Andromaque in Racine's treatment of the myth.

[75] Kamerbeek (1943) 52.

[76] Cf. Méridier (1927) 99 on the 'pessimistic, illusionless insight' of the
play.

of Andromache, Peleus and Neoptolemus into sharper relief, and intensifies the pathos of their suffering.

Euripides could do—and did—anything he wanted with myth.[77] He has chosen (for reasons we will discuss further in Chapter 8) to respect the tradition of Neoptolemus' burial at Delphi, where pilgrims will have seen the hero's *temenos* (cf. Pind. *Nem*. 7. 44–7; Pherecydes, *FGrH* 3 F 64a). However, Euripides gives the tomb of Neoptolemus a novel aetiology in the hostility of Orestes.[78] The heightening of pathos effected by the hero's perverted *nostos* is worth the minor inconcinnity of having the corpse shuttled back and forth between Delphi and Phthia. (Like so many problems discovered in the study, this would not strike the audience as a problem in performance.) A hideously maltreated Neoptolemus (1153, recalling the desecrated corpse of Hector, *Il*. 22. 371) is lamented by his kin in Phthia before his interment back in Delphi. The transportation of Neoptolemus to Phthia is an emotionally powerful innovation in the myth of Neoptolemus' death. The hero, whose absence has made possible the crises of Andromache and Hermione, makes a grand entrance; but it is very different from the entrance which we have been led to expect by the suspense surrounding his decisive return. The warrior who would rescue his concubine and son, or punish his wilful wife, is replaced by a mangled corpse on a funeral bier.

Perhaps the most radical reworking of myth in the *Andromache* is the transformation of Neoptolemus. The epic cycle takes up the Iliadic narrative and recounts the events of the sack of Troy. Here Neoptolemus features prominently, but in

---

[77] For example, one might consider the novel effects of joining the boisterous Heracles to the fairy-tale world of *Alcestis*, of making Ion the son of Apollo, or of placing Heracles' labours before his madness, so that Theseus arrives 'as Heracles' φίλος and in his debt' (Yunis (1988) 139 n. 1). The most extreme instance is Euripides' probable invention of the entire myth of Archelaus: cf. Harder (1985) 132–3. So when Aristotle says: τοὺς μὲν οὖν παρειλημμένους μύθους λύειν οὐκ ἔστιν . . . αὐτὸν δὲ εὑρίσκειν δεῖ καὶ τοῖς παραδεδομένοις χρῆσθαι καλῶς ('One cannot alter traditional story-patterns . . . but each poet must work out how to handle even these to pleasing effect', *Poet*. 1453ᵇ22–6), he is too restrictive in his first judgement, but quite correct in his second.

[78] Dunn (1996) 52.

contrast to Homeric epic[79] it is his atrocities which are most
imposing: 'Briefly, Neoptolemus was the first great war crim-
inal of Greek cultural history.'[80] The murder of Priam at the
altar of Zeus Herkeios,[81] and the hurling of Astyanax from the
walls of Troy,[82] are the chief crimes which are widely found in
later art and poetry.[83] Crucially, neither of these murders is
directly ascribed to Neoptolemus in the *Andromache*. Andromache's silence about the identity of Astyanax's killer in her
eye-witness description of his death is notable: παῖδα θ' ὃν τίκτω
πόσει | ῥιφθέντα πύργων Ἀστυάνακτ' ἀπ' ὀρθίων ('[I saw] Astya-
nax, the child I bore my husband, tossed from the high
battlements', 9–10).[84] The ruthless figure of the Cyclic poems
is radically altered.[85] The absence of certain parts of the myth
contributes to the play's general improvement of Neoptolemus;
one of the chief effects of this is to impugn the revenge of
Orestes and Apollo.[86]

[79] At *Od*. 11. 506–37 Odysseus tells Achilles' ghost of his son's Trojan
career, stressing his good counsel, bravery, and safe return to Greece.

[80] Most (1985) 160.

[81] See *Iliup*. 62. 9–10 D. *Il. Parv.* fr. 17 D has Neoptolemus drag Priam to
the doors of his palace before killing him; this somewhat reduces the
heinousness of the murder. Euripides follows the more shocking version at
Tro. 16–17, 481–3 and *Hec*. 23–4. An interesting example of Neoptolemus
repeating his father's deeds can be seen in the story of Eurypylus, son of
Telephus, who is killed by Neoptolemus using the very same spear that had
healed Telephus: cf. Soph. fr. 210. 24 R.

[82] See *Il. Parv.* 20–1 D. The killing is attributed to Odysseus by *Iliup*.
62. 30 D, and *Tro*. 721–5 has Odysseus instigating the motion at the Greek
assembly.

[83] Cf. Stesich. 202, Ibycus 307 *PMGF*, Verg. *Aen*. 2. 506 ff. See *LIMC* VI
I 773–9 and VI II 450–2 for illustrations and commentary. Most (1985) 162
notes of vase-paintings of Neoptolemus: 'There are a multitude of depictions
of all three murders [Priam, Astyanax, Polyxena]—in comparison, there are
only a handful of representations of Neoptolemus in any other connection
whatsoever—and all emphasize their horror and brutality.' On the role of
Neoptolemus in these images, cf. Shapiro (1994) 163–6.

[84] Cf. Pohlenz (1954), ii. 119: 'Line 9 shows that we are not to think of the
murder of Astyanax by Neoptolemus.' The killing of Astyanax was the central
event of Ennius' tragedy *Andromacha*, which, like Euripides' *Troades*, was set
in the Greek camp at Troy; cf. Jocelyn (1967) 235.

[85] Euripides enjoyed unsettling his audience's expectations about the hero's
character: e.g. Heracles the paragon family-man in the *Heracles*, virtuous
Capaneus in the *Suppliants*, and wicked Eteocles in the *Phoenissae*.

[86] *LIMC* Neoptolemus no. 25, an Apulian krater of *c*.370, depicts a

If we look briefly at the literary precedents for Neoptolemus' death at Delphi, we may see where Euripides has innovated and why. The available evidence suggests that Euripides is the first to present Orestes' involvement in Neoptolemus' death at Delphi.[87] In his later *Orestes*, Neoptolemus will fall Δελφικῶι ξίφει ('by Delphian sword', 1656); the tradition of his marriage to Hermione is explicitly negated (*Or.* 1654), and he is presented as petitioning for compensation for the death of his father (*Or.* 1657, Soph. *Herm.*).[88] The explicit denial here of the events of the *Andromache*, 'a play whose plot we are told retroactively will never take place',[89] is

wounded Neoptolemus before the temple (Apollo and the Pythia look on); to his left is an unnamed attacker with a spear, and to his right, crouching behind the omphalos with a drawn sword, is Orestes (named). The influence of the *Andromache* has been disputed, but the artist 'has sought to underline the importance of sacrilege . . . by the abundance of images which recall the sacred: temple facade, two tripods, omphalos, Apollo, priestess' (*LIMC* VII 779).

[87] See Delcourt (1959) 105 f. There is no evidence that Orestes took any part in the plotting of his death in the *Hermione* (*pace* Bornmann (1962) xiv). Pearson goes well beyond the evidence when he says (Sophocles, *Fragments*, i. 141) 'The plot of this play proceeds on parallel lines to that of Euripides' *Andromache*.' Although it is unwise to speculate too much, the indications are that Neoptolemus was not seen in the most positive light in the *Hermione*. Perhaps like Pindar (cf. *Nem.* 7. 42–4) Sophocles emphasized Neoptolemus' fulfilment of his future as a cult-figure at Delphi. Euripides by contrast constructs and locates the action so as to be able to criticize Orestes and Apollo as much as Menelaus and Hermione. As to the state of Sophocles' *Andromache*, 'There is only one quotation, and "Andromache" may be a mistake for "Andromeda"' (Lloyd-Jones (1996) 48). On the problematic *Il. Parv.* fr. dub. 1 D (thought genuine by Fontenrose (1960) 220), see Stephanopoulos (1980) 66, who shows that this text, which involves Orestes in the death of Neoptolemus, is post-Euripidean. Wilamowitz (1962) 374 n. 1 interestingly proposes that Orestes' involvement in the murder of Neoptolemus was invented by the Delphians to rid themselves of blame. In *Andr.*, however, Euripides stresses the shared responsibility of both. (One might compare the version of Medea's story in which the Corinthians killed her children, but spread the rumour that she herself was responsible. Christa Wolf's recent use of this account in her novel *Medea: Stimmen* (1996) is an excellent example of the continuing vitality of Greek myth.)

[88] Cf. Soph. fr. 696 R (from his *Φθιώτιδες*, *The Women of Phthia*): ἡ πατροκτόνος δίκη | κεκλῇιτ' ἂν αὐτῶι ('He may bring an action for the killing of his father'). Apollo's role in the death of Achilles was no doubt familiar from epic (e.g. *Il.* 21. 277, 22. 359).

[89] Zeitlin (1980) 71.

an excellent illustration of Euripides' literary freedom to adapt and invent.[90]

We may extend our notion of the flexibility of myth to another genre (but still with regard to this particular legend) if we turn to the famously controversial treatment by Pindar of the death of Neoptolemus at Delphi.[91] The Pindaric scholia tell us that the account in *Nem.* 7. 40–9 was written as an apology to the Aeginetans for an uncomplimentary portrayal of Neoptolemus in a *Paean* written for the Delphians (*Paean* 6. 104–21).[92] Whatever the explanation—and Pindar can be correcting tradition rather than himself[93]—his two treatments strikingly illustrate lyric's freedom of approach to myths.[94] In *Paean* 6 Neoptolemus offends Apollo by the murder of Priam, a suppliant at the altar of Zeus, and the god swears revenge (6. 113–15). It is Apollo himself who kills Neoptolemus.[95]

But in *Nem.* 7, as in the *Andromache*, the pacific purpose of Neoptolemus' visit is stressed (he offers Apollo the first fruits of his Trojan spoils, 40–1). An anonymous man is responsible

[90] One might compare the virtuous Helen of the *Helen* so soon after the bad one of the *Troades*.

[91] Pindar supplies our earliest references to the death of Neoptolemus: see Gantz (1993) 690–1. The seventh Nemean is dated *c.*485; *Paean* 6 would be sometime earlier.

[92] Drachmann (1927) iii. 123 ff. On the alleged displeasure of the Aeginetans with *Paean* 6, see Hoekstra (1962).

[93] The scholia's explanation is defended by Carey (1981) 135 and by D'Alessio (1994) 136–7, who think the personal reference by the poet more explicable in the light of an earlier treatment by himself; Defradas (1972) 150 calls *Nem.* 7 'a type of palinode'. Lefkowitz (1991) 141 ff., however, makes a good case against this, arguing that (p. 144) 'no external explanations need be sought'. Heath (1993) 188–92 also points out that the scholia offer no independent evidence for the Aeginetans' anger at the paean; the apology has to be *read into* the concluding lines of the poem: τὸ δ' ἐμὸν οὔ ποτε φάσει κέαρ | ἀτρόποισι Νεοπτόλεμον ἑλκύσαι | ἔπεσι ('But my heart will never say that it has defiled Neoptolemus with unseemly words', 102–4). For further discussion see Howie (1998) 109 n. 136.

[94] Pindar's decision in *Nem.* 7 to highlight Neoptolemus' heroic honours rather than his impiety is part of *his* own creative freedom: as Wilamowitz (1970) 156 remarks, 'it was his right to accentuate this or that side of the recognized legend according to his needs'.

[95] Cf. Lloyd-Jones (1973) 131; Radt (1958) 86–7 argues that in *Pae.* 6 Pindar is not worried about the image of Neoptolemus: 'He is here concerned only to present the power and the punishing justice of Apollo as impressively as possible.'

for the killing: ἵνα κρεῶν νιν ὕπερ μάχας | ἔλασεν ἀντιτυχόντ᾽ ἀνήρ μαχαίραι ('a man stabbed him with a knife during a quarrel over the sacrificial meat', 41–2).[96] Significantly, the Delphians are deeply distressed by the incident (43); this is very unlike the mass suspicion and attack depicted by Euripides (1096–9, 1127 ff.). *Nemean* 7 also alludes to the fifth-century Molossian kings' claim to descent from Neoptolemus (38–40), a claim exploited by Euripides in Thetis' speech *ex machina*. His and Andromache's son will found a new dynasty, and so allay Peleus' grief (1243–51). In both *Nemean* 7 and the *Andromache* the tragedy of the hero's death is transfigured by the future honours of his Aeacid descendants.[97] So Pindar has shaped an account in *Nemean* 7 which is favourable to Neoptolemus, and this in itself is a notable revision of the hero as depicted in archaic art and poetry. But Euripides goes much further in this direction than Pindar. Whereas Pindar stresses Neoptolemus' fulfilment of fate and the honour of his cult, Euripides highlights the troubling aspects of Orestes' and Apollo's revenge; Neoptolemus' tomb will stand as a Δελφοῖς ὄνειδος ('a reproach to the Delphians', 1241).

The idea of a subsequent visit by Neoptolemus to try and undo the first is very likely to be secondary and looks like an ingenious fifth-century invention. The *Andromache* is our earliest evidence for it, and it is an obvious possibility (and probably more) that Euripides is responsible for the addition. We are not allowed to forget the first visit (51–5, 1002–4, 1106–8). In formal terms, we might approach this as an instance of Greek poets' typical keenness to keep as much of the old versions as possible.[98] Although the earlier visit of Neoptolemus to Delphi lies well in the past, Euripides' reference to it has important effects on our response to the meaning of the

[96] Howie (1998) 109 n. 136 explains the ritual background to the scene. Sophocles' *Hermione* gives the role of assassin to Machaireus, a significant if obvious name perhaps extrapolated from the Pindaric version. Alternatively, Sophocles may be alluding to an already established legend.

[97] Cf. Finley (1951) 77, Wilamowitz (1970) 138.

[98] Pindar, for example, in his radical rewriting of the myth of Pelops in *Ol.* 1, keeps the traditional story of Tantalus' feast for the gods, and the λέβης ('cauldron', 26), though here it is καθαρός ('pure'), and used for a different purpose. Note how Euripides makes his new Lycus the son of the elder one (*Her.* 31), who was also a usurper in Theban myth.

action: it confirms the connection of father and son in heroic
opposition to Apollo and emphasizes the specific motif of
divine intransigence.[99] This identification is developed in the
presentation of Neoptolemus' brave defence at Delphi. Moreover, by keeping the traditional element of the son's angry
demand for reparation, the surprising novelty of the second
trip and its conciliatory intent are stressed. The passage of time
has brought a cooling of Neoptolemus' temper and a desire to
make good his heated reaction. Apollo, however, remains
unmollified, and the picture of smouldering divine vengeance
which results is far from complimentary: he acts, the messenger says, ὥσπερ ἄνθρωπος κακὸς ('like a bad man', 1164). The
process is paralleled on the human level in Hermione's fester-
ing hostility to Andromache. The delay in her action, and her
timing of it during Neoptolemus' absence, make her seem more
petty and objectionable. Orestes too has been languishing in
self-pity, waiting to strike back at Neoptolemus (note the tense:
ἔμιμνον 961, 'I kept waiting'). The multiple effects of distance
and delay combine to underline the absurdities of a morality
driven by the desire for vengeance.

The death of Neoptolemus and its lamentation by Peleus are
a poignant climax to the play.[100] The appearance of Thetis at
the end is structurally apt: it balances Andromache's supplication of her at the start of the play (πρὸς τόδ' ἄγαλμα θεᾶς ἱκέτις
περὶ χεῖρε βαλοῦσα 115, 'I embrace this statue of the goddess
with a suppliant's arms'). But more germane to the issues of the
drama, and to Andromache's experience in particular, is
Thetis' Iliadic role as a mourning mother. It may also be
significant that she, like Andromache, was compelled into a
marriage away from her kind.[101] But in *Andromache* the

---

[99] Paus. 10. 7. 1 and Apollod. *Epit.* 6. 14 record a version in which
Neoptolemus came to ransack the Delphic sanctuary; cf. Most (1985) 164 n.
140. Orestes uses this to arouse suspicion (*Andr.* 1092–5) but he is clearly
lying. Nevertheless, this example illustrates how Euripides easily combines
and alters several versions of events in one play.

[100] The scholiast on *Andr.* 32 (op. cit. n. 55) recognizes the tragic power of
Neoptolemus' death and its mourning.

[101] Thetis herself complains bitterly to Hephaestus of her unwanted
marriage, not least because it has brought her a mortal son and so involved
her in human death and sorrow (*Il.* 18. 429 ff.): cf. *Andr.* 1235–7. The scholia
on Apol. Rhod. *Arg.* 4. 816 record Sophocles' treatment of the marriage in

standard sequence of marriage, quarrel and return to the sea is reworked: Thetis will live with Peleus once deified, and their marriage proves a source of salvation. Thus the mythical paradigm of faithless spouses which has recurred throughout the play in various forms (Helen, Hermione, Clytemnestra) is confounded: the faithful Peleus wins immortality, and the devoted Andromache marries back into her own kind, to Helenus, another son of Priam and Hecuba. This is the earliest source for the union,[102] and may well be a Euripidean innovation to honour Andromache with a second Trojan marriage.[103] The wedding of Peleus and Thetis, where the myth of the fateful judgement began, has become a force for resolution: Πηλεῦ, χάριν σοι τῶν πάρος νυμφευμάτων | ἥκω Θέτις ('Peleus, on account of our former nuptials, I, Thetis, have come', 1231–2; cf. 1253). Peleus' line is saved, and the heroic races of Troy (both Phthian and Trojan, discounting the cowardly Atreidae) are united in the child whose descendants will flourish as kings of Molossia (1247–9).

The specific mythical past of Thetis and her mortal family also guides our response to the *Andromache*'s criticisms of Apollo. He betrayed Peleus and Thetis, who had been his hosts at their wedding; Hera berates him for this in the *Iliad*: πάντες δ' ἀντιάασθε, θεοί, γάμου· ἐν δὲ σὺ τοῖσι | δαίνυ' ἔχων φόρμιγγα, κακῶν ἕταρ', αἰὲν ἄπιστε ('All of you gods were present at the wedding. And you too were there at the feast, playing your lyre—you comrade of the base, always a traitor!', *Il.* 24. 62–3).[104] Aeschylus has Thetis recall Apollo's prophecy of happy motherhood and his betrayal in killing Achilles (a speech

---

The Lovers of Achilles (fr. 151 R), in which Thetis is said to have left Peleus because he insulted her. Cf. [Hes] fr. 300 MW.

[102] See Gantz (1993) 689–90.

[103] The idea is present in Aeneas' presentation of the couple: cf. *Aen.* 3. 297 *et patrio Andromachen iterum cessisse marito* ('And Andromache had once again married among her people'). Euripides presents the marriage to Helenus as a positive consolation, whereas Virgil has an arrogant Pyrrhus abandon Andromache to a servile union as soon as he marries Hermione: *me famulo famulam Heleno transmisit habendam* ('he gave me, his slave, to his slave Helenus', *Aen.* 3. 329).

[104] *LIMC* Apollo nos. 843–50 show Apollo at the wedding. See Reid (1993) ii. 1027–31 for the rich artistic *Nachleben* of the wedding as a scene of discord.

famously cited by Plato as coming from the sort of tragedy to which he would refuse to grant a chorus, *Rep.* 383a–c):

> ὁ δ' αὐτὸς ὑμνῶν, αὐτὸς ἐν θοινῆι παρών,
> αὐτὸς τάδ' εἰπών, αὐτός ἐστιν ὁ κτανὼν
> τὸν παῖδα τὸν ἐμόν.

Aesch. fr. 350 R

But he, the very one who sang, who took part in the feast, who uttered these words, he it is who has killed my son.

In the *Andromache* the hostility of Apollo extends to the next generation of Thetis' line, but is countered by divine intervention; this intervention is based specifically on the ties of marriage and more generally on an affirmation of the gods' care, even for the vanquished Troy: καὶ γὰρ θεοῖσι κἀκείνης μέλει | καίπερ πεσούσης Παλλάδος προθυμίαι ('Indeed the gods care for Troy as well, although it fell by the strong desire of Pallas', 1251–2). The play's interesting and thought-provoking refinement is its insistence on the disgrace of Neoptolemus' murder. Apollo is a god and so invulnerable, but his human agents are shamed and his collaboration with Orestes discredited: Neoptolemus is returned to Delphi and buried at the god's altar ὡς ἀπαγγέλληι τάφος | φόνον βίαιον τῆς Ὀρεστείας χερός ('so that his grave may announce the violent murder wrought by Orestes', 1241–2).

The future of Andromache and her son is grounded in a mythical *aition* (1243–9): the foundation of the kingship in Molossia, which is first attested in Pindar (cf. *Paean* 6. 109–10, *Nem.* 4. 51–3). In Pindar, Neoptolemus does not return from Troy to Phthia but is blown off course by a storm to Molossia, where he personally founds the dynasty (*Nem.* 7. 36–9).[105] Euripides, however, places his murder at Delphi before the foundation and thus enhances the role played by Andromache and their son, 'Molossus'. In addition, their postponed arrival allows the Molossian charter-myth to be presented as a divinely sanctioned reward for the Aeacid royal house, and so further elevates the future Epirote dynasty: βασιλέα δ' ἐκ τοῦδε

---

[105] The *Nostoi* (fr. 67. 20–4 D) mention his arrival in Molossia and recognition by Peleus. Eratosthenes *FGrH* 241 F 42 has Neoptolemus sack Molossia and Andromache give birth to Molossus; Stephanopoulos (1980) 70 thinks this an old version.

χρὴ | ἄλλον δι' ἄλλου διαπερᾶν Μολοσσίας | εὐδαιμονοῦντας ('It is fated that his descendants one after another will enjoy a prosperous rule in Molossia', 1247–9).[106]

Turning to the fate of Peleus, it is appropriate that his concern for the future of his line is rewarded with the reunion of his own family. To this end Euripides takes up the myth of Achilles' immortality and innovatively awards Peleus the same status. According to Proclus' summary, the *Aethiopis* of Arctinus related how Thetis snatched Achilles from the pyre and transported him to Leuce, the White Island, in the Black Sea:

καὶ Θέτις ἀφικομένη σὺν Μούσαις καὶ ταῖς ἀδελφαῖς θρηνεῖ τὸν παῖδα· καὶ μετὰ ταῦτα ἐκ τῆς πυρᾶς ἡ Θέτις ἀναρπάσασα τὸν παῖδα εἰς τὴν Λευκὴν νῆσον διακομίζει ('And Thetis arrived with the Muses and her sisters and mourned her son. After this Thetis snatched her son from the pyre and took him to the island of Leuce', p. 47, ll. 26–8 D; cf. *Nem.* 4. 49–50 ἐν δ' Εὐξείνωι πελάγει φαεννὰν Ἀχιλεύς | νᾶσον, 'And Achilles [rules] an island shining in the Euxine Sea').[107] Euripides adapts this version here (1260–2):

> τὸν φίλτατον σοὶ παῖδ' ἐμοί τ' Ἀχιλλέα
> ὄψηι δόμους ναίοντα νησιωτικοὺς
> Λευκὴν κατ' ἀκτὴν ἐντὸς ἀξένου πόρου.

You will see your beloved son and mine, Achilles, dwelling in his island home on the shore of Leuce within the inhospitable sea.

As with the end of Neoptolemus, the aetiologial grounding relates to cult. Leuce was sacred to Achilles,[108] and the Greek community of the region worshipped the hero as Ruler of the Black Sea.[109] By contrast with Homer, who generally suppresses

---

[106] See Ch. 5.

[107] There were other myths surrounding the fate of Achilles, e.g. Ibycus fr. 291 D, where he is married to Medea on the Elysian plain.

[108] Cf. Paus. 3. 19. 11–13 (= Stes. TA40 D), where Helen is also set on the island as Achilles' lover.

[109] Burkert (1985) 172, 205. Hommel (1980) regards Achilles as in origin a god of the dead and considers his cult a divine one, but as Hooker (1988) 2 ff. points out, his theory rests on dubious assumptions. Farnell (1921) 289 is right to stress the crucial role of epic: 'his cult was always a hero-cult, and may have begun before Homer, but in post-Homeric times, independently of tribal affinities, was diffused and quickened by the powerful influence of epic.' Archaeology supports the role of epic in the dissemination of many

the daimonic afterlife of his heroes and stresses instead the finality of death,[110] Euripides often engages directly with the cult status of the Greek heroes. The mortality of Achilles (and of Peleus too) is central to the tragic shape of the *Iliad*. Thetis' revelation of an unHomeric immortality for both Achilles and Peleus, and of cult-hero status for Neoptolemus, anchors the resolution in local cult traditions.[111] Most importantly, by using the Leuce cult, which was 'by far the most famous site of Achilles worship in antiquity',[112] and by stressing the idea of immortality, Euripides makes the honouring of the Aeacid house especially emphatic.

Most strikingly, Thetis personally makes Peleus immortal and divine (ἀθάνατον ἄφθιτόν τε ποιήσω θεόν 1256, 'I shall make you a god, deathless and imperishable') and her promise is sanctioned by Zeus: Ζηνὶ γὰρ δοκεῖ τάδε ('for this is the will of Zeus', 1269).[113] The exalted consolation goes beyond his traditional translation to the μακάρων νᾶσος ('Isle of the Blest', cf. Pind. *O.* 2. 78–83).[114] Thus the broken, mourning Peleus familiar from epic finally regains some semblance of his former blessedness.[115]

such hero-cults: see Coldstream (1976). Achilles was worshipped all over the Greek world and had several cult-sites on the Euxine dating from the archaic period on (cf. Hedreen (1991) 315–21).

[110] See Janko (1992) 370 ff. on *Il.* 16. 419–683 (where Sarpedon dies, despite being the son of Zeus).

[111] Cf. Kamerbeek (1960) 11 on Euripides' 'marked taste . . . for aetiological myth'.

[112] Hedreen (1991) 319.

[113] Stevens (1971) 244 on 1256 ascribes Thetis' gift of immortality to the will of Zeus. But they work in harmony. The wording of 1256 ff. and 1265 ff. stresses her initiative and power, as is appropriate to her personal interest in the outcome of events. For a goddess' immortalization of a favourite, cf. Pind. *Nem.* 10. 7: Διομήδεα δ' ἄμβροτον ξαν- | θά ποτε Γλαυκῶπις ἔθηκε θεόν ('Bright-eyed, golden-haired Athena once made Diomedes an immortal god').

[114] It is 'ad hoc invention'; so Willink (1986) 352 on *Or.* 1635–7 (Helen's marine cult).

[115] Cf. Hes. fr. 211. 7 MW, from a wedding song, τρὶς μάκαρ Αἰακίδη καὶ τετράκις ὄλβιε Πηλεῦ, 'Thrice blessed son of Aeacus and four times happy Peleus!' Peleus and Menelaus both enjoy a blessed afterlife because of their marriages: Aélion (1986) 27. Peleus is here given solace for his sufferings, while in Euripidean tragedy Menelaus is less blessed by his wife than in epic; cf. *Od.* 4. 561–9, where the hero is promised conveyance to Elysium: οὕνεκ' ἔχεις Ἑλένην καί σφιν γαμβρὸς Διός ἐσσι ('because you have Helen as wife and are in their [i.e. the gods'] eyes the son-in-law of Zeus', 569; West *et al.* (1988) 228

The place and manner of his transformation is aptly chosen (1265–8):

> ἐλθὼν παλαιᾶς χοιράδος κοῖλον μυχὸν
> Σηπιάδος ἵζου· μίμνε δ' ἔστ' ἂν ἐξ ἁλὸς
> λαβοῦσα πεντήκοντα Νηρήιδων χορὸν
> ἔλθω κομιστήν σου.

Go to the hollow cave on Sepias' ancient cape and sit there. Wait until I come from the sea with a chorus of fifty Nereids who will escort you.

Cape Sepias was known in one tradition as the place where Peleus wrestled with the shape-changing Thetis and took her as his wife (Hdt. 7. 191, cf. Soph. frr. 150, 618 R). The emphasis on force and on the humiliation done to Thetis by the marriage that is found in many sources[116] is here notably undone. Peleus agrees to await her, οὗπερ σὸν εἷλον χερσὶ κάλλιστον δέμας ('where I once took your lovely body in my arms', 1278).[117] Euripides thus ends the play with a positive addition to the myth that connects and contrasts meaningfully with the conduct of Andromache and Hermione, as Thetis' discontent with her husband is replaced by a joyful reunion and the affirmation of noble marriage: ὦ πότνι', ὦ γενναῖα συγκοιμήματα, | Νηρέως γένεθλον, χαῖρε ('My Lady, noble sharer of my bed, child of Nereus, farewell!', 1273–4).

To sum up, the movement of the *Andromache* consists in a series of bold recastings of heroic myth. The plot's surprising turns, which are often denigrated as symptoms of poor episodic structure (and to which we turn in Chapter 2), emphasize the unexpected elaboration of the figures' post-war experience. The servitude of Andromache in the household of Neoptolemus was an established part of the epic cycle. The marriage of Hermione and Neoptolemus is known from the *Odyssey*,[118] the

comment on this line: 'its defective attestation may indicate that the line is a late addition, making explicit what might easily be inferred [from the rest of the passage]').

[116] See Forbes Irving (1990) 181–3.

[117] Wilamowitz (1962) 375 found this a 'beautiful invention'.

[118] The *Cypria* mentions ἔρως ('desire') between Achilles and Helen themselves (Davies (1989a) 48; cf. n. 108 above). It is appropriate that these two, the most glamorous of their sex, should meet. But just as Achilles could take Troy only in the person of his son, so he could marry Helen only in the next generation.

betrothal of Hermione and Orestes from Sophocles, Philocles, and Theognis. Euripides' probably original contribution here is to mesh the stories in such a way as to bring out the impact of the Trojan concubine's presence on the post-war household of a Greek warrior whose young wife is pursued by another man. The combination allows Euripides to focus at length on the clash of Andromache and Hermione. The epic triangle of two men and one woman is recast as the conflict of two women over one man: this complicates the heroic atmosphere in an interesting and provocative way.

There is no evidence in Eustathius' summary for Andromache's presence in Sophocles' *Hermione*, nor for that of Peleus.[119] Most importantly, Sophocles' play does not involve Orestes in the plotting of Neoptolemus' death. This feature is absent from Pindar too, and may be regarded as the most dramatically compelling innovation (or, less plausibly, choice of versions) in the plot. The quarrel of Agamemnon and Achilles is carried on into the next generation—and, again, Achilles–Neoptolemus is right. The atrocities of Neoptolemus in the epic cycle and the various traditions which mention Hermione's prior pregnancy by Orestes, or her forceful abduction by Neoptolemus, suggest that Euripides' presentation of the Phthian hero was original. The expressive force of his positive characterization is underlined by another probable innovation: the attempted conciliation of his second visit to Delphi, which is worked out as a sign of the petty grudgingness of Apollo.[120] In addition, it alters our view of Hermione and our response to Orestes' justification of his plot. Thus the *Andromache* seems, even by Euripides' standards, strikingly original in its alteration and combination of heroic myth.

The greater part of the *Andromache* has, it seems, been freely invented by Euripides to fashion for the play an effective tragic shape. This chapter has sought to illustrate and emphasize the often neglected fact that the picture of myth as a static body of

---

[119] In the *Andromache*, in contrast to his Iliadic passivity (cf. esp. 24. 486 ff.), old Peleus is given a lively role and heroic things to do. His apotheosis fills in more of his story in a striking way.

[120] In *Orestes*, for all its mythical invention, Euripides keeps to the standard version of Neoptolemus' death during the first visit (*Or.* 1657). Its effect in the *Andromache* was most likely a *coup de théâtre*.

heroic 'history' is basically flawed. We are dealing with a pool of interrelated but nevertheless fluid tales whose malleability makes possible their role in creative literature. Without a doubt there were some defining events in the lives of particular heroic figures which were central to many versions of their myth: for example, an Agamemnon who is not killed by Clytemnestra on his return to Greece seems unthinkable in tragedy, but in fact her role in the killing is contested in epic.[121] Such catastrophic events are essential to the power of tragedy,[122] yet how each individual play goes about presenting even these is a matter of literary choice and skill. The details of the individual tragic plot are not preordained by any canonical version of events. The poet is free to borrow and adapt motifs from earlier treatments. Homer himself had done so: 'None of this deprives Homer of originality; rather, it shows him as an active participant in a tradition which thrives on competition and constant reworking of established themes.'[123]

Indeed one can imagine the competing tragic poets eager to engage with the most hallowed or familiar treatments in new, provocative, and entertaining ways. From a relatively small corpus of interrelated heroic families the fifth-century tragedians were able to develop many thousands of plots.[124]

---

[121] *Od.* 1. 35–9, 3. 265–75, 304–10, and 4. 529–37 stress the initiative of Aegisthus, who corrupts a weak woman; at *Od.* 11. 405–34 the ghost of Agamemnon relates how he was killed by Aegisthus, while Clytemnestra kills Cassandra. It was Aeschylus' *Oresteia* which crucially and influentially redefined her role: see March (1987) 81–98.

[122] Cf. Arist. *Poet.* 1453ª35–9 on Orestes and Aegisthus going off as friends at the end of the play (καὶ ἀποθνῄσκει οὐδεὶς ὑπ' οὐδενός, 'and nobody kills anybody'), which would be the stuff of comedy.

[123] Rutherford (1996) 6.

[124] Importantly for tragedy, the network of heroic myth is genealogical. The importance of birth in heroic society is used in tragedy to reflect on various problems of social justice. The *Andromache* explores one aspect of this: the hereditary status of nobility. The pressure of family history draws on a complex mythical background; consider, for example, the dense mythical allusion as Phaedra tries to avoid the transgressive sexual passions of her mother and sister (*Hipp.* 337–43). The genealogical link between the heroes of myth and the world of the audience was itself subject to political or chauvinistic spin: cf. Bremmer (1994) 58. On the possibility of tracing myths to specific interest-groups, see Parker (1996) 59. Yet in tragedy the role of Athens as saviour in the *Eumenides, Oedipus Coloneus, Heracleidae,* and *Suppliants* is not merely propaganda.

Euripides' constant reworking of tragic myth for original and individual effects is evident in each extant play. He is not merely interested in correcting other poets' mistakes in myth.[125] Rather he explores the open-endedness of tragic myth with insight, exuberance, and curiosity. On occasion Euripides directs the audience to reflection on the status of myth itself as a vehicle of traditional wisdom and exemplary morality.[126] And as the *Andromache* illustrates, he is sensitive to the dichotomy between the distant glories of heroic myth and the contemporary experience of war and social crisis.

The notion of a pure, unchanging myth is fundamentally alien to the restless exploration of human conflict, of moral and political disintegration, which lies at the heart of Greek tragedy. It is the fluidity of myth which enables tragedy to engage with matters of interest to the audience, to use the

[125] The rejection of the Aeschylean signs by Electra (*El.* 518 ff. ~ *Cho.* 183 ff.) is often regarded as Euripidean parody. Such passages are best understood neither as polemic nor as simple parody but in terms of their effects within the play: here, to emphasize the hesitancy of Orestes and the stubbornness and self-absorption of Electra, whose sophisticated rejection is mistaken, and who in a sense does not want to believe that Orestes has returned. I follow here the excellent discussion by Cropp (1988) 134–8. The authenticity of the passage has been much debated. Kovacs (1989) 78 thinks their source 'may be Middle Comedy, a play on the Orestes theme'; he brackets them accordingly in his Loeb edition (1998). West (1980) 17–21 claims 'the passage is largely interpolated, but by Euripides himself'. Even this theory seems doubtful, given the scene's dramatic congruence in context. The intertextual reference to Aesch. *Sept.* at *Phoen.* 751–2 has a force beyond that of criticism: it enhances the pace and multiple plot of Euripides' play (in contrast to Aeschylus'). Burian (1997) 196 also observes, 'his [Euripides'] characters consciously pursue destructive and self-destructive ends rather than struggle with destiny'. Theseus' rejection of a *Septem*-like account of the combatants prepares for Adrastus' very different presentation of the Seven as brave, pious heroes (*Suppl.* 846 ff.).

[126] A character's denial of myth, or wish for its dissolution, draws attention to the novelty of the present action. Such remarks may reveal Euripidean tragedy's complex self-consciousness as literary fiction, yet their function in the drama is uppermost: e.g. Lycus' questioning of Heracles' labours (*Her.* 151 ff.) enhances his arrogance and prepares for Heracles' violent revenge. The chorus reject the story of Heracles' death on the pyre (φεύγω λόγον ὡς τὸν "Αι- | δα δόμον κατέβα, πυρὸς | δεινᾶι φλογὶ σῶμα δαισθείς *Hcld.* 912–14, 'I shun the story that he went down to Hades, his body consumed by the terrible flame of the fire'), and thereby endorse his divinity. Cf. Stinton (1990) 254 ff., Goldhill (1994) 68–70.

world of the heroes as a setting for the provocative exploration of contemporary issues. No less flawed than the idea of an unchanging myth is that of a completed one: in effect the story can always be taken further.[127] At the end of the *Electra*, Castor refers briefly to the *eidolon* of Helen in Egypt (*El.* 1280–3). When one considers how in the *Helen* this basic mythical datum is expanded to form the action of a whole play, one gets an impression of the elasticity and richness of tragic myth. This example also illustrates that the myths comprise a complex, interlocking fictional continuum, in which a story may be modified by the poet and added to the mythical chain, if not quite willy-nilly, certainly with a great measure of freedom. As has recently been written of Orestes' experience after the matricide, 'the life of Orestes after the murder was more or less virgin soil . . . the poets were free to imagine what happened next, and did so in various ways'.[128] We see one particular realization of Orestes' history in the *Andromache*. The play's portrayal of new tragic possibilities latent in the experiences of Andromache, Hermione, Peleus, and Neoptolemus is a striking expansion of their post-war fates. Andromache's life remains dominated by the war, but in very different respects from that of Menelaus or Orestes, Peleus or Hermione. Euripides elaborates and combines their several histories, as the disintegration of civilized norms and the horrors consequent upon their collapse extend beyond the war's initial combatants and long into its aftermath.

---

[127] Cf. Steiner (1996) 537: 'it is . . . in the nature of Greek myths to be open-ended, to be part of a complex dynamic reaching forward into further or variant situations.'

[128] van Erp Taalman Kip (1996) 127. Compare also the various stories surrounding the matricide Alcmaeon, handled by Sophocles (perhaps in a trilogy *Epigonoi, Eriphyle, Alcmaeon*, with the *Amphiaraus* as satyr play—so Lloyd-Jones (1996) 73) and by Euripides in two plays, *Alcmaeon in Corinth*, and *Alcmaeon in Psophis* (Austin, p. 83). Thuc. 2. 102. 5–6 records the story of the Delphic oracle which sent Alcmaeon to the delta of Achelous. Thucydides introduces the mythical extract with λέγεται, on which Hornblower (1991a) 378 comments, 'Th. is not so much expressing uncertainty as flagging the story for what it is—a story which like all myths was a *"tertium quid*, neither true nor false".'

2
Structure, Stagecraft, Unity

A text's unity lies not in its origin but in its destination.
Roland Barthes, *The Death of the Author*

A fuller understanding of the unusual (but effective, deliberate, and artful) structure of *Andromache* is sorely needed. In the scholarly literature on the play one of the most frequently repeated criticisms concerns its apparent lack of unity.[1] Even scholars who find the piece excitingly unorthodox are rarely able to get clear of the perceived problem of construction and declare the play a success. Rivier sums up the general feeling: 'One could say that the poet did not succeed in uniting the diverse elements of his inspiration.'[2] Unfortunately, few critics ever endeavour to define what is meant by this catch-all term of praise, 'unity'.[3] As Hutchinson has observed in connection with the 'particularly bold and strange' design of Apollonius' *Argonautica*, 'It seems almost as if lack of unity were a

---

[1] Cf. Bornmann (1962) xvii; see Steidle (1968) 118 n. 1 and Amoroso (1994) 142–3 with n. 10 for bibliography. Burnett (1971) rightly insists on the multiplicity of the plot (ch. 6 *passim*) but her idea that the characters 'appear now in one and now in another of the *conventional parts* during the course of the play' (130; my italics) is insufficiently sensitive to the moral distinctions between them, and blurs the varied reactions which they provoke in the audience. Collard (1981) 5 regards the unity of *Andr.* as 'especially' threatened by the apparent absence of Andromache after 765 (on this see below). Yet, as we will observe, such movement of interest from one character to another is a common feature of many plays. Euripides likes the technique; it is not a slip in dramatic design.

[2] Rivier (1975) 153. Cf. esp. Burnett (1971) 131 n. 2: ' "Downright insanity", said Verrall; "worthless" is Wilamowitz's report, and others have added further adjectives: chaotic, cheap, sensational, *assez vulgaire*.'

[3] An important exception is Heath (1989). Here and in his earlier work (1987) 98–111 he seeks to revise the criteria of unity, arguing for a much broader and more diverse understanding of the term in ancient aesthetics. Generally, on compositional unity as a property of the beautiful, see Gadamer (1986) 88–90, 95–6.

damaging charge against the poet, whose guilt or innocence must be established.' Critical 'prosecutors' of tragedy are often inspired by an 'Aristotelian singleness of action or plot', while defenders of recalcitrant texts, such as the *Andromache, Supplices, Heracles*, or *Orestes*, will often appeal to (the notoriously malleable) 'unity of theme' to save the poet from censure.[4] The result is a narrow and impoverished appreciation of the variety of design in poetic texts: 'Disunity can often be sought and relished by poets; and there are various kinds and areas of unity, which are compatible, and often combined, with various kinds and areas of disunity.'[5] The following discussion of the *Andromache* tries to establish that the play's design is both more artfully complex and more dynamic than commonly assumed.[6] The shifts and surprises in the *Troades* and the *Heracles* have been more generally appreciated because they obviously amount to a total meaning or impact; but what is the total meaning or impact of the *Andromache*? A key element of the answer will emerge, it is hoped, when we consider both how the chaotic and unexpected happenings of the play are articulated by its structure and stagecraft, and how these events combine to illuminate the fragility of fortune.[7]

[4] Mossman (1996b) 144 well asserts the primacy of thematic variety over thematic unity in *Andromache*: 'I do not think the concept of thematic integration . . . can very helpfully be used in describing this play, just because it embraces so many of the themes which Euripides explores singly in other dramas: the effects of war, nationality and difference, women and their relationships with men and with each other, and the relationship between men and gods.' Cf. Phillippo (1995) 355–6, who proposes, in place of one unifying theme, that we consider 'the way certain issues are explored in the context of the play's various elements'.

[5] Hutchinson (1988) 96–7.

[6] Mastronarde's ((1994) 10) remark on the *Phoenissae* could well be applied to the *Andromache*: 'There is no single narrowly defined event or single person as focus, as "classical" critics have so often desired.' On 'mobility of focus' see Heath (1987) 90–8. The open-ended, interrogatory, and disruptive thrust of tragedy has interesting implications for theories of classical closure, which are often in thrall to misleading notions of the organically whole: cf. Fowler (1994) 232 ff.

[7] Racine's version makes the figures seem more predestined to suffer: given the basic premiss that Oreste loves Hermione, who loves Pyrrhus, who loves Andromaque, who loves her dead Hector, the disaster flows almost inevitably from the passions of the characters and the situation (Menelaus, Peleus, and 'Molossus' are absent, so as not to complicate the action). Such tragic logic has

It is important that we should avoid the common critical muddle which equates unity with continuity: this will allow us to appreciate the close relation between the play's structural dissonance and its depiction of multiple tragic reversals. We must also beware of presuppositions based on 'classical' (sub-Aristotelian) order;[8] a more diffuse and complex form will be outlined and promoted instead. The tendency to apply Aristotelian canons of dramatic coherence has biased many critics against the play. Aristotle's criteria of unity are still very influential, but they are over-intellectual. Aristotle himself might be faulted for having elaborated a prescriptive theory of dramatic design which in fact applies to very few extant plays.[9] His plan (as commonly understood by critics and deployed against 'problem' plays) is too diagrammatic. It risks losing touch with the actuality of dramatic performance, where the audience's sense of cohesion is not dictated by an abstract template but will emerge from experience of the density of the action.[10]

The variety of dramatic design in the plays of all three great tragedians of the fifth century is remarkable. The scale of the whole and the arrangement of detail is unique to each work, and each separate structure is geared to particular effects. It is important that the peculiar qualities of an encounter with the bold structure of the *Andromache* be properly assessed and appreciated. Mastronarde has sketched a conception of 'open'

a remorseless horror and fascination of its own, but it is very different from Euripides' handling of events.

[8] Cf. Mossman (1996b) 145 with nn. 15–17.

[9] Cf. Collard (1981) 14, Taplin (1977), Appendix E (who suspects *Poet.* ch. 12 is spurious).

[10] Many confusions arise from critics' text-boundedness: Friedrich (1953) 60 calls *Andr.* a 'play for reading', and Vellacott (1975) 34 claims most bizarrely that the play's tragic design 'reveals itself, not to the general audience, but to the reader'. Bates (1930) 200 tells very movingly of how a production of Murray's *Trojan Women* made him realize the importance of seeing tragic texts as scripts for *performance*: 'the incidents which seemed like disconnected scenes when read appeared [in performance] to be much more closely knit together, so that there actually seemed to be a plot which advanced steadily to a climax. The play was tremendously effective and the spectators deeply moved.' He rightly says of the *Andromache* (p. 69), 'it is clearly a play to be acted rather than read. The lack of unity would be much less apparent on stage.'

and 'closed' forms of composition which can be profitably applied to the *Andromache*.[11] We will have occasion to note the aptness for *Andromache* of his observation: 'the rhythm of complication and resolution is varied and multiplied'. The action of the *Andromache*, like any other Greek tragedy, is to be perceived in terms of independent human response: an approach which roundly states that 'more than anywhere else the characters appear as mere figures of a calculated mechanism',[12] is unlikely to capture the full emotional complexity and distinctive rhythm of the play.

The detailed analysis of tragic *Bauformen* is often an enlightening approach, but its insistence on the organization of disjunct elements occasionally loses sight of the distinctive tone and atmosphere of the individual play. A static principle of arrangement may lead to the unlovely mechanical subdivision of a work into however many parts; we should rather trace dynamic alterations and developments in content, emotion, and style. It will perhaps be helpful for our discussion if we keep one seemingly simple question before us: 'The description of a poem's structure, then, becomes the answer to the question, "What keeps it going?".'[13] The *Andromache* displays perhaps more clearly than any other Euripidean tragedy the inherent quality of narrative which one might call *dolos*, or the poet's *metis*: his ability to keep the audience hooked. 'One wants to know what is going to happen throughout this play: it generates excitement, born of the proper tragic emotions, pity and fear.'[14]

The prevalence of a linear conception of unity (as continuity) means that, for such plays as the *Andromache*, *Heracles*, or *Phoenissae*, one could easily collate a fat anthology of critical complaints.[15] The complex structure of the last named has

---

[11] See Mastronarde (1994) 3.

[12] Strohm (1957) 113, who thinks this technique 'certainly a danger of Euripidean design', although it seems to me more true of Racine's depiction of an inexorable destiny.

[13] Herrnstein Smith (1968) 4.

[14] Mossman (1996b) 153.

[15] Perhaps the most baffling is Brooks and Wimsatt (1957) 33–4: '*Andromache* falls in half (if not into smaller parts) and might easily be viewed as fragments of at least two unfinished plays stuck together by means of the title and certain other abstract indexes.'

occasioned some particularly negative judgements, which seem to expect that '*Phoen*[*issae*] should have been a simple variation on *Septem*'.[16] The variety of character and incident is often perceived as a fault. Yet with so many striking inventions, Euripides has taken especial care to link them together: the effect is not episodic but cumulative. Although the many solutions to the perceived problem of the *Andromache*'s structure create their own difficulties, it will be useful to consider their general approach, if only to be sure not to repeat their mistakes.[17] We will deal first with the English-language critics, who are generally more outspoken, and come later to the comments of non-English-language scholars. Judgements such as 'the play falls feebly and mysteriously to pieces'[18] are rarely argued with any interpretative cogency or finesse.[19] They seem to adopt a somewhat jaundiced and supercilious attitude to the drama, prejudicially bent on discovering nothing but faults and imperfections, perhaps unduly influenced by a reading of the Aristophanic hypothesis's remark τὸ δὲ δρᾶμα τῶν δευτέρων as negative criticism: 'a play of the second rank'.[20]

There are more appreciative views to be heard: the ever iconoclastic Verrall claimed, '[The play is] in dexterous combination and moral interest one of the best among the extant remains of Attic tragedy'.[21] But even he finds fault with the drama's structure, swayed by an Aristotelian insistence on causal connectedness: 'It presents three incidents, (1) the visit of Menelaus to Phthia, (2) the visit of Orestes, (3) the murder of Neoptolemus at Delphi, not one of which is connected as cause or effect with another.'[22] For Grube,

---

[16] Mastronarde (1994) 4 n. 2

[17] Cf. Boulter (1966) 51–2.

[18] Lucas (1959) 182.

[19] Cf. Whitman (1974) 121 on the 'fitful disjointedness of Euripidean dramaturgy'; the claim is not supported by any textual evidence, but by biographical speculation.

[20] Stevens (1971) 27–8 notes that the remark conflicts with the otherwise laudatory tone of the rest of the hypothesis. In any case, the authority of such hypotheses is minimal. For their general features and readership, see Rossum-Steenbeek (1998) 1–32.

[21] Verrall (1905) 3.

[22] Verrall (1905) 8. Most notorious is Verrall's theory that Menelaus and Orestes were already in cahoots, and that Menelaus' shameful retreat before

Euripides expends too much dramatic time on the conflict between Andromache and Hermione and so overbalances the entire play.[23] Kitto argues that the connecting idea is Euripides' patriotic attack on Sparta: the tragedy is 'not incidentally, but fundamentally, a violent attack on the Spartan mind, on *Machtpolitik*'.[24] One should mention here Kitto's basic premiss that in the 'great tragic period' of Euripides' career (from *Med.* to *Tro.*), Euripides constructed works which are 'all but the *Hippolytus* badly constructed, by Aristotelian standards'.[25] The poet is guided not by concern for structure but by some tragic idea, and 'if conflict arises between the development of the idea and the smooth conduct of the action, it is the action that has to give way'.[26] This neat disjunction is not at all plausible. Euripides is a great dramatist; he was capable of crafting plays with purposeful structures. To attempt to hive off certain features as the 'tragic ideas', which are somehow working against an ideal form of tragic structure, is to set up a false opposition.[27]

The expectation that unity will derive from one single, impersonal, and overarching theme is, we have already noted, misleading.[28] Careful reading of any Euripidean tragedy will reveal a far more complex and unsettling dynamic. Each drama

Peleus was a calculated bluff (cf. Vellacott (1975) 39–42); its fancifulness is rightly criticized by Michelini (1987) 14–15.

[23] Grube (1961) 82: 'Andromache and Hermione as we have them may well be worth the price, but the flaw should not be denied.'

[24] Kitto (1961) 230.

[25] Kitto (1961) 188.

[26] Kitto (1961) 227 on the *Suppliants*. And specifically on the *Andr.*, cf. p. 230: 'Nowhere is it more evident that the unity of the play lies in its idea and not in its story.' Conacher (1967) 173 speaks of the opposition between Andromache and Hermione (and their *philoi*) as an 'intellectual theme'.

[27] Luschnig (1988b) 108 argues that in the *Iphigeneia in Aulis* Euripides was 'willing to sacrifice a canonically well-constructed plot to the ideas in the play'; this seems to rely on a questionable preconception of what makes a good plot. Stevens ((1971) 15) thinks the Trojan War to be the unifying idea in the *Andromache* and claims that Euripides has developed the conflict between wife and concubine 'beyond the requirements of his theme'.

[28] Conacher (1967) 175 identifies the impersonal, unifying element in the *Andromache* as the final separation of good (Phthian and Trojan) from evil (Spartan) elements that were disastrously muddled at the beginning of the play (similarly Kovacs (1980) 75–7, (1987) 13–15).

raises a plethora of interdependent issues, and to seek to
confine this abundance under a central theme cannot do justice
to the plays' richness and variety. Nevertheless, there is abund-
ant criticism of the *Andromache* in the 'tragic hero' style.[29] The
obvious candidate for this role as saviour of unity is Andromache herself. The selfless devotion she displays in attempting
to save her son, and the honesty and bravery she displays in her
arguments with Hermione and Menelaus, are indeed magnificent. Her apparent absence after 765, however, presents a
problem to this approach, and so it is dismissed as of no crucial
significance since, it is argued, her moral superiority still
dominates the second half of the play, colouring our view of
the action, and leading us to criticize the shallow remorse of
Hermione and the duplicitous aggression of Orestes.[30] However, this is to overstate the extent to which we focus on her
personally as the play develops:[31] even while she is still on stage
during the *agon* of Peleus and Menelaus, it is the contrasting
values of the men themselves which draw our attention. Taking
the other female figure, scholars have endeavoured to make
Hermione's passage from jealous plotting to despair the core of
the play.[32] But this is hardly tenable. Hermione is not the
innocent victim this account tends to suggest,[33] our sympathies
do not lie particularly with her, and her fate is no part of the
play after 1062.[34]

Perhaps a more plausible candidate is Neoptolemus himself.
Though he does not appear until relatively late in the play, and
only then as a corpse, there can be a persuasive argument made
for saying that the structure of the play depends strongly on the

[29] Cf. Conacher (1967) 125: 'It is true that this play lacks the kind of unity
essential to tragedy proper.' As often this is defined in 'Sophoclean' terms as
some 'universal truth or value in life' which is revealed by the suffering of a
particular hero.

[30] Argued by Kamerbeek (1943) 62 f. and Erbse (1968), esp. 297; criticisms
in Steidle (1968) 119, Mastronarde (1979) 115, Lesky (1983) 255.

[31] Cf. Erbse (1984) 130 (correcting his earlier view of Andromache's role):
'Whoever focuses on her part in the action will find therein no unifying force.'

[32] Garzya (1951) 127–8; Norwood (1906) lx–lxii, (1954) 43 f.; Pagani
(1968).

[33] Garzya (1963) xxxvii speaks of 'a fundamental innocence . . . [and] her
moral integrity'.

[34] Some of these counter-arguments to unity of person are owed to Stevens
(1971) 9–11.

role of the absent hero.[35] Kamerbeek concedes that 'Neoptolemus . . . contributes uniquely to the unity of the tragedy',
but he considers that the dead hero is not 'in the end the figure
who unites the different motifs of the play'.[36] Neoptolemus'
absence certainly emphasizes the dislocation of the family. He
is also the cause of the conflict between Hermione and Andromache, and it is his prolonged absence which gives occasion to
the interventions of Menelaus, Peleus, and Orestes, the last of
which leads to his own death.[37] Moreover, Euripides keeps
Neoptolemus in mind throughout the play,[38] and his role
(albeit through absence) is structurally effective both as a
source of suspense, and 'as a brilliant and surprising idea
which with one stroke connects the events in Thessaly and
Delphi'.[39] Neoptolemus is central to the play's dynamic in so
far as its structure is based on the traditional *nostos* pattern of
the hero's return.[40] (His father, too, is absent but central for
most of the *Iliad*.) As in the *Odyssey*, the absence of the head of
the *oikos* leads to problems at home, and his return is only
effected after much preparation. Odysseus himself is not even
named in the proem to the first book of the *Odyssey*, and
appears in person only at 5. 149. The introduction of Neoptolemus is similarly deferred, and is preceded by, as Lloyd
points out (p. 3), 'an unusually complex sequence of events in
his home: not only the persecution of Andromache by Hermione and Menelaus, but also Hermione's elopement with
Orestes'. Euripides is self-consciously playing with the standard form of the *nostos* pattern, misdirecting his audience, and
encouraging them to foresee a development (the return of
Neoptolemus and his reinstatement of social and domestic
order) which he then frustrates.[41]

---

[35] First proposed by Hartung (1844) ii. 113 f. and developed by Friedländer
(1926) 99–102; criticized by Friedrich (1953) 47 f. and Lee (1975) 6. Grube
(1961) 82 sees unity deriving from the vengeance of Apollo upon Neoptolemus.

[36] Kamerbeek (1943) 67, although 'his body . . . symbolises the corruption
caused by the Trojan war.'

[37] Cf. Friedrich (1953) 47 on Neoptolemus as 'the central point of the myth
that is being handled'.   [38] Mossman (1996b), esp. 149 ff.

[39] Steidle (1968) 129.   [40] See Lloyd (1994) 3–6.

[41] On Euripides' fondness for this 'tantalizing' technique, see Friedrich
(1953) 58–60.

Lesky makes explicit the worries of many critics who fail to
see the point of the double 'plot' (Hermione and Menelaus
against Andromache, Orestes against Neoptolemus): 'Euripides has in this play joined together two plots with greater
indifference to the unity of the work than anywhere else.'[42] Yet
this elaboration is carefully prepared for in Andromache's
opening speech.[43] The play is an artful example of Euripides'
interest in the unorthodox development or coupling of traditional stories, and the use of combination plots built from
inherited and invented material.[44]

Before we look in more detail at the text, we should first
consider the stage topography of *Andromache*.[45] An image of it
is important to our visualization of the stage action. We rely
primarily on Andromache's own fairly detailed description of
the scene in the prologue (16–23):

> Φθίας δὲ τῆσδε καὶ πόλεως Φαρσαλίας
> σύγχορτα ναίω πεδί᾽, ἵν᾽ ἡ θαλασσία
> Πηλεῖ ξυνῴκει χωρὶς ἀνθρώπων Θέτις
> φεύγουσ᾽ ὅμιλον· Θεσσαλὸς δέ νιν λεὼς
> Θετίδειον αὐδᾷ θεᾶς χάριν νυμφευμάτων.
> ἔνθ᾽ οἶκον ἔσχε τόνδε παῖς Ἀχιλλέως,
> Πηλέα δ᾽ ἀνάσσειν γῆς ἐᾷ Φαρσαλίας,
> ζῶντος γέροντος σκῆπτρον οὐ θέλων λαβεῖν.

I live here in Phthia, in the lands that border on the city of Pharsalus,
where the sea-goddess Thetis used to live with Peleus, far from
the company of men and shunning the throng. The people of Thessaly call the place Thetideion in memory of the goddess's marriage.

[42] Lesky (1947) 99.

[43] Our attention is drawn to Neoptolemus and to the unusual (and risky)
nature of his expedition by Andromache's lengthy explanation of his absence
(50–5); note the danger of μανία ('madness') against a god, and the remoteness
of εἴ πως . . . | θεὸν παράσχοιτ᾽ ἐς τὸ λοιπὸν εὐμενῆ ('in the hope that . . . he may
make the god favourable in the future').

[44] Webster (1971) 32 interestingly sees Euripides 'experimenting with a
new form of tragedy, a triangle of characters, Andromache, Hermione, and
Neoptolemus—Hermione with her own background of Menelaus and Orestes,
and Neoptolemus with his own background of Peleus, who in fact represents
him on stage—who are examined in turn, each at a crisis.' Strohm (1957) 112
fails to appreciate the individuality of the play: 'to a remarkable extent only
consequences are played out in *Andromache*'.

[45] On the manipulation of 'tragic space' by Euripides, see Croally (1994)
174 ff.

Achilles' son then took possession of this house, but he allows Peleus to rule over Pharsalus, not wishing to take the sceptre while the old man is still alive.

The extent of the detail is dramatically important: firstly, it explains why Peleus is absent but close enough to lend support, and secondly, it foreshadows the crucial role played by both Peleus and Thetis later in the play. The *skene*[46] represents the house of Neoptolemus at Thetideion in Phthia (a district of Thessaly),[47] bordering on the territory of the city of Pharsalus, where Peleus continues to rule. Though Thetideion is a real place, its 'exact location and nature remain unknown'.[48] Pherecydes (*FGrH* 3 F 1c) calls Thetideion a πόλις Θεσσαλίας ('town of Thessaly'), but here it seems that nothing more than the royal house and shrine of Thetis are meant, complete with an altar and statue of the goddess. In the play-world, at any rate, Thetideion is clearly to be thought of as rather remote (χωρὶς ἀνθρώπων 18, 'far from the company of men'). The action, it has been argued, is set at the edge of the Greek world.[49] However, while there are interesting effects in setting a play at the limits of the Greek world (*Hecuba*), or even beyond them (*IT, Helen*), the boundary for Euripides was usually in the Propontis region, not in mainland Greece. Thessaly was, of course, the setting for the exotic bargaining of Apollo and Death over the fate of Alcestis, but the atmosphere of *Andromache* is very different. What Thetideion, Pharsalus, and Phthia do offer,

---

[46] A simple wooden building, perhaps introduced in the late 460s: see Taplin (1977) Appendix C, Csapo and Slater (1995) 79–80. The symbolic use of the *skene* is discussed by Wiles (1997) ch. 7.

[47] Phthia is familiar from the *Iliad* as the home of Achilles: see Hainsworth (1993) 115 on *Il.* 9. 395 for the ancient debate about its precise position and political status. Hope Simpson and Lazenby (1959) 104, (1970) 128 argue that Phthia is to be understood in epic as referring to a region, not a *polis*. This matches its description in *Andr.* (e.g. 507, 861). The significance of the play's Thessalian setting is discussed further in Chapter 5.

[48] Lloyd (1994) 10. The two likeliest sites are in the Enipeus valley: cf. Stählin, (1924) 141, Dakaris (1964) 68 n. 1. Stählin (*RE s.v.* Thetideion, 205–6), Walbank (1967) 577–8 and Pritchett (1969) 114–17 (with pictures, pp. 233–5) support a site approximately 10 kms. north-east of Pharsalus. Hammond (1988) 67, 70–1 places Thetideion due north of Pharsalus at a site which, appropriately for Thetis, features a spring. Decourt (1990) 205–8 reviews the evidence and gives further bibliography on both locations.

[49] Kuntz (1993) 65.

however, is a *Greek* setting with strong *epic* connections, and
these features advance the play's exploration of both ethnicity
and heroism.

The following discussion of the *Andromache*'s design is
subdivided into smaller sections (usually coinciding with the
entry of new characters). The divisions are intended to give an
impression of the dramatic movement of the whole, while
accentuating the density of detail and individuality of each
scene as it strikes the consciousness of the audience.[50] The
moment-by-moment analysis tries to show that there is an
aesthetic of surprise operating in the text, with broad moral
significance for our interpretation of the characters and their
actions. We are interestingly and thought-provokingly brought
to contemplate the same set of events from a range of distinct
perspectives. Moreover, there are multiple connections and
contrasts between the different parts of the play which cannot
be reduced to a simple message.[51] The intricate, surprising
structure variegates the moral atmosphere and enhances the
multiple impact of its movement.

1–55: The play opens with Andromache at the altar.[52] We do
not need a temple door for Andromache to enter from, since
hers is a 'cancelled entry'.[53] We are immediately plunged into
the emotional tension of a suppliant scene. This is one of
Euripides' favourite openings (cf. *Hcld.*, *Suppl.*, *Her.*, *Hel.*),[54]

---

[50] Discussion of the choral songs is reserved for Ch. 7, but one should
recognize here their distinctive contribution to the structure of the play. The
first, third, and fourth stasima all deal with the *past* (the Judgement of Paris,
the career of Peleus, the abandonment of Troy by the gods, and the sufferings
of the Achaeans). Their reflections add to the constant emphasis on Troy.
Neoptolemus too dies after reproaching Apollo over his father and the past.
Recollection and its subsequent emotions are thus very important to the shape
and atmosphere of the play.

[51] Cf. Mossman (1996b) 154 n. 13.

[52] In suppliant plays the altar was probably placed at or near the centre of
the orchestra: see Rehm (1988) 274, 307; Wiles (1997) 66, 188.

[53] *Contra* Hourmouziades (1965) 50; cf. Taplin (1977) 134.

[54] The situation of Megara offers interesting parallels and contrasts: she
harks back to her happy past in Thebes (*Her.* 63 ff.), as Andromache does to
hers in Thebe and Troy (1–5); in the absence of their 'husbands' both women
are suppliants at altars, but whereas Megara's children are trapped, Andromache has the ingenuity to smuggle her son out (albeit unsuccessfully).

a powerful visual enactment of the helplessness of the victims.[55] But what begins as an orthodox suppliant play turns into something rather remarkable: three distinct suppliant situations develop in a pattern of repeated reversals of fortune.[56] Here it is expressed in a prologue structure of two monologues (1–55, 91–102) separated by a dialogue (56–90) and capped by an elegiac lament (103–16). The last element occurs only here in extant tragedy. The movement from Andromache's past and present crisis in her monologue, through the brief dialogue (stressing the threat to her son and her resourcefulness), to the epic evocations of the lament well illustrates the flexibility of Euripidean composition.[57] Despite the striking element of regularity (burlesqued by Aristophanes' *Frogs*) of a more or less narrative spoken prologue, Euripides' prologue-parados sections as a whole possess great variety.

Surprise and discontinuity are possible because the prologue does not betray the diversity of action to come.[58] The 'table of contents' approach to Euripidean prologues fails to appreciate how crucial details are omitted or events are presented in an order different from the subsequent action.[59] In the prologue of the *Andromache* every principal character is named except, significantly, Orestes (whose name is also absent from the subsequent dialogue and choral lyrics). Euripides carefully prepares a scenario where Orestes' entrance is a plot surprise (but apt to the issues of marriage, revenge, and war's disruption

---

[55] Kopperschmidt (1971), esp. 339–43; Segal (1992) 99.

[56] In *OC* Sophocles shows three suppliant situations (Oedipus, Creon, Polyneices), but our reactions to each are no less distinctly different.

[57] Cf. Schmidt (1971), esp. 34–44; on the importance of the past to Andromache, see Strohm (1977) 125.

[58] See Segal (1992) 97. The suspenseful possibilities of 'predictive' prologues are all too often overlooked (cf. Ar. *Frogs*, 1177–1250, where the humour is generated by the predictability of the ludicrous ἀπὸ ληκυθίου ('from a flask') tag). Friedrich (1953) 60 criticizes the *Andromache* prologue since it denies the possibility of a powerful 'Aeschylean' crescendo to the play's end. But Euripides has a different purpose: it is only with Orestes' promise of revenge (995 ff.) that we have an inkling of the (mythically novel) circumstances of Neoptolemus' death.

[59] For this *suggestio falsi* technique see Dodds (1960) 69 on *Bacch.* 52; cf. also *Ion.* 69–73., *Hipp.* 42. (On Homeric misdirection, see Rutherford (1996) 54 n. 20.)

of social order). Most remarkable is the wealth of information given about Neoptolemus: he is mentioned at 14, 21–3, 33, 36–8, and we are clearly meant to keep him in mind throughout the play despite his absence.[60] The rehabilitation of Neoptolemus is marked: he is deferential to the aged Peleus (22–3), and seen as a source of succour by Andromache (49–50 are critical of his absence but acknowledge his aid). The slave-woman concurs and groups him as one of her mistress's *philoi*: δοκῶ γὰρ οὐκ ἂν ὧδέ σ' ἂν πράσσειν κακῶς | κείνου παρόντος· νῦν δ' ἔρημος εἶ φίλων ('Yes, though if he was here, I don't think you'd be in such a bad state. But as things stand, you are bereft of friends', 77–8; cf. 138 f., where the chorus refer to the absence of Andromache's Trojan *philoi*). It is notable that we get a sense of the complexity of his character although he never speaks (except for brief remarks reported by the messenger). We are asked to reconstruct his persona from the remarks of others; from Andromache, as Mossman notes, we get the interesting assemblage of unwanted lover and loving father.[61] The reasons for his absence are given in particular detail (49–55): the audience is led to ask, how genuine are these motives, will Neoptolemus return from his mission (which we have seen to be a likely Euripidean invention), and what will he make of the turmoil in his home? This initial suspense is part of Euripides' fondness for the drama of surprise and escape.

The prologues of Euripides are not merely expository but affect our response to the ensuing action. Whether mortal or divine, the figures who speak in the prologues are far from being impersonal purveyors of an objective view of events.[62] One critic has argued that 'while nothing in the speech is without point, the close packing of much information does create a typically dry and didactic atmosphere.'[63] Her general claim is dubious, while the specific criticism of *Andromache* is certainly mistaken. Andromache's tale of personal distress is

---

[60] *Contra* Grube (1961) 213: 'When his body is carried in, it is to us the body of a stranger.'

[61] Mossman (1996b) 150–1.

[62] *Pace* Schmidt (1971) 34.

[63] Michelini (1987) 104 n. 45. Davies (1991) 55 seems to emphasize the factual aspect of Euripides' prologues at the expense of their emotional atmosphere. Easterling's ((1982) 71) 'summarizing monologues', her description of the prologues of *Hel.* and *Phoen.*, cannot embrace the *Andromache*.

anything but dry and didactic; on the contrary, with its recollection of carnage and enslavement, and its emphasis on the injustice of Hermione's intent to kill, Andromache's speech is calculated to set up the crisis facing her in the starkest emotional terms.[64] It is also significant that Euripides does not normally have protagonists speak the prologue-rhesis, 'apparently because he preferred to keep this part of the play free from pathos'.[65] Of the three exceptions among the preserved plays (*Andr.*, *IT*, *Hel.*), the monologues of Andromache and Helen are dramatically motivated by the opening suppliant tableau.

Andromache's suppliant position stresses her isolation, while her servile clothing marks her demeaned status.[66] The emphasis on constraint and helplessness before superior force (cf. 36–8) creates 'a mood of constriction . . . *aporia* or *ananke*'[67] which is typical of tragic beginnings. It magnifies at once, and without sentimentality, the heroic endurance of Andromache and the low cowardice of her attackers (who dare to operate only in Neoptolemus' absence). The contrast between Andromache's heroic past and her present unwilling embroilment in the Spartans' nasty plot articulates a central theme of the action, 'the dissonance between εὐγένεια ['inborn nobility'] and δουλοσύνη ['slavery']'.[68] The disruption of heroic standards is implicit in the behaviour of Menelaus, whom Andromache reports to be newly arrived from Sparta and somewhere in the house (40–2). This foreshadows his entry, but more importantly creates tension surrounding its timing. When he does arrive (309), it is not from the house but from the country, where he has intercepted Andromache's son. The dramatic surprise is prepared for in the prologue by Andromache's claim to have smuggled the child away secretly to another house (μὴ θάνηι φοβουμένη 48, 'for fear that he might be killed'). Our

---

[64] Cf. Strohm (1977) 119: 'Hector's widow interprets her suppliant role in a very personal way.' For the 'contrast "formerly fortunate, now wretched"' in prologue speeches, see Mastronarde (1994) 142 on *Phoen.* 3–4.

[65] Harder (1985) 58–9.

[66] Polyxena's pointed refusal to supplicate Odysseus draws attention to her transcendence of slavery: θάρσει· πέφευγας τὸν ἐμὸν Ἱκέσιον Δία ('Do not worry: you have escaped my Zeus of Suppliants', *Hec.* 345).

[67] Segal (1992) 87.

[68] Strohm (1977) 124.

hopes for the child's safety are thus all the more powerfully overturned.[69]

56–116: A slave-woman exits from the house.[70] She is a fellow Trojan, now a slave in the house of Neoptolemus. Her opening word δέσποιν' ('mistress'), and its expansion back to Troy (55–8), make clear her status as a former slave to Andromache: the pathos of her mistress's fallen station is increased, while her insistence on the old title reaffirms the true nobility of the Trojan princess. As is normal in tragedy for someone of her rank, the slave-woman's entry is unannounced, but not of course unmotivated: she comes bringing news of developments in the plot against Andromache's son. Neoptolemus' absence is again cited as a criticism (ὁ δὲ κεκλημένος | πατήρ 75–6, 'your so-called father'; cf. 49–50), but the possibility is raised for the first time of Peleus' arrival instead, creating another source of tension and suspense. We learn that Andromache has already sent many messengers to him (81), but their half-hearted attempts reinforce her helplessness and the extremity of her present encounter with her former slave. The slave-woman describes Hermione's suspicion in words that suggest not merely vigilance but near-paranoia about Andromache: κίνδυ-νος· Ἑρμιόνη γὰρ οὐ σμικρὸν φύλαξ ('It's risky [to get a message out]; Hermione is no push-over as a guard', 86).[71] There is skilful preparation for the overwrought tone of Hermione's entry. When the slave-woman agrees to try and inform Peleus, her willingness rests on the principle of helping one's friends, resourcefully deployed by Andromache (87–8).[72] The slave's

---

[69] In Antiphon's early fourth-century tragedy *Andromache*, the motif of hiding the child is transposed to an earlier point in her story: it is Astyanax who is hidden, not 'Molossus'; see Xanthakis-Karamanos (1980) 41–6; cf. Sen. *Tro.* 461–518.

[70] The prologue pattern of speech followed by formal parodos is rather rare: *Suppl.* and *Bacch.* The *Andromache*'s monologue plus dialogue form is the most common: see Conacher (1988) 155–6 on *Alc.* 1–76. Yet the flexibility of the form can embrace the macabre humour of Apollo's attempt to bargain with Death, the grim contract of Athena with Poseidon, the *teichoskopia* at Thebes, and the multiple ironies of Teucer's summary of the Trojan War for Helen's 'double'.

[71] For the colloquial tenor of the line see Stevens (1976) 27.

[72] In *Trach.* it is the Nurse who urges Deianeira to send Hyllus after her husband (52–7); Hyllus promptly enters. In the *Andromache* the father is

loyal response to the claims of φιλία ('friendship') sets up a standard with which to measure the behaviour of (mostly non-servile) characters who have yet to appear. The slave-woman departs for Pharsalus, and the brief dialogue is framed by Andromache's parting instruction χώρει νυν ('Be on your way, then!', 91).

Andromache is now alone again on stage, prostrated by the news of the Spartans' intentions. Andromache's reflections (93–5) on the pleasure of women in θρῆνοι ('dirges') and γόοι ('lamentations') introduce an 'elemental outburst of vehement lamentation';[73] similar complaints are found in later plays in the female monody sung before, or as part of, the *parodos* (*Hec.* 59 ff., *El.* 112 ff., *Tro.* 98 ff., *Hel.* 164 ff.; cf. *Med.* 131 ff.). As Mossman notes with regard to Hecuba's anapaests (*Hec.* 59–89), the placing of a monody 'near the beginning of a tragedy . . . makes the opening an arresting one'.[74] Andromache's sung elegiacs are no less striking. The transition from direct speech to monody is exceptionally direct. Although it is a versatile form,[75] this is the only instance of the elegiac metre in Greek tragedy. It is highly characteristic of Euripides' individual approach to dramatic structure that 'something new and unexpected [be] added in the second part of the prologue'.[76]

Page well discusses the structure and style of Andromache's lament, though his claims for the influence of an Argive tradition of threnodic elegy are difficult to substantiate: there is simply not enough evidence.[77] As his critics point out, even if some early elegy was threnodic, this remains our only example of the supposed genre.[78] Nevertheless, while it is right to stress

---

absent while his son is in danger; Andromache is forced to look to an old man for help. The slave-woman's remark γέρων ἐκεῖνος ὥστε σ' ὠφελεῖν παρών ('He is too old to aid you by his presence', 80) increases the impact of Peleus' forceful intervention; cf. Mastronarde (1979) 84.

[73] Kannicht (1969) ii. 58 on *Hel.* 164 ff.   [74] Mossman (1995) 52 n. 16.

[75] Cf. Σ *Andr.* 103: ἐλεγείοις οὐ μόνον ἐπὶ θρήνων ἀλλὰ καὶ ἐπ' ἄλλων ἐχρῶντο ('Elegiacs were used not only for laments but for other things too').

[76] Harder (1985) 80.

[77] Page (1936); Harvey (1955) 170–1 supports Page's idea of a 'forgotten school of Dorian elegists, who used the form for a kind of lament', but offers no new arguments.

[78] See Bulloch (1985) 33, Bowie (1986) 22.

that elegy was performed primarily at symposia and public festivals, it would be wrong to discount the possible use of elegiac laments at funerals. Sepulchral epigrams were often written in elegiacs. (Andromache's lament represents, as it were, the 'tomb' of her past.) One could argue that by using the elegiac metre Euripides is simply showing off his versatility. But there is more to it than that. Given Euripides' liking for a heroine's lament at this point in the play, the choice of elegiacs (instead of lyric) is well explained by the dactylic metre's evocation of Andromache's Iliadic grief.[79]

Lloyd points out that the elegiacs 'may also have seemed more dignified and self-controlled'[80] than the lyric alternatives. Yet these are also intensely emotional lines.[81] Sung to the *aulos*, they display the typical features of tragic song, 'intensification of mood . . . [and] heightened delivery . . . with the power to arouse emotion'.[82] Here the modulation in emotional register through music is supported by the content of the song, which situates Andromache's current predicament in Greece within the wider epic narrative of her city's destruction and her husband's piteous death. The atmosphere of constriction and restraint builds as she focuses on her present condition, a weeping suppliant in need of divine protection (113–16):

> ὤμοι ἐγὼ μελέα, τί μ' ἐχρῆν ἔτι φέγγος ὁρᾶσθαι
> Ἑρμιόνας δούλαν; ἇς ὕπο τειρομένα
> πρὸς τόδ' ἄγαλμα θεᾶς ἱκέτις περὶ χεῖρε βαλοῦσα
> τάκομαι ὡς πετρίνα πιδακόεσσα λιβάς.

Alas, alas for my sorrow, why should I still look on the light of day as Hermione's slave? Harassed by her I have come as a suppliant to embrace this statue of the goddess and I dissolve in tears like a streaming rocky spring.

---

[79] The epic tone of the elegy is underscored by Homeric diction. For example, in lines 113–16 quoted below both τάκομαι ('I melt') and λιβάς ('spring [of tears]') are highly reminiscent of epic composition (cf. *Od.* 19. 204 ff., *Il.* 9. 14–15 = 16. 3–4). Cf. Barner (1971) 297.

[80] Lloyd (1994) 111.

[81] Cf. Segal (1993) 16: the tradition of the lament is taken up in tragedy 'to give ritualized expression to intense emotion and to provide comfort, solace, and security amid anxiety, confusion, and loss'.

[82] Easterling (1997a) 158. For similar effects in Roman drama see Jocelyn (1967) 243.

Her personal lament balances and contrasts with the communal *kommos* of Peleus and the chorus over the death of Neoptolemus (1173–1225). The song's metre, content, and structure convey Andromache's overwhelming sorrow, and reinforce the pathos of her prologue speech.[83]

117–308: The chorus of Phthian women enter. In Chapter 7 the metrical coherence of the lyrics is discussed in more detail: here one need only note how easy the transition is from Andromache's elegiacs to the chorus' opening hexameter. Their entry is explicitly motivated, but in such a way as to arise plausibly from the crisis on stage. They have come εἴ τί σοι δυναίμαν | ἄκος τῶν δυσλύτων πόνων τεμεῖν ('in the hope that I might be able to find you a cure for your indissoluble troubles', 120–1). The notion of finding a remedy or cure for the conflict introduces us to a web of interlocking imagery which runs throughout the play, and revolves around drugs, disease, and remedies. Andromache has already told us of Hermione's charge of secret sterilization (φαρμάκοις κεκρυμμένοις 32, 'with secret drugs'). In the *agon* between them Hermione connects this with barbarian witchcraft (157 ff.), while Andromache offers a much more mundane diagnosis: she explains Neoptolemus' disaffection by the absence of the φίλτρον ('love-charm') of wifely excellence (207).

At 147 Hermione enters from the house, richly dressed and bejewelled.[84] The first act is framed by Hermione's entry and exit back into the house at 268. She controls the house, entering from there again at 825. Her nurse uses the *skene* door at 802 and 877: her forceful exit from the house contrasts

---

[83] See Taplin (1977) 246–7 for the 'pathos in isolation' generated by song at the end of the prologue.

[84] I agree with Page (1934) 69, Hunger (1952) 372–3, and Stevens (1971) 114–15 that 154 is an interpolation (cf. Taplin (1977) 364 n. 1) and that Hermione's entry is not prefaced by a lacunose choral announcement after 146. Erbse (1968) 283–4 thinks 147–54 is addressed by Hermione to the chorus, showing 'a special freedom', which marks her arrogance. His is a subtle explanation, but rather forced. Hermione does not turn to Andromache first at 155; she has been addressing her all along. Rehm (1988) 303 sees the effect here of the altar's location in the orchestra: 'A strong upstage position greatly enhances the strident entrance of Hermione from the palace (147), allowing her to talk "down" to Andromache.'

with the terrified and secretive mission of Andromache's slave-
woman at 56 (cf. 61: φόβωι μέν, εἴ τις δεσποτῶν αἰσθήσεται,
'fearing that one of my masters might see'). Andromache's
relation to the house is most telling: she enters it at 463 with
her son, under the control of Menelaus and his retinue. They
re-emerge at 501 after the choral song; she is roughly bound,
and her son clings pathetically to her. The identification of the
house as a source of danger is most powerfully made by
Hermione's grand entry. (Menelaus' presence there had
already started the process: καὶ νῦν κατ᾽ οἴκους ἔστ᾽, ἀπὸ Σπάρτης
μολὼν | ἐπ᾽ αὐτὸ τοῦτο 41–2, 'He's inside now, having come
from Sparta for this very reason [sc. to kill me]'.)

The visual contrast between the two women is symbolic of
their social status, and in inverse relation to their moral
standing. Hermione's exaggerated pride in her costume crucially colours her characterization. We find a similar rags-
versus-riches coding at two other *agones* between opposing
women. Electra, married to a peasant and rejecting fineries
(οὐκ ἐπ᾽ ἀγλαΐαις, φίλαι, | θυμὸν οὐδ᾽ ἐπὶ χρυσέοις | ὅρμοις
ἐκπεπόταμαι | τάλαιν᾽ *El.* 175–8, 'It is not fine clothes or
golden necklaces which make my wretched heart beat fast'),
berates the richly attired Clytemnestra for her concern with her
looks (1072–5). As Clytemnestra is like her sister Helen in this
respect (1062–4), so here Hermione is like her mother, a motif
that extends beyond dress to sexual desire. In *Troades*, Hecuba
accuses Helen of having been driven mad by Paris' rich oriental
costume; her lust for extravagance leads her to abandon a poor
Sparta: οὐδ᾽ ἦν ἱκανά σοι τὰ Μενέλεω | μέλαθρα ταῖς σαῖς ἐγκαθυ-
βρίζειν τρυφαῖς ('nor were Menelaus' halls enough for your
extravagant tastes to run riot in!', 991–7). According to Andromache, Hermione is disappointed by the wealth of Neoptol-
emus: πλουτεῖς δ᾽ ἐν οὐ πλουτοῦσι, Μενέλεως δέ σοι | μείζων
Ἀχιλλέως ('You are wealthy among the poor, and Menelaus is
greater in your eyes than Achilles', 211–12). The opening line
of Hermione's elaborate proem refers to the κόσμον . . . χρυσέας
χλιδῆς ('diadem of luxurious gold') which she has brought from
Sparta, one of many wedding gifts which she claims give her
the right to speak freely (πολλοῖς σὺν ἕδνοις, ὥστ᾽ ἐλευθεροστομεῖν
153, 'with a large dowry, so that I may speak as I choose'). This
recalls and powerfully contrasts with Andromache's own open-

ing speech where she looked back to her wedding journey from Thebe to Troy ἕδνων σὺν πολυχρύσωι χλιδῆι ('with a luxurious dowry of gold', 2).[85] Much as Hermione may try to distance herself from the barbarian slave, Andromache's recollection of her past emphasizes their common status as royal women.[86] The dissonance between Andromache's former felicity and present catastrophe heightens our antipathy to Hermione's reckless abuse of power.

The act is structured as an *agon*, with two opposing speeches, punctuated by choral comment, and followed by an increasingly vituperative stichomythic exchange.[87] The scene (discussed in more detail in Chapter 4) is highly formalized but no less effective: so far we have concentrated on Andromache's desperate plight and now we get the chance to see the person responsible for it. The structure of the scene encourages us to weigh their respective arguments with judicious impartiality, but the content and quality of the speeches, and the characters which they manifest, incline us to discriminate in favour of Andromache. The formalism of Euripidean structure does not imply that he views his plays as separate units calculatingly laid end to end.[88] He is interested in the expressive potential of the structural conventions. There are of course shocks and disruptions (failed recognition scenes such as those in the *Ion* or *Helen*), but these are not intended merely for the intellectual amusement of connoisseurs of dramatic structure. It would be unfair, for example, to dismiss as mere mannerism Euripides' interest in the effects of extended passages of stichomythia. Although these do contribute more central elements of the plot, this does not entail incompetent dramaturgy (where figures

---

[85] For the magnificence of Andromache's wedding procession, cf. Sappho fr. 44. 8–10 Voigt: πόλλα δ᾽[ἐλί]γματα χρύσια κάμματα | πορφύρ[α] καταύτ[με]να, ποίκιλ᾽ ἀθύρματα, | ἀργύρα τ᾽ ἀνάριθμα ποτήρια κάλεφαις ('And [there are] many golden bracelets and fragrant(?) crimson-dyed robes, intricate ornaments, and countless silver goblets and ivory').

[86] Hermione's insistence on her father's power balances the importance of Hector to Andromache (cf. 8 ff., 107–8, 222 ff., etc.), 'with which the centres of both their worlds are marked' (Strohm (1957) 27).

[87] Cf. Schwinge (1968) 33–56, Lloyd (1992) 54.

[88] Aristophanes presents poetry being measured by builders' instruments (*Frogs* 797 ff.); for his influence on perceptions of Euripides the 'artisan' (versus an 'inspired' Aeschylus), see Finkelberg (1998) 8–10.

must baldly and artificially fill in the story). No less than Sophocles, Euripides is interested in the use of such dialogue for the development of character.[89]

Here the exchange between Andromache and Hermione breaks down into a series of insults, threats, and defiant ripostes (245 ff.) which illuminate the contrasting character of each woman. The invocation of the imaginary gaze of Thetis' statue (246–8) reaffirms the thematic significance of the goddess's experience. Among the theories mentioned earlier which seek to find a unifying figure for the play, nobody appears to have raised the possibility of Thetis. This is not actually intended as a serious proposal; we have observed earlier how misleading the search for personal integration can be. But she contributes something to the complex interconnection of the play. Her image makes her visually present throughout; this presence is exploited in the first part of the play (not only before Hermione, but to greater effect before Peleus: καὶ νῦν με βωμοῦ Θέτιδος, ἣ τὸν εὐγενῆ | ἔτικτέ σοι παῖδ᾽, ἣν σὺ θαυμαστὴν σέβεις | ἄγουσ᾽ ἀποσπάσαντες 565–6, 'And now they are taking me away, having torn me from the altar of Thetis, who bore you your noble son and whom you revere and worship') and in the last, where she appears in person. Peleus addresses her image just before her entrance: σύ τ᾽, ὦ κατ᾽ ἄντρα νύχια Νηρέως κόρα, | πανώλεθρόν μ᾽ ὄψεαι πίτνοντα ('And you, daughter of Nereus in your dark caves, you will see me falling in total ruin', 1224–5). Most strikingly, the importance of her image is affirmed by its imagined antipathy to Hermione's despairing request: τίνος ἄγαλμα θεῶν ἱκέτις ὁρμαθῶ; ('Which god's statue shall I rush to as a suppliant?', 859). Thetis also bears thematic relation to Andromache as mother (both have lost a son) and to Hermione as wife. But there are significant contrasts with Hermione, for Thetis is divine and so the rightfully dominant partner in the marriage that she leaves; she will be reunited with her husband, who (thanks to her) will never die.

As Hermione leaves to re-enter the house,[90] she threatens

[89] For Euripidean innovation in the use of stichomythia to create pathos, see Mossman (1995) 57 n. 34.

[90] Garzya is unlikely to be right about Hermione's presence throughout the first ode and episode, as Stevens (1971) 126 on 268 argues. To his points might be added Mastronarde's analysis ((1994) 347–8 on *Phoen.* 690) of

soon to undermine Andromache's suppliant status, and to make her leave her refuge *willingly*, i.e. without applying physical force (262–5):

> ἀλλ' ἐγώ σ' ἕδρας
> ἐκ τῆσδ' ἑκοῦσαν ἐξαναστήσω τάχα·
> τοιόνδ' ἔχω σου δέλεαρ. ἀλλὰ γὰρ λόγους
> κρύψω, τὸ δ' ἔργον αὐτὸ σημανεῖ τάχα.

But I will soon make you leave this sanctuary willingly; such is the lure I have for you. However, I will say no more, the deed will soon speak for itself.

Again our curiosity and apprehension are aroused. Hermione whets them further: she will say no more, for the deed will *soon* reveal itself (note the repetition of τάχα ('soon') at line-end).[91] The boundary between what is shown and what is told, the most important constructor of narrative in tragedy, is being subtly blurred, again to increase the audience's involvement in the crisis. Given what we know already about Andromache's attempt to smuggle her son away and Menelaus' attempt to thwart it (which is to be imagined as going on off-stage in the dramatic 'present'), Hermione's threat intensifies our uncertainty about the child's fate.[92] Andromache delivers a short defiant speech as Hermione exits at 268.[93] Taplin says of this technique that it 'tends to lack dignity, and is often used to lower the tragic or heroic tone'.[94] Here it expresses Andromache's bafflement at the destructiveness of Hermione.

instances where an actor remains on stage during a stasimon, which tells against Hermione's presence. Also, as Burnett (1971) 139 n. 10 perceptively saw, if Hermione were to remain, 'the effect of splitting the villain would be lost'.

[91] Seneca has Andromache hide Astyanax in Hector's tomb (*Tro.* 503 ff.); Ulysses extorts the child by threatening to demolish it (*funditus cuncta eruam* 685, 'I will totally destroy it'). Andromache's asylum is a holy precinct: the Spartans dare not destroy Thetis' shrine and so need a strong bait to lure Andromache from it.

[92] Hermione says she will wrest Andromache from her position even if molten lead (τηκτὸς μόλυβδος 266) holds her there. This makes Andromache sound rather like a statue, and so increases her proximity to Thetis (rather than to Niobe, *pace* Golder (1996) 9).

[93] Note πέποιθα ('Yes, I do trust him', 269), picking up Hermione's dismissive ὧι πέποιθας ('in whom you trust', 268).

[94] Taplin (1977) 222.

309–493: Menelaus enters with Andromache's son and an armed retinue. The Spartans' intention to kill the child, announced by the slave-woman at 68–9, now fully enters the drama. The emotional power of the encounter derives from many features which have parallels in various combinations in other plays of Euripides: the threat of expulsion from a sanctuary (*Hcld.*, *Suppl.*, *Her.*, *Ion*), a hostage scene (*Telephus*, *Or.*, cf. Soph. *OC* 818 ff.), and voluntary self-sacrifice (*Alc.*, *Hcld.*, *Hec.*, *Phoen.*, *IA*). Having in common βία ('violence') and ἀνάγκη ('constraint') applied to the helpless, they are here deployed together to provoke both pity and outrage. Strohm well says of this scene: 'Elements from all related plays are united in one space, but in such a way that no simple mosaic, but something unique, is achieved.'[95] Menelaus is unmoved by Andromache's plea for a fair hearing before Neoptolemus (355–60); he merely repeats his ultimatum that Andromache must choose between her life and that of her son (314–18, 381–3). The selfless choice she makes is underscored by a significant movement, her first beyond the shrine since the play began: ἰδού, προλείπω βωμόν ('There, I leave the altar', 411).[96] The mood suddenly changes to one of maternal loss, as Andromache addresses her final words to her son. Euripides has constructed the scene around this moving lament so that Menelaus' revelation of the child's death (an act whose treachery he unashamedly admits, 436 ff.) will seem as outrageous and morally culpable as possible.[97]

The following stichomythic exchange on the justice of the deception recalls the one between Andromache and Hermione on true self-control (234 ff.). Both father and daughter display contempt for universal justice, and espouse instead a chauvinistic relativism (cf. 243–4, 439–40). Their narrow power politics provoke Andromache's most outspoken outburst (445 ff.), a speech whose strong anti-Spartan tenor has occasioned much talk of a jarring disruption of theatrical illusion by

---

[95] Strohm (1957) 58.

[96] Cf. Creusa: λείψω δὲ βωμὸν τόνδε, κεἰ θανεῖν με χρή ('I will leave this altar, even if I must die', *Ion* 1401). But whereas Andromache moves to save her son, Creusa does so under threat of death from hers.

[97] Cf. Strohm (1957) 59: 'He disrupts the self-sacrifice and so completes his brutality.'

extra-dramatic, anachronistic patriotism. (The relation of the speech to historical events is discussed in Chapter 5.) Nevertheless, the speech is entirely consistent with the action thus far and embodies a firm, compelling response to the treatment Andromache has suffered. Her final words before she and her child are taken under guard into the house are defiant and pithily foreshadow possible reversals in store for her oppressors (461–3):

> ἐπεὶ σὺ μὲν πέφυκας ἐν Σπάρτηι μέγας,
> ἡμεῖς δὲ Τροίαι γ᾽· εἰ δ᾽ ἐγὼ πράσσω κακῶς,
> μηδὲν τόδ᾽ αὔχει· καὶ σὺ γὰρ πράξειας ἄν.

You might be great in Sparta, but I was great in Troy. If I am faring miserably, do not boast of this. The same may come to you as well.

Her warnings to Menelaus are immediately taken up by the chorus, whose ode ends with an apostrophe of the absent Hermione (ἔτι σε, πότνια, μετατροπὰ | τῶνδ᾽ ἔπεισιν ἔργων 492–3, 'Retribution for these deeds, lady, will yet come upon you!'). Andromache and her son stand on the brink of execution; the intimations of reversal for their opponents are mere words, and contrast poignantly with the imminent deeds of her attackers. But they do create a hope that her prediction will prove true. The surprise of the failure of the Spartans' plot and the calamity which overtakes Hermione is not defused; instead their defeat is raised as a desired, but unlikely, possibility that increases the pathos of the present scene and affects our response to Peleus' entry. However, the pattern of what follows is more complex and ironical: it seems at first that Hermione will, indeed, suffer (cf. ὀλεῖ μ᾽ ὀλεῖ με 856, 'He will kill me, kill me!'), but in fact she gets away with it.

494–544: Andromache enters, bound, from the house; her son clings to her. The episode of Andromache's rescue and Menelaus' rout shows a structure similar to that of the saved suppliants in *Her.* 442–636. It has been said that Menelaus' order at 433 ἀλλ᾽ ἕρπ᾽ ἐς οἴκους τούσδ᾽ ('Now get into this house') is unmotivated (so Bond on *Her.* 442 ff.). However, Menelaus' reasoning here is not the issue, although one could argue that he wishes to get Andromache and her son inside the house to kill them, or more subtly that he is aware of his treacherous behaviour and wishes to hide the visible embodiment of it. But there is an excellent dramatic motive for the exit before the choral ode: Andromache and her child can make a pathetic entrance at the beginning of the third act. They do so accompanied by an anapaestic greeting from the chorus (494–500), the metre suited to the condemned pair.[98]

This entry leads into a lamentatory *amoibaion* between Andromache and her child. Their pleas for mercy, sung in lyric metre, are answered by the calm brutality of Menelaus, in two anapaestic units of seven lines each, followed by a paroemiac clausula. The alternating rhythms create tension[99] and underline the personal and moral contrasts between the figures. This is the first of three *amoibaia* which are introduced when the central figure of the action is at his or her lowest ebb, just before their dramatic rescue. However, the similarity of form belies their contrasting effects.[100] By contrast with Hermione's unexpected lyrical outburst of regret (825 ff.), the *kommos* of Peleus and the chorus is pure in its emotional intensity. Similarity and contrast also operate through the motif of supplication. Andromache urges her son to supplicate Menelaus: λίσσου γούνασι δεσπότου | χρίμπτων, ὦ τέκνον ('Clasp your master's knees, my child, and beg for mercy', 529–30). This ritual gesture is repeated by Hermione's supplication of

---

[98] Taplin (1977) 73; cf. Halleran (1985) 13 f. Menelaus is clearly there though not mentioned: see Hourmouziades (1965) 142 for this kind of selective announcement.

[99] As noted by Kannicht (1969) ii. 175 on *Hel.* 625–99, who also observes that 'the non-lyric part is often performed by an already unlyrical person'; this seems an apt assessment of Menelaus' character. It is unclear whether Menelaus' anapaests were spoken or chanted: cf. Pickard-Cambridge (1968) 161: 'it is difficult to be positive whether Menelaus required a flute accompaniment, or whether the metre merely expresses the urgency of his commands'.

[100] Dale (1954) xx remarks: '*Andromache* is one of the few plays which require two adult singing actors, one for Andromache and Hermione, one for Peleus'; if she is right, the similarity between Andromache and Hermione's lyrics extends beyond form to the voice itself, and underlines even more forcefully the contrast in content and emotional effect. (However, the distribution of parts is highly uncertain: for different possibilities see Pickard-Cambridge (1968) 145 and Lloyd (1994) 11.) Dale goes on, 'and there can be little doubt that the latter [Peleus] sang the boy's part off stage'. This, however, seems unlikely, for as Stevens (1971) 159 and Lloyd (1994) 133 point out, boy soloists would have been available and permissible for the role.

Orestes (πρός σε τῶνδε γουνάτων | οἴκτιρον . . . σοῖς προστίθημι γόνασιν ὠλένας ἐμάς 892–5, 'By these knees, have pity . . . I put my arms about your knees'). But whereas the child is ruthlessly rebuffed (τί με προσπίτνεις, ἁλίαν πέτραν | ἢ κῦμα λιταῖς ὡς ἱκετεύων; 537–8, 'Why fall before me? You might as well entreat a wave or a sea-beaten rock'), Hermione's appeal for pity is accepted. The repeated gesture underlines the injustice of both responses.

Stage children are a rich source of dramatic pathos, and Euripides exploits their potential to heighten emotion and to sharpen and focus audience sympathy. They are given singing roles at *Alc.* 393–415 and *Suppl.* 1123–64, while Medea's children shout from within the house at 1271–8. Dale notes on the *Alcestis* passage: 'Childishness on the stage, in anything approaching a realistic sense, would be unthinkable within the Greek tragic convention. Here as in *Andr.* 505 ff. the child sings the sentiments its elders feel for it.' The first part of her remark is obviously true, the second not. Euripides is the only tragedian to give children speaking roles,[101] 'always at a moment of emotional crisis, always in song',[102] and their words are not so purely conventional. Often they express themselves in ways which have an important bearing on the play's central theme (cf. *Alc.* 411–15, *Med.* 1271, *Suppl.* 1149–51). Andromache's son cries ὦ πάτερ, | μόλε φίλοις ἐπίκουρος ('Father, come and save your loved ones!', 507–8; cf. Heracles' supplicating son: Ὦ φίλτατ', αὐδᾷ, μή μ' ἀποκτείνῃς, πάτερ· | σός εἰμι, σὸς παῖς *Her.* 988–9, ' "Dearest father", he cried, "do not kill me! I am yours, your son!" '). This takes up the theme of Neoptolemus' absence, and pointedly contrasts with Andromache's return to invocation of her true husband, ὦ πόσις πόσις, εἴθε σὰν | χεῖρα καὶ δόρυ σύμμαχον | κτησαίμαν, Πριάμου παῖ ('O husband, husband, son of Priam, if only I had your arm and spear as ally!', 523–5).[103] The pathetic impossibility of *this*

---

[101] There are no examples in the extant plays of Aeschylus and Sophocles. When children do appear, like Eurysaces in Sophocles' *Ajax*, they do not speak.

[102] Fantham (1986) 73.

[103] Cf. Andromache to the doomed Astyanax: οὐκ εἶσιν Ἕκτωρ κλεινὸν ἁρπάσας δόρυ | γῆς ἐξανελθὼν σοὶ φέρων σωτηρίαν ('Hector will not come, grasping his famous spear and rising from the earth to save you', *Tro.* 752–3).

return is intensified by the repetition of imagery from her elegiac lament (tears flowing over a rock: 532–4 ~ 116), where Hector's death was graphically portrayed (107–8). But with Menelaus poised to kill them, it is from the most paradoxical source, the father of her husband's killer, that rescue comes.[104]

545–801: Peleus enters from Pharsalus. It would be an effective dramatic connection if the attendant who leads him were the same slave-woman whom Andromache sent to alert him at 91. The entry announcement emphasizes Peleus' age (γηραιὸν πόδα 546, 'old legs'; cf. 80, 551–3, etc.), making his indignant vigour all the more remarkable.[105] Menelaus' insistence on the old man's physical weakness (σκιὰ γὰρ ἀντίστοιχος ὣς φωνὴν ἔχεις, | ἀδύνατος οὐδὲν ἄλλο πλὴν λέγειν μόνον 745–6, 'Your voice is like that of a walking shadow, and all you can do is talk') ironically strengthens the impression of the Spartan's moral defeat. Like his daughter, Menelaus is worsted in an *agon*. But the similar construction comprises a broadening of the social and political issues inherent in the domestic dispute of the first *agon*. The (sexual) selfishness and obsession with power displayed by Hermione is paralleled by Menelaus' weakness for Helen (605–9, 627–31) and his military imperiousness (693 ff.). Here the stichomythia is briefer and comes before the main speeches, of which there are two on either side. The more lavish scale allows amplification of the central themes of the degeneracy of the Spartan royalty, and the separation of true nobility from legitimacy (cf. 632–41). Peleus' adherence to, and embodiment of, the aristocratic conception of innate *physis* is opposed to

---

[104] Cf. Gould (1973) 83 n. 46. The last-minute entry of a rescuer was a favourite motif of Euripides: cf. Amphiareus in the *Hypsipyle* (fr. 60. 22 Bond; Hose (1995) 136). Contrast the suppliant-rescue pattern of the *Heracles*, where the absent father returns in the nick of time but the rescue is overturned by the even more surprising, and sinister, entry of two goddesses. The drama of what 'nearly happens' is a popular theme in Euripides (cf. Nesselrath (1992) on the development of the motif): one thinks particularly of the matricide in *Ion*, the fratricide in *IT*, the infanticide in *Cresphontes* (fr. 464 K). We see this technique being developed in the *Andromache* with especial versatility. It is far from being a sign of the exhaustion of the myths (*pace* Friedrich (1953) 59).

[105] In Sophocles' *Peleus* (frr. 487–94 R) the old man needs Neoptolemus' help against the usurper Acastus. In the *Andromache*, by contrast, it is Peleus who comes to protect Neoptolemus' house.

Menelaus' glib chauvinism (cf. 665–6, echoing Hermione 170–6, 860). Andromache and Peleus both put forward universalizing conceptions of justice against the Spartans' morality of pleasure and convenience (note especially the similar structure in Andromache's and Peleus' arguments at 242 and 586: ναί, | καλῶς γε χρωμέναισιν· εἰ δὲ μή, οὐ καλά ~ ναί, | δρᾶν εὖ, κακῶς δ᾽οὔ, μηδ᾽ἀποκτείνειν βίαι, 'Yes, [it is natural to put love first] for those women who love properly, but not for those who do not' ~ 'Yes, to treat well, but not to damage or to kill illegally!').

Our attention is movingly drawn to Andromache's condition by the disruption of ritual gesture: she had asked her son to supplicate Menelaus, and now she falls to her knees before Peleus, explaining χειρὶ δ᾽ οὐκ ἔξεστί μοι | τῆς σῆς λαβέσθαι φιλτάτης γενειάδος ('I cannot touch your beloved beard with my hand', 573–4).[106] The dramatic moment of Andromache's release from her bonds, which marks visually the defeat of Menelaus' plans, is made more vivid by the dense sequence of symbolic stage action, in which Peleus drives off Menelaus' retinue, unties Andromache, summons the child to help, and berates Menelaus for his cowardice (715–26). Menelaus' addiction to empty formulae of reciprocity and reason approaches a ludicrous density (738–43). The empty expressions suggest his desperate attempt to withdraw with some face saved. His promise to return to claim justice from Neoptolemus (737 ff.) is a subtle instance of deceptive plot prolepsis that again raises the possibility of Neoptolemus' return.[107] Menelaus' retreat to Sparta (746) finally releases the tension, as Peleus offers the still fearful Andromache some stern encouragement and escorts her and her child off the stage for good (765). The triumph of Peleus, γέρων εὔψυχος ('a brave old man', 764), leads naturally to the chorus' encomium of his enduring heroism in the third stasimon.

802–78: Hermione's Nurse enters from the house. As with the slave-woman in the prologue, her entry is unannounced. The

---

[106] Kaimio (1988) 54 compares Hypsipyle's bound supplication of Amphiareus (fr. 60. 25 f. Bond).

[107] Cf. Mossman (1996b) 151: 'could he be about to turn up to pass judgement on the events of the suppliant drama, even though he is now too late to effect a rescue?'

slave-woman had brought news of encroaching danger to an
innocent and sympathetic figure and so raised the emotional
tension of the scene; now the Nurse's urgent report shows the
consequences of that failed action for one of its planners. The
break which occurs with the Nurse's entrance marks a radical
new direction for the play.[108] The discontinuity furthers
exploration of Hermione's insecure character. The Nurse
begins by deploring a series of calamities (802–3):

> ὦ φίλταται γυναῖκες, ὡς κακὸν κακῶι
> διάδοχον ἐν τῆιδ᾽ ἡμέραι πορσύνεται.

Dear ladies, how trouble follows after trouble on this day!

We are immediately made curious to hear her news. What new
evil can this be that has overcome the house? She reveals the
source of concern straight away: δέσποινα γὰρ κατ᾽ οἶκον,
Ἑρμιόνην λέγω, . . . κατθανεῖν θέλει ('For my mistress in the
house, Hermione that is, . . . wants to die', 804 ff.). The shift,
both in dramatic focus and in Hermione's condition, is wholly
surprising. As so often in the play, we are suddenly brought to
view events from a radically new perspective. That this does
not merely mean adopting the viewpoint of the scene's dominant character is well illustrated here, since the shallowness of
Hermione's regret complicates our sympathy. What we gain is
a more critical and synoptic type of understanding.[109] In a
similar way, when we discover Orestes' murderous plot, it is
more a factual than a half-sympathetic understanding that
matters. The Nurse reports the emotional turmoil of her
mistress (compare the Nurses of *Med.* and *Hipp.*), but her
account of Hermione's violent change of mind is far from
uncritical (815–16, 866 ff.). The Nurse's request that the
chorus should enter the house (817–19), an atypical act, centres
our attention on the *skene* door from which Hermione now
enters (825). Hermione's panic and hysteria are communicated

---

[108] Strohm (1957) 113 notes the prologue character of the Nurse's speech,
but there is little cause for this often repeated comparison: hers is a very brief
rhesis, with an addressee already on stage (the chorus).

[109] Compare, for example, the latter part of the *Trachiniae*, where we are
led to see how things look to Heracles; we do not simply drop Deianeira's
viewpoint and embrace his. Instead the contrast between the two magnifies
the tragedy of her decision and his interpretation of it.

aurally and visually: she tosses the veil from her head, tears at her hair, face, and clothes, and sings in dochmiacs, the most impassioned and agitated of lyric metres, while the Nurse responds in reasoning iambic trimeters.[110] As Burnett eloquently says, 'With direct reference to her previous scene, Hermione now tears at the costume she had put on to shame her rival; she is no longer dressed to kill.'[111]

Hermione's extravagant gestures of grief disrupt the pathos of the scene.[112] Yet the imagery of her lament creates significant connections and contrasts between the different parts of the play. Peleus had represented himself as filling Andromache's sails with a favourable wind (554–5); then as a calm harbour after the storm, χείματος γὰρ ἀγρίου | τυχοῦσα λιμένας ἦλθες εἰς εὐηνέμους ('For though you met a fierce storm, you have come to a sheltered harbour', 748–9). When Hermione employs the metaphor, she sets up an ironic parallel between the timely arrival of Peleus as saviour and that of Orestes: ὦ ναυτίλοισι χείματος λιμὴν φανείς | Ἀγαμέμνονος παῖ ('Son of Agamemnon, you are like a harbour appearing to sailors in a storm!', 891–2).[113] Her calamity also furthers the play's criticism of Menelaus: ἔλιπες ἔλιπες, ὦ πάτερ, ἐπακτίαν | μονάδ' ἔρημον οὖσαν ἐνάλου κώπας ('You left me, left me, father, all alone on the shore without a seagoing ship', 854–5).[114] This complaint combines nautical imagery with the idea of abandonment (ἔρημος), a condition that afflicts all three figures in their crises. The Spartans exploit Andromache's isolation (νῦν δ'

---

[110] For Euripides' use of the emotional contrast of these metres, see Mastronarde (1994) 173.

[111] Burnett (1971) 146.

[112] Her fearful reaction to Neoptolemus' return compares unfavourably with the more justified distress of Peleus in response to Neoptolemus' death—note the verbal reminiscences between the two actions: σπάραγμα κόμας ('tearing my hair', 826) ~ οὐ σπαράξομαι κόμαν . . .; ('Shall I not tear my hair?', 1209).

[113] Heracles' children are 'little boats' (ἐφολκίδας) at *Her.* 631; the image of rescue is significantly repeated, marking the contrast in the action, at 1424, where Heracles relies on Theseus.

[114] The repetition of ἔλιπες ('you left') is followed in the next line by ὀλεῖ μ' ὀλεῖ με ('He will kill me, kill me!', 856) and is appropriate to moments of high emotion: here the effect is intentionally strained. Cf. Collard (1991) 187 on *Hec.* 1056–1108 (Polymestor's monody), which contain 'frantically repetitious and redundant language'.

ἔρημος εἶ φίλων 78, 'Now you are bereft of friends'; τὴν ἐμὴν
ἐρημίαν | γνόντες τέκνου τε τοῦδ' 569–70, 'knowing that I and this
child were all alone'); Hermione feels herself πατρός τ' ἐρημ-
ωθεῖσα ('abandoned by my father', 805, cf. 918); and finally, it is
her influence on Orestes which ensures the death of Neoptolemus and so the true desolation of Peleus (ὦ φίλος, δόμον
ἔλιπες ἔρημον 1205, 'My dear boy, you have left the house
bereft'; ἄτεκνος ἔρημος 1216, 'childless and alone'). The three
actions are thus closely linked by language but their peculiar,
significantly different qualities are not elided.[115]

   Hermione's sudden panic is seen as a structural problem by
many critics, who judge it poorly motivated psychologically
and jarringly inserted at the close of Andromache's suppliant
drama. However, Euripides has skilfully constructed a second
suppliant scene which is a self-refuting perversion of the
first.[116] The formal duplication points up the expressive contrast between the response of the two women to danger:
Andromache's is courageous, even bullish, and in the face of
pressing extinction; the danger facing Hermione, however,
follows from her own wickedness and is exaggerated by her
panic.[117] The Nurse makes both aspects very clear (866–8):

> ὦ παῖ, τὸ λίαν οὔτ' ἐκεῖν' ἐπήινεσα,
> ὅτ' ἐς γυναῖκα Τρωιάδ' ἐξημάρτανες,
> οὔτ' αὖ τὸ νῦν σου δεῖμ' ὃ δειμαίνεις ἄγαν.

My girl, I didn't praise your *excessive* behaviour when you were *acting
unjustly* against the Trojan woman, nor do I now approve of your
present *excessive* fear.

The Nurse's reaction to Hermione's repeated suicide attempts
(cf. 815–16 ἐγὼ μὲν οὖν | δέσποιναν εἴργουσ' ἀγχόνης κάμνω, φίλαι,

---

[115] Lee (1975) 8 notes the repeated imagery but sees it as 'a further
indication of the similarity of their respective tragic situations'.

[116] Hermione asks τί με βρόχων εἴργεις; ('Why do you not allow me to hang
myself?', 844). βρόχος ('cord') had been used of Andromache's bonds at 501,
556, and 720. Hermione's near-melodramatic wish for the noose creates a
harsh dissonance when set against the unmerited suffering inflicted on
Andromache by Menelaus.

[117] Hermione perceives herself as abandoned by Menelaus; interestingly, in
the *Orestes* we see 'Or. shockingly left in the lurch by his uncle [Menelaus]
and about to die nobly by suicide' (Willink (1986) l). But in Orestes' case too
the threat of death is real and pressing.

'Well, my friends, I'm exhausted from keeping my mistress away from the noose') suggests that the scene could be played semi-comically.[118] The complication of tone and the mixture of emotions are striking. The *Andromache* is not the earliest surviving Euripidean tragedy to experiment with comic flavour: in the *Heraclidae* old Iolaus' enthusiasm for fighting is met by the amused sarcasm of the servant, θένοις ἄν, ἀλλὰ πρόσθεν αὐτὸς ἂν πέσοις ('You may strike, but you might fall over first', 686). But it is the first to play with comic elements in a bitter-sweet way. (Interestingly, it is also the first Euripidean play to have been seriously misunderstood by critics.) Menelaus justifies his hasty departure with a ludicrous and scarcely believable excuse, but one whose professed purpose of subjugating a recalcitrant city qualifies the humour of his cowardice (732–8). In Hermione's case, the Nurse's semi-comic interjections colour our reaction to her overwrought lament, but do not obscure the genuine surprise and unexpectedness of her reversal.

Hermione's departure with the man who has just confessed that he is plotting her husband's murder further complicates our response to her despair and terror. The unusual sequence of events,[119] in which she leaves with Orestes *before* Neoptolemus' death, encourages us to reflect critically on their actions. Friedrich saw a chance for greater unity in making Hermione a Clytemnestra, urging Orestes on to kill her husband: 'what is now only appearance would become reality'.[120]

---

[118] In Aeschylus' satyr-play *Dictyulci*, Danae briefly contemplates suicide, ἀγχόνην ἄρ' ἄψομαι . . . δέδοικα γάρ ('So shall I knot myself a noose . . .? No, for I'm afraid to!', fr. 47a, 14–17 R). Cf. *Hel.* 298–302 (deleted by Diggle, following Clark), where a melodramatic consideration of suicide methods has been interpolated. Garrison (1995) 99 argues that Hermione's suicide is not typically tragic in so far as it is not 'resolute, noble, socially motivated and therefore understandable and pardonable'. But pardon seems too tame a reaction to the suicides of Ajax or Phaedra, for example.

[119] Noted but not developed by Friedrich (1953) 50.

[120] Friedrich (1953) 54. With the Nurse's complaint (815–16, quoted above) compare Clytemnestra's lie, τοιῶνδ' ἕκατι κληδόνων παλιγκότων | πολλὰς ἄνωθεν ἀρτάνας ἐμῆς δέρης | ἔλυσαν ἄλλοι πρὸς βίαν λελημμένης ('Because of such untoward reports as these, others have often had to release my neck from the high noose which gripped it', *Ag.* 874–6). Whereas Clytemnestra feigns despair at her husband's non-return, Hermione is genuinely panic-stricken by the thought of Neoptolemus' arrival. Racine has Hermione urge

But Euripides' decision to shape a different plot makes for a more interesting portrayal of Hermione's weaknesses, and allows greater scope for examining Orestes' motivation. The nasty persecutor of Andromache is dwelt on unexpectedly; we are suddenly brought to see the complexity of her situation. The unpredictable opening of a new perspective partly challenges our interpretation of the action thus far and Hermione's role in it.[121] The reorientation of our response is effected by concentration on the manipulativeness of Orestes.

879–1046: Orestes enters (from Delphi).[122] His pace recalls Peleus' timely intervention ($\sigma\pi o \upsilon \delta \hat{\eta} \iota$ 546 ~ 880, 'in haste'), and contributes to the pressing atmosphere of crisis. The rescuers, however, like their beneficiaries, are of a very different kind.[123] Euripides is fond of the totally unprepared entry: Iphis and Evadne in the *Suppliants*, Iris and Lyssa in the *Heracles*, Menelaus in the *Troades*, Pythia in the *Ion*.[124] He was evidently

Oreste on to the murder, only to disclaim responsibilty for it with the famous 'Qui te l'a dit?' (Act v, Scene 3). Douglas Dunn's brilliant verse translation (London, 1990) is worth quoting (p. 76): 'HERMIONE: What Fate gives you the right | To send a King into eternal night? | Why did you kill him? What had Pyrrhus done? | Who told you to? | ORESTE: No! No! *You* were the one! | Didn't you, *you*, not long ago command | That Pyrrhus must be murdered by my hand?'

[121] Michelini (1987) 88 claims that 'In Euripidean drama, a moral perspective is denied the audience'; but this does not correspond to the evidence of the texts. Critics seem often to confuse Euripides' interest in the complication of moral situations with a sophistic assault on the process of moral judgement itself.

[122] The Nurse may leave when the others do at 1008, but her departure is more effective at 877, after her advice that Hermione should go inside as well. This leaves the stage free for Hermione and Orestes' encounter.

[123] Aichele (1971) 76 obscures this when he speaks simply of 'the second counter-movement'. There is also an effect of meaningful similarity and contrast in the way the two supplications end. Andromache warns Peleus of the possibility of ambush, but he belittles the threat posed by Menelaus, a coward who is unable to stand up to a brave old man (752 ff.). Hermione in turn warns Orestes that Neoptolemus or Peleus might come any moment and catch them, whereat he dismisses the $\gamma \acute{\epsilon} \rho o \nu \tau o \varsigma \, \chi \epsilon \hat{\iota} \rho a$ ('old man's strength', 993) and reveals his plot against Neoptolemus. His tone of certainty has a powerful and sinister impact, especially after Menelaus' lame retreat.

[124] The Nurse's confident prediction of Menelaus' return (874–5), coupled with his own promise to do so (737 ff.), encourage us to regard him as the likeliest candidate for entry here: the unexpected arrival of Orestes thus

interested in the dramatic effects of unsettled expectations and sudden plot turns, disrupting the course from foreboding to climax. Yet these are never gratuitous: any such change is (and here the Aristotelian terms are apt) 'a reversal that appears to rise paradoxically, yet naturally and inevitably, out of the nature of the *dramatis personae* or out of their intentions, plans, or actions.'[125] Orestes addresses his first words to the chorus, apparently unaware of Hermione's presence. The visual tableau (Hermione about to leave with the Nurse, Orestes entering but not seeing her) increases the impact of her sudden advance and supplication.[126] Her supplication of Orestes is a mirror scene of the earlier plea of Andromache to Peleus: whereas Hermione can make the full ritual gesture of clasping Orestes' knees, Andromache could only fall before Peleus, unable to touch his chin (572–4). The visual contrast within the repeated ritual context invites us to connect the two events while comparing their differences. Although both are successful, our reaction to them is coloured by the character of the participants and the seriousness of their crisis.

The two stichomythic exchanges thus far have been hostile and abusive; they increase the tension between the opponents (Andromache and Hermione, Peleus and Menelaus) and express vividly their polarized beliefs. The exchange between Orestes and Hermione is not on the surface that of a suppliant and her attacker. However, his role as defender is subtly ironized by the content of their dialogue. We learn that Orestes has known of events all along, but has waited for the strategic moment to act (957 ff.; cf. his pretend astonishment at 896 ἔα | τί χρῆμα;, 'Ah, what's going on?'). The delay makes his manipulation of Hermione's emotional state appear quite calculated. The positioning of the scene works unexpectedly to generate sympathy for Hermione. Though her demeanour is

underlines the fraudulence of Menelaus' claims to concern for his φίλοι ('friends'). Kovacs (1980) 48 remarks that 'Menelaus' failure to reassure his daughter before he leaves is a slight irrationality.' But the characterization by Euripides is quite deliberate.

[125] Seidensticker (1996) 381. Cf. Garvie (1978) 80 on Aeschylus' technique of misdirection: 'the surprise is never a crude one, and he never disrupts the basic unity of the play'.

[126] Seen by Kaimio (1988) 56–7.

uncomfortably self-abasing, the character and intentions of her
rescuer alter our response to her. Now Orestes reveals his
intention to make her a widow (993–1008). There is no reason
to suppose that Hermione has departed at 992.[127] Her presence
underlines the jealous, obsessive anger of Orestes: no less than
Menelaus (for Helen) or Hermione (for Neoptolemus), he is
prepared to kill to regain the one he believes to be his. Far from
being a kindly reassurance,[128] the speech exhibits Orestes'
continued embroilment in the murderous consequences of
sexual jealousy in a disordered household. The chorus's final
ode recalls the matricide as a murder disgracefully supported
by Apollo, a crime whose origins lay in the treachery of a wife
(1028–36). Hermione's present betrayal of Neoptolemus compounds the denigration of Orestes' revenge. Expectation of
Neoptolemus' return has already been frustrated by the surrogate action of Peleus. Orestes' speech focuses our attention
once more on Neoptolemus' fate. The danger now so obviously
threatening him helps ease the transition from the double
supplication-and-rescue plot to the new plot at Delphi, and
this 'in turn leads to a more tragic homecoming for him than
had been expected'.[129]

1047–1165: Peleus now re-enters with a retinue from Pharsalus. The final act raises controversies concerning both stagecraft and the handling of narrative time. The first question is:
to whom does the σοί of 1041 refer, and what does this, along
with παῖδα τόνδε (1246), imply about the possible re-entry of
Andromache and her son? The view that σοί refers to Andromache is argued in more detail in Chapter 7. If this is correct,
does it mean that she now returns with Peleus? Stevens
observes that 'unless she is present . . . the reference is
unusually abrupt and obscure'.[130] He therefore reluctantly
follows Kamerbeek (and others) in positing Andromache's
re-entry at this point.[131] His reluctance is understandable

---

[127] So Verrall (1905) 272.
[128] Kovacs (1980) 73.
[129] Heath (1987) 148.
[130] Stevens (1971) 218 on 1041.
[131] Kamerbeek (1943) 63; for a summary of views on this see Lesky
(1972) 346.

because Andromache does not utter again. But as we shall see, there are good dramatic reasons for accepting her presence, despite her silence.[132]

The most powerful case against Andromache's reappearance has been made by Mastronarde. He finds no parallel for such a choral address to an entering character: 'visual contact with Andromache and an address to her would break the integrity of the withdrawn, non-mimetic stance normal for a chorus when singing a generalizing, reflective antistrophic lyric of this kind.'[133] While it is true that there is no exact parallel in the surviving plays for this kind of direct address,[134] one could view it as a striking adaptation of the regular choral practice of apostrophizing a character near the end of an ode.[135] Furthermore, the evidence of what is merely a tiny proportion of all Attic tragedy should not disallow the entry here on such slender grounds if there are good dramatic reasons in its favour. Quite apart from the visual elucidation of σοί, Andromache's re-entry has an interesting effect on the end of the play.

Before exploring this, however, it is necessary to discuss the evidence of line 1246 for the presence of Andromache's son. The deictic pronoun ὅδε ('this') need not refer to someone in view on the stage, but the majority of its uses do. So at face value Thetis' words appear to refer to 'this boy' as present.[136] Yet if linguistic practice is not conclusive, one should again refer to dramatic effect. The presence of both Andromache and her son on stage adds to the force of the play's closure.[137] The messenger's account of Neoptolemus' death has greater pathos in the presence of his son. Nor can Andromache be indifferent

---

[132] Cf. Golder (1983).

[133] Mastronarde (1979) 100.

[134] Cf. Taplin (1977) 174, who notes that there are 'occasional instances in Sophocles and Euripides where an entry occurs *within* a lyric structure', but these are 'exceptional pieces of technique'.

[135] See Kranz (1933) 206–7.

[136] Lloyd (1994) 163 quotes Mastronarde's emendation τῆσδε ('together with her child'); this is an ingenious but unnecessary solution, as sense can be made of the manuscript reading.

[137] Wilamowitz (1962) 375 claims that Andromache's disappearance leads to the play falling apart, and he believes that the child returns alone. But their joint appearance seems more plausible and better suited to Thetis' prophecy.

to it. Her silence need not be interpreted as condemnation of Neoptolemus.[138] It can be adequately explained by the drama's shift of focus from Andromache's suffering to the death of Neoptolemus and its impact on Peleus.

Most striking is the effect their combined presence has on Thetis' closing speech. When Thetis enters, the stage tableau changes from that of a pathetic group centred on the corpse of Neoptolemus to a visual underlining of the survivors' shared good fortune. Not only is Peleus uniquely rewarded, but Andromache and her son hear personally of their glorious role in the future of the Aeacid house.[139] As Wilamowitz sensitively observed, the child embodies this future, 'and experiences the appearance of the goddess, who is also his great-grandmother. That adds considerably to the pleasure of the closing scene.'[140] So the reappearance of Andromache and her son is not intended to give the play a superficial unity (though Euripides might have brought this out), but to underscore the action's final surprising reversal.

There is another aspect of the chorus's song that requires discussion here, since it has implications for the presence of Orestes at Neoptolemus' murder. Even Lesky, the most diligent proponent of the view that Orestes does not return to Delphi, recognizes the regular tragic technique of treating off-stage space and time with as much foreshortening as the plot requires.[141] This device is particularly common before the

---

[138] *Pace* Erbse (1968) 301–2. Dakaris (1964) 76 n. 2 regards her silence as caused by her continued devotion to Hector: ὁ θάνατος τοῦ ἥρωος δὲν τὴν ἤγγισεν εἰς τὸ βάθος τῆς ψυχῆς της ('The death of the hero [Neoptolemus] has not touched the depths of her soul'). But this is perhaps to psychologize too much. Rutherford (1998 xiii) rightly suggests that 'her mute appearance, recalling to the audience her previous suffering and the miseries of Troy, would modify the effect of the end of the play, in which so much is made of the death of Neoptolemus, one of the sackers of Troy.' But as we saw in Chapter 1, Neoptolemus' role in the sack of Troy is far from prominent. Andromache's Trojan past does complicate our attitude to Neoptolemus, but its main purpose here is to underline the unexpected union of Trojan and Phthian royal houses.

[139] Stevens (1971) 243 on 1243 is right to suggest that although the prophecy affects others, it is addressed to Peleus because it concerns the future of his house. The peculiar relationship between him and the divine speaker is also important.　　　　　[140] Wilamowitz (1962) 382.

[141] Lesky (1947) 101. Kovacs (1980) 51 denies Orestes' presence because

entry of the messenger to report the catastrophe: 'the tension of such situations is enough to bridge the gap in terms of dramatic time'.[142] Although he agrees with Lesky that Orestes does not return to Delphi, Stevens (on 1008) recognizes the textual indications of his involvement there: 1061–5, 1242, 1074–5: τοιάσδε φασγάνων πληγὰς ἔχει | Δελφῶν ὑπ' ἀνδρῶν καὶ Μυκηναίου ξένου ('Such are the sword-thrusts he has received from the Delphians and their Mycenaean friend'),[143] 1115–16: ὧν Κλυταιμήστρας τόκος | εἷς ἦν, ἁπάντων τῶνδε μηχανορράφος ('[Men lay in ambush,] one of whom was the son of Clytemnestra, the cunning contriver of all these events').[144]

None of these excerpts is conclusive in itself,[145] but the opposing case relies rather on the *absence* of explicit statement; and if we attend to the movement of the play it is likelier that we are to imagine Orestes as having already set the Delphians against Neoptolemus (so 995 ff.),[146] and then exiting from Thetideion towards Delphi to see his plot through to its conclusion. But why has this been so often disputed? The reason lies not in careless ambiguities in the text.[147] Misunderstanding is rather due to a change of focus that is often overlooked. For in the messenger's report, Euripides has deliberately guided our attention to Apollo and the Delphians (the traditional killers of Neoptolemus). Orestes, however, still plays a major part: all three share the blame for Neoptolemus' death.[148]

we are 'therefore not forced to assume that the fourth stasimon covers a period of a week or more'.

[142] Taplin (1977) 293. On the flexibility of temporal levels in drama, see Elam (1980) 117–19.

[143] 1075 is omitted in some manuscripts and deleted by Wecklein. Stevens (1971) 221 defends it, but notes its only partial support for the presence of Orestes.

[144] Diggle places a comma after ἦν (1116) and so secures Orestes' presence. As Lloyd (1994) 138–9 notes (on 649–50), Stevens's defence of the rare relative form (without a comma) in 1116 is weakened by Diggle's emendations at the other two places in the play where it is alleged to occur.

[145] Nor is the evidence of vase-paintings: see Lesky (1947) 108 on the possibility of a 'non-Euripidean version' there.

[146] See Pohlenz (1954) ii. 85.

[147] Stevens (1971) 213 even suggests that the ambiguities may indicate the lack of a final revision.

[148] The messenger's speech opens up the *oikos* drama to reveal Delphi, the

Yet why does Orestes make the journey to Thetideion in the middle of his plot? Motivation for Orestes can be supplied without difficulty: to check (and exploit) the development of Hermione's plans (959–63) and to secure his position as her 'saviour'. In more dramaturgical terms, his appearance at this point entices the audience with the story of his plot, which is only partially revealed: ἣν πάρος μὲν οὐκ ἐρῶ, | τελουμένων δὲ Δελφὶς εἴσεται πέτρα ('I will not reveal the trap beforehand, but when things are accomplished, the rock of Delphi will know of it', 997–8). Perhaps most significantly, Orestes' visit forges a link between the crisis in Neoptolemus' household and his death at Delphi. The multiple connections that we have noticed throughout the play ensure that the origins of each action can be perceived in the one before, and that the new direction does not appear merely jarring or irrelevant. The invigorating effects of dislocation and excursion emerge from the larger design and are enhanced by it.

Peleus hears rumour of Hermione's departure and comes for a second time from Pharsalus, τῶν γὰρ ἐκδήμων φίλων | δεῖ τοὺς κατ᾽ οἶκον ὄντας ἐκπονεῖν τύχας ('For when family members are away, those at home should exert themselves to defend their interests', 1051–2). But we see him tragically unable to protect his absent grandson. His attempt to send Neoptolemus a warning message is dramatically reversed. His command οὐχ ὅσον τάχος | χωρήσεταί τις Πυθικὴν πρὸς ἑστίαν ('Let someone go as quickly as possible to the Pythian altar', 1066 f.) is visually answered by the entry of the messenger from Delphi reporting his death (1070). The technique of an intended exit which is prevented by a new entry is a powerful dramatic moment.[149] It well expresses the catastrophe which has suddenly come upon the house of Peleus. Its force is increased by the entry being unannounced (unusual after dialogue), and by the messenger's immediate cry of lamentation, ὤμοι μοι ('Ah, what misery is mine!', 1070). The play has so far presented two (contrasting) dramatic escapes, but there is none for Neoptolemus.

international sanctuary *par excellence*; but the public world depicted is every bit as plot-ridden, suspicious, and murderous as that of the malfunctioning private sphere.

[149] Vickers (1973) 466 comments: 'Prediction and fulfilment merge into one.'

The expectation of Neoptolemus' return, which has been kept constantly in mind through the hopes and fears of Andromache and Hermione, is thus shockingly subverted. Its effect on Peleus is immediate: he collapses with the words οὐδέν εἰμ' ('I am nothing', 1077). The chorus's injunction ἔπαιρε σαυτόν ('Raise yourself', 1077) recalls his own instruction to Andromache: ἔπαιρε σαυτήν (717). The visual and verbal similarities underline Peleus' calamity. The cause is then graphically recounted in the messenger's speech, an incident-filled narrative whose epic motifs evoke a heroism sadly past. Of the description of Neoptolemus' murder at Delphi, it has been said 'No element of the sinister and hateful is wanting; it is a fine climax to a deadly play.'[150] With lavish and piquant unorthodoxy, Euripides presents a noble, heroic Neoptolemus under attack from a treacherous and cowardly Orestes. Structurally, the narrative form of this episode is unexceptional: 'This kind of *angelos*, who might be called an "aftermath" messenger, figures in nearly every surviving tragedy of Euripides.'[151] His moral revulsion at the behaviour of Orestes is unmistakable: 'he is anxious to call attention to Orestes' scheming right from the beginning. In other words, he uses this narrative technique to indict Orestes.'[152] Most strikingly, the messenger's rapid narrative brings the absent hero to life before we see him dead.[153] The presentation of Neoptolemus' brave defence intensifies the grief of Peleus and compounds the pathos of the entry of his grandson's corpse. We have already discussed the unexpected exploration of events from Hermione's viewpoint. The last part of the play exploits the technique of multiple focus to striking effect: Orestes, Apollo, Neoptolemus, and Peleus all bring in different perspectives. The turbulent structure forces our attention to shift rapidly; this challenges our moral capacity to discriminate between competing motives, and invigorates our contrasting response to the characters.

---

[150] Kitto (1961) 235. Conacher (1967) 179 remarks that 'it is important that this necessary death should not be mistaken for a tragic event'. However, this is to underestimate the heroic quality of Neoptolemus' death and the pathos of Peleus' response to it. [151] Taplin (1977) 83.

[152] de Jong (1991) 53–4; de Jong (1990) 10–14 also shows how Neoptolemus is made the centre of the audience's pity. [153] So Mossman (1996b) 152.

1166–1225: a procession enters bearing the body of Neoptolemus. Stevens comments on the chorus's remark to Peleus, αὐτὸς δὲ κακοῖς | εἰς ἓν μοίρας συνέκυρσας ('and you yourself in your troubles have come to share his fate', 1171–2), 'it is rather forced to say that Peleus and Neoptolemus share the same fate'.[154] But the phrase forcefully expresses the intensity of the old man's grief at his grandson's death.[155] The *kommos* is carefully constructed to combine the personal sorrow of Peleus with the communal lament of the responsive *threnos*. The emotional effect of such appropriation of ritual practice was surely very powerful; hence the popularity of lament in tragedy as a device for arousing emotional involvement in the deaths on stage. Hutchinson's remark is pertinent: 'The οἶκτος ["lamentation"] which tragedy aims to excite may have been less detached and philosophical than is sometimes imagined.'[156] Segal's notion of ritual closure defines another important aspect of the lamentatory form: the end marked in funerary practice by lament is transformed dramatically to round off a phase of the plot action.[157] Here, however, the emotionally stirring end of the house of Peleus is itself powerfully reversed by the appearance of Thetis. The disruption of ritual closure underlines the multiple and contrary reversals of fortune which continually propel the action forward.

Like Andromache, and, more problematically, Hermione before him, Peleus is reduced to despair and desolation (1216; cf. 78, 918). Important to the experience of all three is the fear or reality of childlessness: Andromache has lost one son and barely saved another; Hermione is made frantic by her barrenness; and Peleus, who has lost the only son of his only son (1083), expresses his grief at the extinction of his line (1212), which leaves him a pathetic γέροντ' ἄπαιδα ('childless old man', 1207).[158] Visually, the disaster is communicated by Peleus throwing his sceptre to the ground: what had been a

---

[154] Stevens (1971) 236.

[155] Kovacs's translation ((1995) 379), 'and you yourself have met with the same fate as the wicked', introduces an inferior, moralizing thought which is alien to the context.

[156] Hutchinson (1985) 178 on *Sept.* 822–1004.

[157] Segal (1996) 153–9.

[158] For unity derived from the suffering of Peleus' family through the generations, see Hartung (1844) ii. 108–25.

weapon against Menelaus (588) is now a symbol of both personal and civic catastrophe: οὐκέτ' ἐστί μοι πόλις, | σκῆπτρά τ' ἐρρέτω τάδε ('No longer do I have a city; away with this sceptre!', 1222–3).

1226 ff.: Thetis enters, λευκὴν αἰθέρα | πορθμευόμενος ('borne through the bright sky', 1228–9).[159] Her appearance complements the stage tableau of her shrine; particularly pointed is the juxtaposition of both statue and 'live' goddess.[160] The play, which began with a suppliant action at Thetis' shrine, ends with her intervention, creating a balanced close to a disrupted and unsettling sequence of events. The broken and mournful Peleus, a former rescuer, is rescued himself. In his personal vicissitudes from rescuer to tragic victim to survivor, Peleus articulates a key theme (of virtue rewarded) and illuminates an important aspect of the play's fluctuating and disjunctive structure. Thetis' opening words indicate the provenance of this succour: Πηλεῦ, χάριν σοι τῶν πάρος νυμφευμάτων | ἥκω ('Peleus, I have come in memory of our former marriage', 1231–2). Marriage, the root of so much devastation in the characters' past, is now supernaturally reaffirmed.[161] Andromache is returned to a son of Priam and Hecuba (1245), recovering a semblance of her former felicity (the union of Orestes and Hermione, part of established legend, but

---

[159] Both *Andr.* (1226–30) and *El.* (1233–7) suggest flying. Taplin (1977) 443–5 suggests that such announcements may have been added later to match fourth-century theatre practice. However, Mastronarde (1990) 272 has shown that the entrance announcements in *Andr.*, *El.*, and *Her.* 815 ff. have a dramatic purpose: 'the poet wants to portray the panic and surprise of his characters and chorus'. Mastronarde has also persuasively demonstrated that the use of the crane in *Medea* is 'not at all problematic' (p. 265). Thus, he argues (pp. 269–70), the earliest fixed date is 431, but its effects there suggest that it is already 'an established convention'. (Csapo and Slater (1995) 258 push the date back to c.435.) So Stevens (1971) 241–2 is probably right to see Thetis transported by the μηχανή ('crane') on to the θεολογεῖον ('platform'; note ἐπιβαίνει 1230, 'she sets foot'). Hourmouziades (1965) 164–5 even suggests suitable vehicles: either a chariot or a sea-creature!

[160] The technique is used to great effect in the *Hippolytus*, where both goddesses have a statue on stage (cf. 82–3, 101) and both appear, framing the action of the play.

[161] This continuity of theme is missed by Strohm (1957) 111, who says of Thetis' appearance that it 'stands entirely outside the drama'.

disparaged in this play, is passed over in silence). The stress on the continuity of the *oikos* is now crowned by the prediction of a flourishing future for the Molossians: it is a union of two formerly inimical lines (Trojan and Phthian) in which Hermione the Spartan has no share. The characteristic concern of tragic endings with burial honours and commemoration is united here with an *aition* motif, grounding the cult of Neoptolemus at Delphi (1239–42). The eventful, intriguing, and shocking period of the play is set within a larger narrative time which stretches beyond it. The blissful futures predicted for Peleus and Andromache (immortality and return to a Trojan husband) emphasize by their very stability the surprising divagations and variously affecting reversals of the previous action.

Our sequential analysis of the *Andromache* has sought to highlight the disconcerting movement and varied impact of the play. Each play's individual patterning of imagery and scenic motifs promotes coherence and meaning.[162] But even more prominent in the *Andromache* is the expressive force of discontinuity and surprise, which has escaped a good many critics. Thematic and personal motifs do play a part but these are subsumed in an aesthetics of contrast, interruption and excursion. The element of the unexpected is harnessed to forward-looking preparation; this combines the tightening emotional tension of expectation with the shock of its rupture. It now seems likely that the general search for a 'more or less hidden structural element . . . that is common to all tragedies',[163] a unitarian ambition that has influenced many critics, is in danger of obscuring the individual and positive effects of diverse structure in works like the *Andromache*.[164]

We noticed earlier the problems encountered in some other plays by too narrow a conception of dramatic coherence. This point may profitably be expanded. The *Andromache* is not alone in deploying sudden shifts of focus for particular expressive ends. This is a fundamental feature of the ground-pattern

---

[162] On the malleability of metaphor and imagery in poetic texts, see Mossman (1996a) 58–61.

[163] Szondi (1978) 205, quoted by Seidensticker (1996) 379.

[164] See Rutherford (1995) 266.

of many tragedies.[165] In the *Heracles* the entry of Iris and Lyssa begins a reversal of momentum whose structural strangeness is underlined by the disagreements among the goddesses themselves (822–73). Yet the play's movement from persecution to rescue, then from unexpected destruction to an acceptance of suffering, is undeniably moving. The play's force owes much to its shape. The lack of conventional unity is not a fault or an oversight, but a deliberate artistic decision. The unsettling of generic norms enhances both the impact of individual scenes and the larger weight of the whole work.

Like the *Andromache*, the *Troades* is often disparaged for being, in Aristotelian terms, episodic.[166] Yet neither play falls apart into unconnected sections. In the *Troades* in particular the cumulative effect of the imagery is crucial. The concrete envisioning of the city's topography presents the systematic destruction of the acropolis and the desecration of temples. Both are linked to imagery of sexual violation: the city and its women are symbolically and literally raped (cf. 44, 70, 616 ff.).[167] Hecuba's encounters with Cassandra, Andromache, and Helen form a well-designed complex, within which each contrasting character illuminates further aspects of the war's disruptive violence. The play is set amidst a mood of anxious waiting as the Greeks prepare to return home; yet the action, though static in place, is propelled by unexpected movements, such as Talthybius' announcement that Astyanax must die (which itself conveys a surprising tone of sympathy: ἔδοξε τόνδε παῖδα . . . πῶς εἴπω λόγον; 713, 'It has been decided that the boy here—how am I to say it?') or Menelaus' on-stage encounter with his adulterous wife.

By contrast, where one has a central figure, as in the *Hecuba*, the power of a sudden plot shift is intensified by concentration on her response. Hecuba's movement from suffering to revenge, far from indicating a weak, disjointed plot, is brilliantly handled: the mourning mother uncovers the corpse of her dead child, but not the one she expected (681 ff.). The

---

[165] Cf. Collard (1975) i. 25–6 on the 'varying intensity of focus' characteristic of many tragedies, not just of Euripides' 'episodic' ones.

[166] On *Andr.*, cf. e.g. Page (1934) 66, Michelini (1987) 102. For a defence of *Andr.* on this charge, see Mossman (1996b) 145–7.

[167] See Craik (1990) 13.

series of blows is unbearable (ἄπιστ' ἄπιστα, καινὰ καινὰ δέρκομαι. | ἔτερα δ' ἀφ' ἐτέρων κακὰ κακῶν κυρεῖ 689–90, 'Beyond, beyond belief are the things I see, new, unprecedented! Fresh evils follow upon one another'); its structural intensity makes the bereaved queen's sudden resolve for revenge morally engaging and emotionally magnificent.[168]

This chapter has suggested that rather than seek for thematic or personal unity in the *Andromache* one should ask what particular effects the play's deliberate profusion of incident and overlapping of myths are designed to create. The *Andromache* depicts a series of events whose rapid change of focus sustains the production of suspense and significant surprise. One of the chief virtues of *Andromache*'s bold design is the skill with which Euripides has fashioned a combination plot:[169] we start with a suppliant drama (cf. *Hcld.*, *Suppl.*, *Her.*, *Hel.*), then move to a sacrifice-plot (as Andromache offers herself to save her child; *Alc.*, *Hcld.*, *Phoen.*, *IA*). Enter a saviour (*Alc.*, *Med.*, *Hcld.*, *Suppl.*, *Her.* (twice)). Then comes the reversal and (attempted) suicide (*Hipp.*, *Her.*, *Phoen.*), escape (*Cycl.*, *IT*, *Hel.*; in *Andr.* it involves less sympathetic figures) and revenge-plot (*Med.*, *Hec.*, *El.*, *Ion*), all imbued with the tarnished moral atmosphere of a war-play (*Hec.*, *Tro.*, *IA*). (The parallels in each case could be expanded.) Euripides succeeds in making a well-constructed and powerful tragedy from this complex sequence of elements. Discontinuity and artful frustration of expectations work together to produce intriguing and disconcerting results.

The play coheres in its parts, yet the ensemble is a dynamic structure. Here one is combining two opposing but mutually stimulating points. Firstly, the play evinces an aesthetic of

---

[168] See Hutchinson (1988) 13 on the 'complications . . . of moral texture' in the second half of *Andr.* and *Hec.*

[169] The *IT*'s extended recognition scene, for example, differs from that of the Electra plays in that neither participant knows the identity of the other, and suspense surrounds the avoidance of fratricide (cf. 777 ff.). The *Ion*'s first recognition scene, between Ion and Xuthus, is a false one (517 ff.), while the second, between Ion and Creusa, though real, is disrupted by the threat of (unwitting) matricide (1395 ff.). For popular admiration of Euripides' recognition scenes and their dramatic legacy in New and Roman comedy, see Cave (1988) 58, 257.

surprise, with philosophical significance.[170] Secondly, there are manifold connections and contrasts between the different parts of its structure. A closer analysis was necessary since these, as in many works, cannot be satisfactorily reduced to a single meaning. Salient connections include a series of mirror-scenes involving supplication and rescue; important too is the motif of vengeance: Hermione wants revenge on Andromache, she comes to fear Neoptolemus' reprisals, and this in turn aids Orestes' vengeful killing of Neoptolemus.[171] One is brought to reappraise the same set of events from new perspectives, but the rapid shifts of focus alert us to the distinct moral ordering of our response. Thought-provoking surprises and mobile focus are very common in Euripides. To separate the more extreme examples like the *Andromache*, and regard them as aberrations from some good Aristotelian norm of the probable and necessary, is to distort a major feature of Euripides' art. He clearly has a positive concern with alteration and surprise, but not in a random, meaningless, or, as is often claimed, sensationalist manner. Surprising thrusts of structure are combined with acute sensitivity to the cohesion of the whole design. It is this combination, seen to manifold effect in the *Andromache*, but present in different proportions in other plays, that lends Euripidean tragedy much of its dissonant force and intriguing greatness.

---

[170] Its implications for a view of the world dominated by τύχη ('chance') are developed more fully in Euripides' later work.

[171] So de Romilly (1961) 115.

3

Characterization

Shakespeares Werke sind in diesem Sinne am meisten dramatisch; durch seine Behandlungsart, das innerste Leben hervorzukehren, gewinnt er den Leser; die theatralischen Forderungen erscheinen ihm nichtig, und so macht er sich's bequem, und man läßt sich's, geistig genommen, mit ihm bequem werden.

Goethe, 'Shakespeare und Kein Ende', HA xii. 296

The individuality and inwardness of characters is of no importance whatever in this play.

D. Kovacs[1]

Goethe's praise of the dramatic art of Shakespeare appeals to a standard of characterization which once influenced many readers of Euripidean tragedy. We are now aware that to demand that the tragic poet should create people with a past, with a depth and textured reality, is to show the influence of an alien aesthetic, one embodied most strikingly in the nineteenth-century novel, which is eminently interested in the development of character in terms of moral progress and decline. A strong reaction against this unitary conception of characterization was inevitable; it proclaimed, in essence, 'that any overarching notion of consistent or plausible "character" is subordinated to the particular concerns of individual scenes'.[2] The salutary restraint of this approach is evident, but so are some basic objections to it. For how is the individual scene to attain maximum dramatic effect on the audience without some

---

[1] Kovacs (1980) 82–3.

[2] Hunter (1993) xxix. Goldhill (1990a) 112 sums up the common view of Euripides as 'sacrificing consistency or credibility of characterization to a desire for good plots or even just good rhetorical arguments'. Conversely, Euripides has often been hailed as the first dramatist to explore the details of his characters' inner world. The explanation for these contrary judgements lies in the author's great variety in the handling of characterization: see Griffin (1990) 128.

input from coherent persons? It will be argued here that in Euripides' plays person and dramatic effect are interwoven. No less than Homeric epic, tragedy depends for its effects on 'the unity of the person as thinking, acting, and bodily present'.[3]

However, we must be clear that the effectiveness of a dramatic person need not consist in being complicated, and that the dramatic 'reality' need not be complex to be rewarding for the audience. Andromache as presented is by no means complex: she is always noble, but her simplicity is made admirable and moving. Menelaus is an essentially shallow, dislikeable figure; no deep understanding of him is required. But he is, nevertheless, hardly two-dimensional; in the dramatic context he makes an interesting figure.[4] We can point to one general feature: Euripides is less interested in depicting inner experience as such than in exploring (and exploiting) the contrasts between characters, and our moral reactions to them. But this too needs refining. We can distinguish in the *Andromache*

---

[3] Williams (1993) 49. On 'tragic characterization' in Homer, see Griffin (1980) ch. 2, Rutherford (1982), Gill (1996) 89–93. For the historians' interest in character, in terms of 'individualism, as well as individuation', see Pelling (1990) 259–61, Westlake (1968) 5–19. The concept of developing character is clearly present in Greek literature (cf. Rutherford (1986) 147). There is also evidence for an independent awareness in antiquity of the key role played by characterization in dramatic works. Sophocles was considered one of the masters of the art of character portrayal: (*Vita* §21, p. 40 Radt): οἶδε δὲ καιρὸν συμμετρῆσαι καὶ πράγματα, ὥστ' ἐκ μικροῦ ἡμιστιχίου ἢ λέξεως μιᾶς ὅλον ἠθοποιεῖν πρόσωπον. ἔστι δὲ τοῦτο μέγιστον ἐν τῆι ποιητικῆι, δηλοῦν ἦθος ἢ πάθος. ('And he knows how to compose the action with such a sense of timing that he builds an entire character from a mere half-line or a single expression. This is the most important thing in poetry, to depict character or feelings.') It is important to observe that this observation also implies something very like our own notion of character-building by deft, economical means within a literary text (cf. e.g. ΣD on *Il.* 8. 85, ΣT on 1. 348). At Σ *Aj.* 354 the critic suggests that 'one should guess at the character' (δεῖ τοῦ ἤθους στοχάζεσθαι) in order to decide who might speak a disputed line. For both Plato and Aristotle, character (interpreted on an ethical, rather than a psychological or aesthetic, level) is a main category of tragic analysis.

[4] Contrast Kovacs (1987) 22, who comments on the *Hippolytus* that 'the characters are less abstract and more lifelike [than in *Andr.*]'. Luschnig's ((1988a) 61–2) claim that there is a tension between individual and type in tragic characterization is not supported by any evidence. Menelaus is no more a stagey villain than is the Creon of *OC*, for example. The tawdry self-interest and brutal violence of both figures are used to illuminate the greatness of their opponents, Andromache and Oedipus.

between degrees of evolution and wholeness, psychological depth or complexity. Characters vary in the impression that they give of density and history. Hermione, for example, is comprehended far more in terms of her past than, say, Neoptolemus is, and her character so formed is a central determinant of the shape of the action.

This complexity of interest is closely bound up with the tragic genre itself. Critics who search for the innermost life ('das innerste Leben') of a figure are too little sensitive to the stylization of the literary medium. Dramatic persons are constructs of language, gesture, and action.[5] Character cannot be understood simply as 'a closed and predictable totality of internal qualities'[6] since, as Aristotle noted, it is revealed by action.[7] And this action is simultaneously interaction with other figures. So concentration on the internal experience of persons is misleading; our idea of a person is worked up through that person's contact with, and impact on, other persons. It is crucial that we should see each figure not in isolation, but as playing a part in a larger whole.

Another important feature of the dramatic medium is the intriguing indeterminacy of motivation we are at times presented with: the reasons for a person's actions are not spelled out; we must fill in the gaps, constructing an account of the decision which suits our understanding of events.[8] Hermione's departure with Orestes, for example, is open to various readings: we can see her as a tool of another's will or as more duplicitous and shallow. Far from being a source of irritating obscurity, this ambiguity expands the intellectual and emotional significance of the drama.[9]

So far we have insisted on the interconnection of person,

---

[5] Cf. Gould (1978) 43.

[6] Mogyoródi (1996) 365.

[7] Aristotle is often misinterpreted as downgrading character in favour of action. Cf. Nussbaum (1986) 379: 'He says that there might be a tragedy without full character-development; but this is clearly not what he himself prefers.'

[8] Docherty (1983) 218–19 rightly stresses the involvement of the audience, which is necessary to a play's dynamism, meaning and 'genuine "experience"'.

[9] Cf. Halliwell (1997) 137 on the 'degree of interpretative opaqueness' found in many tragic agons.

action, and effect; the importance of the dramatic context of interaction and response; and the intriguing, expansive effect of motivational uncertainty. We are claiming that Euripides is less interested in interior complexity than in doing interesting things with people. But clearly this does not exclude his also being interested in strange twists of character and unpredictable behaviour. These too have their peculiar effect and value. Hermione's sudden change of mind will concern us later. Here we might note the terms in which the volte-face of Iphigeneia in *IA* is discussed (Aristotle's example of character inconsistency, *Poet.* 1454^{a}32 ~ *IA* 1246:1375). Mellert-Hoffmann rightly criticizes Zürcher, who rejected the girl's 'new psychological structure', but he himself goes on to argue for 'the unity of the Iphigeneia-figure'.[10] Luschnig stresses the plausibility of this change of mind in a play where few decisions are final.[11] But talk of plausibility does not ring true to the tenor of the work.[12] Aristotle was right to be surprised; Euripides wants us to be. We encounter a nobility we did not expect, and our view of the other characters (especially the Atreidae) is significantly altered.[13]

As was suggested above, the debate over the priority of plot or character is misleading: the plays repose upon, and articulate, an interdependence of the two elements. The one is inconceivable without the other: it is the dialectical relationship of plot and character which makes the drama.[14] P. E. Easterling has correctly encouraged us to 'attend to the *dynamics of action and interaction* rather than look for static "character portraits" with the notion of a unitary character as our starting point'.[15]

[10] Mellert-Hoffmann (1969) 74–5, 80–89.

[11] Luschnig (1988b) 106–7.

[12] Griffin (1990) rightly stresses that credibility, rather than plausibility, is what matters.

[13] One could compare the effect of Polyxena's willing sacrifice on our perception of the Greeks in *Hecuba*.

[14] Pfister (1988) 160 ff. argues that the 'thing done' is understood as the development of a situation (plot, at its barest) through the changing relationships between the figures. Cf. Mossman (1995) 102: 'the Greeks described changing responses, not changing characters'.

[15] Easterling (1990) 88. Docherty (1983) xii–xiv also emphasizes change and mobility, rather than 'trying to discover the singular simple essence of character'.

Related to this is the consideration, familiar from everyday life, and also significant for the texture of literary personality, that one's character is influenced by others. The chorus of the *Wasps* express this most clearly when reflecting on the change in Philocleon (1457–61):

> τὸ γὰρ ἀποστῆναι χαλεπὸν
> φύσεως, ἣν ἔχοι τις ἀεί.
> καίτοι πολλοὶ ταῦτ' ἔπαθον·
> ξυνόντες γνώμαις ἑτέρων
> μετεβάλοντο τοὺς τρόπους.

For it is difficult to deviate from the natural character one has always had. And yet this has happened to many people: through exposure to others' opinions they have changed their ways.

In the *Andromache* this feature of character moulding is exploited by Hermione in her defence. She explains to Orestes that she was not responsible for the plot to kill Andromache; instead she blames the influence of wicked women, αἵ μοι λέγουσαι τούσδ' ἐχαύνωσαν λόγους ('who filled me with conceit by speaking like this', 931). Yet her self-exculpation is frustrated by our previous impression of her motives. The attempt itself makes sense in terms of what we know of her tendency (shared by Menelaus) to blame others for her own failings. But her claim that she was misled by Σειρήνων λόγους ('Sirens' words', 936) strikes us as grotesque. So while the excuse itself fits Hermione's psychology well, the appeal is rendered dubious by the identity of the speaker.

We might pause to reflect on the complex relationship of stage figures to reality. One of the chief merits of recent literary theory has been to illustrate the slipperiness of concepts of character in literary texts. Simply saying that stage figures are not real people (and cannot be treated as such) seems obvious, but it has interesting ramifications. The issues raised here relating to identity and self-construction are complex. It has been said of self-fashioning, or the 'topography of the self', that 'probably, for most of us, self-creation is a matter of a fairly disorganized cluster of smaller aims: more like building a medieval town than a planned garden city'.[16]

---

[16] Glover (1988) 135.

When one considers the literary construction of character, these concerns are raised to a further level of difficulty. But we should not therefore become distanced, purely intellectual observers, because tragedy presents lived experience.[17] And there is surely something strange about not responding to the humanity of dramatic characters who come to life before us in performance.[18] Yet at the same time we must accept that there are constraints and limits to the idea of character (even if it is an indispensable key to understanding the texts): it operates within each individual play-world and cannot be separated from 'the pervasive metaphorical colouring of the whole language of the play'.[19]

The ontological difference between fictional and real characters has important implications for our perception of dramatic time and the significance of dramatic action. The closed, finite universe of the play-world means that each piece of information we receive becomes much more important for our construction of character. This heightened concentration allows the poet to communicate character more swiftly than in real life. Importantly, this sense of a person need not be minutely detailed for the action to flow credibly from the figure's motivations and choices. What matters is that figures should be clearly and vividly portrayed; often 'a few basic traits' are enough to carry dramatic conviction.[20] The simplicity of technique lends expressive strength.

The status of tragedy as a 'theatre of *public* events'[21] does not

---

[17] See Herington (1985) 133–50 on the novelty of early tragedy, where (p. 150) 'the ancient mythological figures have acquired legs' and act before a watching audience. The role of the actors is often forgotten in the debate over character. One need not presume the intensity of modern 'method acting' techniques. Yet ancient Greek performers surely attempted to invest their roles with some nuance of personality. The skill involved is evident if one considers that the same actor played, for example, both Heracles and Alcestis!

[18] One must beware of leaning too heavily on a timeless view of static 'human nature' to explain the plays' continuing force as vehicles of human action and response. The cultural dependency of categories of the self is now generally recognized (cf. Easterling (1990) 89, Goldhill (1990a) 100–1.). Nevertheless, it will be argued that to ignore the psychology of dramatic figures risks adopting a blandly depersonalized approach to Greek tragedy.

[19] Gould (1978) 60.   [20] Heath (1987) 119.

[21] Gould (1978) 46, who observes that there is nothing in tragedy to approach the self-analysis of Shakespearian soliloquies.

exclude the exploration of internal motivation. Particularly when a crisis-decision must be made, we are permitted an insight into characters' deliberations through the use of monologue. At the dramatic crux of the *Medea*, where the play's ultimate conflict lies in Medea's self-resistance, her great monologue (1021–80) lays bare the opposition of maternal sensitivity and vengeful self-assertion: like a Homeric warrior,[22] she addresses her *thumos*—μὴ δῆτα, θυμέ, μὴ σύ γ᾽ ἐργάσηι τάδε ('Do not, my heart, do not do this deed!', 1056).[23] She changes her mind as to whether she should kill or spare her children, οὐκ ἂν δυναίμην . . . χαιρέτω βουλεύματα ('I could not do it . . . Farewell to my plans', 1044–8), καίτοι τί πάσχω; . . . χεῖρα δ᾽ οὐ διαφθερῶ ('What is wrong with me? . . . I will not weaken my arm', 1049–55), an oscillation which manifests the agony of her dilemma. But the dilemma itself only occurs because of the type of person Medea is; it is the combination of her ἦθος ('character') with the σύστασις τῶν πραγμάτων ('state of affairs') which makes her decision seem both credible and harrowing.[24] And it is all the more poignant for Medea's painful awareness of her fatal character: ὦ δυστάλαινα τῆς ἐμῆς αὐθαδίας ('Alas, how miserable my stubbornness has made me!', 1028; cf. 1078–80).

The example of Medea also alerts us to the poet's fabrication of personality to suit the particular effects of the drama. The mythical innovation of the infanticide is shocking, but to claim that Euripides is 'manipulating his audience's emotions through the violence he does to characterizations they have come to accept as true'[25] is very misleading. For it assumes that the mythical tradition apportions 'true', fixed, or definite patterns of motivation and response to individual figures. (Of course one need not deny that the intertextual comparison of a character's history can occasionally create effects of dissonance or congruence. What is being stressed here is the free-standing effect of each individual text as perceived in performance.)

---

[22] See Easterling (1977) 183 on Medea's 'self-image as a hero of the old style'.

[23] 1056–80 del. Bergk, and bracketed by Diggle (OCT); 1056–64 bracketed by Kovacs (Loeb; cf. Kovacs (1986)). But see Williams (1993) 205 n. 39.

[24] Medea's near-divine status represents an approach to her character that is much overplayed. She certainly escapes like a god, but cannot escape suffering, as a god would.

[25] McDermott (1989) 41.

Such personal attributes as do construct and sustain each work are inherent to the peculiar texture and atmosphere of the play. Medea's combination of an acute moral sensibility with the passionate desire for revenge is the basis of her tragedy.[26] This brings us again to the notion of 'complexity' (which will be discussed more fully later). Here we may observe that Medea's character is simply delineated; so too the conflict she faces in undertaking the most painful form of vengeance possible. From the contrary workings of a few bold elements (Medea's honour, her devotion to Jason, and his betrayal) comes a drama of overwhelming emotional power.

The *Andromache* is particularly notable for the way it takes characters familiar from the Trojan War myths and projects them into unfamiliar territory in the post-war period. Each figure is faced with new dilemmas in the aftermath, and the responses of each display their respective characteristics, some of which diverge quite markedly from their epic precedents (this is especially true of Neoptolemus). The tendency to view the play as directed primarily by *polis* or ethnic features distorts the action too far in the direction of a general schematic (anti-Spartan) meaning. This vitiates a fuller understanding of the acute and careful description of motives which are at the very centre of the play's movement and meaning. Friedrich said of the *Andromache* and the *Electra*, 'the psychological peculiarities are a means of winning new possibilities from used materials'. This claim we will explore and to some extent confirm, though without accepting the continuation of Friedrich's view, 'and they are in this respect symptoms which announce the end of the art form'.[27]

Jacqueline de Romilly has sensitively outlined the development of the figure of Andromache in European poetry from Homer to Baudelaire.[28] She shows how the basic characteristics, established by Homer, of loving wife, grieving widow,

---

[26] See Easterling (1977) 183.

[27] Friedrich (1953) 86. Far from being a symptom of decline, psychological penetration is central to Aeschylus' treatment of Clytemnestra, *vis-à-vis* the story of Agamemnon's return as told in the *Odyssey*. (I owe this point to Professor Griffin.)

[28] de Romilly (1995) ch. 2, entitled, after Baudelaire, 'Andromaque, je pense à vous'.

and mother, have endured, pointing to the constant relevance of her experience: 'the character of Andromache has scarcely ceased to live. It renews itself from work to work, perhaps more than any other. . . . Even in our age these traits confer upon it an exceptional presence and actuality. Its variety results in a kind of reawakening of an archetype.'[29] For those of us who have not lived through war or suffered the disintegration of civic order, loss of family, and moral anarchy which it threatens, de Romilly's words will perhaps have a slightly unfashionable air of humanist universalism about them. But for the Athenian audience of the mid-420s, and those of later war generations regardless of locality, the figure of Andromache speaks directly to such feelings of loss and victimization.

The process of the Greek audience's identification with the Trojan captive is enhanced by various factors, not least by the character and actions of her Greek persecutors. Their Greekness, of course, is part of the play's transcendence of the polarity of Greek and Trojan. The words and actions of both actors and chorus direct us to sympathize with the Trojan slave. And since there is a 'strong measure of self-definition in Hermione and Menelaus' treatment of Andromache',[30] our negative view of them emerges forcefully from their actions.

Euripides constructs his characters, like his plots, from a skilful blend of the traditional and invented. Consideration of Andromache's opening speech illustrates this most clearly. Evocation of her past as loved and loving wife and mother emphasizes the tragedy of her unfamiliar position in the household of Neoptolemus. Her present status as concubine sets her traditional virtues in an alien context: the repetition of δοθεῖσα ('given in marriage'/'awarded as a prize', 4 ∼ 15) enhances the contrast between the two journeys. Most striking in this regard are lines 5–6:

> ζηλωτὸς ἔν γε τῶι πρὶν Ἀνδρομάχη χρόνωι,
> νῦν δ', εἴ τις ἄλλη, δυστυχεστάτη γυνή.

I, Andromache, was formerly a woman to be envied, but now my misery is greater than any other's.[31]

---

[29] de Romilly (1995) 29.
[30] Kuntz (1993) 72–3.
[31] Line 7: ἐμοῦ πέφυκεν ἢ γενήσεταί ποτε ('[no woman more miserable] than

The recollection of her happy past culminates in her name; the temporal juxtaposition reveals a sharp dissonance in her condition then and now. The contrast is significant, for the first part of the play will explore how Andromache's noble character endures despite her changed circumstances. Euripides takes care to place Andromache in her larger history of suffering.[32]

Unlike the prologues to the *Alcestis*, *Electra*, or *Telephus*, Andromache addresses in her opening words not the stage locale, but her ancestral home in Asia, Ἀσιάτιδος γῆς σχῆμα, Θηβαία πόλις ('O my Asian homeland, city of Thebe!', 1). The dissonance between past prosperity and present catastrophe is striking. Once again, but now in a post-war Greek scenario, her son is threatened with death; by contrast with Astyanax's fate, however, stress is here laid specifically on Spartan responsibility (39–42). Andromache describes herself as having become dependent on her son (ἐλπίς μ᾽ ἀεὶ προῆγε σωθέντος τέκνου | ἀλκήν τιν᾽ εὑρεῖν κἀπικούρησιν κακῶν 27–8, 'I was always led on by hope to believe that as long as my child was safe I would find some sort of help and protection from misfortune'), a pathetic hope which Hermione's jealousy now threatens to annihilate.

The speech brings out in various ways the victimization of Andromache. She recounts the latest turn in her fortunes thus (29–31):

> ἐπεὶ δὲ τὴν Λάκαιναν Ἑρμιόνην γαμεῖ
> τοὐμὸν παρώσας δεσπότης δοῦλον λέχος,
> κακοῖς πρὸς αὐτῆς σχετλίοις ἐλαύνομαι.

But ever since my master married the Spartan Hermione, rejecting union with me, a slave woman, I have been cruelly accused by her.

The language emphasizes the decisive control of others and the precariousness of her status as a slave (both ideas are fundamental to the chorus's view of Andromache's position: 126–34;

me has been born or ever will be born') is, as the scholia note, an actor's interpolation (which has made its way into all the manuscripts: see Zuntz (1965) 269). It adds nothing to the bold contrast of the previous lines.

[32] Kuntz (1993) 69 well notes how Andromache's thoughts of the past echo a feature of her Iliadic character, comparing her account of the sack of her home by Achilles (6. 406–23). Easterling's ((1984) 8) remarks on the end of Soph. *Aj.* might very well be applied to *Andr.*: 'the power of the themes relating to Hector and Andromache is still paramount: birth, friends and enemies, stubbornness and σωφροσύνη, time and change'.

cf. also 390–3). Neoptolemus' marriage had nothing to do with Andromache, yet she is unjustly persecuted as a result of it. Her attackers are strongly characterized as irrationally bent on her destruction. Hermione's charges are met by Andromache's persuasive defence (32–8), but the futility of argument is clear (39–40):

> ἀλλ' οὔ σφε πείθω, βούλεται δέ με κτανεῖν,
> πατήρ τε θυγατρὶ Μενέλεως συνδρᾶι τάδε.

But I cannot persuade her of this, indeed she wants to kill me, and her father, Menelaus, is abetting his daughter in this plot.

The arrival of Menelaus creates an atmosphere of fear (δειμα-τουμένη δ' ἐγώ 42 'I in terror'; μὴ θάνηι φοβουμένη 48, 'fearing he will be killed'), and this is heightened in the exchange with the slave, who makes explicit the threat to Andromache's son (φόβωι μέν, εἴ τις δεσποτῶν αἰσθήσεται 61, 'in fear that one of my masters might find me out'). Andromache identifies herself with her former slave (64–5), although the latter had pointedly begun her speech with a long justification of the title δέσποινα (56–9). This suggests a warm humanity whose dramatic significance is developed in the next scene; there it significantly contrasts with Hermione's contempt for slaves. The importance of the present scene for our impression of Andromache and her opponents is concentrated in her response to the news that Menelaus has just set out to intercept Andromache's son (74–6):

> ἀπωλόμην ἄρ'. ὦ τέκνον, κτενοῦσί σε
> δισσοὶ λαβόντες γῦπες, ὁ δὲ κεκλημένος
> πατὴρ ἔτ' ἐν Δελφοῖσι τυγχάνει μένων.

Then I am destroyed. My child, they will take and kill you, those two vultures, while your so-called father still lingers in Delphi!

She likens Menelaus and Hermione to a pair of vultures, an unusual image[33] which vividly captures their cowardice and opportunism:[34] they only dare act in Neoptolemus' absence,

---

[33] Stevens (1971) 103 ad loc. notes that the metaphor is much rarer in Greek than in English.

[34] Cf. Dunbar (1995) 517 on Ar. *Birds* 890–1: 'Vultures devouring carrion would be a familiar sight in Attica'; also *Tro.* 599–600.

when their victim is defenceless. The remaining part of the dialogue communicates Andromache's resourcefulness; we learn that she has already sent appeals for help to Peleus several times (81) and now observe her ingenuity and determination as she persuades the servant to make one more attempt. Her acceptance of the difficult mission (κίνδυνος 86, 'It's a dangerous task') underlines the justice of Andromache's cause and the loyalty she still arouses.

Andromache's speech carefully sets her in specific relationships to the other main figures of the play; at the same time, through the sympathetic depiction of her endurance and innocence (cf. οὐχ ἑκοῦσα 36 and 38, 'unwilling'), it orientates our attitude to the other characters. In the case of her persecutors, the reaction of the audience is straightforwardly negative—though this will be refined in Hermione's case as the play develops.[35] For Neoptolemus, despite Andromache's insistence that she had to sleep with him against her will, the signals are more complex. On the one hand, he is absent when his mistress and son need him most (49–50), but on the other, his refusal to take up full regal powers while Peleus still lives (22–3) is unusual in the heroic world, where old rulers often abdicate to make way for a son (Pheres and Admetus in *Alc.*) or grandson (Cadmus and Pentheus in *Bacch.*), and suggests Neoptolemus' sense of respect and piety. Though the detail clearly has a plot function to explain the closeness of Peleus and his ability to help, it also begins to create the impression of an unexpectedly sympathetic Neoptolemus.

An interesting feature of characterization in the *Andromache* is the varying techniques of self-definition employed. That of the Spartans is particularly revealing. Both Hermione and Menelaus continually affirm their status as royal, Greek, and free (cf. esp. 153 ~ 155, 243, 665–6, 860).[36] But the lowness of their plot implicitly undermines their right to these honours. Both Hermione and Menelaus are reduced to blustering threats

---

[35] Cf. the complication of our response to Eurystheus at *Hcld.* 998 ff., or (most strikingly) to Clytemnestra, who rescued Electra from Aegisthus (*El.* 27–8) and regrets the murder of Agamemnon (1105–10).

[36] On slave vocabulary in the play, see Kuch (1974) 46 with nn. 1 and 3. One is reminded of the historical Spartans' 'stark "othering" of the Messenians through the helot status' (Osborne (1996) 184).

by Andromache's superior case and skill in arguing for it: σοφὴ σοφὴ σύ· κατθανεῖν δ' ὅμως σε δεῖ ('You're so very clever! But still you must die', 245) ~ ὅταν τάδ' ἦι, τότ' οἴσομεν· σὲ δὲ κτενῶ ('When that [divine judgement] comes, I'll bear it. But right now I will kill you', 440).

Yet we sense a difference in the characters of Menelaus and Hermione emerging from their language. Menelaus is shallow like his daughter, but far more calculating and brutal. He preaches a policy of retaliation to justify killing Andromache and her son: καὶ τοῖς γε Τροίαι (sc. σοφά), τοὺς παθόντας ἀντιδρᾶν ('Yes, and [it is thought wise] among the Trojans as well for the injured to strike back', 438).[37] The magnanimity of the final scenes of the *Iliad* is unknown to him. Juxtaposed to the generosity of Andromache in dying for her son,[38] and to the nobility of Peleus in rescuing them, Menelaus' claim that his murder attempt is motivated by the interests of Greece (645 ff.) is exposed as a crass deception.

Although Hermione is on stage for a comparatively short time, it is important to consider how Euripides manages to make her character both intriguing and central to several major issues of the action. Even before she appears, the chorus alert us to her suspicious nature (142–6). Her first speech begins with a self-description which is remarkable for its intricacy and length (147 ff.). But we note that it is purely exterior; as Barlow rightly says, 'Hermione's desperate self-advertisement in fact masks a certain barrenness of body and soul'.[39] Her pride in her precious possessions is excessive and suggests her insecurity and fragility. Hermione explains why she remains childless: στυγοῦμαι δ' ἀνδρὶ φαρμάκοισι σοῖς, | νηδὺς δ' ἀκύμων διὰ σέ μοι διόλλυται· | δεινὴ γὰρ ἠπειρῶτις ἐς τὰ τοιάδε | ψυχὴ γυναικῶν ('I am detested by my husband because of your drugs, because of you my womb is fruitless and withers away. For the minds of Asiatic women are terribly skilled in such things', 157–60). In the light of the prologue, where Andromache is emphatically not presented as a barbarian witch, the charge is grotesque.

---

[37] Cf. 519 ff. and Kassel (1954) 51 on the motif of killing one's enemies' children to avert vengeance.

[38] Polyxena's nobility is evident when she thinks of Hecuba first (*Hec.* 197 ff.).

[39] Barlow (1971) 86.

Hermione's overwrought imagination even extends to fantasies of abasement: she vividly depicts the demeaning tasks she will set Andromache, should she escape with her life (a significant qualification: 163–7).

The hysterical excess of Hermione's anti-barbarian tirade (170 ff.) suggests a fundamental insecurity, which we might sympathize with if she were not now being so destructive.[40] The source of her hysteria will be discussed further in Chapter 6. There too we will analyse how this scene, perhaps more than any other in his plays, displays Euripides' acute interest in feminine psychology and sexuality. Andromache repeatedly calls attention to Hermione's youth (184–5, 192, 238, 326); this is a factor in both her moral and sexual immaturity. Though it does not prevent us condemning her actions against Andromache, Hermione's immaturity alters our understanding of her panic and insecurity. Wilamowitz says, 'She is ἀντίπαις 326 ['like a child'], that is, seventeen years old at most, full of childish vanity.'[41] But 'childish vanity' is too dismissive an explanation of Hermione's behaviour. Her age, sex, Spartanness, and silliness all contribute to our initially negative impression. But this is surprisingly and interestingly modified as the play develops.

Pertinent to Hermione's behaviour, and to the rhetoric of Peleus later in the play, is the notion of inherited character. Andromache is provoked by Hermione's jealous fury into raising the negative example of her mother's conduct (229–31):

> μὴ τὴν τεκοῦσαν τῆι φιλανδρίαι, γύναι,
> ζήτει παρελθεῖν· τῶν κακῶν γὰρ μητέρων
> φεύγειν τρόπους χρὴ τέκν᾽ ὅσοις ἔνεστι νοῦς.[42]

Do not try to outdo your mother in man-loving. For if mothers act deplorably, their children should avoid mimicking their ways, if they have any sense.

Hermione shows great sensitivity about her mother's past: ἦ καὶ πρόσω γὰρ τῶν ἐμῶν ψαύσεις κακῶν; ('Ah, will you even touch on

---

[40] Electra's wallowing in hatred and self-abasement has a similarly alienating effect (Eur. *El.* 300 ff.; cf. 647 for her murderous keenness).

[41] Wilamowitz (1962) 379.

[42] On the violation of Porson's law in 230 see Diggle (1994) 457.

my misfortunes?', 249).[43] As Andromache's ambivalent use of
φιλανδρία ('man-loving', 229–30) suggests, Hermione has com-
pensated for her mother's sexual licence[44] by demanding too
strict a form of monogamy from her husband. Tellingly, when
her plans collapse, Hermione's abandoned behaviour is unexpectedly sexy: τί δὲ στέρνα δεῖ καλύπτειν πέπλοις; ('Why should I
cover my breasts with my dress?', 833). While the psychological ramifications of Hermione's personal background are
not minutely analysed, her obsession with sexual matters (cf.
240–1) is set within a larger, and thought-provoking, history.[45]
One might compare Hippolytus, the son of an Amazon and a
bastard, and so rather awkward about τὰ Ἀφροδίσια ('sexual
pleasures'). There, too, Euripides plays up sensitivities of this
kind.[46]

Menelaus is, of course, complementary to Helen as parent of
Hermione. However, he is portrayed not just as an origin of
Hermione's faults but as an interesting, albeit repellent, character in himself.[47] His very first words capture his unheroic
pride in a petty triumph (309–10):

> ἥκω λαβὼν σὸν παῖδ', ὃν εἰς ἄλλους δόμους
> λάθραι θυγατρὸς τῆς ἐμῆς ὑπεξέθου.

I have come bringing your son, whom you sent secretly to another
house to escape my daughter.

He offers Andromache a choice between saving herself or her
son (ταῦτ' οὖν λογίζου 316, 'So think about this'). The bogus

[43] Despite her desperate situation, Andromache answers, ἰδοὺ σιωπῶ
κἀπιλάζυμαι στόμα ('Fine, I am silent and hold my tongue', 250). λάζυμαι ('I
seize') is a Homeric word, expressing a strong grasp. The force of Andromache's self-control is amplified by the rare compound.

[44] For Euripides' multifaceted use of Helen, see Homeyer (1977) 26–37,
Austin (1994) ch. 6.

[45] Later, in Peleus' first speech, Hermione's parents are also seen in
subjection to Kypris (esp. 629–31). Solmsen (1975) 137 notes the psychological acuteness of Hermione's violent jealousy. The imbalance is reflected in
her diametrically opposed rhetoric (of female submissiveness) after the failure
of her plot.

[46] For further examples of Euripides' sensitivity to psychological factors,
see *Or.* 251–2 and Foley (1985) 215 with n. 14 (on Pentheus' destruction by
his mother).

[47] Verrall (1905) 9 thought that Menelaus' actions simply disfigure the
play: '*Incredulus odi*: it is incredible and disgusting.'

claim to fairness is typical of his attitude throughout the scene (contrast Andromache's genuine appeal to just process: αὐτοὶ τὴν δίκην ὑφέξομεν 358–60, 'I will willingly submit myself to judgement'). The scene of Andromache's ruthless extortion from the shrine movingly presents her mental and emotional turmoil as she debates whether to offer up her own life to save (as she thinks) that of her son.[48]

Andromache is an effective foil, stressing the brutality and moral cynicism of Menelaus. The contours of her character are confirmed by the encounter, but it is the personality of Menelaus which now occupies the centre of our attention.[49] He is quite convinced of his own cleverness: ἀλλ' ἐφηυρέθης | ἧσσον φρονοῦσα τοῦδε Μενέλεω, γύναι ('But you have been found to be less clever than Menelaus here, woman', 312–13; cf. 378–9).[50] Yet his cleverness consists in blackmail and murder disguised as concern for his *philoi*. The ethics of retaliation, the claim to be doing both Neoptolemus and Greece a favour, are shown to be merely a front for petty revenge and self-aggrandizement.[51]

In the post-war world of the play, where Menelaus proclaims his arrival as σύμμαχος ('ally', 370–1) to his daughter, the moral

[48] Cf. Griffin (1990) 144 n. 28, quoting Kumaniecki on 'Euripides' accurate representation of *animus titubans*, a mind indecisive'.

[49] Menelaus' capture of Andromache's child might be compared to his interception of Agamemnon's second letter in *IA*. Agamemnon, like Peleus, is provoked to denounce his officious and self-regarding interest in a kinsman's household: οὐχὶ δεινά; τὸν ἐμὸν οἰκεῖν οἶκον οὐκ ἐάσομαι; ('Isn't this terrible? Am I not to be allowed to run my own household?', *IA* 331) ~ πῶς; ἢ τὸν ἀμὸν οἶκον οἰκήσεις μολὼν | δεῦρ'; οὐχ ἅλις σοι τῶν κατὰ Σπάρτην κρατεῖν; ('What? Will you come here and try to run my household? Isn't it enough for you to rule those in Sparta?', *Andr.* 581–2). Such remarks suggest reflection about Spartan interference in other *poleis*. Cf. *Telephus* fr. 723 K (Agamemnon to Menelaus): Σπάρτην ἔλαχες, κείνην κόσμει· | τὰς δὲ Μυκήνας ἡμεῖς ἰδίαι ('Sparta fell to your lot, so govern her! I have Mycenae for myself').

[50] γύναι ('woman') is repeated at the beginning of Menelaus' next speech (366). Like Creon in *Antigone*, he is acutely conscious of his opponent being a woman, and is anxious to assert his superiority. Cf. also *Or.* 488, where Menelaus implies his inclusion ἐν τοῖς σοφοῖς ('among the clever').

[51] One might compare Polymestor, whose impatient greed is skilfully portrayed (*Hec.* 998 ff.), as are his bogus pro-Greek motives for killing Polydorus. Menelaus' materialism undermines his anti-barbarian rhetoric (cf. Soph. fr. 587 R φιλάργυρον μὲν πᾶν τὸ βάρβαρον γένος, 'The entire barbarian race loves money').

fabric of society is still dominated by the exigencies of conflict. Those with power gratify their passing passions as best they can (368–9).[52] Menelaus' moral decadence is subtly marked by language: he selfishly misappropriates the rhetoric of communality and reciprocity (cf. 376–7, 438, 585). He also attempts to distance himself from any real responsibility for their deaths with talk of 'necessity': δυοῖν δ' ἀνάγκη θατέρωι λιπεῖν βίον ('It is necessary that one of you two die', 383), δύο δ' ἐκ δισσαῖν | θνήισκετ' ἀνάγκαιν ('Twin necessities compel the two of you to die', 516–17; cf. 431–2, 442). Andromache, by contrast, does not spare Menelaus' conscience the bloody reality of his intentions (note the unremitting asyndeton of 412: σφάζειν φονεύειν δεῖν ἀπαρτῆσαι δέρην, 'to slaughter, to murder, to tie up, to hang by the neck').[53] The perversion of language by Menelaus (the attempted double execution is called προμηθία ('forethought', 690)!) reveals with Thucydidean precision 'the pressure of sophistry and the corrupted . . . individualism'[54] of a society disfigured by war.

The chorus's expression of pity for Andromache (421–2) accentuates the brutality of Menelaus' conduct. He has Andromache bound before revealing that her son will die too. Just as he breaks his word, he lectures Andromache on *hybris* (433–4). His hypocrisy is manifest. Indeed, he appears almost proud of his treachery: κήρυσσ' ἅπασιν· οὐ γὰρ ἐξαρνούμεθα ('Proclaim it to everybody; I do not deny it', 436). Significantly for our image of Menelaus, even Hermione accuses him of betrayal and abandonment (854–7). And betrayal is one of the charges also laid against Menelaus by Orestes (967).[55]

When Menelaus is forced to defend his actions before

---

[52] See Cropp (1995) 144 on *Cresph.* fr. 452 K (Polyphontes to Merope: ἐκεῖνο γὰρ πέπονθ' ὅπερ πάντες βροτοί· | φιλῶν μάλιστ' ἐμαυτὸν οὐκ αἰσχύνομαι, 'My experience is that of all mankind: I am not ashamed to love myself above all') for the distinction between a 'crude egotism' and 'an acceptably balanced self-interest'.

[53] Mastronarde (1994) 480 on *Pho.* 1193 notes 'verbal asyndeton at the start of a trimeter is an intensifying stylistic device used by all three tragedians, frequently in narratives of violence'.

[54] Foley (1985) 256 (on *Phoen.*); she explicitly relates the reflection to contemporary Athens.

[55] The motif of Spartan betrayal of allies recurs in Orestes' attack on Menelaus at *Or.* 717 ff.

Peleus, his argument is revealing. The strained logic and clumsy structure of 655–6 undermine his efforts to forge any compelling link between Andromache's and Achilles' death:

Πάρις γάρ, ὃς σὸν παῖδ' ἔπεφν' Ἀχιλλέα,
Ἕκτορος ἀδελφὸς ἦν, δάμαρ δ' ἥδ' Ἕκτορος.[56]

For Paris, who killed your son Achilles, was Hector's brother, and she was Hector's wife.

He berates Peleus for 'sharing his table' with Andromache (καὶ ξυντράπεζον ἀξιοῖς ἔχειν βίον 658); the image recalls again the last book of the *Iliad*, where Achilles insists on sharing a meal with Priam (24. 601–19). The father's generosity is here modelled on the son's, while Menelaus' disgust forcefully and critically displays his lack of the virtue. His defence of Helen and the Trojan War is gruesomely inappropriate before a man who had lost his son there: καὶ τοῦτο πλεῖστον ὠφέλησεν Ἑλλάδα ('and this greatly benefited Greece', 681). In this way Menelaus' reasoning is discredited not only by his own conduct and the character it reveals, but also by the identity of his audience.

Peleus takes up the theme of the Trojan War and echoes Andromache's earlier claim that Menelaus is unworthy of such fame (328–9).[57] As if to prove his general point in action, he challenges Menelaus' vaunted toughness by moving to untie Andromache: φθείρεσθε τῆσδε, δμῶες, ὡς ἂν ἐκμάθω | εἴ τίς με λύειν τῆσδε κωλύσει χέρας ('Let go of this woman, slaves, so that I can find out whether anyone will stop me untying her hands', 715–16). Her mutilated wrists, which Peleus remarks on in disgust (719–20), emphasize Menelaus' own barbarism, while the presence of her son allows for 'the tender tableau of the child helping to untie his mother's hands'.[58] Menelaus attempts to disguise his retreat under the *ad hoc* pretence of prior military obligations (732–6),[59] and

[56] The lines are deleted by Nauck. They offer, as Stevens (1971) 175 notes, a laboured explanation, but this is appropriate to the content of Menelaus' claim. Hose (1995) 158 notes how Menelaus' racist rhetoric is undermined by his character. (However, his comparison of *IA* 1400–1 is not so straightforward as he seems to think.)

[57] Cf. *Hel.* 393–6, where Menelaus puts his contribution to the Trojan War above that of Agamemnon.   [58] Kaimio (1988) 71.

[59] On the alleged contemporary reference of these military manœuvres, see Ch. 5.

adds a vague, long-winded threat (737 ff.).[60] This is an excellent example of a situation where the audience construes character to explain action: Menelaus' sudden withdrawal before an aged opponent (cf. 678 γέρων γέρων εἶ, 'Oh, you are an old, old man!') supports Peleus' accusation of cowardice (note the sarcasm of 721–2: ἢ μὴ ξίφος λαβοῦσ' ἀμυνάθοιτό σε | ἔδεισας;, 'Or did you fear that she might grab a sword and take revenge on you?').

Peleus' rout of Menelaus parallels the moral and intellectual victory of Andromache, a woman and a slave, over her 'superiors'.[61] The victory of Peleus represents the validation of *eugeneia*, or 'superior pedigree'. As Edith Hall has noted, 'on balance the statements on nature versus nurture [in tragedy] are surprisingly reactionary'.[62] Nevertheless, the aristocratic play-world may generate surprises and contradictions. In the *Andromache* the notion of inherited character is not presented as merely serving those in power. The shared nobility of Peleus and Andromache strongly discredits the Spartans' insistence on ethnic distinctions. Similarly, the play's handling of legitimacy cuts across simple categories of good and bad birth.

To line 801 the play concentrates on letting the characters establish and reveal themselves through a series of disputes.[63] However, with the entry of the Nurse, the conflict between characters is transformed and focused in a single figure. In a brilliant stroke of plot manipulation and surprise, the tormentor of the first action becomes the victim of the second. Hermione's regret at her attack on Andromache is not merely a device used to connect the crisis in Phthia to Orestes' plot at Delphi: the scene is important in itself and positively interesting. Hermione is a character of extremes. But in so

---

[60] Cf. Gibert (1995) 116 on 'the not uncommon situation of a character whose bluster seems to signal imminent collapse'; also Mossman (1996b) 156 n. 40 on the use here of polyptoton to make Menelaus sound 'splendidly pompous'.

[61] In the context of Peleus' battle with age, his eventual immortalization by Thetis is fitting reward for his last heroic victory (cf. 790 ff.).

[62] Hall (1997b) 99.

[63] Strohm (1957) 28 finds 'an abundance of psychological dissonances'. The first half, the tragedy of Andromache, has traditionally been the more preferred: Friedrich (1953) 53, for example, claims that 'the *Andromache* reaches its peak in the first action and falls away markedly in the second'.

far as she is so, she is recognizably human: the sudden reversal in her fortunes springs from a psychologically plausible reaction.[64]

The first crisis of the play (supplication followed by rescue) arose from Hermione's excessive jealousy, and so now her exaggerated fear creates a second crisis, with the former persecutor now in despair and in need of rescue herself. The impact of Hermione's reversal is complicated but not effaced by the character she has presented in the first part of the play. It has been suggested that hers is a fake suicide, that Hermione is merely acting; but this is to ask the audience to do too much work.[65] The change of mind is remarkable, but not arbitrary: Hermione's fragile self-confidence collapses with the failure of her plot. Her words at 267–8, ἐξαναστήσω σ' ἐγώ | πρὶν ὧι πέποιθας παῖδ' Ἀχιλλέως μολεῖν ('I will make you move before the arrival of Achilles' son, in whom you trust'), imply an awareness that her plot would be unpleasing to Neoptolemus. Her disregard of his wishes is part of her extreme independence and youthful brashness. Now her calamity pushes her to the other extreme, dependent on Orestes and vociferously critical of wayward women (her over-insistent tone disrupts her message: ἀλλ' οὔποτ' οὔποτ' (οὐ γὰρ εἰσάπαξ ἐρῶ) 943 ff., 'But never, never (I will never tire of saying it)').

The Nurse reports that Hermione feels remorse at the attempted murder (συννοίαι θ' ἅμα | οἷον δέδρακεν ἔργον 805–6, 'and also aware of the dreadful deed she has done', οὕτω μεταλγεῖ καὶ τὰ πρὶν δεδραμένα | ἔγνωκε πράξασ' οὐ καλῶς 814–15, 'So great is her remorse and she has realized that what she did before was not right'). The emotion is unexpected and striking in this ruthless princess.[66] From what we have seen so

---

[64] Contrast Gibert (1995) 63, who detects 'a feeling of arbitrariness about this change'.

[65] Stevens (1971) 193 on 825 ff. sees the effect of Hermione's high tragic language as 'to present Hermione as rather hysterical and perhaps "putting on an act", hoping that before she meets Neoptolemus he will hear of her wild grief and self-reproach'. Gibert (1995) 57 goes too far when he argues that Euripides 'makes fun' of Hermione.

[66] Cf. Kumaniecki (1930) 41. Hermione seems also to have been portrayed as experiencing remorse in Pacuvius' play: cf. fr. 183 (Warmington (1936) 230) *quantamque ex discorditate cladem inportem familiae* ('What damage I have done to my family by quarrelling!').

far of Hermione's self-obsession, it is remarkable that her emotions are now directed towards others.

As a result of this startling change, some critics have been unwilling to accept the new Hermione. Douglas Cairns has argued that the Nurse is putting a positive, but false, construction on her mistress's reaction. He rightly notes that it is fear of punishment and dishonour (808–9) which propels Hermione's panic.[67] Yet this need not imply that Hermione's motives for her change of mind are morally negligible, even if she remains a rather shallow person.[68] She is both repentant and terrified, as her own lament makes clear (837–40):[69]

> Τρ. ἀλγεῖς φόνον ῥάψασα συγγάμωι σέθεν;
> Ερ. κατὰ μὲν οὖν τόλμας στένω δαΐας,
>   ἂν ῥέξ' ἁ κατάρατος ἐγὼ κατά-
>   ρατος ἀνθρώποις.

NURSE: Are you in distress because you plotted against your rival?
HERMIONE: Much more: I groan for the daring, hostile act I committed, I the accursed, accursed in the eyes of mankind.

Just as in the *Medea* we are surprised to find ourselves in the end feeling some pity for Jason, so the transformation of Hermione challenges our moral response.[70] Her cruelty and hauteur crumble in adversity to reveal a weak and unstable

---

[67] Cairns (1993) 304–5. Whereas Andromache (344), Peleus (710), and the Nurse (809) envisage Neoptolemus expelling Hermione from their married home, Hermione herself fears being killed by him: ὀλεῖ γάρ μ' ἐνδίκως ('For he will rightly kill me', 920).

[68] Cf. Lesky (1947) 100: 'It is not the knowledge of the reprehensibleness of her action, but the fear of the consequences, which weighs upon her'. Steidle (1968) 123, however, sees Hermione gripped 'by real feelings of guilt'.

[69] Hermione's intense agitation is reflected in her emotional dochmiacs; on the metre's urgency and excitement, see Wilamowitz (1921) 404–8 and Koster (1962) 274. Dale (1968) 169 contrasts the Nurse's reasoning trimeters. The dochmiac is the only metre of tragedy which cannot be paralleled in earlier lyric: see Herington (1985) 114–15. Hutchinson (1985) xxxvii implies that the metre can help in conveying a 'female atmosphere'. In the *Andromache* the metre's association with 'horror and acute pain' (Rosenmeyer (1982) 34) is suited to Hermione's frantic state of mind.

[70] Compare the unexpected movements towards sympathy for the tormentor(s) in *Hcld.*, *Hec.*, *El.*, and *Bacch.* In the *Hippolytus* the excessive and insecure hero becomes a focus of pity and respect by the end of the play.

young woman.[71] An interesting complexity is thus revealed by her reaction.

Furthermore, acute observation of Hermione's psychological state is itself immediately exploited by Orestes. His sudden arrival parallels that of Peleus, but it is even more of a surprise because it is completely unprepared. We might have expected the entry of Neoptolemus (to confirm Hermione's fears) or the reappearance of Peleus or Menelaus (to refute her claims of abandonment). As we saw in Chapter 2, the multiple links between the three movements of the play combine with discontinuities such as the sudden breakdown of Hermione and Orestes' unexpected entry. Euripides makes the structure clear and intelligible, but not predictable. Most strikingly, he strives to realize the varied expressive potential of surprise; structure is used to create contrasts of character.

The jealous fiend of the first part of the play now emerges as an insecure young wife. Her naïveté and susceptibility to social pressure emerge most strikingly. The impact of others is vividly conveyed by direct quotation of what they (allegedly) said (932–5).[72] The revelation of outside interference allows us to see Hermione from a different viewpoint. These interesting new details alter our understanding of both her earlier behaviour and her present (excessively anti-female) reaction. Hermione is suddenly seen as a victim herself, an

---

[71] Pelling (1997) 13 n. 56 usefully distinguishes emotional engagement (depending on shifting focus and producing sympathy) from cognitive engagement (seeing events from a character's perspective: otherwise known as 'focalization'). One may easily operate without the other: we come to see the past through Orestes' eyes but feel little sympathy for him. In Hermione's case, however, the change of perspective modifies our attitude to her a great deal.

[72] The Homeric quotation of imagined future speeches is related (cf. *Od.* 6. 276–84, where Nausicaa imagines the response of critics to her 'husband' Odysseus). In the *Iliad*, Hector in particular is constantly worried about what people will say (6. 459–62, 7. 87–91, 16. 838–42, 22. 106–8). Some anonymous speaker, he predicts, will look at the captive Andromache after Troy's fall, and say, Ἕκτορος ἥδε γυνή, ὃς ἀριστεύεσκε μάχεσθαι | Τρώων ἱπποδάμων, ὅτε Ἴλιον ἀμφιμάχοντο ('This is the wife of Hector, who was the greatest warrior of the horse-taming Trojans, when they were fighting over Ilion', 6. 460–1). Cf. Martin (1989) 136: 'Hektor is creating the exact format of his own reputation, like a poet writing his own epitaph.' In contrast to Hermione, Hector's quotations (of praise or blame) are geared to motivate selfless action.

unstable young woman made vulnerable by a jealous mistake; and this surprise is multiplied by the abuser's identity: we find ourselves for once not sympathizing with Orestes.[73] His deceitful arrival, his manipulation of Hermione's emotional state, and the underhand cowardice of the ambush at Delphi, give Orestes' character a less admirable side which is new in extant tragedy.[74]

To appreciate fully the impact of this scene, we should consider more closely Euripides' choice of Orestes to fill the role of rescuer. The character of Orestes in Greek tragedy is a focus for various dilemmas relating to justice within the family and the *polis*. The dilemma thrust upon Orestes by the avenging of Agamemnon's murder entails a dramatic character of problematic and compelling interest. As we saw in Chapter 1, there is a clear attempt in the *Andromache* to weave the mythical background of the house of Atreus, the family 'welded to destruction' (Aesch. *Ag.* 1566: κεκόλληται γένος πρὸς ἄται), into the story-pattern of the play.[75] The myth of Orestes' matricide deals provocatively with the idea of gods sharing responsibility for human crimes. In the *Andromache* this motif is adapted to question Orestes' involvement in a new death, that of Neoptolemus.[76]

The Phthian chorus announces Orestes' entry in a remarkable manner (879–80):

> καὶ μὴν ὅδ' ἀλλόχρως τις ἔκδημος ξένος
> σπουδῆι πρὸς ἡμᾶς βημάτων πορεύεται.

Look, here comes a stranger, not one of our people but foreign looking, moving towards us at a quick pace.

In the preserved tragic accounts of Orestes' return to kill his mother and Aegisthus, he is regularly disguised as a foreigner

---

[73] Cf. Kuntz (1993) 74 on Orestes' 'cocky, self-satisfied tone'.

[74] This looks forward to the very ambiguous hero of the *Orestes*.

[75] For the technique of using the *later* stages of a myth to inform the response to events on stage, see Winnington-Ingram (1980) 227–8 (on the ending of Soph. *El.*).

[76] It is misleading to deprive Orestes of freely determined action; cf. Kovacs (1980) 80: 'Orestes, when all is said and done, is merely Apollo's tool'. But we will see that as an independent figure he is adequately furnished with plausible (albeit questionable) motivation for revenge.

(*Cho.* 560–4, Soph. *El.* 1106–7, Eur. *El.* 216 ff., 781–2). In the *Andromache* his foreign appearance triggers the pattern of deceit and murder, but we now see them being practised in less justifiable circumstances.[77] In addition, Orestes introduces himself in a significant way: Ἀγαμέμνονός τε καὶ Κλυταιμήστρας τόκος, | ὄνομα δ' Ὀρέστης ('I am the son of Agamemnon and Clytemnestra; Orestes is my name', 884–5). The mention of Clytemnestra, unnecessary and striking on the lips of Orestes, recalls the matricide. In Pacuvius' *Hermiona* and Virgil's *Aeneid* (3. 330–2), Orestes is motivated to kill Neoptolemus both by anger at the loss of Hermione and by madness brought on by the matricide. Euripides does not explicitly mention such madness in the *Andromache* (cf. *Or.* 36–7, 338, Aesch. *Cho.* 1055 ff.), but Orestes' savage past, which is invoked with incredulous revulsion by the chorus just after his appearance (1031–5), informs our response to his cold-blooded determination for revenge at Delphi.

In support of his hostility, Orestes recalls that when Neoptolemus returned from Troy he not only refused to return Hermione but also taunted Orestes over the murder of his mother (971–8). By deepening the temporal perspective of their quarrel, and insisting that it caused him pain (980), Orestes' recollection adds an extra layer to the depth and the characterization of both men. Neoptolemus is portrayed as arrogant, but the impact is defused both by his presentation so far (above all by Andromache, whom one could hardly call unduly biased in his favour) and by the character of the speaker and his crime. Orestes' identity is thus a significantly altered version of that familiar in extant tragedy: he is here an avenger whose motives are purely selfish. The concept of revenge is repeatedly questioned in the course of the play: Andromache's husband dies as a result of it, the Greek forces raze Troy for it, Hermione is driven by it to destroy Andromache, and Orestes proclaims it as his reason for killing Neoptolemus. In each case the character of the agents orientates us to criticism. In Orestes' case, this is done by a striking adaptation of the matricide myth: the avenger of his father is approaching the role of

---

[77] Orestes' subterfuge is part of his traditional role as the avenger who returns to kill with the aid of Apollo. Here too he is reunited with a female relative, his would-be wife (Hermione) instead of the usual sister (Electra).

Aegisthus, the husband killer. The ironies are stark, and lead us to condemnation of his third vengeful murder.

The technique of characterization by opposition and interaction which we discussed earlier is used to round out every major figure of *Andromache*. Orestes' dark prediction of the plot at Delphi (ἦν πάρος μὲν οὐκ ἐρῶ 997, 'I will not reveal the trap beforehand') creates an unflattering comparison with Neoptolemus' openness and heroism. Returning to the contrast of the two rescuers, Peleus and Orestes, we observe how their entrances point to very different intentions: Peleus is direct and gets straight to the point (ὑμᾶς ἐρωτῶ τόν τ' ἐφεστῶτα σφαγῆι, | τί ταῦτα, πῶς ταῦτ'; 547–8, 'You men there, and you who are in charge of the butchery, what is this, how did it come about?'). Orestes' explanation for the casual call (885–6) proves to be guarded deception, and he only reveals his real intentions when he is sure of Hermione's compliance (959 ff.). The sudden revelation of Orestes' true motives is a shock. The fact that he has come, οὐ σέβων ἐπιστολάς ('not in response to messages [from you, Hermione]', 964), makes clear his independent initiative and alerts us to his self-interested motives.[78]

Characterization by opposition is also present in the messenger's report of events at Delphi. Peleus' presence as audience greatly increases the pathos of the narration. Throughout the speech, Neoptolemus is called παῖς Ἀχιλλέως (1119, 1149–50).[79] Achilles, of course, was a highly complex character: he could behave and fight in appalling ways, but he was universally recognized as the most formidable Greek fighter and as admirable for his freedom from δόλος ('cunning'). Both his excellence as a warrior and his animosity towards Apollo are echoed in his son. Tragically these inherited

---

[78] Note too the stress on Andromache's getting a message through to Peleus (καὶ μὴν ἔπεμψ' ἐπ' αὐτὸν οὐχ ἅπαξ μόνον 81, 'Well, I've sent a message to him more than once'), who, unlike Orestes, comes in response to a truly urgent and moving threat.

[79] Cf. Stevens (1971) 90 on line 14: 'Though N is repeatedly mentioned in this play the name occurs only here, partly on metrical grounds, but periphrases reminding us of his lineage are sometimes dramatically effective.' The other thirteen references to him in the play are in the form 'son of Achilles'; see Phillippo (1995) 367. Further, Gould (1996b) 222 with n. 22. For Neoptolemus presented in Homer as repeating his father's heroic prowess, see *Od.* 11. 519–22 with Heubeck and Hoekstra (1989) 108 ad loc.

features lead to Neoptolemus' death, though it is one magnified by the heroism of his self-defence.[80] Conversely, Orestes is called Agamemnon's son (1090), but also Κλυταιμήστρας τόκος (1115), an appellation which recalls his deceitful and murderous past in alliance with Apollo (cf. 1027–36).[81]

The brief passage 1117–19 shows the messenger making a clear distinction between the unarmed, surprised victim and his primed, stealthy assailants:

> χὠ μὲν κατ᾽ ὄμμα στὰς προσεύχεται θεῶι,
> οἱ δ᾽ ὀξυθήκτοις φασγάνοις ὡπλισμένοι
> κεντοῦσ᾽ ἀτευχῆ παῖδ᾽ Ἀχιλλέως λάθραι.

Neoptolemus was standing *in full view*, praying to the god, but they, *armed* with sharpened swords, stabbbed the *unarmed* son of Achilles from their place of *ambush*.[82]

The lies spread by Orestes at Delphi (1090 ff.) contrast with the plain motives of Neoptolemus (1106–8). Neoptolemus fills the heroic role set by his father, and stands his ground against heavy odds (1129–31, a Homeric metaphor comparing missiles to hail). The direct second-person address to Peleus creates pathos as the audience is reminded of the close relationship between the old man and the young fighter: δεινὰς δ᾽ ἂν εἶδες πυρρίχας φρουρουμένου | βέλεμνα παιδός ('You would have seen a

---

[80] Burnett (1985) 33 interestingly contrasts 'the tragic effects that are contrived in the report of Neoptolemus' death' with the messenger's unheroic tale of 'Rhesus' last moments on earth'.

[81] The messenger calls Orestes ἁπάντων τῶνδε μηχανορράφος ('contriver [literally, plot-weaver] of all these things', 1116), recalling Orestes' own boast, τοία γὰρ αὐτῶι μηχανὴ πεπλεγμένη ('For such a trap has been contrived against him', 995). The imagery of plots and traps likens Orestes to the Spartans: cf. 66–7 (Andromache) τί δρῶσι; ποίας μηχανὰς πλέκουσιν αὖ, | κτεῖναι θέλοντες τὴν παναθλίαν ἐμέ; ('What are they up to? What plots are they weaving now? Do they want to kill me, wretched as I am?'), 549 (Peleus) τί πράσσετ᾽ ἄκριτα μηχανώμενοι; ('What plot are you contriving without a trial?'), and, most forcefully, Andromache's denunciation of her treacherous attackers, ψευδῶν ἄνακτες, μηχανορράφοι κακῶν ('Lords of lies, cunning weavers of evil schemes', 447).

[82] In Ch. 2 it was argued that we should see Orestes as present at Delphi, though not actually foregrounded in the messenger's account. One effect of this is to stress Orestes' cowardice: he is not brave enough to face Neoptolemus man-to-man.

grim war-dance as the boy moved to ward off the missiles', 1135–6).[83]

The death of Neoptolemus, like those of Patroclus, Hector, and Achilles, is only possible with the intervention of a god. Neoptolemus' initial complaint at Delphi recalls his father's attitude to Apollo: ἦ σ' ἂν τεισαίμην, εἴ μοι δύναμίς γε παρείη ('I would surely pay you out, if only I had the power', *Il.* 22. 20). Crucially, however, the basic innocence of Neoptolemus' second visit is unquestioned. This in itself is enough to raise serious questions about the character of his opponents and their revenge. Despite his 'change of mind' (μετάστασις | γνώμης 1003–4)[84] and his decision to return to Delphi to apologize, Neoptolemus is confronted by a god who harbours grudges: ἐμνημόνευσε δ' ὥσπερ ἄνθρωπος κακὸς | παλαιὰ νείκη ('He remembered old grievances like a bad man', 1164–5). The second thoughts of Hermione and Neoptolemus thus have very different outcomes. Neoptolemus finds no escape, despite his recognition of error.

Most significantly, both for our attitude to the murder and for our view of the Spartans' opposition of Greek and barbarian, the series of Homeric reminiscences[85] ends with a striking and poignant allusion that compares Neoptolemus to Hector (1152–5):

> ὡς δὲ πρὸς γαῖαν πίτνει,
> τίς οὐ σίδηρον προσφέρει, τίς οὐ πέτρον,
> βάλλων ἀράσσων; πᾶν δ' ἀνήλωται δέμας
> τὸ καλλίμορφον τραυμάτων ὑπ' ἀγρίων.

When he fell to the ground, who did not bring up a sword, who did not bring up a rock to strike and tear him? His whole beautiful young body has been destroyed by savage wounds.

In the *Iliad*, the Greeks marvel at Hector's beauty and stab his corpse: οὐδ' ἄρα οἵ τις ἀνουτητί γε παρέστη ('and nobody approached the body without stabbing it', 22. 371). However, unlike Neoptolemus, Hector's body is not disfigured (24. 405–

---

[83] See Stevens (1971) 231 on 1135 for the technique's epic origin. Also de Jong (1991) Appendix G 195–7: 'Signs of the "you"'.

[84] Knox (1979) 243 comments that this expression 'gives us the nearest Greek equivalent of our phrase "change of mind"'.

[85] See Garner (1990) 134 for the relevant passages.

21). Among the several scenes of mutilation in the *Iliad*, Homer 'has reserved the more moving and solemn effect for Hector',[86] using enjambment and alliteration (22. 401–4). Euripides deploys insistent questions (hypophora), whose emotion is heightened by the final asyndetic participles ('striking and tearing'), to express the messenger's horror and disgust. Andromache's second 'husband' is identified with her first in the moment of death, a hero's defining hour. The effect is intentionally shocking and arresting. It magnifies the grief of Peleus to come, and enhances in hindsight our respect for the relationship of Andromache and Neoptolemus. Most importantly, the comparison furthers the approximation of Trojan and Phthian interests that powerfully overturns the Spartans' anti-barbarian programme.

As was discussed in Chapter 1, the *Andromache* presents a range of figures who are familiar from the epic myths, and who thus are to some extent already inscribed with a past and with certain characteristic patterns of motivation and outlook. Euripides may freely modify their more or less traditional features (as with Neoptolemus, whose brutal past is suppressed). Or he may project their prominent qualities (for example, Andromache's maternal affection) into a new situation where novel pressures complicate the familiar portraits of the figures. The extent of this varies from figure to figure: Hermione does not feature much in the epic tradition, and so Euripides is free there to be particularly inventive and original.[87] But we should beware of setting constraints to his freedom in proportion to a figure's bulk in the mythical tradition: the varied handling of Menelaus by Euripides (*Andr.*, *Tro.*, *Helen*, *Or.*, *IA*) shows the extent to which he can depart from a particular character's epic portrayal. Who could have foreseen the paragon of a wife in the Clytemnestra of *Iphigenia in Aulis*? Or the 'civic virtues of the Seven'[88] in the *Supplices*?

This chapter has tried to bring out the importance of both

---

[86] Segal (1971b) 42.

[87] Compare the innocent and naïve figure she cuts in *Orestes*.

[88] Hutchinson (1985) 105 on *Sept.* 369–652. Euripides makes the surprise clearest in the first figure of the funeral oration, Capaneus, whose reckless arrogance and godlessness (cf. Aesch. *Sept.* 422–56, Eur. *Phoen.* 1172–86) is replaced by modesty and self-restraint (Eur. *Suppl.* 860–71).

structure and context in the formation of dramatic character. Structure is here meant in a very basic sense, namely, the order in which we learn things about the figures. Hermione and Neoptolemus are most striking in this respect. The heroism of the latter is gradually disclosed; he is an off-stage, but nevertheless powerful, presence, whose imagined reaction to events in Phthia underlines the low and nasty behaviour of Menelaus and Hermione. He remains, however, a fairly straightforward figure; his uncomplicated heroism stands opposed to the deceit and cowardice of the Spartans and Orestes.[89] By contrast, the sudden interest in the calamity of Hermione, thus far an unpleasant personality, is highly provocative. The dramatic frame does not encourage us to speculate on minute details of motivation (nor is this necessary to the impact of the scene), but her remorse and fear are surprising enough to modify our otherwise decisive moral response to her.

Closely tied to structure is context; that is, again at a basic level, who says what to whom. The importance of interaction, the dynamic relation of self-presentation and comment which works both between the major figures and between them and the chorus, has been stressed throughout the chapter. When one person comments to another on the actions of a third, this should make us think about how figures perceive others. The importance of this feature for the creation of character cannot be stressed too heavily.[90] When, for example, Orestes quizzes Hermione on the events preceding the crisis in Neoptolemus' household, he touches on the reason for Menelaus' hasty departure, κἄπειτα τοῦ γέροντος ἡσσήθη χερί; ('So was he *worsted in combat* by the old man?'), to which Hermione replies, αἰδοῖ γε ('*No, by respect for his age*', 917–18). Her attribution to Menelaus of a sense of shame collides forcefully with the character we have observed scorning an innocent child on the brink of execution (535–44). We register the dissonance;

---

[89] Cf. Segal (1993) 157 on Neoptolemus' inheritance in *Hecuba*: 'The great feat of Troy's capture is over. Achilles is only a shade. He and his son, Neoptolemus, are distinctly marked as remnants, traces of a lost grandeur.'

[90] Cf. Mitchell-Boyask (1996) 431: 'A character, the locus of a set of cultural roles, myths, and traditions, depends on other characters for intelligibility.'

the simple incongruity has a striking impact on the character-ization of both figures.

It is hoped that something of the skill with which Euripides leads the spectator to develop an impression of significant character in the *Andromache* will now be clear. Standard approaches to the play tend to underestimate this. Zürcher, for example, has claimed of pathos in *Andromache*: 'even if it is deeply and inwardly felt, it corresponds on the one hand simply to the objective situation and on the other has quite conventional or typical characteristics; thus it offers no insight into a personally unique nature'.[91] This is too depersonalized, even if it is a healthy change from the presumption of rich interiority.

Critics guided by a belief in the clinical exactitude of Euripides' character-drawing have offered many suggestive, but too often fanciful, accounts of the figures' psychological make-up. The *Hippolytus* and *Bacchae* especially have pro-voked much interpretation of this kind.[92] Commenting on 'the grippingly staged dissolution of the king's [Pentheus] personal identity', Charles Segal argues that 'Euripides here deliberately fragments the unitary heroic personality as we know it from earlier tragedy and from earlier Euripidean plays like *Medea*, *Hippolytus* or *Heracles*'.[93] We might dispute whether Pentheus' demise is really a product of psychological fragmentation, rather than being more closely linked to his repudiation of Dionysus' right to divine honour (the source too of Hippolytus' destruction: τιμώμενοι χαίρουσιν ἀνθρώπων ὕπο *Hipp*. 8, 'They delight in being honoured by mortals').[94] Richard Seaford has discussed the various psychoanalytic concepts applied to Pentheus (projection, splitting, narcissism, etc.) but reminds us that the application of such categories to Pentheus 'suffers from the disadvantage that he has no existence beyond the

[91] Zürcher (1947) 183; cf. Kovacs (1980) 97 n. 29.

[92] Segal (1986) 268–93 is a sensitive and comparatively sober example of the psychoanalytic approach. Devereux (1985) on the other hand illustrates the extremes to which this method can be taken; cf. esp. pp. 10–18, concluding 'The second Euripidean Hippolytos, an "orphic" quasi-Platonist, is also a forerunner of the ashram-dwelling psycho-terrorists of our age.'

[93] Segal (1982) 346. Gould (1996a) 571–2 has some interesting remarks on Euripides' 'vision of human experience as inherently fragmented'.

[94] See Heath (1987) 121–2.

drama'. This very basic point is often forgotten. Seaford goes on to comment: 'But the power of the representation of a character may reside precisely in its concentration on a coherent set of symptoms (*as if* the character had an unconscious mind formed over time).'[95] This is a reasonable formulation of the value and limits of the psychological model of criticism. But even here the language of 'symptoms' and the 'unconscious mind' suggests a clinical finesse which is not strictly necessary to our understanding of the characters.[96]

This can be illustrated from the *Andromache*. Critics may be tempted, for example, to psychoanalyse Hermione for her feelings of sexual inadequacy and her passive dependence on her father. There is certainly evidence in the text for her insecurity, isolation, and hysteria.[97] The portrayal of unstable youth and sexual-reproductive jealousy is compelling.[98] But it actually consists in a few bold and clear features which are illuminated and strengthened by the interactions and contrasts of the drama. This is why talk of 'complexity' or the 'unconscious mind' is hazardous. The sense of a 'deeply private consciousness' is for the study of tragedy 'a secondary and often inappropriate issue'.[99]

Malcolm Heath has argued that in so far as we have a sense of 'subtlety of characterisation' in tragedy, this is in fact a product of the 'vividness and conviction' with which 'a simple and easily grasped conception has been realised in textual details'.[100] While this approach has its merits, we should be

---

[95] Seaford (1996) 33–5.

[96] Interestingly, contemporary philosophy of mind has broadly adopted Wittgenstein's 'enduring hostility to the idea of an individuated, substantive self' (Sluga (1996) 321). Cf. also Gill (1995) 8–11 on recent anti-Cartesian accounts of Greek models of human psychology.

[97] Racine portrays Hermione's uncertainty most vividly by making her unsure whether she wants to see Pyrrhus die (cf. Hawcroft (1992) 198–200).

[98] Sophocles' reported remark on the reality of Euripides' characters makes sense in the context of such psychological acuity (Arist. *Poet.* 1460^{b}33–5).

[99] Hutchinson (1985) xxxiv. The poetry of looking within is the hallmark of a later and very different age. Cf. Wordsworth, *Prelude*, Book VII, ll. 462–6 on 'the ties | That bind the perishable hours of life | Each to the other, & the curious props | By which the world of memory & thought | Exists & is sustained.'

[100] Heath (1987) 119.

wary of the word 'simple' in the context of Euripides' character portrayal. The word has various meanings, and we may hesitate to accept Heath's view in its full rigour. What is being stressed here, since it is ultimately more important to the atmosphere and impact of the drama, is Euripides' use of character to achieve varied and striking effects: these include the creation of suspense and pathos, rapid changes in plot direction, and the ordering of our moral response.[101]

To sum up, the varied techniques of characterization used in the *Andromache* set forth striking patterns of individual motivation and expression and thus secure the coherence and interest that are necessary to the workings of the play. This chapter has tried to show how distinct individuals are worked out with clarity and significant connection in the play. The impact of interacting figures provides the basis for the powerful effects of the drama. Euripides' skilful fabrication of character guides our response to the play, and ensures that we are engaged, and profoundly moved, by tragic ἀπάτη ('illusion', cf. Gorgias fr. 23 DK).

---

[101] We do not need to postulate any detailed interiority to understand and evaluate the dramatic figures; however, we must in some sense recognize them as centres of purposeful action if their experience in the drama is to have any meaning and impact beyond that of random events. Cf. Foucault (1986) 28: 'all moral action involves a relationship with the self'. As Griffin (1990) 149 eloquently comments, some sense of plausible and involving human experience is required, 'or we shall be unmoved as we should be by a tragedy set among ants'.

4

Rhetoric

ἁπλοῦς ὁ μῦθος τῆς ἀληθείας ἔφυ,
κοὐ ποικίλων δεῖ τἄνδιχ᾽ ἑρμηνευμάτων.

Simple is the account which is true, and the right needs no subtle elucidating.

Eur. *Phoen.* 469–70

The peculiar tenor of Euripidean rhetoric, more specifically its overt and self-conscious technicality, has excited great suspicion among critics both ancient and modern. Behind this uneasiness there often lurks an ill-examined prejudice which automatically links such a style to sophistic cleverness and, therefore (it is assumed), theatrical frigidity.[1] Aristophanes in particular lampooned Euripides' skill as a 'composer of little lawcourt phrases' (ποιητῆι ῥηματίων δικανικῶν, *Peace*, 534).[2] However, such criticisms typically underestimate (or entirely ignore) the key rhetorical elements in the work of his dramatic predecessors and contemporaries, and so misleadingly portray Euripides' tragedies as 'a regrettable fall from the purity and passion of a putative Aeschylean *Gesamtkunstwerk*'.[3] This

---

[1] On the need for further 'rehabilitation' of Euripides' use of sophistic rhetoric, see Goldhill (1986) 225. On Euripides as a 'bookish' person, and the association of books with the educational techniques of the sophists, see Thomas (1989) 19–20. Henrichs (1986) 383 discusses Nietzsche's influential view that it was his 'insistence on knowledge and self-consciousness that made Euripides a bedfellow of Socrates and alienated both men from the true tragic spirit, which appealed to the emotions rather than the intellect.' For telling criticisms of such notions as the 'true tragic spirit' see van Erp Taalman Kip (1996) 131–6, who remarks (p. 132) 'the [tragic] corpus as a whole . . . is far too diverse to yield an all-embracing view'.

[2] Aristophanes himself is prone to an ambivalence similar to Plato's with regard to rhetoric (cf. Cic. *de Or.* 1. 47). Bowie (1993) 100 observes of Bdelycleon's attack on the courts: 'His warnings about the power of rhetoric to pervert the course of justice are cast, like Dicaeopolis', in an admirable example of the genre.'

[*See p. 119 for n. 3*]

chapter aims to reappraise the functions and importance of Euripidean rhetoric (defined more broadly than the mere use of forensic topoi) by placing it within the larger dramatic context of the plays, and by viewing them within the wider rhetorical context of fifth-century Athenian culture.[4]

Literary rhetoric extends back beyond Aeschylus, of course. We find spectacular displays of speech and counter-speech in the *Iliad* (especially Books 1 and 9). Nevertheless, people clearly felt that in some way the rhetoric of the late fifth century was new and different. This novelty and difference derived from an emphasis on *systematizing*. The most detailed recent study of formal debate in Euripides has admirably analysed the influence of contemporary rhetoric on its style and structure.[5] In its discussion of the thirteen major *agones* one finds a serious attempt to link these detached episodes to the larger meaning of the play.[6] Necessarily, many of the things said here will bear on the topic of characterization which was discussed in Chapter 3. I hope to avoid repetition and rather to stress the intimate connection between the topics in a way which should be illuminating for both. Such overt orations as Electra's 'kakology'[7] of Aegisthus (*El.* 907–56) make us ask not only to what extent there is a rhetorical language which is generalized between genres but also provoke the question whether the use of rhetorical topoi marks out a character as peculiar.

There is nothing unnatural in the union of tragedy and rhetoric.[8] Indeed the dialectical relationship between drama

---

[3] Goldhill (1997b) 135, who goes on: 'it is Aeschylus, after all, who stages the first trial.'

[4] The point is made with force (and a little exaggeration) by Winnington-Ingram (1969) 136: 'The rhetoric which pervades his theatre was not a personal idiosyncrasy, but an addiction of the Athenian people.' Cf. Hall (1997b) 119 on the Athenians' 'inherently dialogic' imagination. Halliwell (1997) 141 considers rhetoric 'among the most basic categories with which we interpret ancient cultures'.

[5] Lloyd (1992) 19–36. Cf. also Usher (1999) 18–20.

[6] A positive departure from earlier treatments which immediately suspected such passages: cf. Jaeger (1947) 346–8 on 'the invasion of tragedy by rhetoric' heralded by Euripides.

[7] The term proposed by Cropp (1988) 160 for Electra's 'inversion of the formal eulogy'.

[8] Cf. Mossman (1995) 94, 204: 'Disagreement and diversity are fundamental to drama.' Cole (1991) 15–18 stresses the similarities between tragic

and the lawcourt has recently been reasserted.[9] The influence of legal language and rhetorical techniques on drama is extensive: both tragedy and rhetoric are genres which rely on persuasion. But here we may distinguish between the sort of persuasion which is part of all drama, and the more ostentatiously patterned, and schematized, persuasion in Euripides, which sets him apart even from the other tragic dramatists. His rhetoric is ostentatious in drawing attention to its own adherence to modern, recently devised, systems. Euripides takes up the structure, tropes, vocabulary, and overtness of fifth-century rhetoric, which both displays its wares and expects its audience to be swept along by it. However, his dramatic mode concentrates on the *failure* of persuasion and its abuse. No one is ever converted by an *agon* in Euripides (contrast Aristophanes' persuasive *agones*). So too the speeches of Thucydides often fail of their effect.[10]

Dramatic rhetoric is peculiar in another respect:[11] one has various figures trying to persuade others of specific points, and this series of exchanges takes place before an audience which is itself being persuaded of the plausibility and (theatrical) reality of events, and which is forming moral judgements about characters. The situation is more complex than that of an orator proposing a course of action. There the author and persuader are one, while in tragedy the rhetorical effect is channelled through independent characters and seen to work in their immediate on-stage sufferings. The embodiedness of persuasion (or the failure of persuasion) in tragedy makes the poetry and oratory, both of which rely on verisimilitude of plot and argument for their success.

[9] Cf. Halliwell (1997) 122–3, and Hall (1995) who notes the similarities between oratory and drama by describing legal speeches as (p. 40) 'the written records of competitive quasi-dramatic *performances* by individual speakers, before responsive audiences, in a particular social context'. Wiles (1997) 34–5 discusses the theatricality of the Pnyx. On the other hand, fourth-century orators simplify Euripidean rhetoric for their own purposes when they quote him: on their 'particularly edifying' Euripides, see Wilson (1996) 314–15. Cf. also Cartledge (1997) 34 on the 'theatricality of fourth-century democratic rhetoric'.

[10] See Macleod (1983) 146–7.

[11] Thucydides, for example, presents a pattern of opposition between matching speeches, but in tragedy the absence of an authoritative narrator makes them even less defined and more open.

observed drama of frustrated or abused rhetoric peculiarly moving and disturbing.

As preliminaries to the discussion of *Andromache* we will consider the background of earlier poetry, the rise of the sophists, and the role of legal and political rhetoric in fifth-century Athens. This can be little more than a sketch of a vast and complex terrain, but even an outline will help us trace more accurately the particular texture of Euripides' rhetorical atmosphere and style. Criticism of the *Andromache* (like that of *Hcld.* and *Suppl.*) has been dominated by political interpretation of the action in terms of 'das Lob Athens'.[12] While one may say that in the *Andromache* 'the Spartans have gravitated to the conceptual space elsewhere occupied by non-Greeks',[13] it is not certain that Euripides has made this polarity the main dramatic interest of the play. Thus such criticisms of Euripides' 'bias' as that made by Pohlenz: 'He has thereby destroyed the artistic unity of his tragedy', exaggerate the disruption of the dramatic world by unrestrained 'patriotic motives'.[14] The scope and merits of a political reading will be appraised at the relevant points in the main discussion and in Chapter 5. Here we may pause to remind ourselves that the understanding of tragic rhetoric in predominantly political terms represents a debilitating constraint.[15] Moreover, we should be wary of taking too narrow a line on what constitutes rhetorical technique (it clearly extends beyond set-piece confrontations), and so underestimating its capacity to articulate character, advance action, and direct emotion.

Homeric epic, along with much early Greek poetry, displays an expert use, and a connoisseur's enjoyment, of persuasive speech.[16] Characters are often singled out for their skill as speakers. Indeed, as Richard Rutherford has calculated, 'we find that some 55 per cent of the Homeric corpus consists of direct speech'.[17] This high proportion 'goes

[12] So Zimmermann (1992) 123–5.

[13] Hall (1989) 214.   [14] Pohlenz (1954) i. 289.

[15] Cf. Taplin (1986) 167, who is sceptical of 'any direct reference to the immediate politicking of the Athenian audience at any one particular time'.

[16] The variety of persuasive registers in the 'ranked society' of the *Iliad* is discussed by Osborne (1996) 154.

[17] Rutherford (1992) 58. Aristotle considered Homer's narrative style supremely dramatic (*Poet.* 1460^{a}9–11).

with the conception of Homeric people as articulate and complex'.[18] In the progress of the disguised hero of the *Odyssey*, success often depends on the 'masterly plausibility'[19] of his lying stories. As Segal has shown, the poem itself displays an acute self-consciousness about the way this persuasive lying is fabricated and accepted as truth. Most strikingly, because Odysseus' accounts contain much material which is adapted from his actual past, the borderline between fact and fiction is subtly blurred.[20]

However, the self-consciousness of Euripides' tragic rhetoric clearly goes beyond the eloquence and formal oratory of epic. It must be seen in the context of the new legal and political institutions of the democracy, where public debate determined success or failure (which, importantly for tragedy, could mean death). Thought about the paradoxes and problems of rhetoric, especially the worry thrown up by the idea that one can persuade people of things that are immoral or untrue, animates many discussions in the sophistic, historical, and dramatic literature of the fifth century.[21] The arguments for paradoxical conclusions—for example, Antiphon's demonstration that it is unjust to keep one's oath (87 44B, 2 col. 1 DK)—or the construction of equally plausible arguments for opposing theses (e.g. Prot. 80 A1, B6a DK, Eur. *Antiope*, fr. 189 N, the anonymous *Dissoi Logoi*, Antisthenes' speeches for Ajax and Odysseus) point to a broad debate (and to a climate of anxiety: cf., e.g., *Med.* 576 ff., *Hipp.* 486–9, *Hec.* 254–7) about the proper uses of persuasion.

The atmosphere of uncertainty and curiosity manifests itself in both the serious intellectual interest of Protagoras and the playful self-deconstruction of Gorgias' *On Not Being* (82 B3 DK).[22] The ambiguous, morally malleable power of *logos*,

---

[18] Griffin (1995) 42.   [19] Emphasized by Gould (1983) 44.

[20] Segal (1994) ch. 8.

[21] On fifth-century suspicion of rhetoric's 'possible artifices, snares, and partialities' see Halliwell (1997) 121 f.

[22] Guthrie (1969) 197 n. 2 remarks: 'It is all, of course, engaging nonsense'! For the possibility of a more serious reading see Croally (1994) 227. Radermacher (1951) 42–66 collects most Gorgianic texts and testimonia, including the criticism of Gorgias' precious style by [Long.] *de subl.* 3. 2. De Romilly (1992) 63–5 contrasts Gorgias' wearisome artifice with the forceful antitheses and density of thought to be found in Thucydides.

strikingly displayed by Gorgias' defence of the notorious Helen,[23] sent shock-waves through the intellectual circles of late fifth-century Athens (compare the stunning impact of Gorgias' first visit there, 82 A4 DK) and was subjected to fierce criticism by Plato among others.[24]

If the *Tetralogies* of Antiphon are dated to the 440s,[25] then we can see Euripides' work against a background of opposing fictitious speeches that are full of ingenious argumentation and deeply conscious of the paradoxical nature of rhetoric. The first speech handles a murder case where circumstantial evidence is disputed and so everything hangs on probability (τὰ εἰκότα).[26] The second and third meanwhile are a matter of disputed responsibility: a man's death is admitted but the defendant argues that he is not criminally culpable. Here, crucially, we come upon the concept of responsibility, which unites forensic oratory and much of the rhetoric of tragedy. Both debate 'the complexities of responsibility, choice, causation and reasoning',[27] and this is especially true of those plays of Euripides which are set in the aftermath of the Trojan War (cf. *Andr.* 247–8, 388 ff., 614–15; *Hec.* 269–70; *Tro.* 914 ff.).

One scholar has observed that the sophists 'emerged from the womb of Greek argumentativeness; they did not create it'.[28] Euripides engages with this dialogic tradition and exploits the sophists' insights for his own dramatic purposes, particularly their reflections on the role (and abuse) of language as a tool of political power.[29] The public discourse of Athenian culture is stressed by Pericles in the Funeral Speech (Thuc. 2. 40. 2),

[23] Cf. MacDowell (1982) 12–13, Kerferd (1981) 78–82, Croally (1994) 31–2.

[24] e.g. *Phdr.* 272e–273a (plausibility in lawcourts at the expense of truth). See further Wardy (1996).

[25] Cf. Dover (1989) 29–34. On Antiphon's (critically split) identity, see Rutherford (1995) 109 n. 26. Antiphon refers to tragedy in his oratory: cf. §17 of his *Prosecution for Poisoning* (Clytemnestra); also Andoc. *Myst.* 129 (Oedipus, Aegisthus). For the practice, see Bers (1994) 189–90.

[26] Cf. I. 2 γιγνώσκοντας οὖν ὑμᾶς ταῦτα, κἂν ὁτιοῦν εἰκὸς παραλάβητε, σφόδρα πιστεύειν αὐτῶι ('So knowing this, you must place firm confidence in whatever probability indicates'); on εἰκός see Gagarin (1997) 14, 16.

[27] Goldhill (1997b) 132.

[28] Rankin (1983) 122.

[29] Relevant too is the sophists' own role as political figures and ambassadors (cf. Pl. *Hipp. Ma.* 281a–282c).

where quietists are disparaged. Pride in their *parrhesia* (freedom of speech) was a common Athenian boast. In the democratic *polis*, where the lawcourts and popular assembly were the focus of political discourse, mastery of language was a major factor in success.[30] Indeed, in the lawcourts, as often in tragedy, speakers may in fact be arguing for their lives. The forensic scenario, familiar to many of the audience from their state jury-service, enlivens the stage events with the immediacy of a crucial, real-life situation.

The ideal of democratic persuasion outlined by Pericles is not allowed to stand unqualified by Thucydides, whose portrayal of the horror of its collapse has many points in common with Euripides' own reflections on the morality of power.[31] Odysseus, the ἡδυλόγος δημοχαριστής ('sweet-tongued crowd-pleaser', *Hec.* 132),[32] represents a type of unscrupulous politician that Thucydides often disparages (particularly in the scramble for power following Pericles' death).[33] Hecuba reminds Odysseus of the status that lends his words persuasiveness (*Hec.* 294–5). The contrast with her own powerlessness to persuade is uppermost, but the sense that 'justice' is in the hands of the powerful is also present.

Thucydides' interest in the changing meaning of evaluative terms (cf. esp. 3. 82–3) is also mirrored in Euripides' exploration of the way figures like Menelaus in *Andromache* appropriate the positive rhetoric of *philia* for their own selfish ends: 'politics speaks the language of kinship'.[34] In Thucydides' narrative the change in values brought about by *stasis* is the

[30] Cf. de Romilly (1992) 57: 'Speech was thus an important mode of action, and it became increasingly so as democracy developed.'

[31] At 3. 38. 4–7 Cleon describes speeches in the Assembly as mere occasions for sophistic display, but as Halliwell (1997) 122 points out, the scene reveals 'the suspicion of rhetoric which lay cheek by jowl with the institutionalized Athenian reliance on the medium of public speech'. Cleon is himself called πιθανώτατος ('most persuasive', 3. 36. 6), which in context is not a term of praise: see Cawkwell (1997) 63. On Thucydides and the sophists, see Hornblower (1987) 110–35.

[32] The background to this description (Odysseus' victory over Ajax for Achilles' arms) is frequent in Pindar (e.g. *Nem.* 7. 20 ff.) and elaborated in Sophocles' *Ajax*.

[33] Cf. Odysseus' presentation in *Tro.* 721, *IT* 24–5, *IA* 523–6.

[34] Loraux (1993) 8 (in a discussion of Athenian autochthony).

result of 'greed and ambition'.[35] In a similar way, Menelaus exploits the opportunity furnished by the conditions of war to advance his own interests through a calculated use of anti-barbarian rhetoric (representing Andromache and her son as enemies on Greek soil).

What are the moral implications of Andromache's presentation as a master of rhetoric? Her argumentative skill extorts from Hermione the very charge made against sophists: σοφὴ σοφὴ σύ ('How very clever you are!', 245).[36] Euripides, it seems, is pointing at such moments to the moral neutrality of skilful speech *per se*.[37] What matters is in fact the identity of the speaker.[38] Tragedy does not consist in a collection of examples from a rhetorical handbook, but works with interacting and contrasting personalities, whose particular arguments are a complex product of their character and situation, and their words are intended to elicit distinct reactions from the other participants, as well as from the audience.[39] So here we see how interdependent rhetoric and character are, and how flexible our definition of rhetoric must be if we are to capture the dramatist's skill in choosing the proper words to create a particular effect on the audience.[40]

---

[35] Hornblower (1991a) 479.

[36] On the pejorative connotations of *sophos* in the later fifth century, see Rutherford (1995) 103; cf. *Alc.* 58, *Med.* 295 ff. (here its dangers are emphasized by Medea, but in a brilliant deception speech!), 579 ff., 1225–7 (on the folly of clever speech writers), *Hec.* 1187 ff.

[37] Cf. Rutherford (1995) 147 on the defence of rhetoric as morally neutral by Plato's Gorgias and by Aristotle.

[38] This was also recognized by ancient critics. According to the scholiast on *Andr.* 330, Didymus (*c.*50 BC) objected to the language here (330–2, an interpolated passage: 330–1 are also found in Menander): σεμνότεροι γὰρ οἱ λόγοι ἢ κατὰ βάρβαρον γυναῖκα καὶ δυστυχοῦσαν ('For the words are too lofty for a barbarian woman in misery').

[39] In addition, we must bear in mind the role played by the chorus in orientating our response to the speeches. Jason's self-righteous defence of his conduct is denied by the Corinthian women, who insist on his treachery (δοκεῖς προδοὺς σὴν ἄλοχον οὐ δίκαια δρᾶν *Med.* 576–8, 'you are doing wrong in betraying your wife'), while Helen's shameless justification provokes from the chorus of Trojan captives a reflection on the particular disgrace of skilful speech being used by a guilty person (ἐπεὶ λέγει | καλῶς κακοῦργος οὖσα· δεινὸν οὖν τόδε *Tro.* 967–8, 'since she speaks well but is herself wicked, which is truly terrifying').

[40] Just as rhetoric and character support one another in tragedy, so too in

Yet even if we focus on the more formal aspects of public speech within the tragedies, it is important that we recognize the range of effects achieved. Medea's articulation of rhetorical structure, for example, makes her argument seem even more dense and forceful, piling up her grievances against Jason, and emphasizing his treachery (ἐκ τῶν δὲ πρώτων πρῶτον ἄρξομαι λέγειν *Med.* 475 ff., 'I shall start my speech from the very beginning'). Theseus' overt signalling of the *agon* format (*Suppl.* 426–8) prepares us for the opposed conceptions of government (democratic monarchy versus tyranny) in the debate with Creon's herald.[41] Hecuba's remarks on the unlimited power of persuasion read like a pointed wish for up-to-date sophistic training, yet the words magnify our sense of her desperation (*Hec.* 812–19; at 1195 ff. the signposted structure marks Hecuba's confidence in the justice of her revenge on Polymestor). Most spectacularly, Cassandra's proof of the defeated Trojans' better fortune (*Tro.* 365 ff.) adds the force of sophistic paradox to the play's insistence on the deceptiveness of such categories as victor and vanquished, slave and free, Greek and barbarian. As we shall see, the *Andromache* is particularly notable for its display of the full range of these effects.

As we look in more detail at the verbal constitution of the *Andromache*, we can see how heavily laden it is with styles of expression (threats, appeals, insinuations, insults) which might be termed rhetorical. The first episode consists of two set speeches: first Hermione's grievances, then Andromache's response, followed by lengthy stichomythia. The adversarial framework is fully operative here, producing much rhetorical flourish and exaggeration, but the attempt to produce a memorable confrontation does not distort the characters involved; rather, their conflict is so acute because of who they are and the attitudes they espouse. The relationship

---

oratory: *ethopoiia* was a standard feature of rhetorical training (for which Lysias was particularly renowned, cf. Dion. Hal. *Lys.* 8). The prejudices and emotions of the audience were recognized somewhat reluctantly by Aristotle as factors in composition (cf. *Rhetoric* 1404[a]4–11).

[41] *Hcld.* 36 shows a similarly democratic Athens in mythical times (cf. 80). The pro-Athenian bias of the myth made it popular with the orators: e.g. Lys. 2. 11–16.

between rhetoric and speaker is mutually reinforcing: our knowledge of the speaker's personality is itself a product of his or her self-presentation and comment by others, and so in a broad sense it is a rhetorical construct; while in turn the identity of the speaker influences our attitude to his or her attempts to persuade.[42]

Many critics detect a degree of rhetorical self-indulgence in such agonistic *rheseis*. But Euripides' use of rhetorical techniques, even when pointedly overt, shapes character in a specific manner, even to the extent that 'he uses their own rhetoric to undercut their moral standing'.[43] The idea of Euripides λογογράφος, who 'promises to do the best for each of his clients in turn as the situations change and succeed one another',[44] has been justly criticized.[45] It has two major flaws: firstly, it reduces the plays to largely impersonal structures dominated by the 'rhetoric of the situation';[46] and secondly, it is too relativist on moral evaluation.

Rhetoric itself is just one of many formal elements of tragedy. To see its usefulness, one should regard rhetoric as one part of the stylization of the genre, whose result is not frigidity or alienation from the action, but rather lucidity and brevity of exposition, along with the excitement of confrontation and cut-and-thrust argument. The verbal skills of rhetoric are evident, and linked to them in Euripides is 'an ability to understand broad laws of individual and social conduct'.[47] However, while this universalizing tendency can be detected, and is indeed implicit in the argumentative technique of likelihood, one must insist on the appropriateness of these generalizable ideas for the concrete situation of the individual scene and its effect within the plot.

If the speakers' words do not elucidate motivation or relate to the larger themes of the play, we may fairly speak of rhetorical irrelevance. The 'air of uncertain abstraction'[48] which some detect in the more philosophical passages of

[42] See Carey (1994) 39 on dramatic character as a means of persuasion.
[43] Mossman (1995) 94.
[44] Dale (1954) xxviii.
[45] Cf. Mossman (1995) 97–102, Halliwell (1997) 123 n. 10.
[46] Dale (1954) xxv.
[47] Conacher (1981) 9.
[48] Gould (1978) 53.

Euripidean rhetoric is invariably taken to mean jarring formality of tone and expression. However, Conacher has well illustrated how passages of philosophical rhetoric are in fact entirely relevant to the speaker's individual motives and decisions.[49] His discussion of the speeches of Phaedra and Hippolytus is an excellent exegesis of the balance between abstract reflection and emotional expression. We shall damage understanding of the characters' perception of their situation, and their means of coping with it, if we divorce these two aspects of their deliberation.

Euripidean debates display considerable flexibility of form.[50] The first *agon* of *Andromache* begins without a formal introduction. Instead Hermione launches straight into her attack, in 'a scene so spirited that it has distracted many critics from seeking further meaning in the play'.[51] It is only with Andromache's reply that the *agon*-form is explicitly marked (cf. ὅμως δ'ἐμαυτὴν οὐ προδοῦσ'ἁλώσομαι 191, 'None the less I shall not be guilty of failing to defend myself').[52] It may seem a naïve question, but it is in fact quite illuminating to ask whether Hermione is actually attempting to persuade. After all she is bent on Andromache's death.[53] Her determination is expressed by the forceful triple negative, followed by a blunt, and deadly, asseveration (161–2):

> κοὐδέν σ' ὀνήσει δῶμα Νηρῆιδος τόδε,
> οὐ βωμὸς οὐδὲ ναός, ἀλλὰ κατθανῆι.

[49] Conacher (1981) 11–15.

[50] Cf. Duchemin (1968) 156–66. Collard (1975) ii. 134–5 gives an apt warning against using too rigid rhetorical canons to analyse Euripides' unsystematic technique.

[51] Conacher (1967) 167.

[52] At *Med.* 522–5 Jason draws attention to the contest of words that Medea has begun, δεῖ μ', ὡς ἔοικε, μὴ κακὸν φῦναι λέγειν ('It appears I must prove myself a skilled speaker'); cf. *Hipp.* 990–1: ὅμως δ'ἀνάγκη, ξυμφορᾶς ἀφιγμένης, | γλῶσσάν μ' ἀφεῖναι ('Nevertheless, as a crisis has occurred, I must loosen my tongue').

[53] Her digression on the humiliating servitude of Andromache is presented as a remote hypothesis (163–9: ἢν δ' οὖν βροτῶν τίς σ' ἢ θεῶν σῶσαι θέληι . . . 'If some god or mortal intends to save you'). The motif of 'sweeping' (166) frequently expresses servitude: e.g. *Cycl.* 29, *Hec.* 363, *Phaeth.* 55–6 Diggle. The image underlines Hermione's wish to degrade her (once royal) opponent.

This house of the Nereid will not protect you, nor will her altar or her shrine, but you shall die.

Dramatic *agones* seldom in fact resolve the disputed issues.[54] The conflict of argument clarifies our sense of the individuals and their grievances, and provokes our reflection and response. It is often difficult to judge who is in the right, or whether both parties have a claim (Admetus or Pheres in *Alcestis*, Clytemnestra or Electra in *Electra*?), but the dilemma sharpens our conception of the wider issues raised by the play. Occasionally we can in fact judge with confidence that one figure has the better case (Medea, Hecuba in the *Trojan Women*, or Andromache), yet their arguments are in vain. The failure of persuasion shows provocatively how power and self-interest may override considerations of justice.[55]

Hermione's speech, as often in oratory, begins by establishing the ἦθος ('character') of the speaker. In oratory this is intended to arouse sympathy and support from the audience, and the use of ethnic stereotypes is fair game if this will further the speaker's cause (or, in Aristophanes, raise a laugh). But when Euripidean figures use such arguments, the broader dramatic context often alerts us to the inconsistencies and injustice of their remarks. Hermione trumpets her Spartan origins and wealth, and denigrates her opponent as a slave and a foreigner (155, 159).[56] But her excess is repellent and we know that Andromache was a princess and is σπουδαία ('good')

[54] Strohm (1957) 37–8, Lloyd (1992) 15; Goff (1990) 69 detects 'parody of the judicial, rational rhetoric that it employs', but parody is too frivolous a word for the majority of such conflicts.

[55] Cf. Lloyd-Jones (1971) 150–1 on the *agon* of *Troades*: 'So too in the Euripidean agon both sides are right; how much more powerful is its tragic effect if this is realised!' But Helen's use of the Gorgianic idea of *eros* excluding free will (Gorg. *Hel.* 15) is rebutted by Hecuba's insistence on human responsibility. The notion of the 'tragic' as springing from an irresolvable conflict (typified by Hegel's interpretation of the *Antigone*) is still influential, but it risks obscuring the effect of moral distinctions which the audience will have formed in the course of characters' opposing arguments.

[56] Hermione even sees Andromache sprinkling water from *golden* jars (166–7). She is eager to prove that Sparta can outdo Troy in every respect. Phrygian wealth was proverbial, cf. *Hec.* 492, *El.* 314 ff. With Hermione's ἀλλ' Ἑλλὰς πόλις ('this is a Greek city', 168) contrast the pro-Athenian force of *Hcld.* 193 f.: οὐ γάρ τι Τραχίς ἐστιν οὐδ' Ἀχαιικὸν | πόλισμ' ('This is not Trachis or some Achaean township').

as a character: Hermione's sneers are to be seen against what we have seen of Andromache, not just as intrinsically nasty. Although we sense that she is plagued by feelings of jealousy and alienation (an awareness that is relevant to her later calamity), such insecurity does not justify her present intentions.

Hermione's elaborate proem (147–53) peaks rhetorically with the final word ἐλευθεροστομεῖν ('to speak freely', 153). She revealingly defines her right to free speech by reference to the prestige of her wealthy dowry and Spartan origin, while denying Andromache this same right.[57] The connection of independent wealth to free speech is characteristic of the aristocratic world of heroic myth.[58] Hermione classes Andromache as the very antithesis of the free Greek ideal. By speaking out on her own behalf, and by worsting Hermione in debate, Andromache subverts her opponent's simple-minded distinctions.

Hermione's style is punchy, studded with anaphora (161–2, 168–9), and ruthlessly decisive. Yet her control is tenuous, and her cutting speech belies a seething temper which promptly bursts forth in a series of increasingly exaggerated and grotesque insults (171 ff.). Hermione's attack on barbarian sexual and social mores has rightly been called 'the most flamboyant passage of anti-barbarian rhetoric in extant tragedy'.[59] Yet the allegedly barbarian practices of kin-killing and incest are familiar events in Greek myth.[60] Moreover, the charges are rebutted by the action of the play itself. Andromache clearly has no choice but to sleep with Neoptolemus (cf. 36–8), while it

---

[57] Such is the force of the delayed μέν . . . δέ construction (147 ~ 155). Line 154 is a 'pedantic reader's addition' (Mastronarde (1979) 116).

[58] For the importance of wealth to noble status, cf. *El.* 37–8: λαμπροὶ γὰρ ἐς γένος γε, χρημάτων δὲ δὴ | πένητες, ἔνθεν ηὑγένει' ἀπόλλυται ('I have an illustrious lineage, but no wealth, and nobility is destroyed by poverty') and Denniston (1939) 80 f. on *El.* 253. In the context of fifth-century democracy, the exercise of παρρησία is one of the foremost benefits of citizenship; cf. Democritus B 226 DK, *Ion* 674–5, and Theseus' anachronistic vision of Athenian *isonomia* and *parrhesia* at Eur. *Suppl.* 429 ff. On the *Orestes'* portrayal of *parrhesia* as a dangerous freedom, see Dunn (1989) 239–40.

[59] Hall (1989) 188.

[60] And they were exploited in oratory: cf. And. 1. 129 (on the marital life of Callias) τίς ἂν εἴη οὗτος; Οἰδίπους, ἢ Αἴγισθος; ἢ τί χρὴ αὐτὸν ὀνομάσαι; ('Who is he then? Oedipus or Aegisthus? What should he be called?').

is Hermione who of her own will leaves with Orestes and, according to established tradition, goes on to bear children not just to the son of the man who killed her husband (cf. 171–3) but to the murderer himself. Indeed, nobody fits the charge διὰ φόνου δ᾽ οἱ φίλτατοι | χωροῦσι ('close relatives kill each other', 175–6) better than Orestes, whose sordid and brutal history is recalled at his first entry (884).[61]

Hermione's ethnic evaluations are undermined both by her own actions and by the response of Andromache.[62] The Spartans' rigid categories of Greek self-definition are exposed as rhetorical constructs (in a negative sense) in the course of the play. This process is illuminated and enforced by the play's contemporary background. Unlike the conflict of the Persian Wars, which solidified, if it did not invent, the polarity of Greek and barbarian, the Peloponnesian War 'was an especially rigorous test of the security of self/other, especially Greek/ barbarian, distinctions'.[63] The *Andromache* shows these oppositions in crisis, then in breakdown, and finally reconstitutes *philia* relations along radically new lines.

Hermione's speech ends with a general reflection (177–80, a regular rhesis device in Euripides),[64] whose emphasis on fidelity and restraint as guarantees of domestic happiness represents an important motif of the play (cf. 619–23, 639–40, [1279–82]).[65] However, as will be seen more clearly in Chapter 6, Hermione's confrontation with Andromache shows

---

[61] The stereotype is pointedly subverted by Thoas' response to the news of Orestes' matricide in *IT*, Ἄπολλον, οὐδ᾽ ἐν βαρβάροις ἔτλη τις ἄν ('By Apollo, not even a foreigner would have brought himself to do this!', 1174). Compare Andromache's reaction to the demand for Astyanax's death, ὦ βάρβαρ᾽ ἐξευρόντες Ἕλληνες κακά ('O Greeks, you have invented atrocities worthy of savages!', *Tro.* 764).

[62] The importance of character and context for our response to such rhetoric is well illustrated by Jason's claim, οὐκ ἔστιν ἥτις τοῦτ᾽ ἂν Ἑλληνὶς γυνὴ | ἔτλη ποθ᾽ ('No Greek woman would ever have committed this', *Med.* 1339–40). The play's exposure of Greek chauvinism and betrayal means we cannot share Jason's opinion, even if we are horrified by Medea's revenge.

[63] Croally (1994) 55.

[64] See Friis Johansen (1959) 151–9.

[65] Lines 1279–82, deleted by Stevens (1971) 246, are defended by Sommerstein (1988). But his argument for them involves positing that (p. 245) 'two or three lines that once preceded them have dropped out of the text'. κᾆτ᾽ ('So then', 1279) suggests a closing summary by a moralizing interpolator.

her torn between two radically opposed visions of women's role (independence versus strict control). Michelini argues that 'the balance in the arguments is more significant than the imbalance in Hermione's psyche',[66] but it is a mistake to divorce the two or set up priorities between them. Hermione's confusion (reflected in her contradictory arguments) contrasts with the stability of Andromache, and leads us to understand her later reversal.

Andromache's reply (184 ff.) would do credit to the law-courts. It clearly shows the influence on Euripides of recent advances in speech construction. But rather than fault the writer for creating a jarring conflict between the complexity of rhetorical argumentation and psychological plausibility, we should ask why Euripides has chosen to portray Andromache in this way. As we noted above, the tension between status and expression is productive: Andromache's rhetorical sophistication is at ironic odds with her condition as a foreign slave. One might compare and contrast the way Aeschylus in the *Agamemnon* presents Cassandra: she is both foreign and enslaved but divines the history of the house and is understanding and accepting, whereas the conqueror Agamemnon goes blindly to his doom. Euripides substitutes a superiority in self-conscious rhetoric, which is equally paradoxical, but in a (characteristically) different way. Euripides is fond of exploring 'the ambiguity of the concept of barbarian logos',[67] and in the confrontations between Andromache, Hermione, and Menelaus the conventional (Greek) opposition of foreign guile versus the rational power of logical exposition and persuasion is provocatively deconstructed.[68]

Andromache begins with a gnomic expression, but the conventional criticism of youth is modified to fit the context (184–5; cf. νέα πέφυκας ('You are young', 238), θυγατρὸς ἀντί-παιδος ('[on the word of] your daughter, a mere child', 326):

$$κακόν \; γε \; θνητοῖς \; τὸ \; νέον \; ἔν \; τε \; τῶι \; νέωι$$
$$τὸ \; μὴ \; δίκαιον \; ὅστις \; ἀνθρώπων \; ἔχει.$$

[66] Michelini (1987) 115.
[67] Hall (1989) 200.
[68] For barbarian deficiency in rational *peitho*, see Buxton (1982) 58–9, 161–3.

What an affliction on mankind is youth, and especially those of the young who act unjustly!

Like many forensic compositions, the defence opens with a προοίμιον ('introduction', 184–91), emphasizing the strength of her case (πόλλ' ἔχουσαν ἔνδικα 187, 'even though my case is just'), but stressing the peculiar difficulties and disadvantages of her position (τὸ δουλεύειν 186, 'my status as a slave'). Such introductions are more than routine copies of fifth-century rhetoric: they are 'an interesting instance of that art's propensity to self-exposure'.[69] Euripidean speakers often sense that their words will offend and seek to defuse the effect,[70] but Andromache's response is remarkably forthright and courageous. Although she knows victory to be counter-productive, Andromache decides on principle to make the best and truest defence possible, since it would be cowardly to let condemnation follow by default (191).[71]

Theseus' condemnation of Hippolytus, and the latter's defence, are couched in terms which evoke forensic oratory: cf. κἀξελέγχεται . . . ἐμφανῶς ('he is clearly convicted', *Hipp.* 944–5), ἁλίσκηι ('you are convicted', 959), ὅρκοι . . . λόγοι . . . αἰτίαν ('oaths . . . arguments . . . charge', 960–1), μάρτυρος ('witness', 972), μάρτυς . . . ἠγωνιζόμην . . . διεξιών ('witness . . . plead my case . . . investigating', 1022–4). The legal atmosphere makes the perversion of justice more marked. In Andromache's case the legal language of her proem (ὄφλω βλάβην 188, 'I suffer harm'; ἁλώσομαι 191, 'I am convicted', ἐχεγγύωι λόγωι 192, 'justifiable argument')[72] stresses the ironic bind of her dilemma: victory in argument will do nothing to avert her defeat and death. Indeed given the character of her opponent, sure to resent being bested τῶν ἐλασσόνων ὕπο ('by her inferiors', 190), a victory is only likely to confirm her fate. The ironies, ambivalences, and dangers of rhetorical skill mark Euripides' recurring use of it.

Andromache begins by addressing Hermione, εἴπ', ὦ νεᾶνι ('Tell me, young woman', 192), words that are far from the

---

[69] Michelini (1987) 156.

[70] Cf. *Tro.* 914 ff., *El.* 1013–17, *Or.* 544 ff.

[71] Cf. Dem. 21. 106, where Demosthenes refuses προσκυνεῖν τοὺς ὑβρίζοντας ὥσπερ ἐν τοῖς βαρβάροις ('to kowtow to assailants, as foreigners do').

[72] For ἁλίσκεσθαι ('to be caught', 191) as legal terminology, cf. *OT* 576.

language of a slave. The severity of her circumstances and the ingenuity of her response alter our attitude to her use of elaborate argument. One might contrast the speech of Helen at *Tro.* 914 ff. In Helen's case we interpret it as special pleading, in Andromache's as an elaboration of her crisis. Andromache deploys anthypophora (rhetorical questions which propose and deny solutions to a problem) and arguments ἐκ τοῦ εἰκότος (from probability) in a telling series of questions which illustrate the absurdity of her alleged designs on Hermione's position.[73] It is a brilliant passage, sustained over twelve lines (192–204), which illustrates the absurdity of her alleged motives. One might compare Creon's defence against Oedipus' charge of conspiracy in the *Oedipus Tyrannus*, where his series of questions concentrates on asking why he would want to be king (592 ff.). Andromache's strategy is to ask why she would wish to supplant Hermione. It is important not to be distracted by technical considerations from the content and significance of the language itself. Andromache's questions relate to marriage, sex, the female body, reproduction, inheritance, and the opposition of Greece and Troy, all major issues in the dynamic of the plot.

The second part of Andromache's defence (205–31) is less obviously rhetorical in texture, but it is going too far to say that 'this part of Andromache's speech contains neither argument nor explicit response to Hermione'.[74] Andromache's telling *reductio ad absurdum* of Hermione's obsessive jealousy (215–20) defuses the Spartan's earlier charge of Trojan polygamy. The boastful description of Hermione's apparel indicated an obsession with appearances, which Andromache pointedly corrects: οὐ τὸ κάλλος, ὦ γύναι, | ἀλλ' ἀρεταὶ τέρπουσι τοὺς ξυνευνέτας ('It is not our beauty, woman, but our goodness which pleases our husbands', 207–8). The paradox is enforced by the language: physical allure (τὸ κάλλος) is more often the delight of a bed-mate (ξυνευνέτας) than the abstract virtues of a good wife (and Euripides chooses the word ξυνευνέτας to bring this out). This is an unexpected refinement to the debate on sexual mores initiated by Hermione.[75]

---

[73] Goebel (1989) 32–5 finds a parallel with Gorgias' *Palamedes*, of which Kovacs (1996) 42–3 is sceptical.　　　　[74] Lloyd (1992) 54.

[75] Cf. Sappho fr. 50 Voigt: ὀ μὲν γὰρ κάλος ὄσσον ἴδην πέλεται ⟨κάλος⟩ | ὀ δὲ

Yet more surprising is Andromache's recollection of her tolerance of, indeed support for, Hector's adultery (σοὶ καὶ ξυνήρων 223, 'I even helped you in your affairs'). She presents his infidelities as natural, trivial slips, the work of Aphrodite, εἴ τί σε σφάλλοι Κύπρις ('if Aphrodite should trip you up', 223). Although the Athenians had a relaxed moral attitude to extra-marital sexual relationships (on the part of Athenian men),[76] Andromache's laissez-faire attitude is an unexpected addition to her epic history. What gives it such rhetorical power is precisely its mythical setting and the unexpected recasting of the marital devotion which so strongly characterizes Hector and Andromache's union in the *Iliad*. Clearly, we are not meant to concentrate on Hector's affairs as an affirmation of manliness; what the parallel illustrates is Andromache's gen-erosity and her less destructive method of coping with sexual rivalry. Yet the deviation from the literary background, as we shall see in Chapter 6, has more than a purely rhetorical effect.

Hermione's response is to accuse Andromache of manufac-turing an *agon*: τί σεμνομυθεῖς κἀς ἀγῶν' ἔρχηι λόγων, | ὡς δὴ σὺ σώφρων, τἀμὰ δ' οὐχὶ σώφρονα; ('Why do you indulge in lofty moralizing and begin a contest of arguments, claiming that you are chaste, but I am not?', 234–5).[77] The use of ἀγών ('contest') as a 'headline to a rhetorical showpiece'[78] normally introduces extended *rheseis*; here it is used to herald the combative stichomythia between Hermione and Andromache.[79] The core terms of the stichomythia are *sophrosyne* and *nomos*. Both Hermione and Menelaus appropriate the virtues of restraint and lawfulness for themselves; this is particularly

κἀγαθὸς αὐτίκα καὶ κάλος ἔσσεται ('For the beautiful person is beautiful in appearance, but the good person will as a result also be beautiful').

[76] Cohen (1991) 98–132 is a detailed analysis of Athenian attitudes to adultery. He argues that notions of 'inherent moral wrongness' (p. 123) do not apply to Athenian sexual mores.

[77] Halleran (1995) 191 on *Hipp.* 490–1a notes 'σεμνομυθέω is rare, appearing only here and at *And.* 234 in archaic and classical literature; it may be a Eur. coinage.'

[78] Mossman (1995) 103 n. 29 on *Hec.* 229.

[79] The *Andromache* lacks the very long passages of stichomythia found in late Euripides, but those it has effectively express the tension attendant on the conflict of the *agon*, whether after the *rheseis* (236–60, 435–44) or before (583–9).

striking in the light of the oligarchic overtones of the words in Athenian thought.[80] Spartan Εὐνομία ('lawfulness'), the 'abstraction that typifies the so-called Lycurgan constitution',[81] was a proud boast. Sparta was 'widely admired for the rigid domination she exerted over (and by) her citizens'.[82] Here, however, Hermione's rigid, chauvinist division between Greek and barbarian laws is trumped by Andromache's universalist perspective on morality: κἀκεῖ τά γ' αἰσχρὰ κἀνθάδ' αἰσχύνην ἔχει ('Foreigners regard what is shameful as a disgrace, no less than Greeks', 244). Herodotus in particular shows us that the question of competing *nomoi* was being discussed in the second half of the fifth century.[83] The existence of such a refined discourse on 'normality' undercuts Hermione's position. In any case, Spartan claims to both self-control and lawfulness are soon made to seem hypocritical, as Menelaus enters holding an innocent child hostage, and then reneges on his promise to spare the child's life.

In her confrontation with Menelaus, Andromache is given three speeches of considerable length (319–63, 384–420, 445–63) which build in emotional intensity and culminate in her passionate condemnation of the Spartans.[84] Again the range of her rhetorical skills is fully explored, from rational persuasion and sarcasm to begging and invective. By contrast, Menelaus' contributions are peculiarly low, a blend of the ruthless and the

---

[80] See Rutherford (1995) 94 on *sophrosyne*, who brings out the political connotations of the slogan, referring to the 'better class' or 'decent ones'. On the word's 'concealed oligarchic or elitist attitudes' (present at *Hipp.* 79–80?), see Croally (1994) 66–7. (North (1966) 85–120 stresses that the word was deployed by democrats as well.)

[81] Bowra (1961) 72.

[82] Thomas (1994) 37. The tradition goes back to Tyrtaeus.

[83] At 3. 38 he remarks that each people naturally take their own *nomoi* as standard (cf. *IA* 558–9). Greek and non-Greek are not rigidly divided: the Greeks share some customs with the Egyptians (2. 35 ff.). The Old Oligarch remarks on the Athenians' mixture of various Greek and foreign elements in their speech, dress, and lifestyle, [Xen.] *Ath. Pol.* 2. 8.

[84] Andromache's confidence in argument and in her own innocence is signalled by her readiness to submit to trial and punishment—only before Neoptolemus, whose right it is to deal with her (358–60). Menelaus' rejection of any fair judicial process is telling. The existence of similar life-or-death arguments in Athenian political history (cf. Thuc. 3. 52 ff., 5. 84 ff.) heightens the impact of such scenes.

self-congratulatory.[85] As Lloyd observes, Menelaus' speech 'is characterized by clichés, proverbs, and tricks of style'.[86] His public acclaim is challenged by Andromache on the grounds of his domestic interference (319–29).[87] Andromache's mastery of language now goes beyond the Greek/barbarian polarity and challenges the stereotypes of gender role. Her powerful female rhetoric destroys Menelaus' claims to political power.

As in her speech before Hermione, Andromache adopts an explicitly forensic tone (334 ff.).[88] With oratorical precision she distinguishes the various undesirable consequences of her death: pollution for Hermione ($\mu\iota\alpha\iota\phi\acute{o}\nu o\nu$ . . . $\mu\acute{v}\sigma o\varsigma$ 335, 'the taint of murder') and condemnation by association for Menelaus.[89] She pictures Menelaus standing trial as an accomplice to murder before the judgement of the community (336–7):

> ἐν τοῖς δὲ πολλοῖς καὶ σὺ τόνδ' ἀγωνιῆι
> φόνον· τὸ συνδρῶν γάρ σ' ἀναγκάσει χρέος.

You will go on public trial for this murder; your taking part will force you to accept responsibility.

The court of public opinion, the tribunal of heroic shame culture, is emphasized by its position at the start of line, as is the charge of murder ($\phi\acute{o}\nu o\varsigma$). The responsibility for the crime is expressed in the compact certainty of 337, where each word

---

[85] One might compare his low style in Sophocles' *Ajax* (1120 ff.).

[86] Lloyd (1994) 126 on 366–83. De Romilly (1961) 32–3 notes how the pathos of the scene is intensified by Menelaus' deceitfulness; cf. Di Benedetto (1971) 98–9.

[87] I do not intend to set up a rigid dichotomy between *oikos* and *polis*. Friedrich (1996) 273 well comments: 'both institutions define one another and are interdependent as well as reciprocal'. Cf. Croally (1994) 117: 'Ideologically, the public and the personal aspects of *philia* do not interpenetrate, but . . . as in *Andromache*, . . . we are shown how the public and the personal can be in conflict in terms of *philia*.'

[88] The three resolutions of the formal opening, Μενέλαε, φέρε δὴ διαπεράνω- μεν λόγους ('Menelaus, come, let us discuss the arguments', 333) led to its deletion by Wilamowitz (cf. (1875) 190 n. 5 ad loc. 'the *Andromache* is among the heavily interpolated plays'), who is followed by Diggle. The interpolation of a formal debate header derives from the legal tone of Andromache's speech.

[89] For the dangers of wrongful execution, cf. Antiph. *Tetr.* Γ β 8, δ 10: οὗτός τε ἀνοσίως διαφθαρεὶς διπλάσιον καθίστησι τὸ μίασμα τῶν ἀλιτηρίων τοῖς ἀποκτείνασιν αὐτόν ('If the defendant is put to death unscrupulously, he doubles the pollution brought upon his killers by the spirits of vengeance').

lays an extra burden of obligation on Menelaus. Hypophora is once again extensively deployed, this time to outline the various undesirable consequences of the murder of Neoptolemus' son for both Menelaus and Hermione (339–51). Andromache exploits the rhetorical technique of imagining a person's probable reaction to events, καῖτα πῶς πατὴρ | τέκνου θανόντος ῥαιδίως ἀνέξεται; ('And do you think his father will accept his son's death lightly?', 339–40). The structural conjunction of father and dead child adds pathos to the father's natural grief, and vividness to his imagined revenge.

Menelaus' appropriation of the rhetoric of kinship is marked (374–7). His interference, however, is clearly motivated by self-interest and regard for Spartan power rather than concern for the good of his son-in-law.[90] Bluntly stated, Menelaus' behaviour is at odds with his rhetoric: his self-interest undermines his claim to the values of kinship and communality.[91] Thucydides' observations on the process are apt: 'the Spartans may be described in the pages of Thucydides as assimilating τὸ καλόν to what is purely expedient'.[92] In the *Andromache* the superior force of the Spartans and their distortion of moral language in the service of violence reminds us most vividly that civilized order is fragile and can always disintegrate.

The debate rises to a more intense emotional level in Andromache's next speech, at the end of which she leaves the sanctuary of Thetis' shrine. She bombards Menelaus with a series of questions which are remarkable for their combination of emotional passion with forensic precision and penetration (387–93).[93] Andromache's demands, τίνα σῶν ἔκτανον παίδων ἐγώ; | ποῖον δ' ἔπρησα δῶμ'; ('Which child of yours did I kill? Which house did I burn down?', 389–90) reinforce our impres-

---

[90] In *Orestes*, Menelaus is cool to Orestes' own appeals on the basis of *philia* and its obligations (651 ff.). He fails even to turn up in court to support him, putting political ambition before duty to his kin (1058–9).

[91] Xen. *Lac. Pol.* 5. 1 records the Spartan practice of communal authority (among male adults) over children and servants. Andromache, however, is in a special position as ex-concubine of Neoptolemus and mother of his only son. For the ambiguities of appeals to jurisdiction over suppliants by members of alien communities, see Wilkins (1993) 69 on *Hcld.* 142 ff.

[92] Creed (1973) 231; cf. Cawkwell (1997) 7.

[93] Mossman (1995) 106–7 explains how the frequent short questions at 387 ff. (and 192 ff.) effectively portray Andromache's emotion and distress.

sion of her miserable past and throw into relief (both temporal and moral) the injustice of Menelaus' continuing persecution of her.[94] The heroism and nobility of Andromache's departure from the altar are marked by the accumulation of infinitives, which express both the brutality of her opponents and her forceful defiance of them (411–12).[95] The structure of Andromache's *rhesis* (384 ff.) is highly crafted and there is a careful change of ἦθος ('character') from point to point. The excellence (both moral and technical) of her argument is visible in its effect: the chorus pity Andromache and urge Menelaus to reach a peaceful agreement (421–4). He responds with shameless manipulation of a basic canon of Greek morality (return like for like, 438). The scene's indictment of the abuse of ethical clichés by the powerful is peculiarly forceful.

The much debated relevance of Andromache's subsequent anti-Spartan outburst will emerge clearly from closer observation of its verbal detail.[96] The metonymy of δόλια βουλευτήρια ('cunning plotters', 446) is striking, and its denunciation of deception is amplified in the cumulative barrage of 447–9:

> ψευδῶν ἄνακτες, μηχανορράφοι κακῶν,
> ἑλικτὰ κοὐδὲν ὑγιὲς ἀλλὰ πᾶν πέριξ
> φρονοῦντες . . .

Lords of lies, weavers of wicked schemes, whose thoughts are crooked and rotten, utterly twisted . . .

The patterning of 447 draws attention to the violence and cunning of the Spartans.[97] Their devious thoughts are mirrored

---

[94] Andromache's 'but what have I done?' defence is paralleled in other scenes of unjust killing: *Hec.* 264 (Polyxena has done Achilles no harm), *Her.* 207 (the innocence of Heracles' children).

[95] Compare her injunction in *Troades* to the Greek killers of her first son, Astyanax: ἄγετε φέρετε ῥίπτετ', εἰ ῥίπτειν δοκεῖ | δαίνυσθε τοῦδε σάρκας ('Take him, carry him off, throw him to his death, if you have so decreed! Feast on his flesh!', *Tro.* 774–5).

[96] The passage's relationship to contemporary events is discussed in Ch. 5.

[97] The stereotype of the duplicitous Spartan is a staple of Athenian tragedy, comedy, historiography and philosophy: see Bradford (1994), Mills (1997) 67–8. With 451–2 compare Hdt. 9. 54 ἐπιστώμενοι τὰ Λακεδαιμονίων φρονήματα ὡς ἄλλα φρονεόντων καὶ ἄλλα λεγόντων ('[The Athenians] were aware of the Spartan habit of saying one thing and meaning another'). Yet Herodotus' view of Periclean Athens was itself ambivalent: see Gould (1989) 117–18. The

in the structure of 447, the metaphor of twisting (ἑλικτὰ ... ἀλλὰ
πᾶν πέριξ) enclosing the charge of rottenness (κοὐδὲν ὑγιές).
Andromache's recollection of Hector's death leads to an inglor-
ious image, ναύτην ἔθηκεν ἀντὶ χερσαίου κακόν ('he made you a
cowardly sailor, not a soldier by land', 457; the adjective's
impact is greater for its delay). In this way Menelaus' unheroic
deportment, both then and now, is connected and clarified.[98]

The force and passion of the following lines display the sort
of vigour that marks the expressive difference between poetic
drama and a prose text (458–60):

> νῦν δ' ἐς γυναῖκα γοργὸς ὁπλίτης φανεὶς
> κτείνεις μ᾽· ἀπόκτειν᾽· ὡς ἀθώπευτόν γέ σε
> γλώσσης ἀφήσω τῆς ἐμῆς καὶ παῖδα σήν.

Now you appear as a dashing warrior against a woman and are trying
to kill me. Kill me then! I will leave you and your daughter without a
single word of flattery from my mouth.

The sarcasm of γοργὸς ὁπλίτης ('dashing warrior') is cutting.
What sounds alarming at the start of 459 ('you are killing me')
is scornfully made a command by the victim. Her imperative
marks her powerful and principled defiance.[99] Her refusal to
fawn draws attention to her own commitment to the truth and
contrasts the Spartans' self-serving use of moral language and
legal rhetoric.

The lyric ἀμοιβαῖον ('exchange') which follows the second
stasimon is geared to raise the emotional tension to a pitch of
pathos. The child's simple plea to Menelaus suits this admir-
ably, ὦ φίλος | φίλος, ἄνες θάνατον μοι ('O friend, friend, please
spare me from death', 530–1).[100] Andromache calls their

translation 'lords of lies' is taken from Lloyd (1994). For the Semitic origins of
such expressions see West (1997) 545–6.

[98] Poole (1994) 21–9 discusses the various (and variously critical) depictions of Menelaus from *Andromache* to *IA*. Cf. Seidensticker (1982) 89 f. on
Menelaus' insensitivity at *Tro.* 1050.

[99] Perhaps the ἀπο- has more confective force as against the more
imperfective κτείνεις; cf. *OC* 993–5: εἴ τίς σε τὸν δίκαιον αὐτίκ᾽ ἐνθάδε | κτείνοι
παραστάς, πότερα πυνθάνοι᾽ ἂν εἰ | πατήρ σ᾽ ὁ καίνων, ἢ τίνοι᾽ ἂν εὐθέως; ('If
someone here and now stood by you, the righteous one, and tried to kill you,
would you enquire whether the killer was your father, or would you retaliate
at once?').

[100] The scene contrasts with the calculated use of children as objects of pity

murder a 'cruel blood-offering' (θῦμα δάιον, 506); the perversion of sacrificial language marks the abnormal brutality of Menelaus' intentions. He attempts once more to mask his violence with a specious hint at legality (σὲ μὲν ἡμετέρα | ψῆφος ἀναιρεῖ, παῖδα δ' ἐμὴ παῖς | τόνδ' Ἑρμιόνη 517–19, 'You are put to death by my verdict and your son here by my daughter Hermione').[101]

The violent emotion of the scene is channelled through a second full *agon*, as Peleus questions the justice of Menelaus' murderous interference in his son-in-law's affairs. This *agon* has two pairs of speeches with the subordinate pair taking the place of the angry dialogue which often concludes an *agon* (cf. 234 ff.). Each speaker is thus able to react more fully to the other's arguments: Peleus' speeches in particular cover much ground, reflecting on Menelaus' disgraceful role in the Trojan War, from the sacrifice of Iphigenia (624–5)[102] to the present crisis over a prisoner of war in the house of Neoptolemus. Peleus speaks first, and as in the agonistic scene between Andromache and Menelaus, there is no formal indication that a debate is underway.[103] As Lloyd remarks, 'In this play, unusually for Euripides, the distinctness of the *agon* form is blurred.'[104] Given the frequency of scenes of personal conflict in the first half of the play, this lack of rhetorical signposting averts the impression of stiffness or excessive formality. Each separate confrontation is shaped to illuminate the various aspects of individual motivation and reaction. The series has

in real trials (cf. Lys. 20. 34–5, And. 1. 148), an emotive technique parodied by Aristophanes in his *Wasps* of 422 (976–8), and criticized by Socrates in Pl. *Apol.* 34c–d.

[101] Hutchinson (1985) 77 on Aesch. *Sept.* 198 says of ψῆφος: 'The word is often used of an individual's decision to punish or acquit.' Here, however, the word's connotations of an open vote for condemnation are rhetorically exploited by Menelaus (but rebound against him). The juxtaposed forms of παῖς , meaning 'son' and 'daughter', poignantly underline the contrasting fortunes of the two young people.

[102] Compare Orestes' rhetorical use of his sister's death as a lever on Menelaus, ἃ δ' Αὐλὶς ἔλαβε σφάγι' ἐμῆς ὁμοσπόρου, | ἐῶ σ' ἔχειν ταῦθ'· Ἑρμιόνην μὴ κτεῖνε σύ ('As to what Aulis took, the slaughter of my sister, I'll give you that, you don't have to kill Hermione', *Or.* 658–9).

[103] The marked difference in the length of the speeches again connotes the feebleness of Menelaus' case.

[104] Lloyd (1992) 6.

a cumulative force: it enriches our impression of Andromache's predicament, her heroic response, and the lowness of her persecutors.

Peleus' first speech concentrates its venom on the unheroic conduct of Menelaus, whom he witheringly addresses as ὦ κάκιστε κἀκ κακῶν ('you coward descended from cowards', 590), ending some fifty lines later with the no less pungent σὺ δ᾽ οὐδὲν εἶ ('You are a nothing!', 641).[105] There is much thematic coherence between Peleus' and Andromache's earlier attack on Menelaus. Both stress his unheroic conduct at Troy and his current interest in a sordid matter of sexual jealousy. Both remark on his unheroic subordination to women, whether to wife or daughter (cf. 326–9, 629–31).

Notably, Menelaus' reply recalls Hermione's anti-barbarian rhetoric in its rigid adherence to stereotypes and simplistic ethical divisions (647 ff.). Of course, this kind of thing may not discredit the speaker automatically: we should not forget Peleus' own stereotype of Spartan females (595 ff.). Our response to their rhetoric is guided by our judgement of their intentions. Menelaus' pedantic insistence on the ethnic guilt of Andromache (655–6) is fully characteristic, and ironically dissonant with the play's illustration of the instability of such rigid categories of φίλος and ἐχθρός (cf. *Hec.* 846–9). Peleus' own view of the death of Achilles had reversed the nationalistic paradigm (611–15):

> ψυχὰς δὲ πολλὰς κἀγαθὰς ἀπώλεσας
> παίδων τ᾽ ἄπαιδας γραῦς ἔθηκας ἐν δόμοις
> πολιούς τ᾽ ἀφείλου πατέρας εὐγενῆ τέκνα.
> ὧν εἷς ἐγὼ δύστηνος· αὐθέντην δέ σε
> μιάστορ᾽ ὥς τιν᾽ ἐσδέδορκ᾽ Ἀχιλλέως.

You destroyed many brave souls, you made old mothers childless in their homes and robbed grey-haired fathers of noble sons. Of these fathers, I, my wretched self, am one. And I regard you as the defiled murderer of Achilles.

---

[105] Stevens (1971) 167 notes the common καὶ ἐκ plus adjective construction and is sceptical of any wider meaning here; but the reference to Menelaus' ancestors (Pelops and Atreus) is particularly apt in a play so centrally concerned with the continuity of family characteristics.

The evocation of the *Iliad* in 611 (πολλὰς δ' ἰφθίμους ψυχὰς "Αιδι προΐαψεν | ἡρώων 1. 3–4, '[Achilles' anger] cast many powerful souls of heroes down to Hades') lends Peleus' statement a particular poignancy and authority, and this is confirmed by his personal grief; he is able to point to himself as proof of his charge (614), which culminates with the name of his dead son (615).

Menelaus' wish to wipe out the last traces of Troy, and with it the slightest possibility of Trojan resurgence and revenge (cf. 519–22), may be compared to Polymestor's lying justification of his murder of Polydorus (*Hec.* 1138–44). As with Poly-mestor, Menelaus is really much more concerned to further his own interests than the cause of Greece, especially as the child is, equally, all that survives of Achilles. His defence of Helen on the grounds that her rape benefited Greece (680; cf. *Tro.* 932–4) is worthy of Gorgias himself. The paradox is shocking and both the content of the claim and the character of the speaker guide us to reject it.[106] Peleus ignores Menelaus' warning against γλωσσαλγία ('garrulousness', 689), and con-demns the Atreidae's generalship as thoroughly 'undemocratic' (693–705).[107]

In Hermione's speech of self-justification before Orestes it is the very power of *logos* which is ultimately made the scapegoat

---

[106] Menelaus' argument reduces the Trojan War to a military training course; as often, he supports his point with a banality (683–4). Cf. Collard (1993) 157 on the prevalence of 'sententious or self-righteous recourse to moral truths' in debates, both in tragedy and in the lawcourts. Menelaus even uses an *ad hominem* attack on the murder of Phocus to secure Peleus' characteristic virtue of self-control for himself (ἐσωφρόνουν 686, 'I showed restraint'). On Peleus' chastity, and the accusation of rape made by his host Acastus' wife Hippolyte (or Astydameia), see Σ Pind. *Nem.* 4. 57, Ar. *Clouds* 1063, Pl. *Rep.* 391c.

[107] Mossman (1995) 115 n. 56 well remarks that the Homeric background to this speech is more important than contemporary allusion: Peleus echoes Achilles' attack on Agamemnon's inferior prowess and greed (*Il.* 1. 163–71) and extends it to Menelaus. But the emphasis on generalship (στρατός . . . στρατηγός . . . στρατηγίαι, 'army . . . general . . . generalship') has an added bite when one considers that fifth-century generals were answerable to the *demos*, and could be disciplined unless their activities received prior approval: see Hamel (1998) 44–6, 128–30. The role of the generals in the pre-play ceremonies is less significant; cf. Goldhill (1990b) 100–1. (Plut. *Alex.* 51. 8 records the story of Cleitus' quotation of *Andr.* 693–8, for which he was killed by Alexander; cf. Cameron (1995) 74.)

for her reckless action (cf. Gorg. *Hel.* 8). First she evokes the
urgent danger facing her in a vivid image of the palace taking
voice to drive her out (923–5). Then, as a prelude to her
defence, she rhetorically asks how she came to commit such
an error: πῶς οὖν τάδ᾽, ὡς εἴποι τις, ἐξημάρτανον; ('How then, as
someone might say, did I go wrong in this way?', 929).[108] The
words of the meddling gossips are quoted directly, a technique
familiar from epic to build up a sense of the pressure of public
evaluation (930–5):

> κακῶν γυναικῶν εἴσοδοί μ᾽ ἀπώλεσαν,
> αἵ μοι λέγουσαι τούσδ᾽ ἐχαύνωσαν λόγους·
> Σὺ τὴν κακίστην αἰχμάλωτον ἐν δόμοις
> δούλην ἀνέξηι σοὶ λέχους κοινουμένην;
> μὰ τὴν ἄνασσαν, οὐκ ἂν ἔν γ᾽ ἐμοῖς δόμοις
> βλέπουσ᾽ ἂν αὐγὰς τἄμ᾽ ἐκαρποῦτ᾽ ἂν λέχη.

The visits of wicked women undid me, who inflated me with folly by
speaking like this, 'Are you going to put up with this vile captive in
your house, a slave-woman sharing your marriage-bed? By Hera,
goddess of marriage, she wouldn't have enjoyed my bed under my
roof and lived to see the light!

Their first question is sharpened by the pronoun placed bluntly
at the start of the line; the shame of sharing a bed with a slave is
compounded by the enclosing structure of 933 (δούλην . . .
κοινουμένην, 'slave . . . sharing'). Their oath is, according to
Dover, 'the only tragic approximation to the banal oaths of
conversation'.[109] The colloquialism adds to the 'psychological
realism'[110] of the imagined scene, with which Hermione
attempts to persuade Orestes of the culpability of others.

Hermione invokes typical male fears of corruption from
outside, very like the admonitory husband of several Attic
orations. Her address to husbands (950–1) recalls Peleus'
advice to suitors (622–3). As we recall Hermione's previous

---

[108] The manuscripts at 929 read ἐξημάρτανες ('you commited a crime') and
attribute the line to Orestes. In their texts Stevens and Diggle both accept
Vitelli's ἐξημάρτανον ('I committed a crime') and Lenting's attribution to
Hermione. Kovacs (1996) 49–51 rejects Vitelli's change and supports a one-
line interruption by Orestes. But, as Stevens (1971) 202 notes, the words are
more effective as a rhetorical anticipation of an outsider's question.

[109] Dover (1987) 48, quoted by Lloyd (1994) 150.

[110] West (1990) 5, discussing the effects of colloquial language in tragedy.

wilfulness, the rhetoric of female control seems forced, but the change makes sense in a character of extremes. Her rhetoric thus develops the psychology of her characterization. Such moralizing, cast in the form of general reflection, stands in a complex relationship to the dramatic situation.[111] It is at once internally coherent and externally directed to a hypothetical audience of 'imaginary listeners'.[112] Such apparent breaches of dramatic illusion have encouraged some critics to detect authorial rhetoric for one viewpoint or another. This approach, however, not only assumes a simplistic identification of character and author, but also diminishes the interrogative complexity of the texts: the world of the play is distinct, yet the audience can, if it chooses, place itself in the position of the address's implied audience.

As we saw in Chapter 3, Orestes' rhetoric of revenge (999–1008) represents a disturbing extension of his murderous history into another *oikos*. Our potential sympathy for his condition is undermined by his own language, whose plangent excess, marked by repetition, frustrates his intentions, ἤλγουν μὲν ἤλγουν ('I was pained, sorely pained', 980; cf. φεύγων ἀπ' οἴκων ἃς ἐγὼ φεύγω φυγάς 976, 'fleeing from my home as an exile flees'). Like Menelaus before him, Orestes hides his selfish desires behind the rhetoric of concern for kin (cf. 889–90, 985–6). He subtly leads Hermione's narration (εὖ μ' ὑπηγάγου 906, 'You have prompted me well') and plays purposefully on her jealousy (909–10). Through Orestes' deception we are disturbingly brought to see rhetoric as 'a medium of exploited confidence and emotional duplicity at the very heart of human relationships'.[113]

In considering the criticism of Apollo which closes the messenger's speech (1161–5) one must not ignore either the rhetoric of the situation (the hero's final hour related to his grieving relatives) or the character of the speaker (a servant of the dead man).[114] The criticism is the climax to a vivid and

---

[111] Cf. Bain (1987), esp. p. 4.

[112] Bain's phrase, discussed by Croally (1994) 242–3, on whom my next point is based.

[113] Halliwell (1997) 126, discussing Clytemnestra in the *Oresteia*.

[114] Heath (1987) 153–7 counters the view of the messenger as 'an unengaged, unindividualised figure' (p. 154).

enthralling narrative. The excitement of the messenger's
account relies on careful preparation of the scene, which
makes full use of a range of voices, lying (Orestes' δυσμενεῖς
. . . λόγους 1091, 'malicious words'), resentful (the Delphian
ῥόθιον . . . κακόν 1096, 'wave of anger'), and apologetic (Neo-
ptolemus' wish τῆς πάροιθ' ἁμαρτίας | δίκας παρασχεῖν 1106–7, 'to
make amends for my past error'). Each voice is appraised from,
and directed through, the personal viewpoint of the messenger.

The picture of intrigue and murder at one of Greece's most
famous shrines expands the narrative perspective of the domestic tragedy.[115] By contrast with Hermione's quotation of the
gossiping women, the messenger's report of Neoptolemus'
reply to his (ominously) anonymous questioner shows emotional rhetoric creating a positive moral evaluation of the victim
(compare the force of Neoptolemus' baffled question, 1125–6).
His account (1104–11) arouses anger at Orestes' manipulation
of μῦθος (1109, 'rumour'), and pity for the death of his master.
Neoptolemus places the god first (Φοίβωι 1106, 'Phoebus'),
stressing in vain the sincerity of his apology. The account of
the murder itself is detailed with heroic resonances which
elevate the self-defence of Neoptolemus (these were discussed
in Chapter 3). As a whole the speech illustrates a strong
consonance of poetic register and rhetorical impact.

We began this chapter by noting the close connection
between rhetoric and characterization. The ensuing study of
the *Andromache* has sought to show that Euripidean rhetoric is
not as dramatically stultifying as is sometimes alleged. While
figures do make use of elaborate argumentative structures or
particular terms which draw on fifth-century philosophical
enquiry and politico-legal oratory, their speeches cannot be
divorced from the fictive world of the play. The arguments
gain their peculiar dynamic from the specific relations between
figures. The *Andromache* also reveals how characters variously
use or abuse rhetoric to manipulate their environment.[116]
Rhetoric emerges as something eminently adaptable (according
to the moral constitution of the speakers and their intentions).
And this includes the positive aspects of the art which illuminate the intellectual superiority and heroic fortitude of Andro-

[115] See Diller (1960) 95–7.
[116] Cf. Burian (1997) 200: 'Words are tools of power in tragedy.'

mache and Peleus. Their use of rhetoric stands apart from, and guides our negative response to, the cynical exploitation of political and personal slogans by their opponents.[117]

The disturbing picture of human beings manipulated by *logos* emerges clearly from the brittle word-play with which Menelaus seeks to justify violence and murder. Andromache's argumentative skill and her rhetorical victories align our sympathies, and work not only emotionally but also cognitively[118] to explore major issues of power, not least its responsibilities and the moral implications of their neglect. The disturbing impression of Euripides' war-plays is well summed up by Colin Macleod: 'We see both that there can be no other basis for justice than convention, and that conventions can easily be manipulated in argument or rejected in fact by men in their own interest.'[119]

Tragic rhetoric interacts with the theatricality of the Athenian institutions for public debate and decision-making.[120] The spatial and rhetorical similarities of stage *agones,* assembly meetings, and legal trials highlight the way in which each tragedy challenges the audience to judge the characters' behaviour as it is presented by the agent or criticized by an opponent. The plays themselves often call into question the process of apportioning responsibility. Tragedy stresses the plurality and complexity of human motivation and choice. It presents the difficulty (and the challenge) of judging between competing *logoi*, and it makes the energy of rhetorical conflict an engine of dramatic momentum. Rhetoric in its various uses, sometimes principled, at other times equivocal, both enhances Andromache's struggle to resist degradation, and emphasizes

---

[117] In the last book of the *Iliad*, the opposition of enemy peoples is transcended by the realization of common loss and suffering. The epic's moment of humane fellowship is expanded; the descendants of Peleus and Priam are united in a way that refutes the Spartans' rhetoric of barbarian inferiority. Cf. Strohm (1977) 124: 'The former enemies, Achilles and Hector, are brought together—Hector's widow is needed to keep the Aeacid dynasty alive!'

[118] For the inextricability of both levels of audience response to Greek tragedy, see Lada (1996) 409.

[119] Macleod (1983) 156, discussing Thucydides' Plataean debate and Melian dialogue.

[120] See Ober and Strauss (1990) 238–9, 248.

the debased values of her attackers. Defeated in war, Andromache is victorious in *logos*. The play does not optimistically reassure us that such a victory is enough to save her life, but it expresses her resilience, ingenuity, and nobility with both pathos and power.

5

The *Andromache* and the Spread
of Attic Tragedy

Discussion of the *Andromache* in relation to its historical
context has generally concentrated on those passages where
Sparta is condemned, and these have been taken to reflect the
propaganda of the Archidamian War.[1] In this brief chapter I
shall argue that while the play certainly reflects the war atmosphere of its time, it does so in a more provocative and complex
manner than any anti-Spartan reading can convey.[2] In doing so
I shall broaden the discussion of the play's historical relevance
by relating it to the popularity and spread of tragedy outside
Athens.

One may start by reviewing the evidence for the date and
place of *Andromache*'s first production. Metrical and stylistic
evidence point to a date of *c*.425.[3] It is perhaps unlikely that

---

[1] Cf. e.g. Page (1938) viii on the 'fierce joyous patriotism' of the *Andromache* (among other plays of this decade).

[2] Cf. Eagleton (1976) 3: 'The painter Henri Matisse once remarked that all
art bears the imprint of its historical epoch, but that great art is that in which
this imprint is most deeply marked.'

[3] For metrical evidence see Stevens (1971) 18–19, Cropp and Fick (1985) 5.
Poole (1994) 4 warns that 'Attempts to date the plays simply on the basis of
supposed contemporary allusions have been numerous, divergent and subjective.' Di Benedetto (1971) 127 n. 55 claims that the date of the *Andromache*
is more disputed than that of any other Euripidean tragedy. Pohlenz (1954) i.
290 offers a solution which is typical of many critics' imaginative reconstruc-
tions of the evidence: the scholiast's reference (on 445) to a broken treaty is
identified with Brasidas' actions in 423 (cf. *Hcld.* 1035 f. and the breaking of
the Thirty-Year Peace); production elsewhere than in Athens 'is, however,
scarcely to be considered. Thus one can imagine that in 423 Euripides wrote
down this song of hate (Haßgesang) in rash anger, but then dispensed with its
performance.' Interestingly, Webster (1967) 137 thought that the *Andromache*
and *Cresphontes* might have been produced in the same year, and Cropp
(1995) 124 comments that *Cresph.* 'may well have had a political thrust
comparable with that of *Heraclidae*' (i.e. anti-Spartan). But not enough is

anyone would have presumed a first production outside Athens were it not for the comment in the scholion on line 445: εἰλικρινῶς δὲ τοὺς τοῦ δράματος χρόνους οὐκ ἔστι λαβεῖν· οὐ δεδίδακται γὰρ ᾿Αθήνησιν. ὁ δὲ Καλλίμαχος ἐπιγραφῆναί φησι τῆι τραγωιδίαι Δημοκράτην . . . φαίνεται δὲ γεγραμμένον τὸ δρᾶμα ἐν ἀρχαῖς τοῦ Πελοποννησιακοῦ πολέμου ('One cannot determine the date of the play precisely, because it was not produced in Athens. Callimachus says the tragedy was ascribed to Democrates . . . The play appears to have been written towards the beginning of the Peloponnesian War'). This is a striking collection of information. The scholiast may be drawing on technical information and should not be lightly ignored.

It is usually believed on the basis of the scholion that the didascalia did not record the play (at least not under Euripides' name).[4] Unfortunately we cannot verify this as the relevant dramatic records are lost.[5] Callimachus (fr. 451 Pf.) says the play was ascribed to Democrates, and a tragedian of that name is recorded (*TrGF* i. 124); but Snell dates him to the late third century and is rightly sceptical of any connection between him and the scholion on *Andr.* 445.[6] The suggestion that this is a pseudonym for Euripides is not convincing.[7] Wilamowitz suggested that it might be the name of the διδάσκαλος (director), but the playwright himself usually directed his own work.[8] Certainty here is impossible, but this seems the likeliest explanation of the name's association with the play.[9] Most

known about the action of *Cresph.* (see Harder (1985) 7–12 for the mythical raw material), nor are its date and fellow plays certain (cf. Wilkins (1993) xxxiv–xxxv, Harder (1985) 4, who dates it between 430 and 424). As a point against very specific political interpretations of the *Andromache*, one should stress that the date is only approximate.

[4] Taplin (1993) 3 n. 8, reading *Andromache* for *Andromeda*.

[5] Crucially, as Harder (1985) 126 n. 4 saw, since the records are incomplete, '"absence from the didascalia" cannot be used as a positive argument against production at Athens.'

[6] *TrGF* i. 124. 2 (p. 284).

[7] Robertson (1923) 59 thought it 'easy to suppose that Euripides was not very proud of *Andromache* and preferred to disguise his authorship'.

[8] Wilamowitz (1875) 148. As the didascalia gave prominence to the victorious *choregos* and director, Democrates might be the name of either. (The name might even be that of a man responsible in either of these roles for a later fourth-century revival of the play.)

[9] Csapo and Slater (1995) 15 have revived Bergk's emendation of Demo-

importantly, the remark of Callimachus, if correctly reported and based on didascalic records, suggests that the play was produced in Athens.[10] As Michael Lloyd points out, critics have yet to find convincing evidence of theatrical or stylistic features which set the *Andromache* apart from the rest of Euripides' work produced in Athens.[11] However, as we shall see, the play has been written so as to appeal to audiences beyond Athens.

Of course, productions of tragedies outside Athens were not unprecedented in the 420s. It is a remarkable thought that Aeschylus' production of the *Women of Aetna* in Sicily, if dated *c.*476/5,[12] would predate our earliest surviving tragedy, the *Persians* of 472.[13] In any case, these (re)performances certainly predate the *Andromache* by more than a generation and show an interest in, and audience for, tragedy well beyond Attica. In the case of the *Andromache*, even if we retain a first production at Athens, it is certainly possible (and in fact, as I shall argue, perhaps probable) that the play was reperformed outside Attica and was written with this in mind.

In a thought-provoking exploratory article Pat Easterling has suggested that we might be 'less inclined to define the ideology of fifth-century tragedy as almost obsessively Athenocentric and pay more attention to the potential interest and relevance of Attic drama to contemporary audiences elsewhere. The shift of perspective could be liberating.'[14] It may also be very

crates to Timocrates, on the basis of the latter's alleged authorship of Euripides' songs (*Life* §5, Kovacs (1994) 2). The story, of course, is pure (comic?) invention.

[10] See Pfeiffer (1968) 132 on Callimachus' chronological list of dramatists which was 'based on Aristotle's διδασκαλίαι taken from the documents in the archon's archives'.

[11] Lloyd (1994) 12.

[12] See *CAH*² v. 150.

[13] Cf. *TrGF* i. T1, ll. 33–4, where the biographer records that the play was written for Hieron's new city of Aetna, οἰωνιζόμενος βίον ἀγαθὸν τοῖς συνοικί-ζουσι τὴν πόλιν ('auguring a good life for the settlers in the city'). According to a scholion on Ar. *Frogs* 1028, the *Persians* was itself reproduced in Syracuse before Aeschylus' death.

[14] Easterling (1994) 80. Accordingly, she considers the chorus of Trojan women's laudatory references to Sicily (*Tro.* 220–9) and relates them to reperformance 'at some Sicilian location and at Thurii' (p. 76). Taplin (1999) 44 suggests that Thurii (founded by Pericles in 444/3, cf. Plut. *Per.* 11. 5–6) was

fruitful for understanding some aspects of the *Andromache* which have puzzled critics. The two Greek states which feature most prominently in the play are Thessaly and Molossia. Of these it is Molossia which has generally received most attention. Yet the play is set in Phthia and, as we saw in Chapter 2, the setting is quite explicitly described. Oliver Taplin has drawn attention to the localization of Thessaly in several Euripidean plays including the *Andromache*.[15] While I would give more weight than Taplin does to the significance of the Molossian genealogy announced by Thetis (1243–9), his suggestion of a 'secondary Thessalian audience' is one I find quite convincing.[16]

In order to understand the significance of the material in the *Andromache* that is of cultural interest to non-Athenian audiences, one needs to outline the relations of Athens to the states concerned. We will look first at Molossia. Of course one should not forget that Euripides did not invent the story of the Molossians' descent from Neoptolemus (cf. Pind. *Nem.* 7. 38–40).[17] However, he has purposefully innovated in having Neoptolemus settle in Thessaly (rather than passing straight from Molossia to his death in Delphi, cf. Pind. *Pae.* 6. 98–120), thus not only allowing for Thessalian localization but also presenting the Molossian dynasty as a divinely sanctioned consolation for the Aeacid house.

As Nilsson saw, 'It seems to be most likely that the Molossians appropriated the myth of the wandering of Neoptolemus from Thessaly and made him an ancestor of their royal house.'[18] Why should they want to do this? As we shall see, the Molossians became increasingly involved in Greek politics during the fifth century. From this developed a desire

'very likely to have been one of the first places to have hosted performances of Athenian tragedy'.

[15] Taplin (1999) 44–8.

[16] Taplin (1999) 45. Professor Taplin kindly allowed me to read his article before publication. I had already arrived independently at the idea of reperformance outside Athens, but had envisaged the second possible venue (Molossia) with more certainty than he does.

[17] Howie (1998) 111 shows how *Nem.* 7 satisfies several communities at once, including the Molossian royal audience.

[18] Nilsson (1951) 106. On the general importance of heroic genealogies for Greek states, see Hall (1989) 172–81.

to anchor their genealogy in the Greek mythical and heroic past. Pindar is the first writer to record Neoptolemus' kingship there, but his brief description does not elaborate the myth's Thessalian or Trojan connections. Euripides' work, by contrast, played a decisive role in shaping and validating the Molossian tribe's genealogical myth,[19] and it did so at a time when Athenian interest in the area was particularly keen.

According to Thucydides (2. 80), in the summer of 429 the Spartans were persuaded by the Ambraciots and the Chaonians to launch an attack on Acarnania in the north west. Among Sparta's allies was a contingent of Molossians, led by Sabylinthus, the guardian of king Tharyps (2. 80. 6). Shortly after this, however, Tharyps came to Athens (perhaps fleeing hostile forces at home) and was granted Athenian citizenship sometime between 428 and 424.[20] This was an exceptional honour in the fifth century (much rarer than the grant of proxeny), particularly to one so young,[21] and can best be explained as an attempt to court Molossian support.[22] It seems to have worked. Athenian relations with Molossia remained friendly for the rest of the war.[23]

The Hellenization[24] of the north-western tribes is said to have begun with Tharyps, whose reign lasted *c.*423–390. In his *Life of Pyrrhus*, Plutarch relates the historical tradition that

[19] This is seen at the most basic level in the replacement of Pielus (eponym of an old Epirote tribe) by Molossus as the founder of the kingship: see Dakaris (1964) 21–3, 77. The child is not named in the play but the emphasis on the name Molossia (1244, 1248) makes clear who is meant.

[20] See Hammond (1967) 506–7, Osborne (1983) 29–30, and Hall (1989) 180–1. Dakaris (1964) 51–2 makes a good case for 427. As Hammond (1967) 501 observes, 'Thucydides does not say which tribe had Tharyps as its king. He assumed his readers would know that Tharyps was a member of the Molossian royal house.' His presence in Athens will have been well known.

[21] But as Osborne (1983) 29 observes 'in the case of monarchs, with whom Athens desired good relations and who were unlikely to need their citizenship as a practical benefit, such technicalities were doubtless capable of being ignored.'

[22] In 431 at the start of the war the Athenians had done a similar thing in Thrace, granting citizenship to Sadocus, the son of King Sitalces: Thuc. 2. 29. 5.

[23] And beyond—in 375 Tharyps' son Alcetas joined the Second Athenian Confederacy, and in 342 his grandson Arybbas fled to Athens and claimed his right to Athenian citizenship: Osborne (1983) 30.

[24] See Hornblower (1991a) 352 on this term, first attested in Thucydides.

attributed to Tharyps responsibility for introducing Greek customs, laws, and letters to the cities of Molossia (Plut. *Pyrrh.* 1. 3). The late Roman epitomist Justin claims that Tharyps *primus itaque leges et senatum annuosque magistratus . . . composuit* ('first set up laws, the senate and annual magistracies', 17. 3. 11). The extent of Tharyps' reforms may well have become exaggerated (there was a tendency to ascribe most constitutional reform to one early figure), but the evidence certainly suggests that he remodelled the Molossian state partially along Athenian lines, while retaining a hereditary monarchy.[25]

The tribes of Epirus spoke Greek, but Thucydides classed all Epirote tribes as barbarians because of their lack of culture.[26] The new influence of Athenian culture is evident on the Molossian writing script, coins, pottery, and temple architecture.[27] It is appropriate that the reorientation of Molossian culture towards the south, and towards Athens in particular, should be reflected in the most distinctly Athenian of all cultural forms, that of tragedy. One need not assume that the *Andromache* had its premiere in Molossia to see Euripides writing a play which would have a strong appeal to (and influence upon) the young King Tharyps and his entourage.

The Molossian dynasty is linked to one of the most famous Greek families (the Aeacidae), while its heroic credentials are confirmed by the commixture of Trojan nobility.[28] Though the play works on many levels and should not be interpreted as propaganda, the repudiation of Spartan interference and the criticism of Delphi would have a forceful extra-dramatic point. As part of his programme of Hellenization, one can easily imagine Tharyps encouraging future performances of the

[25] Cf. Rhodes and Lewis (1997) 184: 'according to Aristotle the monarchy survived because it was not despotic (*Pol.* v. 1313 A [18–]23–4)'.

[26] Hammond in *CAH* III.² iii. 284.

[27] Dakaris (1964) 58–9.

[28] As Woodbury (1979) 122 notes, the names Tharyps and Sabylinthus are not Greek. It is a measure of the Molossians' absorption of heroic myth that later kings bore names drawn from the Trojan myth (the earliest inscriptions date from the reign of Neoptolemus in 370–368). Nilsson (1951) 108 thinks this shows 'the overdone eagerness of a barbarian house to appear as heroic Greeks'. But they were just as ready to adopt Trojan names: e.g. Alexandros, Teucros (also Achaean, in Homer), Helenus.

Andromache in Molossia, appropriating the dignity and kudos of tragedy, and the force of the play's finale, for his own ends.[29]

The invention of flattering genealogies is something we meet with again in the *Archelaus*, produced in 408/7 for King Archelaus of Macedon. The work has a Hellenizing aspect similar to that of the *Andromache*.[30] The Greek ancestry of the Macedonian king is strongly asserted: in the prologue his mythical namesake traces his lineage back eleven generations to Danaus, king of Argos.[31] As Aeschylus' career shows, the prestige of tragedy was already recognized outside Athens in the 470s. In the *Andromache*, the cultural respectability of the genre embraces two further ethnic groups, Molossians and Thessalians, who are united in an anti-Spartan alliance. This is not the whole meaning of the play, but it is certainly a bonus from an Athenian point of view.

In the mid-420s Aristophanes 'mocked the ambitions of Athenian statesmen in the north-western area, when he produced *Acharnians* and *Knights*'.[32] At about the same time, Athens was keen to gain, or to maintain, the support of as

[29] Hammond (1967) 505 argues that the play was intended to bring the Chaonians into a closer relationship with the Molossians (both groups had fought for the Spartans in 429). The Chaonians were descended from Helenus. Euripides has Helenus marry Andromache in Epirus (1245), and this may well be his own invention. It is not impossible that an Epirote audience would see here an affirmation of tribal unity (and Molossian dominance). Robertson (1923) 60 ingeniously reads Orestes' role as an attack on the Orestians, another Molossian tribe. But their name in fact has a different derivation (see Hornblower (1991a) 363 on Thuc. 2. 80. 6). Dakaris (1964) 93 n. 1 endorses the conjecture that Antiochus, the Orestian king, had plotted against Tharyps, which would make the play a charter myth for the domination of the Aeacidae over other ethnic groups in Molossia. However, one may remain sceptical about such precise political readings, yet accept that the play contains positive references of cultural interest to the Molossians. Whether or not Tharyps or his supporters actually commissioned the work, a performance in Molossia would make an excellent overture to the beginning of his reign in 423.

[30] Cf. Hammond (1997) 58: 'Thus the foundations were being laid for the entry of the Epirotes and the Macedonians into the Greek world.'

[31] Harder (1985) 178 notes Euripides' fondness for genealogies in prologue speeches and points out that Archelaus' genealogy is unusually long. Its purpose was no doubt to impress the audience with Archelaus' extensive Greek ancestry.

[32] Hammond (1997) 58.

many of the powerful Thessalian city-states as possible. Thessaly was by virtue of its Dorian language and Heraclid descent linked to Sparta.[33] Spartan attempts to gain control of Thessaly's wealth and strategic position began in the late sixth century and continued throughout the fifth.[34] In 462 Thessaly made an alliance with Athens (Thuc. 1. 102. 4) and this was invoked in 431 when Thessalian troops fought on the Athenian side (2. 22. 3).[35]

In the fifth century the individual city-states became the main units of power in Thessaly. Since the sixth century the tetrad of Phthiotis was controlled by Pharsalus, '[b]y far the most impressive of Thessalian cities'.[36] The chief ruler of the Thessalian confederacy from c.440 to 413 was Daochus of Pharsalus; Thessaly remained favourable to Athens throughout his tenure of office (cf. 4. 78, 132; 8. 3).[37] It is over Pharsalus that Peleus rules (*Andr.* 22). The portrayal of a noble Thessalian hero prepared to fend off unwarranted Spartan aggression will have struck a chord in both Athens and Thessaly. In 426 Athenian interests in Thessaly were threatened by a new Spartan colony at Heraclea in Trachis. According to Thucydides, the foundation initially caused the Athenians alarm, but its effects were neutralized by frequent attacks from the neighbouring Thessalians (3. 93. 1; cf. 5. 51).[38]

The Spartan colony of Heraclea was intended partly as a move to control the Delphic Amphictiony, normally in the hands of the Thessalians.[39] In 426 the Spartans assembled their army at Delphi (Thuc. 3. 101. 1). Thus the *Andromache*'s criticisms of Delphi are illuminated by awareness of the oracle's well-known Spartan sympathies. Of course the refer-

---

[33] Snodgrass (1980) 89–90 outlines some shared features of the Dorian states in the archaic period.

[34] Hornblower (1991b) 80–2, (1992) 181. For Thessaly's fertility see Thuc. 1. 2. 3.

[35] See Helly (1995) 233–40 on the Thessalian cavalry support of 431.

[36] Westlake (1969) 11–12. There is insufficient archaeological evidence for the frequent identification of Pharsalus with the Homeric Phthia.

[37] Pharsalus did not Medize but was allied to Athens in the Persian Wars as well.

[38] Ar. *Wasps* 1271–4 pokes fun at an Athenian embassy to Pharsalus in 423/2.

[39] Cf. Westlake (1969) 29, Hornblower (1991a) 501–3, (1992) 182.

ences to Delphi, Thessaly, and Molossia must be primarily understood in terms of the action of the play. But their impact on a contemporary audience should not be ignored. The *Andromache* is a key play in the debate about performance outside Athens. Our arguments so far has suggested that both Thessaly and Molossia would make effective venues for the play.[40]

Oliver Taplin has discussed several example of Thessalian localization in Sophocles and Euripides, and argues that they

are there, at least on some level, to promote the Athenian cause in that area. They may be seen, that is, as a kind of 'cultural propaganda', suggesting to [Thessalians] . . . that they should wish to be closely affiliated with the city which has created such a superb new art-form, and which has celebrated their localities within it.[41]

As Taplin points out, this form of 'cultural propaganda' is conventionally seen as operating on audiences in Athens, but 'if it is once accepted that tragedy had been reperformed in the fifth century at Isthmia or Aigai, then why not at the Pylaia, or even in Thessalian Magnesia?'[42] In the case of the *Andromache*, I would argue, the same arguments apply to Molossia as to Thessaly. The play will have been pleasing to both ethnic

[40] No elaborate buildings were required for the production of tragedy; cf. Wiles (1997) 53 with n. 111 on the portable *skene*. So plays could be put on in any town. The Agora was said to be the site of Athens' first theatre; cf. Wiles (1997) 25. Rossetto and Sartori (1994) ii. 112 ff. provide a helpful map of the many dozens of theatres in Greece with plans and descriptions. The large stone theatres of Molossia and Thessaly date from the fourth and third centuries but were often superimposed on smaller venues; cf. Hammond (1967) 582 on the theatre at Dodona built for the Molossians. The point of Orestes' lying reference to Dodona (*Andr.* 886) might be partly to provide a 'zooming effect' for future Epirote audiences. In Thessaly the most likely venue is Pharsalus itself. If the *Life of Euripides* can be trusted (§10, Kovacs (1994) 2; treated sceptically by Lefkowitz (1981) 92–3, but more favourably by Easterling (1994) 76 and Taplin (1999) 42), Euripides was honoured late in life when he moved to Magnesia. This indicates great appreciation of his work in Thessaly. Magnesia itself enters the play at 1265–8, when Thetis instructs Peleus to go to Cape Sepias. This was well known as the place where Peleus won Thetis as his bride and so it is appropriate to the reaffirmation of their union at the end of the play, but the implicit aetiology of Peleus' hero-cult will have appealed to Thessalians, and to Magnesians in particular.

[41] Taplin (1999) 48.
[42] Taplin (1999) 48.

groups and reperformance in both places is certainly possible. It will in this way have been most effective, as the dramatic localizations would have the greatest impact on regional audiences.[43]

Nevertheless, as we saw, there is not enough evidence to rule out categorically an initial performance in Athens. Unlike the *Archelaus*, there is no conclusive external evidence for the *Andromache*'s first production taking place abroad.[44] Perhaps one should mention the possibility that even if the play was not produced at the Dionysia, it could have been performed elsewhere in Attica.[45] However, the *Andromache*, with its non-Attic cultural references, is better suited to the cosmopolitan character of the Dionysia.[46] If produced there, it is plausible, in my view, that influential Molossians and Thessalians, impressed by its sentiments, might have arranged for the play to be performed in their home-cities.

The relationship between the world of the play and that of its (first) audience is a notoriously complex question.[47] In our discussion of the *Andromache*'s place of production, the work's connection to the events of the period has emerged as import-

---

[43] Taplin (1999) 38–9 discusses Plato's references to the theatrical 'circuit' (Csapo and Slater (1995) 13) and, significantly, extends this beyond the local demes to cities outside Attica. Wiles (1997) 8 sees the *Athenian* audience as an integral 'semantic element' of the plays. If we think of non-Athenian audiences too, this may potentially enrich our readings of the works.

[44] Could the scholion's claim that the play was not performed in Athens have arisen as a result of a later reproduction abroad?

[45] On dramatic festivals in Attica see Csapo and Slater (1995) 121–32; on deme theatres see Wiles (1997) ch. 2. Whitehead (1986) 16 notes that 'few demes, comparatively speaking, are known to have possessed a theater'. He calculates that of the 139 demes there is direct evidence for 7 having theatres, and 7 more are almost certain (pp. 212–13, 219–20). But as Whitehead observes (p. 220), many more deme theatres doubtless existed. Moreover, those certainly possessing a theatre include the largest demes (Acharnae, Salamis, Eleusis, Piraeus). There is evidence for Euripides producing a play at the Piraeus, and for Sophocles and Aristophanes at Eleusis (Csapo and Slater (1995) 125 49G, 129 52A), though we cannot be certain that these were premières. In the case of such major dramatists, they were probably reproductions of plays which had been successful in the city.

[46] For the pan-Hellenic audience of the Dionysia see Pickard-Cambridge (1968) 58–9.

[47] For an argument that 'a play about the end of the Trojan War [can] really refer to the Peloponnesian War', see Croally (1994) 233–4.

ant. However, the *Andromache* does not primarily articulate a particular view on current political events or social conditions. Euripides is not taking sides, but reflecting on dramatic crises which have a relevance to 'his own time and society'.[48]

Hall states the important points succinctly: 'It is significant that the plays where Greeks are shown in a poor light are always concerned not with Athenians but with their enemies in the Peloponnesian war, especially the family of the Atridae (increasingly associated not with Argos but with Sparta), or Thebans.'[49] With the *Andromache*, the temptation to read off a simple 'message' from the words of the characters has always been great.[50] One can perhaps see Euripides as playing to the gallery somewhat with Andromache's speech at 445 ff. In some members of the Athenian audience, themselves victims of Spartan aggression, Andromache's tirade may have prompted a cheer.[51] But it must be stressed that the crescendo of accusations and rhetorical questions is clearly an integral part of the drama and a natural response to the actions of her aggressors.[52]

As Pat Easterling has pointed out, the tragedians 'devised ingenious and often subtle ways of suiting [the world of the epic poets] to their contemporary purposes'.[53] The *Andromache*, like all other tragedies, reflects contemporary thought,

[48] Macleod (1983) 149 (on *Suppl.*), who continues 'In that sense, the tragedian is a sort of historian.'

[49] Hall (1989) 213.

[50] Garzya (1951) 110 observes: 'many have seen in the play nothing other than . . . a kind of anti-Spartan theatrical pamphlet'. Cf. e.g. Méridier (1927) 99.

[51] Bowie (1993) 20–1 (on Ar. *Acharn.*, produced in 425) notes the violence of the play and the violent attitude in Athens in the play. Events such as the massacre of 200 Plataean and 25 Athenian prisoners in 427, despite a promise that nobody would be unjustly treated (Thuc. 3. 68. 2), were evidence enough of Spartan treachery and brutality.

[52] Erbse (1968) 286 is going too far when he says: 'the frame of the tragedy is broken because the poet could not control himself'. Cf. Kamerbeek (1960) 17: 'contemporary concern has so overridden the dramatic proprieties that one may justly hold it against the poet.' Nevertheless, if the extra-theatrical resonances of Andromache's words make her appear a more sympathetic character in the eyes of the audience, this is all to the good for the overall interpretation of the play. She generates an atmosphere of epic integrity against which her shallow persecutors are measured.

[53] Easterling (1985) 10.

including its political aspects.[54] Yet although the play engages with Sparta, Molossia, and Thessaly in ways that are relevant to contemporary Athenian concerns, these references are part of an integrated and wide-ranging dramatization of divine and heroic myth. The combination of the distance of myth with contemporary relevance allows the audience 'to see the events in a double perspective, making it possible for them to apply what happens in the drama to their own times, but not forcing a single interpretation'.[55] Neither the play's pleasing references to Thessaly and Molossia, nor its anti-Spartan tenor, can be interpreted purely as propaganda.[56] Such a reading would be both artless and dull, and would risk reducing (this particular) tragedy to a mere tool of political power. So we should not let the cultural references obscure the dramatic point of these moments; nor can we make the contemporary bearing the origin and goal of the play.

[54] Compare, for example, the Archidamian War overtones of *Hcld.* 278–81, or the representation of competing political voices in the Argive assembly of *Orestes* (902–16).

[55] Easterling (1997b) 35.

[56] In the case of Euripides' *Supplices* Bowie (1997) shows that the play does not present 'the Athenian behaviour [as] simply justifiable' (p. 49).

6
Gender

Ἐλ. ἄκουσον, ἤν τι καὶ γυνὴ λέξηι σοφόν.

HELEN: Listen, if a woman too may make a clever proposal.

Euripides, *Helen* 1049

Tragedy, more than any other ancient Greek genre, shows 'an overwhelming insistence on the troubled relationships between women and men'.[1] Like comedy, though less explicitly, tragedy 'invites the audience to compare their contemporary social order with that of the myth'.[2] In respect of issues of gender, this comparison is strikingly provocative, especially in Euripides. The subject of tragic women has in recent years attracted the bulk of critical attention. This chapter will seek to test some of its insights against the *Andromache* (which is problematic in several ways), and will stress the need to take tragic men and issues of masculinity seriously as well.[3] Given the shape of the play, discussion of its presentation of women will form the main part of the chapter, but the interdependence of concepts of femininity and masculinity will clearly emerge.

The idea of women controlling or defying men, a fecund source of humour in Aristophanes' fantasy world, is presented as a reversal of both nature's and the state's legitimate order.[4]

---

[1] Hall (1997b) 95.

[2] Wiles (1997) 52.

[3] As Dover (1993) 18 n. 21 has observed, 'What message about men is communicated by most tragedies is a matter on which the ancient world is silent.' A recent work, edited by Foxhall and Salmon (1998), explores (p. 1) 'artistic and intellectual expression as the *self*-representation of man'. Foxhall goes on to claim that (p. 5) 'the creation of man/subject disallows the creation of woman/subject, denying her an identity.' (Do Medea, Hermione, Phaedra, Deianeira, etc., lack a coherent and compelling identity?) Such a rigid approach confuses male authorship with support for patriarchal ideology. The tragedians' engagement with issues of gender, however, is far more complex.

[4] Cf. Konstan (1993).

Yet comedy plays with stereotypes, and the audience can see outside them. The women of tragedy, on the other hand, relate in a more complex way to stereotypes of female behaviour and ideologies of sexual control in fifth-century Athens.[5] The prominence of women in the heroic world of tragic myth sets tragedy apart from comedy; and as the heroic society of tragedy encounters various forms of crisis, the female figures become essential for exploring the tensions, both domestic and political, that emerge.[6]

The *Andromache* explores through myth the conflicts and tensions underlying the status and experience of women in classical Athens. What we know of the opportunities and powers possessed by fifth-century women of citizen status presents a complex picture which is composed of 'economic, social and political structures, cultural priorities and biological premisses'.[7] This dense nexus of cultural preconceptions is illuminated by a study of the *Andromache*. By our standards the lot of most fifth-century women, notably in Athens, was no doubt a straitened one, but it is of limited help simply to say that women were subservient to 'male law-givers—medical, moral, or marital'.[8] While one may say, 'Formally speaking, they were not part of the *polis*, for women were not registered in the register of the deme, nor were they, in all probability, registered as members of the phratry',[9] this needs to be balanced against what the same scholar has called women's 'private influence and the actual exercise of informal power',[10] which it is difficult to calibrate but would be hazardous to dismiss.[11]

---

[5] Cf. Clark (1989) 10: 'In Athenian myth, and fifth-century art, the Amazons are a threat to the city, and are defeated or raped by Athenian heroes.'

[6] Redfield (1995) 154 remarks that drama reveals the domestic interior as always 'broken or in crisis'. He also notes (p. 157): 'The most contented married couple in all tragedy is probably (before the moment of truth) Oedipus and his mother!'

[7] des Bouvrie (1990) 58.

[8] Winkler (1990) 6.

[9] Seidensticker (1995) 151.

[10] Seidensticker (1995) 154.

[11] Hunter (1994) 38–42 offers a view of female autonomy which is more generous than most. Foxhall (1996) 134 questions the common assumption of

Among literary representations of women in Greek culture it is the striking and varied female figures of Euripidean tragedy which have excited most discussion and disagreement.[12] And this is no new phenomenon: Euripides' shocking fictional women were a popular target of Aristophanic humour and a topic of controversy from their first production.[13] To ask ourselves whether Euripides was a feminist or misogynist will not take us very far (although critics never tire of taking sides on the issue).[14] Euripides has recently been called 'the most eloquent and most insistent advocate of women's cause'.[15] It is easy to understand why such remarks are made: Medea, for example, is the most incisive, and certainly the most famous, critic of sexual double standards in Greek literature (perhaps in all literature).[16]

To formulate our inquiry in terms of misogyny or feminism involves blurring the shape and impact of the texts by viewing them through a peculiarly modern set of concerns, while it also presupposes an erroneous correspondence between the views espoused by fictional characters and those of the author.[17] This chapter will instead try to appraise Euripides' handling of female characters in its historical context. It is only by seeing

women's 'derivative, familial identities (as opposed to the personal, individual identities of men)'.

[12] Cf. Pomeroy (1975) 103.

[13] Indeed, ever since Aristophanes the most common complaints concern Euripides' 'insistence on ugly realism and his fascination with bad women' (Goff (1990) 94).

[14] For bibliography see des Bouvrie (1990) 28 nn. 6 and 7.

[15] Seidensticker (1995) 167.

[16] Such criticism is not without its precedents in Greek literature; cf. Williams (1993) 119, who mentions *Od.* 5. 117 ff. and Soph. fr 524 N [= 583 Radt (*Tereus*)]. Remarkably, the Medea contains a daring choral ode on the male bias of the literary tradition itself, *Med.* 410–30; cf. West (1996) 10. Euripides was clearly aware that one could argue that statements about gender were partly dependent on the sex of their authors and that women had unequal access to this important means of expression.

[17] Cf. Cameron (1995) 318–19 on Euripides in the *Vitae* as the misogynist ironically caught in the toils of love. Cantarella (1987) 67 (on Hippolytus' misogynistic tirade, *Hipp.* 617–48) remarks: 'The very bitterness of the attack leads one to assume an identification of Euripides with his character.' She goes on to conclude that Euripides' reputation for misogyny was 'perhaps not altogether without basis' (p. 69), using Ar. *Thesm.* as evidence for his unpopularity among women!

his works from a historical perspective that their exceptionally challenging force can be fully understood. Tragedy is indeed a 'genre of ambiguity',[18] in the sense that it presents questions rather than answers and exposes 'tensions within the city's stock of concepts and guiding images'.[19] The female figures of tragedy present a variety of possible roles, many of which challenge the audience to reflect critically on the role and status of women in their own society.

Instead of speculating on the author's own views, what we should rather ask is, what is new about the treatment of women by Euripides? After all, as Sir Kenneth Dover has remarked, the Clytemnestra of Aeschylus' *Agamemnon* is an adulterous killer, but it is Euripides who acquired the reputation for portraying wicked women.[20] To what extent then 'does Euripidean tragedy really slander women?'[21] Even if we accept the claim that 'Euripides reveals some murky aspects of female psychology which had previously received little attention',[22] we must go on to ask why he did so and why it was so controversial. More generally, why has Euripides deliberately invented or accentuated the role of women in so many tragic myths?[23] The *Andromache* is an important text for this inquiry; not only does it show myth being constructed to foreground the women's role, but it also raises a wide range of interlocking issues relating to desire, sex, and marriage ('that key institution of normative sexual discourse and social practice'),[24] as well as to the social and political importance of legitimacy (consolidated by Pericles' citizenship law of 451).

Recent criticism has made much of the fact that women were present on stage only as representations (the chorus and actors being men). But it seems unlikely that this dramatic convention will have affected audience response as much as some critics claim; slaves, for instance, were played on stage by free men. But the latter point is not fastened on so readily, because (for

[18] See Vernant and Vidal-Naquet (1988) 29 ff.
[19] Williams (1993) 15.
[20] Dover (1993) 17.
[21] Bowie (1993) 227.
[22] MacDowell (1995) 253.
[23] See March (1990) 35 (Medea), 47 (Phaedra), 49 (Agave), 63 (*Stheneboea* and the first *Hippolytus*).
[24] Goldhill (1995) 113.

reasons grounded in our culture) this is not what critics are so interested in. A related critical trend, which we have briefly noted above, argues that women are represented as catalysts for male self-analysis and for the education of male citizens: 'From the outset, it is essential to understand that in Greek theater, as in fact in Shakespearian theater, the self that is regularly at stake is to be identified with the male, while the woman is assigned the role of the radical other.'[25] Thus female characters are seen as a useful way of exploring and reconstructing essentially male behaviour and values. Yet this is too constrictive an account of the dissolution of social order presented in tragedy. The 'male project of selfhood'[26] is too narrow an end for tragedy.[27]

Such accounts illustrate the danger of taking too schematic a view of Euripides' treatment of women.[28] They obscure the particularity of the text and the individual texture of each work. The neat division of female figures into 'fetishized victims' (Alcestis, Polyxena, Iphigenia) or 'vengeful destroyers' (Medea, Phaedra, Hecuba) reduces complex and questioning texts to tools of propaganda.[29] Even when Euripides' skill in

[25] Zeitlin (1990) 68.

[26] Zeitlin (1990) 69.

[27] Thus I would dispute Hall's ((1997b) 95) claim that tragedy 'defines the male citizen self and both produces and reproduces the ideology of the civic community'. While Hall rightly stresses the democratic polyphony of tragedy (pp. 118 ff.), which gives voice to women, slaves, and foreigners, she claims that tragedy nevertheless affirms the inferiority of these groups (pp. 93, 125). Tragedy thus 'challenges the very notions which it simultaneously legitimises' (p. 118; cf. Griffith (1995) 111–12 on the *Oresteia*'s alleged 'affirmation of social hierarchy and inequality' which he extends to the genre as a whole). I shall argue that the challenge of tragedy operates without such ideological legitimation. Cf. Rehm (1994) 137: 'Although no fully "liberated" women appear in these scenarios, it would be unfair to conclude that female characters simply affirm the structures of power that constrained their real-world counterparts.'

[28] Cf. March (1990) 65 n. 8: 'These kinds of fashionable polarities often prove to be very unilluminating tools of analysis, and it should certainly not be assumed that Euripides viewed the world in this way, nor that he saw the human race as being divided into two separated halves.'

[29] Rabinowitz (1993) 22–7 develops this division; her extreme hostility to any suggestion of Euripides' sensitivity to the experience of women is consolidated by an impoverished view of the genre as 'male fantasy, which I take tragedy to be' (p. 26).

creating forceful, intelligent and disruptive women is admitted, these figures are there merely to reaffirm the patriarchal order: 'their experience is shaped to the end of supporting male power'.[30] Perhaps the most serious distortion effected by this approach is to limit (indeed deny) the importance of women as centres of interest in their own right. Zeitlin goes on to write that '*functionally* women are never an end in themselves . . . they play the roles of catalysts, agents, blockers, spoilers, destroyers, and sometimes helpers or saviors for male characters'.[31] But does this description match our response to the experience of Medea, Hecuba or Andromache?[32] The *Andromache* is an example of a text which cannot be tidily interpreted in terms of state-sponsored control of sexuality: the text endorses no one view of the role of women (or men), but rather presents problems arising between and within conflicting conceptions.

Andromache is more noble, resourceful, and self-sacrificing than any other character in the play. This is a regular feature of many Euripidean heroines, who are equal, if not superior, to any male figures on the stage. Yet this pre-eminence has a varied moral force: it may be a victory of endurance, of ruthlessness and revenge, or less murderously, of cleverness ensuring escape (*IT* and *Hel.*). Hermione's murder attempt is one of many near-fatal (or fatal) plots by women. She attempts to kill another's child because of her own childlessness. Hermione's revenge, however, lacks the horrendous, cumulative motivation of Alcmene, Hecuba, or Electra, while her resentment is more reprehensible, because it is in truth groundless. Her jealousy and selfishness throw Andromache's modesty, tolerance, and selfless heroism into greater relief.

As one of Euripides' post-Trojan War plays, the *Andromache* reflects on the experience of captured women who are made slaves by the defeat of their people. *Hecuba* (*c*.424) and *Troades* (415) are the most striking parallels to this theme, and they offer valuable insights into the psychological effects of defeat and degradation. The *Andromache* focuses on a later and

---

[30] Rabinowitz (1993) 14.

[31] Zeitlin (1990) 69.

[32] See Griffin (1998) 45–6 for further pertinent criticisms of Zeitlin's approach.

separate stage in the process of conquest, both military and sexual, while the *Troades* dramatizes the immediate aftermath of the war against the background of the still smoking ruins of Troy (*Tro.* 8–9, 1291–2). The grief of the women over the defeat and death of the menfolk, and their uncertainty as to which Greek commander will take them into slavery, contribute to a sombre and pained atmosphere of loss and foreboding. The experience of Andromache is central to the play's study of mourning and resilience. We see her wrestling with the dilemmas of slavery which form the basis of her later crisis in the household of Neoptolemus. Her exemplary behaviour as wife of Hector has led to her high value as a war prize (*Tro.* 643–60). Her disgust at the idea of sex with another man (the son of her husband's killer no less, *Tro.* 661–72) echoes her protestations of unwilling union in the *Andromache* (36–8). There is a dense weave of anticipation and recollection between the two plays, the *Troades* recalling the earlier play, the *Andromache* the earlier myths. The contrast between Andromache and Helen at Troy has its Phthian counterpart in the contrast between Andromache and Hermione. Both mother and daughter have sexual problems, though, as we shall see, they are of a radically different kind.

In the *Andromache* we are presented with a conflict between two contrasting women, one bad and both unhappy. The root of their conflict is sexual jealousy and the fear of childlessness. Both the marriage of Neoptolemus and Hermione and his relationship to Andromache as concubine are established parts of heroic myth. The conjunction of the stories of the two women affords a dramatic conflict generated by opposed views on a husband's liaisons with other women. The play's exploration of the experience of women focuses on concubinage and fertility; both ideas are linked to the classical *polis*'s concern with legitimacy as defined by birth from two citizen parents.

The heroes of epic (excepting Priam) are monogamous, but female slaves were sexually available to their masters, as in fifth-century Athens.[33] Menelaus is presented in the *Odyssey* as celebrating a double wedding for Hermione and Megapenthes,

---

[33] See Pomeroy's ((1994) 297–300) excellent note on Xen. *Oec.* 5. 5: τεκνοποιῶνται οἱ οἰκέται ('the slaves breed').

his son by a slave-woman (*Od.* 4. 10–14).[34] The son suffers no
obvious disadvantage as a result of his mother's servility.[35]
Epic does, however, make clear the potential displeasure felt by
a wife who feels herself displaced by the entry of a concubine.
In Book 9 of the *Iliad* Phoenix relates how he was persuaded by
his mother to seduce his father's concubine, and so alienate the
slave from his father's affections (*Il.* 9. 447–63). The *Odyssey*
presents the prudent Laertes as refraining from sex with the
maidservant Eurycleia: εὐνῆι δ' οὔ ποτ' ἔμικτο, χόλον δ' ἀλέεινε
γυναικός ('But he never slept with her: he avoided his wife's
anger', *Od.* 1. 433).[36] Nevertheless, the opposition (and potential for antagonism) between wife and concubine is very much
greater in tragedy than it is in Homer. Not only does tragedy
concentrate much more than epic on breakdowns within
families,[37] but the classical *polis*, in which tragedy matured,
limited full civic rights to the male offspring of a legitimate
citizen marriage, debarring such children as Menelaus' son
from becoming 'full members of *oikos* and *polis*'.[38]

In the Homeric world, as Vernant has observed, 'the opposition between the legitimate wife and the concubine appears
much less marked than in the classical period.'[39] However,
such passages as *Od.* 14. 199 ff. show that there was a distinction made, though one centred not on the women, but on
the children ('Odysseus' inherits very little from his Cretan
father, Castor).[40] In fifth-century Athenian society, despite the
variety of relationships classifiable as concubinage, there was a
marked gap in the relative status and rights of wife and
concubine.[41] This is reflected in the position of illegitimate

[34] Other versions record additional children of Menelaus and Helen; cf.
RE, s.v. 'Hermione' (vol. 15, cols. 841–3).

[35] As Harrison (1968) i. 13 observes, 'the status of their offspring, though
these were called νόθοι, could, if the father so willed, be much the same as that
of his legitimate children'.

[36] The displeasure of wives at their husbands' liaisons with slave-concu-
bines is illustrated on a ghoulish scale by the Lemnian women's slaughter of
their husbands; cf. Apoll. *Argo.* 1. 790 ff., where Hypsipyle speaks of the
'bastard race' imposed upon them.

[37] Arist. *Poet.* 1453[b]19–22 locates the best tragic plots in crises within the
family.

[38] See Seaford (1990) 159–60.

[39] Vernant (1980) 51.   [40] See also n. 99 below.

[41] Pericles' citizenship law helped cement this distinction. Osborne (1997) 4

children. A great deal of evidence (particularly forensic oratory) testifies that there was much debate as to their legal status and right to inheritance.[42] Peleus confronts the question forthrightly: νόθοι τε πολλοὶ γνησίων ἀμείνονες ('Many bastards are better than legitimate children', 638).[43] But the play is hardly a political tract for bastards' rights (cf. *Hipp.* 1082–3, 1455).[44] Rather it recognizes the real disadvantages of those born to (foreign) *pallakai* in fifth-century Athens,[45] and explores these in terms of heroic society's more flexible attitude towards such children. In this way the play touches upon Athenian concerns about illegitimate or foreign interlopers. Euripides saw the connection between this problem and the role of women as preservers of the *oikos,* and has so constructed Hermione's anxiety as to throw a thought-provoking light on both of them. The more lenient regime covering legitimacy in the heroic world[46] underlies Hermione's fear that Andromache will supplant her as mother of the next generation of the Aeacid line.[47] The heroic world is thus used to explore current Athenian anxieties about bastardy and legitimacy.[48]

argues that it changed 'how Athenian citizens thought of their wives in particular, and of their families more generally'.

[42] Under Solon's law (see Ruschenbusch (1966) 86), Athenian men could have legitimate children by foreign wives, and there was no distinction between wives and free concubines. The exclusion of bastards from Athenian citizenship in the classical period was due to the high membership value of this exclusive political community; as Davies (1977–8) 106 observes, 'Athenian citizens were not merely a descent group but also an interest group, disposing of privileges which were worth defending.' He also argues (p. 121) that 'pressure from outsiders could just be accommodated inside the descent system providing that the inflow remained only a trickle'.

[43] Euripides was fond of this provocative idea: see Ogden (1996) 204.

[44] Contrast Amoroso (1994) 150, who sees it as exposing 'the insensitivity of the existing legislation', while Andromache triumphs 'by overcoming every judicial aspect'. Barrett (1964) 363 well notes the psychological effects of Hippolytus' νοθεία ('bastardy').

[45] For these see Todd (1993) 179, 211.

[46] Cf. *Il.* 8. 283–4; *Od.* 14. 202–4, 15. 365, 18. 321–5.

[47] Andromache is of course a slave-captive and not a citizen *pallake,* but in the heroic world her royal status and fertility are enough to provoke Hermione's fear of displacement. That she is of aristocratic birth is also reflected in her being presented as singing, if Hall (1997b) 111 is right about this distinction.

[48] By contrast with Hermione, Deianeira in Sophocles' *Trachiniae* does not

Yet despite the endorsement of citizen marriage in the classical *polis*, the status of concubines was not necessarily low.[49] The privileging of legitimate wives did not mean that a 'positive opposition' between the two was practically possible.[50] The Athenian concubine potentially enjoyed certain benefits (cf. Isaeus 3. 39), and children born to her might even be regarded as legitimate (Lys. 1. 30–1).[51] A concubine was protected by certain legal standards: it was illegal for another man to have sex with her.[52] An offender could be killed if the παλλακή ('concubine') was being kept for the production of free children (cf. Dem. 23. 53–5).[53] Thus both the Athenian and the heroic background explain Hermione's fear of retaliation by Neoptolemus.

Nevertheless, the separate status of concubines is reflected in the general tendency to house them separately from wives. At

mention possible children as her grievance. The focus there is more on the wife's sexual jealousy (cf. 539 ff.) and its consequences than on her fears for her own children.

[49] What sort of women became *pallakai*? One can imagine various scenarios: a woman abandoned as a child (cf. e.g. Men. *Perikeir.*), a *hetaera* whom somebody got involved with, or a woman who cannot marry for some reason. She may well have been a foreign citizen brought to Athens as a captive, and so of some status. Presumably the role is more respectable than that of a 'flute-girl'. At Dem. 19. 161 ff. Aeschines is said to have beaten up an Olynthian captive who was ἐλευθέρα ('free') and σώφρων ('modest') because she could not sing or entertain.

[50] Vernant (1980) 47; he describes the concubine as (p. 68 n. 26) 'oscillating between the courtesan with whom she may often be confused and the wife from whom she is often not clearly distinguished from an institutional point of view'. Davidson (1997) 132 argues that many Athenians cohabited with foreigners so that 'on a day-to-day basis, for some men and perhaps for many women too, the difference between wives and mistresses could be rather blurred'.

[51] MacDowell (1978) 90 defends the idea that legitimate children might be born of citizen *pallakai* in times of crisis (e.g. to counter the losses of war). Sealey (1984) 130 thinks that no special decree was needed for a man to beget legitimate children by a citizen *pallake*. On this complex question see Harrison (1968) i. 67–8 and Blundell (1995) 206 n. 23. Even if, as Ogden (1996) 158 argues, citizen *pallakai* were rare, concubines could still be of variable status.

[52] Cf. Cohen (1991) 106, 128.

[53] Davidson (1997) 98 dates this law back to the time of Draco. Cf. Keuls (1985) 272–3: 'the law protected not the woman but her keeper's interest in her'.

[Dem.] 59. 22 Apollodorus praises a man for not taking his girlfriends home out of respect for his wife and mother. The potential conflict between wife and concubine is invariably presented in tragedy as disastrous for the *oikos*.[54] Each instance of actual or projected cohabitation in tragedy ends in disaster: Cassandra and Agamemnon are murdered by Clytemnestra (cf. *El*. 1032–4),[55] Heracles is killed unintentionally by Deianeira who then commits suicide, while Hermione's attempt on Andromache's life fails but contributes to the death of Neoptolemus.

Whether we should see the plays, however, as in this way generating norms and ideals of masculine conduct is far from clear. Is the *Andromache* really saying it is fine to have a concubine as long as you keep her in a separate establishment? In connection with this approach, Edith Hall has interpreted the *Andromache*, among other tragedies, as endorsing the notion that it is dangerous for a husband or *kurios* to leave his *oikos* unsupervised.[56] While the pattern stands, it is essentially a plot device which only has meaning when embodied in interesting people. And these figures are very different: Clytemnestra, Deianeira, and Hermione, for example, stand in very individual relationships to their husbands. One should be wary of drawing general moral lessons for fifth-century Athenian men from texts that are so detailed and so various.[57]

There is a striking difference between the inter-state, aristocratic marriages of the Homeric world and those of democratic Athens. Vernant traces the shift from archaic marriages which trade in power and connections to later unions whose purpose is 'to perpetuate the households'.[58] The heightened emphasis on reproduction (of the citizen stock) is highly relevant to the impact of Hermione's dilemma. Each marriage was a union of

---

[54] See Lloyd (1994) 7–8.

[55] Tragic myth exceeds epic in the transgressive behaviour of women: according to *Od*. 11. 405 ff., Clytemnestra kills the concubine Cassandra, while Aegisthus murders Agamemnon.

[56] Hall (1997b) 106–8

[57] There was, for example, very strong public condemnation of female adultery and this is reflected in tragedy. But in real life a more flexible approach to extra-marital sex was often necessary: see Roy (1997), esp. 19.

[58] Vernant (1980) 50. Griffith (1995) 69 discusses the more locally focused loyalties of the democratic *polis*.

two *oikoi*, and the possibility of competing demands is a potential source of conflict.[59] Hermione's continuing devotion to her father's household proves disastrous and is marked by her insistence on the impressiveness of her dowry (a link to the paternal home) and by her failure to produce offspring, a lack which renders her integration into the new household of her husband abnormal and incomplete (cf. 211–12). Her ambiguous status confirms her estrangement and frustration. Yet we are gradually brought to realize the complexity of her situation and the various pressures working upon her, not only from men but from other women too.

In the *Andromache* we see Homer's good wife surprisingly set up in the role of the other woman. The marriage of Hector and Andromache was long since enshrined as a poetic ideal.[60] She is still the loyal 'wife' and mother, and repeats the Iliadic pattern of seeing her child's life endangered, and his father killed. But she is now a paradoxically virtuous mistress.[61] As we saw in Chapter 1, Euripides is probably the first writer to explore the domestic antagonisms between Andromache and Neoptolemus' new wife. With characteristic ingenuity he initially frustrates our concern for the neglected Greek wife, and enlists it on behalf of the Trojan concubine (compare Cassandra in the *Agamemnon*) by presenting the chaos from her point of view.[62]

Andromache's perspective on the action is established by her prologue speech. The first twenty lines are remarkable for the density of vocabulary relating to marriage or its disruption:

[59] Seaford (1990) 151–2.

[60] Cf. Amoroso (1994) 140, North (1979) 48: 'Homer . . . supplies the two primary exemplars [of the good wife] for later times, Penelope and Andromache . . . and each is much more than a stereotype.' On the Homeric poems' sensitivity to the suffering of women in war, see Taplin (1992) 32 n. 35.

[61] Euripides here foreshadows a theme of New and Roman Comedy; cf. Zagagi (1994) 21, 113 ff. on Chrysis in Men. *Sam.*

[62] One might contrast the centrality of the wife's point of view in *Trach.* (where Iole has no lines whatsoever). Deianeira complains, τὸ δ' αὖ ξυνοικεῖν τῆιδ' ὁμοῦ τίς ἂν γυνὴ | δύναιτο, κοινωνοῦσα τῶν αὐτῶν γάμων; ('What woman could live with this girl, sharing the same marriage?', 545–6). Yet despite her silence, Iole's experience illustrates the sexual powerlessness of the concubine: Heracles orders a disgusted Hyllus to do him the χάριν βραχεῖαν ('little favour', *Trach.* 1218) of marrying Iole, since he has slept with her. Even after his death, she remains an object of Heracles' sexual possessiveness.

Andromache's dowry (2) and happy past as a 'child-bearing' wife (παιδοποιός 4),[63] her dead husband and son (9), her enforced union with Neoptolemus (15), and the marriage of Peleus and Thetis (17–20). The recollection of her past revolves around two diametrically opposed unions; the first voluntary and enviable, the second a product of violence and impressing upon a former princess the shame of slavery.[64] (The demeaning fate in store for captive women is expressed by Nestor (*Il.* 2. 354–6, where he holds out the prospect of every Greek sleeping with a Trojan wife).)

The contrast of both situation and affection is underlined by the use of the same word, δοθεῖσα ('handed over'), to describe Andromache's divergent experience as female object of exchange:[65] first given in marriage to Hector, then as booty to Neoptolemus (4, 14–15). Andromache's perfect *oikos*[66] was destroyed (8–11) and this sets a pattern of disruption which runs throughout the play, where the Trojan War, including the *Iliad*'s depiction of the marriage of Hector and Andromache, functions as 'a secondary field of reference'[67] for events in Phthia. The union of Andromache and Neoptolemus, as well as the marriages of Hermione and Neoptolemus, and Menelaus and Helen (the origin of the war: cf. 605–6, *Tro.* 498–9), are separately and critically appraised by the repeated reminiscences of Andromache's first happy, but tragically short,

---

[63] Pòrtulas (1988) 285 exaggerates the connection here to 'the terms of the marriage contract in ancient law'.

[64] Cf. *Tro.* 645 ff., where 'Andromache reviews the past as exclusively the history of her marriage' (Croally (1994) 86). Andromache still defines herself and is defined by others (principally her Spartan opponents) as 'wife of Hector' (4, 107, 656, 908); cf. Storey (1993) 182: 'Characters in this play are more frequently called by their relationship than by their actual name. . . . The domestic relationship is as important as one's actual identity.' Further, Phillippo (1995) 369–70.

[65] See Easterling (1987) 15 on women as objects of exchange in archaic literature; cf. *Hipp.* 618 ff. for the idea of replacing women's reproductive function with money.

[66] Cf. Storey (1993) 181: 'The key words to watch for in *Andromache* are *domos, oikos, gamos, lechos, posis,* and the rare, but significant, *nympheumata.* Of these *oikos* is found more often in *Andromache* than in any other extant play; *lechos* is widely used in only three plays (*Medea, Andr., Helen*); of the eight instances of *nympheumata* in extant Euripides, four occur in this play.'

[67] Kuntz (1993) 67–8.

marriage.[68] Importantly, not only are the women involved in these marriages explicitly compared, but the men are too.

The unsatisfactoriness of Neoptolemus as a 'husband' is emphasized by his absence at a critical time of need (49): he is the child's κεκλημένος | πατήρ ('so-called father', 75–6). However, there is an ironic tension in Andromache's situation. The defeat of Troy meant the destruction of her family and city, the death of her husband and only son, and the loss of her freedom. Moreover, she was forced to sleep with the son of her husband's killer.[69] Nevertheless, this unwanted union has given her a second son, a source of hope and security for the future (cf. 27–8). So the child, a bond between Andromache and Neoptolemus and the focus of Hermione's jealousy, is both his mother's defence and her destruction. It is an excruciating paradox. The contradiction at the centre of Andromache's situation is how to remain both loyal to the memory of her dead husband and true to the new family ties imposed by her role as the mother of Neoptolemus' only son.

The typically female duty of mourning and preserving the memory of dead kin, a major motif of several tragedies, is bound in the *Andromache* to the other major determinants of

---

[68] Homer gives Helen and Paris no children—theirs is distinguished from a real marriage by sterility (cf. Neoptolemus and Hermione). This contrasts with Hector and Andromache.

[69] *Contra* Kovacs (1980) 9–20, who has propounded three notions that do not agree with the text (noted by Erbse (1984) 139): firstly, he argues that Andromache was a willing concubine; secondly, that her relations with Neoptolemus continued after the marriage to Hermione; and thirdly, that Hermione does not think herself sterile but merely neglected by Neoptolemus. However, on each point Andromache says otherwise, as an alert reading of 30–8 shows. Amoroso (1994) 142 claims that Andromache is triumphant 'in the contest for the bed', but this is to impute motives she does not have. The lot of Andromache contrasts with that of Briseïs in the *Iliad*. Achilles had killed Briseïs' husband and three brothers (*Il.* 19. 291–3), yet Patroclus consoled her by saying that he would make her Achilles' κουριδίην ἄλοχον ('wedded wife') back in Phthia (19. 298). Achilles himself refers to her as his ἄλοχον θυμαρέα ('heart-loved wife', 9. 336; well discussed by Taplin (1992) 213–16). In *Andromache* the theme of affection for one's husband's slayer is more problematic (cf. Hermione and Orestes). In general the impression of Andromache's 'affection' for Neoptolemus is a product of her child's peril; she stresses the ties between father and son in order to safeguard the boy's life.

[70] Cf. *Il.* 6. 55–60, where Menelaus would have spared the suppliant, but Agamemnon urges him to kill even the boys still in their mothers' wombs.

women's experience: marriage and motherhood. This is itself connected to the play's more general concern with the relations of parents and children. The loss of Achilles and Neoptolemus constitutes Peleus' tragedy and prompts Thetis' saving response; Andromache succeeds this time in saving her son from murder by Greeks; Hermione's doubly-troubled inheritance informs our interpretation of her actions; and Orestes' transgressive past as matricide colours his latest revenge. Most strikingly, Menelaus' mission to continue the extermination of every Trojan child[70] is exposed as a corruption of revenge rhetoric for selfish ends, which appeals to the duties of *philia* while suppressing the Greek nationality of Andromache's son.

By her unique elegiac lament, Andromache is placed at the heart of the (sexual) 'politics of tragic lamentation'.[71] Solon and Thucydides offer evidence of Athenian concern to limit the extravagant emotion of public lamentation by women.[72] In his funeral speech Pericles instructs the women of Athens not to 'parade their grief excessively'.[73] Robert Parker reviews the evidence of Plutarch for the Solonian 'control of women' in religion and society and remarks: 'He [Plutarch] also speaks in a related context of "removing what is harsh and barbarian from mourning practices".'[74] Andromache's own lament, however, although unique in extant tragedy, is characterized by its formal conventionality.[75] Far from being full of wild repetition, Andromache's song is all the more intense for its dignified

---

[71] See Foley (1993); with regard to Hermione's fear, compare esp. 143: 'A mourning woman is not simply a producer of pity, but dangerous.' Andromache's grief has proved an enduring poetic image: cf. Baudelaire, 'Le Cygne', *Les Fleurs du Mal*: 'Andromaque, je pense à vous! Ce petit fleuve, | Pauvre et triste miroir où jadis resplendit | L'immense majesté de vos douleurs de veuve, | Ce Simoïs menteur qui par vos pleurs grandit' ('Andromache, I think of you! This little river, a poor and sad mirror where in times past the immense majesty of your widow's sorrows shone, this false Simoïs which grows with your tears'); and Wallace Stevens' 'Another Weeping Woman', *Harmonium*.

[72] Cf. Solon frr. 72a–c in Ruschenbusch (1966); also Eteocles in *Sept.* 236–43, Theseus in *Suppl.* 837–43.

[73] Hornblower (1991a) 314 on Thuc. 2. 45. 2. Cf. *Her.* 533 ff., *Or.* 1022–3. Seaford (1994) 74–86 discusses in detail the funerary legislation of Solon.

[74] Parker (1996) 50.

[75] Cf. West (1982) 128.

control.[76] The formality of expression is contrapuntal to the horror of the events described.

Among the main features of the elegiac metre were its simplicity and 'the ease with which the riches of the epic vocabulary could be adapted to it'.[77] The evocation of Andromache's epic past is facilitated by Homeric vocabulary, while the song's coupling of the Trojan War with the post-epic present allows for a poignant pattern of repetition and dissonance. As in the prologue, the destruction or perversion of marriage is a major theme: οὐ γάμον ἀλλά τιν' ἄταν ('[Paris brought to Troy] not a marriage, but a curse', 103).[78] The key image of the (marriage) bed as symbol of women's destiny, a focus which is developed throughout the play (cf. 30, 904–5), is used here to contrast the experiences of Helen and Andromache: Helen abandons her Greek home for the bedroom of a Trojan (104), while Andromache is forcibly expelled from hers (109, 111–12) and brought to serve the bed of a Greek.[79] Finally, and most strikingly, the corrupted wedding imagery of δουλοσύναν στυγερὰν ἀμφιβαλοῦσα κάραι ('casting hateful slavery around my neck', 110) depicts Andromache's passage from Troy to Greece as a perverted bridal procession (cf. Cassandra's 'wedding march', *Tro.* 308 ff.).[80]

---

[76] The no less 'tragic' effects of Euripides' later astrophic songs are suggestively discussed by Gould (1996a) 573. He points out that they 'seem to float without ultimate closure'. Andromache's lament is tightly structured and well integrated into its context: the chorus take up her closing reference to Thetis in their opening words. The elegy's final image may suggest the Niobe legend (τάκομαι ὡς πετρίνα πιδακόεσσα λιβάς 116 'I melt in tears like a gushing mountain spring', cf. 532–4). If so, it is Niobe's grief for her children, not her boasting of them, which is recalled.

[77] West (1974) 18.

[78] In the *Agamemnon* Helen brings to Troy 'a dowry of death' (ἀντίφερνον ... φθορὰν, 406): see Rehm (1994) 43–58. Cf. Ach. Tat. *Clitophon and Leucippe* 1. 8. 6: τὸ μὲν γὰρ Ἑλένης τῶν γάμων πῦρ ἀνῆψε κατὰ τῆς Τροίας ἄλλο πῦρ ('For Helen's wedding-torch lit another kind of torch in Troy'). On the importance of marriage, both good and bad, to the background of *Andromache*, see Albini (1974) 94.

[79] Cantarella (1987) 69 notes that words for bed are 'repeated about 20 times in the play'; she describes it as a key word in Euripides for the man-woman relationship, but does not explore the complex uses to which it is put in the *Andromache*. Loraux (1993) 201 comments: 'the bed (*lechos*), an institutional reality, is kept distinct from the couch (*eunê*), a place of sexual pleasure'.

[*See opposite page for n. 80*]

The lament juxtaposes the adulterous union of Paris and Helen with the harmonious marriage of Andromache and Hector which it destroyed. It then moves from the mother to her daughter, concludes with Hermione's persecution of Andromache (113–14), and suggests for the first time the idea that Hermione has inherited the role (and the selfish, sexual destructiveness) of her mother. The idea is elaborated by both Andromache and Peleus (cf. 361–3, 621–3), strengthened by Hermione's desertion of her marital home, and then undercut in her final appearance as a passive follower of Menelaus' will: νυμφευμάτων μὲν τῶν ἐμῶν πατὴρ ἐμὸς | μέριμναν ἕξει, κοὐκ ἐμὸν κρίνειν τόδε ('As for my marriage, my father will consider it; it is not my right to judge about this', 987–8).

Hermione sees herself as ἄπαιδα καὶ πόσει μισουμένην ('childless and hateful to her husband', 33); that is, as part of a marriage which is an outright failure.[81] This prompts her to constant emphasis on her status as the legitimate wife, contrasted with that of Andromache as a foreign slave (e.g. 155, 927–8). The repetition of the distinction marks Hermione's insecurity. As Hall notes, 'when women in tragedy "get out of hand"', as Hermione thinks Andromache has done, 'reference is frequently made, whether explicitly or implicitly, to barbarian mores'.[82] Here though, interestingly, the stereotype is subverted, as it is Andromache who is presented as the better wife, while Hermione's independence and luxuriousness marks her as the more 'barbarian', or rather, tyrannical. We are not encouraged to sympathize with Hermione as we do with Medea (another barbarian) when another woman (again, a Greek) is put over her. The interconnection of sexual, political, and ethnic rhetoric (Andromache is emphatically 'other' in free Greek male terms, as woman, slave, and barbarian) is characteristic of Hermione's outlook and part

[80] The image contrasts poignantly with the 'veil normally *shed* by the departing bride' (Seaford (1987) 130).

[81] In Greek thought marriage is a woman's inevitable fate: cf. Creon to Antigone, πολλή σ' ἀνάγκη· ποῖ γὰρ ἐκφεύξηι λέχος; ('You must marry my son; for where could you go to escape it?', *Phoen.* 1674). The single life for a woman 'was considered pitiable' (Demand (1994) 26). For the particular importance of reproduction to Spartan women, see Xen. *Lac. Pol.* 1. 4.

[82] Hall (1989) 202–3.

of her shallow Spartan inheritance, as the arguments of Menelaus make clear.[83]

Hermione's opening speech echoes Andromache's prologue in evoking a bridal procession, but with revealing differences. Andromache apostrophized the city of her birth, Asian Thebe, whence she was successfully transferred to her husband's *oikos* in Troy. Hermione by contrast is never entirely integrated into her new household: she remains a Spartan, conscious, indeed proud, of her separateness (cf. 209–12). What gives her the right to speak freely (153), she thinks, is her impressive dowry. Dowry has been described as 'a fund or an estate created by the bride's relatives to give her as it were a stake in the *oikos* to which she is by marriage transferred'.[84] Not only that, it also gives the bride's family some influence in the marriage, a power we see abused in Menelaus' subsequent conduct. Well-dowered women could also have considerable power in a relationship.[85] The connection between her dowry and her power in the household is strongly made by Hermione, but again we see rather her misuse of such power.

Aristotle attributes the political decline of Sparta in his own era to the excessive influence of women, and remarks on their great wealth and right to own and inherit property (*Pol.* 1269[b]39–1270[a]31). The luxury they enjoy is seen as deleterious to the well-being of the state.[86] The same passage also explains that the licentiousness of Spartan women is only to be expected when the men are always off at war; Redfield remarks: 'To the disciplined asceticism of the men was contrasted the disorder and luxury of the women.'[87] But in the *Andromache* Menelaus does not fit this contrast. The mere sight of Helen's breast disarms him: ἀλλ' ὡς ἐσεῖδες μαστόν, ἐκβαλὼν ξίφος | φίλημ' ἐδέξω, προδότιν αἰκάλλων κύνα ('But when you saw her breast, you dropped your sword and let her kiss you, fawning on the

---

[83] For the Greek 'other' in these terms, see Williams (1993) 112.

[84] Harrison (1968) 45, cf. Foxhall (1989) 32, 38. Pomeroy (1994) 58–61 discusses the capital contribution of a dowry to the *oikos*.

[85] Compare, in a Roman context, Plaut. *Aul.* 475–536; Leo (1912) 122 thinks that Menander is perhaps the original source.

[86] Blundell (1995) 155–6. On Plato's keenness to abolish dowries from his model state see Saunders (1995) 599.

[87] Redfield (1995) 174.

treacherous bitch', 629–30). He is emasculated by the defeat (cf. 327–9).

Hermione has inherited her mother's weakness for extravagance and wealth (cf. *Tro.* 991–7). She is preoccupied with the economic aspects of marriage (with its role in maintaining her status), and she lacks the insight of Medea, who trenchantly notes the injustice of a woman having to buy a husband, a 'master of her body', with her dowry (*Med.* 232–4; cf. Soph. fr. 583 R).[88] The Spartan practice of wife-sharing (cf. Xen. *Lac. Pol.* 1. 7–9, Plut. *Lyc.* 15. 6–9) is forcefully reversed by Euripides, who presents Hermione as highly monogamous (177–80). This is far from being a negative characteristic.[89] The innovation of Hector's affairs, and Andromache's tolerant compliance (discussed further below), complicates our response to the contrasting visions of what marriage means for a woman. This is not just a simple conflict of good versus bad types of woman. There is some truth in the assertion that both women are 'equally robbed of dignity by what war and society—both the creation of the male—have done to them'.[90] But 'equally' is an extravagant exaggeration: we do not perceive the women as morally equal, and we should beware of saying (as Vellacott does) that Hermione is merely the innocent tool of Menelaus and Orestes. Her responsibility is real and is closely connected to her view of herself as a threatened wife and failed mother. Her sense of inadequacy is used to portray the asymmetry of expectations at the heart of marriage.

Hermione's charge of poisoning (157–8) illustrates how female characters can criticize other women using stock arguments ultimately derived from male-generated stereotypes (e.g. *El.* 1052–4).[91] In fact, Andromache herself is not immune to

---

[88] Medea also powerfully confronts the hypocrisy of a sexual morality which allows the husband but not the wife to take another partner (*Med.* 244–7, cf. *El.* 1036–40). The chorus of *Hipp.* wonder whether Phaedra's affliction is the result of Theseus' infidelity (151–4; the Nurse makes a similar surmise, 320).

[89] Patterson (1991) 57 reminds us that despite the sexual freedom of Greek men, marriage was highly valued as a relationship between two persons. For the ideal, cf. *Od.* 6. 182–4.

[90] Vellacott (1975) 119.

[91] But these may be used by women for a specific rhetorical purpose which transforms their bare content. Medea is again the most striking example, e.g.

this form of thought: in urging the servant-woman to relay a message to Peleus, she says, πολλὰς ἂν εὕροις μηχανάς· γυνὴ γὰρ εἶ ('You'll find many schemes, for you're a woman', 85; cf. 93–5, 181–2, 220–1, 269–72, 353–4). For such remarks to be uttered by a woman is unexpected and arresting. Andromache's use of such male-serving rhetoric led Sarah Pomeroy to refer to 'masochists like Andromache'.[92] As we shall see, her submissiveness is indeed problematic.

Hermione accuses Andromache of plotting to supplant her as the wife of Neoptolemus (34–5, 155–7, 192 ff.). As we saw, such a remarriage was unnecessary in the more lenient marital world of epic. But given the emphasis in classical Athens on the grounding of legitimate reproduction within marriage, Hermione's barrenness will have appeared not only as unfortunate but also as a threat to her status as wife. Richard Seaford argues that one cannot simply transfer Pericles' citizenship law wholesale to heroic Phthia, since it would denigrate Neoptolemus' marriage to the Spartan Hermione.[93] Peleus does criticize Neoptolemus' choice, but this is because of Hermione's inherited faults (619–22), not as an endorsement of citizen marriage. The law is in this sense universally alien to tragedy. Thus nobody denies that Medea is married to Jason (or that the Corinthian princess can marry him).[94] Though Andromache is not even Greek, Peleus regards her son as his offspring even if he is a *nothos* (cf. 636, 711–14).[95]

Remarkably, at various points, Andromache, Hermione, and Menelaus all express 'an absolute rather than a relative model

---

Med. 889–90. When Aethra says πάντα γὰρ δι᾽ ἀρσένων | γυναιξὶ πράσσειν εἰκὸς αἵτινες σοφαί ('Women who are wise should achieve everything through men', *Suppl.* 40–1), this topos is transformed by her own crucial initiative in making Theseus change his mind about helping the Argive mothers. Clytemnestra's criticism of bad wives at *IA* 1162–3 is in context self-praise and increases the moral pressure on Agamemnon to accept her plea for Iphigenia's life.

[92] Pomeroy (1975) 105.

[93] Seaford (1990) 169.

[94] Cf. Easterling (1977) 180–1.

[95] It is the Spartans Hermione and Menelaus who show an 'Athenian' obsession with legitimacy. Ogden (1996) 250 notes that contemporary 'common' Spartans had only 'a minimal conception of bastardy', while (p. 262) 'vicious bastardy disputes' occurred in the royal stratum of Spartan society.

of legitimacy'[96] which asserts that her son will always be a slave. But these remarks have a specific rhetorical context. Thus Andromache naturally attempts to play down the threat posed to Hermione's position by her half-Trojan child, referring sarcastically to her slave children as an ἀθλίαν ἐφολκίδα ('a wretched appendage', 199–200).[97] Menelaus uses the idea to argue unconvincingly for the scandal of barbarians ruling over Greeks (663–6). Hermione's awareness of it is most interesting: she initially fears Andromache's son but later recognizes in regret that such offspring would have been ἡμιδούλους τοῖς ἐμοῖς νοθαγενεῖς ('bastards of half-servile origin and slaves to my own children', 941–2).[98] The change of perspective is part of Hermione's dramatically effective breakdown.[99]

The *agon* between Andromache and Hermione focuses the issues of marriage and sexuality on the idea of *sophrosyne* ('self-control', 'modesty'), which in the (male) Greek value-system was the 'archetypal female quality',[100] and to which the women make rival and contrasting claims. Andromache rejects Hermione's charge of sorcery and suggests instead that Neoptolemus is no longer interested in his wife simply because she is 'hard to live with' (ξυνεῖναι μὴ 'πιτηδεία, 206). She implies that Hermione is too dependent on her looks, and unaware of the importance of correct behaviour (207–8).[101] However, while Hermione's concern with beauty seems superficial and

---

[96] Ogden (1996) 196.

[97] Ogden (1996) 102 sees Andromache exploiting in her defence 'the extremity and the impossibility of the paradox of the "married courtesan"'.

[98] Earlier in the action the possibility of Hermione having her own children is not stressed so that her position in the house will seem all the more insecure.

[99] Seaford (1990) 170 even suggests that 'It may also to some extent reflect the historical shifts in attitudes to marriage during the transmission of the myth, in the period in which the city-state was formed'. But this is already ambiguous in epic: cf. *Il.* 5. 69–71, 8. 284 (hostile), 11. 101 ff. (note the name Ἶσος, 'equal'), *Od.* 14. 202 ff. Easterling (1997b) 25–6 shows how in Sophocles' *Ajax* '"heroic vagueness" is used both to gloss over an issue and to make it prominent within the same play. This is the matter of the status of a concubine and her child: Tecmessa and Eurysaces, Teucer and his mother.'

[100] Goldhill (1994) 68. Cf. Gregory (1991) 167.

[101] Cf. Lucr. 4. 1278–82: the ugly girl manages by her compliant behaviour to make herself loved.

immature, Andromache goes on to outline a model of wifely submission that complicates her defence (213–14):

χρὴ γὰρ γυναῖκα, κἂν κακῶι πόσει δοθῆι,
στέργειν ἅμιλλάν τ' οὐκ ἔχειν φρονήματος.

A woman must cherish her husband, even if she has been given to an inferior man, and must not compete with him in pride.

Andromache is espousing an essentially male-generated ideology of female submission. In many traditional societies it is often older oppressed women who transmit support for patriarchal values. Andromache has internalized such qualities very thoroughly.[102] However, the incongruity of her extreme submission calls her views into question. In the *Iliad* Hector fathers no children outside his marriage to Andromache. Here their exemplary relationship is distorted. Her repeated suckling of Hector's various bastards seems grotesquely self-abasing (222–5). Despite its rhetorical function, her boasting of such conduct shocks.[103] Thus in a daring way Euripides uses an unexpectedly extreme form of the ideal epic wife and mother to challenge women's reproduction of the dominant (male) values of their culture.[104]

It is remarkable that our sympathy for Andromache is refined in this manner. But as the subsequent stichomythia shows, both wife and concubine, despite their opposed views,

---

[102] I owe this point to Edith Hall. She compares the example of older women's support for clitoridectomy in conservative Muslim society.

[103] The impact on female spectators will have been especially forceful. The evidence for women's attendance at the theatre is unfortunately far from conclusive (Pickard-Cambridge (1968) 263–5), though Csapo and Slater (1995) 286–305 make a good case for it. Nevertheless, many critics write as if the 'male, adult, enfranchised perspective' (Goldhill (1997a) 66) were the sole determinant of meaning: cf. Wiles (1997), ix: 'I have assumed throughout that the Greek spectator was male.' Goldhill ((1997a) 66) goes on to claim that even if the presence of women is accepted, it is still possible that male citizens remain 'the "proper or intended" audience' and that 'the citizen perspective remains dominant'. But it is debatable whether the plays actually support such a one-sided, tendentious reading. The related notion that tragedy is all about teaching lessons to male citizens is hardly tenable.

[104] Of course it is hard to counter the argument that part of the audience would be delighted with her. Perhaps (as with the suttee of Evadne in *Supplices*) different spectators responded very differently. Cf. Pelling (1997b) 221 on the various possible responses to Medea.

embody a range of problematic aspects of women's experience. Hermione picks up on Andromache's priggish, moralizing tone (τί σεμνομυθεῖς 234, 'Why do you adopt lofty words . . .?'). The women dispute whose conception of sensible behaviour is right. Hermione assumes that an unhappy sex-life is what women think of as first in importance (241). We see an insecure young woman whose identity and self-worth are contingent upon reproductive success. As a result she is driven to murder by jealousy and fear. From our perspective it is tempting to read these events as critical of (male) bracketing of child-bearing as women's supreme function. However, we must remember that in the past having children was central to women's lives. This makes Hermione's anxiety credible to an ancient audience, but it does not excuse her actions.

Andromache admits that all women give priority to their sexual problems, but commends only those whose response is of the right kind; that is, those who are as silently compliant as she is (238–42).[105] Interestingly, Hermione's insecurity is connected to her mother's past. She pleads with Andromache, ἦ καὶ πρόσω γὰρ τῶν ἐμῶν ψαύσεις κακῶν; ('Will you keep on touching my woes?', 249). The mother's notorious promiscuity[106] seems to have affected her daughter.[107] Andromache insinuates that Hermione's monogamous jealousy is really just another form of her mother's sexual insatiability (218–19, 229–31). However, the extreme self-denial of her own attitude to Hector's bastards complicates the accusation.

The entrance of Menelaus with Andromache's son explores the ambiguities and dangers of Andromache's position from a

---

[105] On alleged textual problems here, see Kovacs (1996) 45–7. He argues (p. 46, against 242 as a reply to 241): 'Andromache does not think that sex is of first importance to good women'. But Andromache says exactly that.

[106] E.g. Stes. fr. 223 D, *Ag.* 62, *Cycl.* 179–82; also Derek Walcott's poem 'Menelaus' (Walcott (1987) 101): 'I would not wish her curse | on any: that necks should spurt, | limbs hacked to driftwood, because | a wave hoists its frilled skirt.'

[107] Cf. Electra's wish (*Cho.* 139–41) to be a better woman than her mother. In terms of heroic male ideology, one might compare Hector's wish for Astyanax: καί ποτέ εἴποι "πατρός γ' ὅδε πολλὸν ἀμείνων" | ἐκ πολέμου ἀνιόντα· φέροι δ' ἔναρα βροτόεντα | κτείνας δήϊον ἄνδρα, χαρείη δὲ φρένα μήτηρ ('And may people say, as he returns from war, "This man is far better than his father." And let him bring home the bloody spoils of a slain enemy so that his mother may rejoice in her heart', *Il.* 6. 479–81).

new perspective.[108] Like the *Medea*, the play shows not merely a domestic quarrel, but constitutes a 'family drama in which the future and even the safety of the children are at stake.'[109] As in the *Medea*, children are made tools of revenge, with the important difference that here the mother is the passive victim. In both plays Euripides uses the foreignness, isolation, and vulnerability of the heroine to reflect critically on the reality of the opposition between Greek and barbarian.

The speech of Andromache is notable for the way she uses the constraints affecting female conduct in her favour. She exploits the shame of being unmarried which faces Hermione if expelled by Neoptolemus. She alleges that even repeated infidelities by the husband are preferable to the life of an ageing unmarried woman left at home (347–51).[110] As with her remark on the evil nature of women which men should avoid (353–4; cf. *Med.* 890–1), we are brought to reflect on these clichés of sexual difference by the speaker's extreme formulation of them.

Nevertheless, we certainly sympathize with Andromache and appreciate her moral victory over Menelaus, which subverts his own rhetoric of gender and ethnicity. His attack on a defenceless foreign slave undermines his claim to heroism. Andromache's recollection of Hector's conduct at Troy, where he exposed Menelaus' cowardice (456–7), presents a model of masculinity which completely discredits Menelaus. The model goes beyond bravery, however, to a

[108] The bond between a father and his children was sometimes promoted above that of the mother, who becomes a mere 'surrogate parent' (cf. Walker (1995) 88–9). However, commenting on *Eum.* 657–66, Sommerstein (1989) 206–8 shows that this was not the normal Athenian view, despite the (p. 207) 'basically patriarchal and patrilineal' structure of Athenian scoiety. As Ogden (1995) 219 remarks, 'in the imaginary world of Euripidean tragedy . . . the status of offspring rose and fell with that of their mothers'. On the ironies of Electra's trap, which lures her mother to her death by the lying tale of a new-born son, see Hall (1997a). The mother–child bond (cf. Soph. fr. 685 R, and for its disruption, *Cho.* 189–91) is parodied by Aristophanes: (Myrrhine comes down to Cinesias from the Acropolis) οἷον τὸ τεκεῖν. καταβατέον. τί γὰρ πάθω; ('What a thing it is to have given birth! I must go down. For what else can I do?', *Lys.* 884).

[109] Easterling (1977) 181.

[110] Cf. *Hel.* 689–90, where Helen laments that her reputation has ruined Hermione's chance of a husband and child.

valuing of Andromache as a person. Menelaus equates her with a piece of property (κοινὰ χρήματα 377, 'the goods are shared'), which he may treat as he likes (note Peleus' criticism at 586). But her generous self-sacrifice puts his rhetoric of reification to shame.

As with Polyxena's proud act in the *Hecuba*, Andromache's self-sacrifice reaffirms her nobility in overcoming degradation.[111] Andromache and her son sing a moving lyric lament, punctuated by brutal interjections from Menelaus.[112] The effect is wholly pathetic and stirring.[113] As Mastronarde notes (on *Phoen.* 355–6), 'That Eur[ipides] dwells explicitly in many of his plays on the love of children and the pathos of separation from them shows his greater interest in domestic emotions and women's emotions.' Here the child appeals in vain to his father (508–9). Neoptolemus' absence from his *oikos* is the catalyst of the action, but we should not ignore its critical aspect. Andromache has already drawn attention to her dissatisfaction (49–50). Menelaus is censured by Peleus for leaving Helen at home unguarded (592–5), and Neoptolemus was arguably unwise to leave Andromache and their son alone with Hermione.[114] However, as we saw earlier, the criticism (of a husband's absence) need not be abstracted to condone a general principle discouraging Athenian men from leaving their homes unsupervised. The play deals with specific characters in a peculiar situation. Women are not simply portrayed as dangerous when

[111] Some of Euripides' plays of voluntary self-sacrifice by women (*Alc.*, *IA*) are structured 'so as to leave us doubtful whether the men for whom the women sacrificed themselves were worth it' (Pomeroy (1975) 110).

[112] On Euripides' use of children for pathetic effect, cf. Kassel (1954) 58 on the 'permagna caterva parvulorum' ('great number of children') in his work. On children as avengers (note Menelaus' justification, 519–22, 659, and Peleus' threat, 723–4), see Kassel (1954) 51–2, Fantham (1986) 268, and Menu (1992) 258. Trendall (1991) 170 notes the practice of including children in vase-painting illustrations of tragedy 'to heighten the emotion'.

[113] Racine keeps Astyanax; his explanation in the second preface underestimates the pathos of the present scene: 'I doubt that the tears of Andromache would have made the impression they did on the mind of the audience, if they had flown for a son other than the one she had by Hector.'

[114] Peleus reveals that he had vainly warned Neoptolemus against marriage to Hermione: μήτε δώμασιν λαβεῖν | κακῆς γυναικὸς πῶλον· ἐκφέρουσι γὰρ | μητρῷι' ὀνείδη (' . . . nor to take into his house a filly of such a wicked mother; for the daughters carry on their mother's faults', 620–2).

left alone. Hermione is subject to different pressures from her Spartan past and from Orestes.

When Peleus arrives, he argues with Menelaus over who has the greater claim to control over Andromache; the term *kurios* is used (cf. 558, 580), as in fifth-century legal language, to mark the man in charge. Peleus concentrates his criticisms on Spartan *sophrosyne*, principally on Hermione's and Helen's failure to achieve it, and this is expanded in a striking claim: οὐδ' ἂν εἰ βούλοιτό τις | σώφρων γένοιτο Σπαρτιατίδων κόρη ('No Spartan girl could be virtuous, even if she wanted to', 595–6). The irascible old man adopts the rhetoric of Athenian disapproval of Spartan women's freedoms (597–601).[115] It is likely that many prejudices about Spartan education prevailed in popular Athenian thought, and enough for such moralizing by Peleus to be easily concocted.[116] But as with Andromache, Peleus' laudable aims do not mean that his arguments about female modesty are totally compelling.

The system of moral values founded on distinctions of birth and wealth, a hallmark of tragedy's heroic setting, is frequently explored by Euripides.[117] Peleus' speech subverts the Spartans' connection of wealth and moral superiority, and stresses instead inborn excellence and the priority of personal over material values (639–41):[118]

ἀλλ' ἐκκομίζου παῖδα. κύδιον βροτοῖς
πένητα χρηστὸν ἢ κακὸν καὶ πλούσιον
γαμβρὸν πεπᾶσθαι καὶ φίλον·

[115] The perception of Spartan women as less bound by marriage ties than other Greek women (cf. Xen. *Lac. Pol.* 1. 3–10) led some to idealize their lives as pure service to the state. However, as de Beauvoir (1949) 89 comments: 'such examples as Sparta and the Nazi regime prove that [woman] can be none the less oppressed by the males, for all her direct attachment to the state'.

[116] On Spartan women's revealing clothes, see Anacr. fr. 399 *PMG*; Soph. fr. 872 R specifically mentions Hermione. In Athens it was men and boys who exercised; cf. Dover (1974) 97.

[117] See Collard *et al.* (1995) 92 on *Sthen.* fr. 661. 2–3 K, Wilkins (1993) 88–9 on *Hcld.* 297–303.

[118] Wealth and family prestige, the bedrock of the Spartans' self-confidence, are transitory; what really counts, as Electra points out in words which are highly relevant to the action of the *Andromache*, is natural virtue: ἡ γὰρ φύσις βέβαιος, οὐ τὰ χρήματα ('Character is secure, not wealth', *El.* 941; cf. *Hec.* 592–8).

Take you daughter back home. It is better for people to have marriage-relations who are poor and honest rather than rich and unscrupulous.

He supports Andromache's son κεἰ τρὶς νόθος πέφυκε ('even if he's a bastard three times over', 636). In the contemporary terms of *nomos* and *physis*,[119] many fragments of Euripides claim that *physis* refuses to grant legitimate birth any particular privileges (frs. 141, 168, 377 N²). Peleus' remarks reflect such debates but his attitude is traditional in its insistence on inborn nobility.

The scene of Hermione's breakdown is interesting in several ways. The Nurse's account of it is, of course, primary: her father's departure and her consciousness of what she did to Andromache has made Hermione fear her husband's revenge (805 ff.; cf. 833 ff., 856). Nevertheless, one might tentatively suggest that there is also a gynaecological aetiology operating in the background. In the Hippocratic corpus physical and psychological disorders in female patients are regularly ascribed to the woman's lack of sexual intercourse.[120] Hermione has been shunned by Neoptolemus and the deprivation of sexual intercourse and pregnancy might be interpreted as a cause of her irrational state of mind. Hermione describes herself as 'puffed up with foolishness' (ἐξηνεμώθην μωρίαι, 938). Lloyd well notes the gynaecological connotations of the image: Hermione's womb is made big by folly instead of by a child.[121] In her distress she casts off her mantle (829–31), tears at her clothes, and exposes her breasts (832–5). She and Andromache have now changed places definitively, Andromache being associated with the wifely duty of child-bearing, and Hermione with the eroticism of the concubine (she is still semi-clad when Orestes, her future husband, appears).[122]

[119] The complex debate is succinctly set out by Rutherford (1995) 161–3.

[120] Dean-Jones (1994) 69–70, Hall (1997b) 109. Dean-Jones (1994) 109 points out that Greek 'science' contrived to 'construct a female body inherently weak and in need of supervision'.   [121] Lloyd (1994) 150.

[122] For this division in the 'ideology' of classical marriage see Vernant (1980) 67 n. 25. Hermione has also adopted the earlier suppliant status of Andromache (859), but she cannot seek refuge at the altar of Thetis on stage. Wiles (1997) 201 interestingly suggests that 'The statue of the sea-nymph may simultaneously be a mother like Andromache, and erotically under-dressed like Hermione.'

Previous chapters have already explored Orestes' manipulation of Hermione's calamity. Here we may explore in more detail what his actions both in Phthia and Delphi tell us about expectations and models of male behaviour. His interrogation of Hermione reveals a typically male view of women's presumed range of concerns, but he takes care not to insult his future wife: τίς οὖν ἂν εἴη μὴ πεφυκότων γέ πω | παίδων γυναικὶ συμφορὰ πλὴν ἐς λέχος; ('What misfortune could afflict a childless woman apart from one involving her marriage?', 904–5).[123] Less measured is his association of women and plotting: μῶν ἐς γυναῖκ' ἔρραψας οἷα δὴ γυνή; ('Did you act as a woman would and plot against the other woman?', 911). But Hermione is in no position to disagree. His carefully planned exploitation of her situation is intensely alienating.

Unexpected as Hermione's reversal is, her submissiveness and criticism of other women are just as extreme as her earlier jealousy and persecution of Andromache. She is desperate to persuade Orestes to escort her from Neoptolemus' house back to Sparta (922–3). Her speech of diminished responsibility is largely wasted on Orestes, since he cares about her responsibility for attacking Andromache only in so far as it furthers his own plans. Nevertheless, her speech is remarkable for what it reveals about 'the polarisation of incompatible aspects of the female role'.[124] The opposition between the two women as independent wife and dutiful concubine collapses. Hermione reacts in a remarkable manner to the failure of her plot against Andromache by adopting the Trojan's extreme submissiveness (as if to reassure her returning suitor that she has learnt her lesson). But as with Andromache's earlier speeches, Hermione's tirade against the corrupting influence of other women makes use of patriarchal ideology in such an extravagant fashion as potentially to call it into question.

To explain her disastrous misjudgement, Hermione invokes typically male fears of promiscuous women and their dangerous influence (946–50):[125]

---

[123] Cf. Stevens (1971) 201: 'The conditional μὴ is due either to politeness or feigned ignorance, and πω softens the implied reproach.'

[124] See Lloyd (1994) 9, quoting Gould (1980) 56.

[125] On the corruption of women by their peers, cf. Sem fr. 7. 90–1 W (the bee woman does not enjoy sitting with women talking about sex), *Phoen.* 198–

αὗται γὰρ διδάσκαλοι κακῶν·
ἡ μέν τι κερδαίνουσα συμφθείρει λέχος,
ἡ δ' ἀμπλακοῦσα συννοσεῖν αὑτῆι θέλει,
πολλαὶ δὲ μαργότητι· κἀντεῦθεν δόμοι
νοσοῦσιν ἀνδρῶν.

These women teach wives to be wicked. One corrupts a marriage in hope of some profit; another, an adulteress herself, wants someone to share her disease, while many are motivated by sheer promiscuity. As a result the houses of husbands are diseased.

The imagery of illness and disease recalls Andromache's remark that womanhood itself brings the affliction of lust (220–1, cf. 269–72). The character and history of the speakers, though very different in each case, expose the partial thinking that feeds such male-generated prejudice.[126] Hermione's panicked reaction reveals an insecure, childless young wife who is sensitive to the rumours and opinions of society.[127] Hermione's dilemma, response, and counter-response do not represent a lesson in feminine conduct. Euripides is rather using her experience and her conflict with Andromache to explore various domestic and social pressures on women.[128]

Importantly, Hermione's sudden submissiveness proves destructive. Her departure with Orestes ensures that her possible divorce will never happen.[129] Instead it promotes the death of her husband. Andromache invoked Hector's greatness

201. Hall (1997b) 109 well discusses Aristotle's formalization of the 'frailty of the female psyche' which made women especially susceptible to invasive influence; cf. Padel (1992) 110–13.

[126] The idea that one should not generalize about women from one unflattering example is well expressed in Euripides' *Protesilaus*: ὅστις δὲ πάσας συντιθεὶς ψέγει λόγωι | γυναῖκας ἑξῆς, σκαιός ἐστι κοὐ σοφός ('Whoever lumps all women together and berates them is a fool and not wise', fr. 657. 1–2 N²): cf. *Mel. Desm.* fr. 493 K, *Ion* 398–400.

[127] Garrison (1995) 98 is perhaps too harsh: 'her quick abandonment of the idea [suicide] when a new opportunity for escape in the person of Orestes presents itself shows her as all too human, all too ready to live with whatever moral adjustments are necessary'.

[128] Hunter (1994) 115 observes of Athenian society that 'Examples of gossip about women usually relate to two issues: sexual mores and status as an Athenian.'

[129] A father had the right to terminate his daughter's marriage whenever he wished, but as Dean-Jones (1994) 244 points out, 'in the Classical period there are only three cases known where divorce did proceed from the woman's side'.

as a warrior and thereby diminished Menelaus' stature (523–5).
Now the heroism of her second 'husband' discredits the cowardly Orestes. Peleus' response to Neoptolemus' death makes
clear where the responsibility lies in his eyes : ὦ γάμος, ὦ γάμος,
ὃς τάδε δώματα | καὶ πόλιν ὤλεσας ὤλεσας ἁμάν ('Oh marriage,
marriage that has destroyed, destroyed this house and my city',
1186–7). The play now turns to his loss, but in a notable
reversal of the marriage of Neoptolemus, Peleus' own union
proves a source of consolation.

The marriage of Peleus and Thetis appeared to be yet
another instance of fractured union. In the prologue Andromache referred in the past tense to Thetis' living with Peleus
(ξυνώικει 18, 'used to live together'). As was discussed in
Chapter 1, Thetis left her husband and returned to live with
her father (cf. 1224).[130] This pattern connects and contrasts
with the actions of Helen and Hermione. Hermione returns to
her father but will never see her husband again. Helen leaves
her husband but eventually returns to him in shame.[131] Thetis
is a goddess and can combine both marriage and freedom to do
as she wishes.[132] Her enviable position highlights the constraints that operate on mortal women.

Despite the ambivalent impact of Andromache's male-serving rhetoric, it is necessary that she be included in her child's
glorious future. It is also appropriate that her innocence and
resilience be rewarded. Moreover, the identity of Thetis as
benefactor contributes to the criticism of Menelaus' rhetoric of
Greek and barbarian, since Thetis resembles Andromache in
being 'an exotic non-Grecian partner but of high social
status'.[133] Andromache regains her freedom and is to establish

---

[130] For a comic version of Thetis' reasons see Ar. *Clouds*, 1067–9. Thetis'
aversion to the marriage underlies the myth of her shape-changing (cf. Soph.
fr. 150 R, variations discussed by Forbes Irving (1990) 181–4), which is a
popular scene on vase-paintings: see March (1987) 11–18, *LIMC* Peleus nos.
61–107. Fifth-century vases bring out the role of Aphrodite (with Peitho and
Eros) as an ally of Peleus: see Krieger (1973), esp. 138–40.

[131] Alc. fr. 42 Voigt makes a moral contrast between the pure, child-bearing
Thetis and the adulteress Helen, who is ultimately responsible for Achilles'
death.

[132] Peleus' journey to the depths of the sea (1257–8) reverses the traditional
passage of wife to husband's home.

[133] Wiles (1997) 201.

a new *oikos* that will regenerate the two war-scarred houses (1249–51). 'Molossus' physically unites the chief enemy families of the Trojan War, and his paradoxical inheritance enhances the impact of the reconciliation.[134] The restoration of domesticity thus represents a release from the reciprocity of violence and revenge that has shaped the play.

It is generally recognized that in Athenian society of the classical period 'the primacy of males was pervasive; marriage was patrilocal as inheritance was patrilinear and authority patriarchal'.[135] This chapter has tried to show that Euripides' work challenges his audience to reflect critically on certain core assumptions of sexual politics in their society. In the *Andromache* Neoptolemus' absence and eventual death play down the relationship between father and son so that Andromache's role as protector and heroic exemplar is enhanced.[136] While it may be true in some cases that 'there is a discernible "masculinisation" of women in Greek tragedy',[137] Andromache exemplifies the way in which the 'feminine' qualities of duty to children and domestic harmony may be no less a source of courage, endurance, and survival. But as we have seen, if we leave things there, we risk reading a rather cosy conformism in the text. One scholar has recently tried to show that women 'who are in total conformity with the social norms and ideals' are very common in tragedy. He goes on: 'good wives (and mothers) may not be material for tragedy, but they are an important part

---

[134] As Osborne (1996) 148 points out, in the Homeric poems 'marriages are one of the most important means by which networks of alliance have been created on both Greek and Trojan sides.' Such wartime alliances are unilateral. In this respect the Molossian dynasty of Andromache and Neoptolemus is unique; the divine prophecy of its success transcends, and at the same time discredits, the lingering, post-war hostility of the Spartans.

[135] Redfield (1995) 175. Cf. Whitehead (1986) 77: 'In the strictest sense women were simply ignored by the deme system and, through it, by the polis itself.' However, the importance of women in the sphere of religion and cult must not be overlooked (cf. Kron (1996) 139). It is often reflected in tragedy: see Gould (1980) 50. In the *Antigone*, most famously, a woman's ritual duties challenge the priorities of a self-consciously male authority.

[136] Two vases, an Attic kylix by the Brygos Painter (*c*.495, *LIMC* Andromache no. 46, Beazley *ARV*² 369 no. 1) and an Attic hydria (*c*.480, *LIMC* Andromache no. 47, Beazley *ARV*² 189, 74), show Andromache physically defending herself (and Astyanax in the former scene) using a large pestle.

[137] Gould (1980) 57.

of the tragic world, from Aeschylus' Atossa and Hypermestra to Sophocles' Tecmessa, Iocaste and Eurydice, and to Euripides' Alcestis, Andromache, Euadne and Iocaste'.[138] Surely, however, in view of this very list (which is by no means comprehensive), we can say that the experience of wives and mothers is in fact excellent material for tragedy. It is often their struggle to be 'good' which reveals certain fundamental tensions and conflicts at the heart of various images of womanhood.

Let us briefly reconsider Andromache and Hermione, whose very different situations and responses can be seen to develop challenges to conventional demands on women. Indeed, the distance between them is not merely a neat opposition but is used to widen the range of the play's questioning. Hermione's portrayal of Andromache as a husband-grabbing *pallake* overturns her epic role as faithful wife and exemplary mourning widow. But we see that Andromache has in fact changed in an even more male-serving manner. To see her as merely conforming to some fifth-century female role is untenable. Was it to be expected that an Athenian wife would give the breast to her husband's bastards? While one should recognize that 'the scene is certainly not a domestic interior in Athens, we are in the time of the myth',[139] this distancing effect does not diminish the surprise of the image. Andromache's frequent recollections and invocations of Hector (e.g. 8–9, 106–7, 222, 399–400, 523–5) keep the memory of their Iliadic relationship alive as a contrast to the fractured household of Neoptolemus; but this very continuity makes his bastard children, unthinkable in the *Iliad*, more disconcerting. Hector's continuing presence as a model of masculinity throws a revealing light on the activities of Menelaus, Orestes, and Neoptolemus.

Importantly, what Hermione does and what is done to her are separate things. We condemn her murder attempt but are brought to realize the pressure on her to reproduce the Spartan line (and not to repeat her mother's typically 'female' mistakes). Her coming to and going from Neoptolemus' *oikos* are both represented as being under male supervision. The words

---

[138] Seidensticker (1995) 158. Cf. Loraux (1987) 28: 'It is true that "good" wives are not material for tragedy.'

[139] Pòrtulas (1988) 289.

and actions of both Menelaus and Orestes make us doubt whether their primary motives have much to do with her own good. The impression that she is not really in control is confirmed when Menelaus takes over the persecution of Andromache, succeeds, where Hermione had failed, in extorting her from the altar, and faces Peleus as the intending killer. We are encouraged to reflect on her 'male' criticisms of women in such a way that their extremism challenges not only her own purpose but also the underlying ideology which polices women sexually and socially.

Euripides has used Andromache's Iliadic past to provoke reflection on the victimization of women. As she tells Hector, Achilles had killed her father and seven brothers (*Il*. 6. 414–24); the opening words of her prologue in the *Andromache* recall her passage from Thebe to her married life in Troy which the Greeks destroyed. Made the unwilling mistress of her husband's killer's son, she endures the degradation of slavery, supported by hope for her own son. But the harrowing experience of the female captive is overshadowed in the play by the strains of domestic demands; these are explored in an interesting and thought-provoking way by making Andromache's main opponent a woman. Further, Hermione's concern with fertility and her emotional response to calamity do not merely pander to male stereotypes of female character. In this context, to claim that Greek tragedy works 'without challenging the traditional casting of social roles and the underlying conceptual assumptions'[140] of fifth-century society seems to underestimate its provocative relation to the tensions inherent in the female role both public and domestic.[141] The *Andromache* suggests the link between the Spartans' domestic misfortunes and their political interference; the link is made not only by the Greek hero Peleus but by a foreign female

[140] Seidensticker (1995) 167. Cf. Loraux (1987) 60: 'Tragedy certainly does transgress and mix things up—this is its rule, its nature—but never to the point of irrevocably overturning the civic order of values.'

[141] Beard (1991) 21–6 discusses the 'normative' images of women in vase-paintings, but also brings out the ability of visual images to subvert such stereotypes (pp. 26–30). This is an enlightening visual parallel to the literary disruptions of tragedy. The *Poetics*' handling of female characters and choruses and its 'lack of interest in the genre's ideological dimension' are well noted by Hall (1996b) 307 n. 23.

slave, whose moral and intellectual virtues 'explore ambiguous and often dangerous moral frontiers . . . [and] reveal in a positive sense important social and ethical alternatives'.[142]

A fascinating scholion tells us that ancient critics disliked the play since it portrayed 'women's suspicions about one another, their jealousies and insults and other things which are part of comedy' (γυναικῶν τε . . . ὑπονοίας κατ' ἀλλήλων καὶ ζήλους καὶ λοιδορίας καὶ ἄλλα ὅσα εἰς κωμωιδίαν συντελεῖ, Σ on 32). Women's jealousies could be handled in tragedy (for example, Clytemnestra and Cassandra, Deianeira and Iole), but on grounds of dignity the poets generally did not focus on women's λοιδορίαι ('insults'). Revealing as it is of tragic ὕψος ('sublimity'), the critics' judgement here is awry because it misses the play's questioning use of female experience. In the *Andromache* and other tragedies the predominantly male audience is challenged to extend its emotional sympathies to the experience of women, judging between them certainly, but also recognizing their right to be taken seriously.

The chapter began by applauding the view 'that at all costs the sterile opposition between feminism and misogyny should be avoided'.[143] Euripides was clearly fascinated by the special position of women that was possible in tragedy; their alternative viewpoint on the male world both of heroic myth and of his own society made fictional women valuable sources of tragic inquiry. Whether as witnesses, victims, or avengers of male violence, they can supply a significantly critical response from an atypical perspective. Their marginal status, often compounded by foreignness and slavery, enhances the impact of their moral and intellectual challenge to 'the dominant orderings of patriarchal society'.[144] If there is one feature which Euripides' work may be said to communicate most penetratingly in this area, it is to stress the distinctive tragic potential of women's constrained experience.

However, our appreciation of such distinctiveness needs to be carried through to the level of individual characters. In the *Troades*, for example, Cassandra, Hecuba, and Andromache all face the same bleak backdrop of Troy in ruins, but each of

---

[142] Foley (1996) 49–50.   [143] Loraux (1987) 62.
[144] Goldhill (1986) 115.

them interprets her situation and reacts to it in a unique way. The contrasting histories of Andromache and Hermione illustrate the many pressures that can affect the lives of women, from social conformity to the consequences of military conquest, and these pressures in turn reveal much about their male agents. Moreover, our sense of the movement and force of the *Andromache* depends in no small way on the individual responses of the female figures, whether murderous and self-deceptive, or heroic and moving.

7

Chorus

'You know, that's why you will always be a chorus-member; because
you don't do anything! I act, I take action, I make things happen!'

Woody Allen, *Mighty Aphrodite*

Recent work on the tragic chorus has stressed the plurality of
interpretative models available on the topic.[1] The richness of
modern debate contrasts with the brief treatment of the matter
by Aristotle in his *Poetics*.[2] The views of the latter, although so
summarily expressed, have influenced criticism of Euripidean
choral technique profoundly.[3] Indeed, Aristotle's disapproval
has arguably held back scholarly appreciation of the variety and
experimental power of Euripides' choruses.[4] This chapter
attempts to give an impression of the flexibility of the Euripidean chorus, and to show this quality at work in the
development and impact of a particular tragedy. As Pat Easterling has remarked, 'we have to be alive to the danger of trying
to arrive at an overall theory independent of the particular

---

[1] Gould (1996b) 217–19, reviewing the work of *inter alios* Vernant,
Winkler, Henrichs and Goldhill.

[2] The relevant passage runs: καὶ τὸν χορὸν δὲ ἕνα δεῖ ὑπολαβεῖν τῶν ὑποκριτῶν,
καὶ μόριον εἶναι τοῦ ὅλου καὶ συναγωνίζεσθαι μὴ ὥσπερ Εὐριπίδηι ἀλλ' ὥσπερ
Σοφοκλεῖ ('And one should handle the chorus as one of the actors, and it
should be a constituent part of the whole and should join in the action, not as
in Euripides, but as in Sophocles', 1456ª25–7).

[3] See Nordheider (1980) 7–11 for this tradition. One should add the parody
of Euripidean choral lyric at Ar. *Frogs* 1309–28, where, L. P. E. Parker (1997)
507 observes, 'Aristophanes is clearly not interested in imitating the archi-
tectonics of Euripidean lyric: he may even be insinuating that they do not
exist.' The regularity (that is, elevation) of Euripidean lyrics is argued for by
Silk (1996) 449 with n. 6.

[4] Despite the fact that ancient sources frequently record expressions of
praise for the beauty of his songs (both choral and monodic): cf. Satyrus, *Vita*
39. 19, Plut. *Nic*. 29. 2–3 (Kovacs (1994) 24, 122–4). The Plutarch passage is
especially notable for its claim that by the year 413 Euripides' lyrics were
famous not only in Sicily but also among the Caunians of south-eastern Caria.

context of each play'.[5] The most recent large-scale study of the subject concludes: 'Euripides uses the chorus in a free manner'.[6] The present chapter applies that study's analytic technique in greater detail to the lyrical structure of the *Andromache*, and seeks to relate the power of the poetry both to the 'rhetorical grounding'[7] of the chorus and to the wider issues and meaning of the play.

The *Andromache* is eminently suitable for this approach; in a drama which has long suffered critical disapproval, the choral songs have languished in even darker neglect. A salutary exception is Stinton's study of the first stasimon; yet even his praise is severely qualified: 'It is among the finest of Euripides' lyrics, a welcome oasis in an indifferent play.'[8] Lattimore writes: 'Against the frigid unpleasantness of the action in *Andromache* is placed a rather appetizing impression of the goddesses appearing before Paris to be judged.'[9] This chapter aspires to indicate how choral contributions function much more provocatively than is often appreciated, not merely as reflections of events, or reactions to them, but with the capacity and intent of modifying our interpretation of the surrounding 'action'.[10]

This is not to accord the chorus a privileged point of view: their response is 'no more protected from fallibility than any other'.[11] They are part of the play in the very strongest sense: the tragic fiction encompasses them (and they are almost always present on stage).[12] They do not stand outside the play, delivering a commentary from some more objective, authoritative position.[13] Indeed, the very fact that the chorus can be

[5] Easterling (1987) 26.

[6] Hose (1990–1) ii. 413.

[7] Goldhill (1996) 247, who glosses Gould's 'social and political rooting' as 'the *place from where a chorus speaks*'.

[8] Stinton (1990) 26–34 (quotation from p. 34).

[9] Lattimore (1958) 119.

[10] Rode (1971) 109 is too simplistic when he states of all choral odes of Euripides between 438 and 420: 'These songs bring no development of thought or contrast with the action; they are not only dependent, but also entirely subordinate to the situation.'

[11] Gould (1996b) 231.

[12] On the five (dramatically motivated) occasions when the chorus leave the orchestra during the play, see Rehm (1994) 88 with n. 17, Burian (1997) 199.

[13] Contrast the distancing effect of the comic parabasis, where the poet can

wrong (misunderstanding or simplifying the situation, say, or being insensitive to a character's dilemma) has an expressive force of its own. In Sophocles' *Antigone*, for example, the chorus's equation of the laws of the city with those of the gods, and their insistence that the temporal ruler must be obeyed (cf. *Ant.* 853–6, 872–5), magnify Antigone's heroic isolation and sharpen our sense of her different hierarchy of moral obligations.

We are continually reminded in tragedy that, despite their use of the mythical tradition in their songs to point parallels or retrace the causative history of the story, the chorus are ignorant of the future. They are in a sense spectators, an internal audience whose response the theatre audience can use as a correlative for its own.[14] But it is, as it were, a subjective correlative: it is tied to the chorus's identity, their particular limitations and preconceptions. Importantly, their presentation and its effects shift from song to song.[15] That is why we must attend above all to the specific circumstances of each play, tracing the chorus's role in (and not mere response to) the action as a dynamic part of that distinct fictional world and its articulation.[16]

The chorus was in many respects the 'most open field of address his audience through the chorus. Gould (1996b) 217 remarks on the 'worn-out and never very fruitful notions of "the ideal spectator" and "the poet's voice"'. Winnington-Ingram (1980) 200 expresses the point well: 'We must always seek—and shall always find—a meaning and a coherence of thought which belongs to the Chorus in its own dramatic entity.'

[14] For an excellent discussion of the chorus as 'a group of "built-in" witnesses', see Easterling (1997a) 163–5.

[15] See further Thiel (1993) 441–56 ('The Chorus as Dramatic Character'). Bacon (1995) 21 n. 3 gives an excellent summary of some major twentieth-century views of the chorus as actor. Dale (1969) 210 is too sweeping when she states that the chorus's 'anonymous collectivity tended to push it away from the centre, where things happened'. Easterling (1987) 26 is right to insist that 'choruses, like individuals, are remarkably chameleon-like, changing according to the dynamics of each particular play'. The multifarious functions of choral song itself (encomium, threnos, prayer, hymn, etc.) are stressed by Calame (1995), esp. 148.

[16] The dynamic role of the chorus is cogently demonstrated by Wiles (1997) in terms of of stage-space (p. 63): 'The notion that the actors performed (principally) on a stage whilst the chorus performed (principally) in the *orchêstra* is [an] important twentieth-century chimaera', which obscures (p. 65) 'the complex and shifting relationship between actors and chorus'.

choice'[17] in the construction of the tragic fiction; Euripides' choice of choral identity and personality is always tuned to the larger framework of the play. The multiplicity of choral identity and experience in Euripides' plays is evident; yet one is also struck by his no less remarkable preference for female choruses.[18] Of seventeen tragic choruses (excluding *Rhesus*) fourteen are female.[19] Frequently their marginal status and their impotence to change events are emphasized by their being slaves or foreigners (or both).[20] Gould has well observed that most of Euripides' plays also have a female protagonist, and this double female perspective produces a peculiarly critical view of the male heroic world which forms the fictional background to the action.[21]

In the *Andromache*, as in *Medea*, the chorus are local women, whose very rootedness underlines the displacement and isolation of the foreign woman protagonist.[22] In both plays the bond of womanhood partially bridges the racial divide.[23] This is

[17] Gould (1996b) 229.

[18] A preference perhaps shared by Aeschylus, but not by Sophocles. The numerical data (embracing lost plays too) are collated and examined by Castellani (1989) 15 nn. 4 and 5.

[19] The preponderance also holds true of the fragmentary or lost plays (whose chorus's sex is known or reasonably conjectured): see Castellani (1989) 16 n. 8.

[20] Cf. Easterling (1987) 23 with n. 30. As Griffin (1998) 42–3 remarks, scholars who regard the tragic chorus as a (somehow exemplary) micro-community of citizens seem blind to the actual constitution of the choruses. Similarly, while it would be unwise to deny the importance of *choreia* as an educational institution in which everyone might participate (cf. West (1992) 14–21), this is very far from making it an 'ideological performance' (Goldhill (1996) 251). On the place of the tragic chorus within the 'broad and ancient current of Greek choral traditions', see Taplin and Wilson (1993) 178.

[21] Gould (1996b) 222.

[22] Medea in fact points out the contrast to the chorus of Corinthian women in the hope of securing their collaboration in her revenge: ἀλλ' οὐ γὰρ αὐτὸς πρὸς σὲ κἄμ' ἥκει λόγος ('But the same story does not apply to you and to me', *Med.* 252). In the *Electra* the chorus's local concerns (proclaiming a sacrifice to Hera (167–74), which the distraught Electra refuses to attend) emphasize the heroine's marginalization from her native community. The motif of swearing the chorus to secrecy (*Med.*, *Hipp.*) or including them as conspirators (*Her.*, *El.*, *IT*, *Hel.*, *Or.*, *Bacch.*) binds them closely to the dramatic action and heightens suspense, and allows for one type of dramatic irony as a result of their superior knowledge.

[23] Cf. *IT* 1061–2 (Iphigenia): γυναῖκές ἐσμεν, φιλόφρον ἀλλήλαις γένος, |

more surprising in the *Andromache*, since 'the protagonist is of enemy race'.[24] The choice of Phthian women (as opposed to non-Greek fellow-slaves of Andromache, as in *Hec.* and *Tro.*)[25] rules out the emotional unity of protagonist and companions united in catastrophe, but produces a more concentrated pathos in the audacity and solitary heroism of Andromache.

In the *Andromache* the response of the audience to the suppliant's prologue is heightened by the sympathetic yet realistic advice of the *parodos*. We see that the chorus's role is, as often, 'not to do and suffer, but to comment, sympathise, support or disapprove'.[26] The chorus enter immediately after Andromache's elegiac lament,[27] and the opening hexameter of their dactylo-iambic song smoothes the transition from Andromache's elegiacs to their view of events.[28] The lament's Doric alpha is a regular feature of tragic lyric but its primary effect here is to distinguish these dactyls from the epic tradition and to add to the delightful novelty. Andromache's lament

σώιζειν τε κοινὰ πράγματ' ἀσφαλέστατα ('We are women, a race well-disposed to one another, and most certain to safeguard our common interests'), *Hel.* 327–9 (Chorus): . . . γυναῖκα γὰρ δὴ συμπονεῖν γυναικὶ χρή ('for woman should work together with woman').

[24] Mossman (1995) 70 n. 4. However, the chorus of the *Medea* is surprisingly willing to go along with the murder of their king and his daughter; it is the infanticide that shocks them (*Med.* 811 ff.).

[25] Contrast also *IT* and *Hel.*, where the fellow-Greek captive chorus enhances the heroine's longing for Greece in a foreign land. By an oversight, de Romilly (1995) 36 says that the chorus of the *Andromache* consists of 'young Trojan women, captives like herself'.

[26] Easterling (1977) 178.

[27] *Andr.* belongs to a group of six Euripidean plays (with four of Sophocles) in which there is 'no anapaestic opening or corresponding formal prelude' to the *parodos* (Pickard-Cambridge (1968) 243). *Med.*, *El.*, *IT.*, and *Hel.* link the entry of the chorus to the prologue by the use of lyric exchange. The *parodos* messenger-speech of *Hec.* is unique: see Mossman (1995) 70–5.

[28] On the metrical unity of the *Andromache*, see Fraenkel (1964) 213–14. Webster (1967) 120–1 well observes how the dactylo-epitrite base of the first, third, and fourth stasima relates 'emotionally and thematically as well as metrically' to the elegiac lament of Andromache and to the first part of Peleus' lament. Cole (1988) 209–10 makes the interesting suggestion that the elegiacs 'may be less a hearkening back to some earlier tradition of ritual laments . . . than an initial experiment, subsequently abandoned, in the innovative use of dactylo-anapaestic that is to become more and more conspicuous in Euripidean lyric'. Or, of course, they may be neither an 'experiment' nor 'nostalgia', but simply a one-off surprise musical feature.

approaches the emotional tension of actor's monody, while the metre and diction, recalling hexameter epic, are an appropriate vehicle for her as a character with a famous lament in the *Iliad*, and for her review of the Trojan War and the implacable continuity of disaster.

As soon as the chorus enter, they reveal their identity as Phthians.[29] More remarkably, they express their exceptional sympathy for the foreign captive: Φθιὰς ὅμως ἔμολον ποτὶ σὰν Ἀσιήτιδα γένναν ('Though I am *Phthian*, I have come to you who are of *Asian* stock', 119). There is careful patterning with the corresponding line of the antistrophe, δεσπόταις ἁμιλλᾶι | Ἰλιὰς οὖσα κόρα Λακεδαίμονος ἐγγενέταισιν; ('Do you contend with your masters, a *Trojan* girl against people born in *Sparta*?', 127–8), which also articulates the opposition of nationalities, and stresses Andromache's temerity in opposing superior Spartan force.[30] They state the reason for their entrance: εἴ τί σοι δυναίμαν | ἄκος τῶν δυσλύτων πόνων τεμεῖν ('in the hope that I might be able to contrive a cure for your difficult troubles', 120–1). The Homeric conditional instead of a purpose clause has here a tentative quality, and suggests the difficulty of their project. The cure (ἄκος)[31] they seek is for troubles (122–5),

> οἵ σε καὶ Ἑρμιόναν ἔριδι στυγερᾶι συνέκλῃσαν,
> τλᾶμον, ἀμφὶ λέκτρων
> διδύμων, ἐπίκοινον ἔχουσαν
> ἄνδρα, παῖδ' Ἀχιλλέως.[32]

which have locked you and Hermione in a hateful struggle, poor woman, over two beds, since you have a husband in common, the son of Achilles.

---

[29] On prompt choral self-description in the *parodos*, see Lefkowitz (1991) 22–3; Anzai (1994) 150 (Appendix D) lists first-person references in the *parodoi* of tragedy. Stinton (1990) 253–4 discusses the differences between the 'I' of choral lyric and the songs of tragedy.

[30] Tragic choruses often counsel submission to the ruling authorities or customs, and so highlight the protagonist's very different choices: e.g. Soph. *El.* 219–20: τάδε—τοῖς δυνατοῖς | οὐκ ἐριστά—τλᾶθι ('You cannot contend with those in power—so put up with these things!').

[31] For the metaphor, see Breitenbach (1934) 135, who gives a full list of metaphorical expressions in Euripidean lyric (pp. 132–61).

[32] Diggle (1994) 204–8 explains his emendation of ἐοῦσαν | ἀμφὶ (124–5).

Thus the first strophe touches on some of the major themes and characters of the play: the conflict of national interests, the harsh distress of sexual jealousy (ἔριδι στυγερᾶι 122, 'hateful struggle', an epicism, underlined by the dactylic hexameter), and the unusual conflict of two women over one man. The vocative τλᾶμον ('poor woman', 123) marks their sympathy.[33] The two women are linked by grammatical co-ordination (σε καὶ Ἑρμιόναν 122, 'you and Hermione'), and the cause of their struggle is climactically placed at the end of the strophe: παῖδ' Ἀχιλλέως ('the son of Achilles', 125). The conflict itself is ἀμφὶ λέκτρων | διδύμων ('over two beds [or 'sexual relatioships']', 123–4), a striking phrase which sets Andromache's enforced union with Neoptolemus on a par with that of Hermione's marriage, while the unusual doubling of the relationship presages jealousy and disaffection.

In the antistrophe the tone changes from sympathy to mild reproach. The chorus are urgent and direct in their advice: γνῶθι τύχαν, λόγισαι τὸ παρὸν κακὸν εἰς ὅπερ ἥκεις ('Realize your fate, consider the present evil into which you have come', 126; the Delphic tone is enhanced by the hexameter, the metre regularly used for oracles). They are also harshly realistic. Andromache's subjection to new masters is repeated in parallel phrases of fruitless conflict: δεσπόταις ἁμιλλᾶι ('it is with your masters that you are contending', 126) ~ δεσποτᾶν ἀνάγκαις ('because of constraints from your masters', 132). The ring composition and the repeated vocabulary of fate, power, and necessity highlight the hopelessness of Andromache's situation. She must recognize the unstoppable momentum of a greater force (133–4):

τὸ κρατοῦν δέ σ' ἔπεισι· τί μόχθον
οὐδὲν οὖσα μοχθεῖς;

---

[33] Cf. Diggle (1994) 208 n. 30: 'Stevens . . . claims that "it is odd that the Chorus should commiserate with her for having to share N. with his lawful wife." I do not find it at all odd.' Compare the mixture of sympathy and advice on submission given to Cassandra by the Argive elders: ἐγὼ δ', ἐποικτίρω γάρ, οὐ θυμώσομαι· | ἴθ', ὦ τάλαινα, τόνδ' ἐρημώσας ὄχον· | εἴκουσ' ἀνάγκηι τῆιδε καίνισον ζυγόν ('I shall not be angry, for I pity her. Come, miserable woman, leave this chariot; yielding to this necessity, try on your new yoke', *Ag.* 1069–71).

Power will come upon you; why are you who are nothing toiling in vain?

The neuter participle construction (τὸ κρατοῦν 133, 'power'), and the pessimistic reflection on might, feel markedly Thucydidean. The future tense of ἔπεισι ('will come upon', 133) is emphatic and expresses the chorus's certainty. Andromache, a mere 'nothing', is placed at the centre of a figure (μόχθον . . . μοχθεῖς 133–4, 'you toil a toil') which bluntly conveys the futility of her resistance.

The shorter lyrical structure of the second strophic pair accompanies an increase of urgency, pace, and emotional tension.[34] It begins with imperatives: ἀλλ' ἴθι λεῖπε θεᾶς Νηρῃίδος ἀγλαὸν ἕδραν ('But come, leave the shining shrine of the Nereid goddess', 135). Again there is an insistence on awareness (γνῶθι 136, 'realize') of altered circumstances, while the accumulation of words expressing foreignness and servility make the point most emphatic: γνῶθι δ' οὖσ' ἐπὶ ξένας | δμωὶς ἀπ' ἀλλοτρίας | πόλεος ('and realize that you are a *slave-woman* from a *hostile* city, and in a *foreign* country', 136–8). The enjambment of ἔνθ' οὐ φίλων τιν' εἰσορᾷς | σῶν ('where you can see none of your friends', 138–9) marks the total isolation of Andromache.[35]

The chorus's reproaches suddenly modulate to intense sympathy; they address her as ὦ δυστυχεστάτα, | ⟨ὦ⟩ παντάλαινα νύμφα ('O most unfortunate, O utterly miserable wife', 139–40). By addressing Andromache as νύμφα ('wife', 140), the chorus recall her marriage to Hector.[36] The dissolution of her marriage

---

[34] The impact of the alternating rhythms and dance movements of the tragic chorus remains elusive. We can be sure, however, that their gestures were appropriate to the content of the song, while the musical accompaniment communicated a similarly suitable 'range of feeling or action' (Pickard-Cambridge (1968) 259). Plato's conservatism points to the power of the various modes and rhythms: cf. esp. *Rep.* 424c, with West (1992) 246 ff. Euripides is said to have introduced the 'soft' chromatic genus into tragedy: see Kovacs (1994) 50. Wiles (1997) 87–113 offers an illuminating discussion of mimetic dance and choreography. Especially interesting is his discussion of the 'infinitely transformable space established primarily in the dance sequences' (p. 119).

[35] Talthybius advises Andromache to give up Astyanax for slaughter in similar terms: ἔχεις γὰρ ἀλκὴν οὐδαμῆι ('For you have no protection at all', *Tro.* 729).

[36] The meaning 'bride' is more common than 'young woman' (see LSJ).

by killing has resulted in a forced and false union to Neoptolemus, so that she is, in two different but mutually compacting respects, an 'utterly miserable wife'.

Finally, the chorus openly declare their pity for Andromache's plight (141–2):

> οἰκτροτάτα γὰρ ἔμοιγ' ἔμολες, γύναι Ἰλιάς, οἴκους
> δεσποτᾶν ἐμῶν·

Most pitiful in my eyes at any rate was your coming, woman of Troy, to the house of my masters.

The revelation is surprising: γύναι Ἰλιάς ('woman of Troy', 141) emphasizes their unexpected sympathy for a member of an enemy ethnic group. But while they offer comfort, the particle γε ('at any rate', 141) hints that their emotion will not be shared by others. The closing words of the *parodos* make clear both the sincerity of their feelings (note the parenthesis and the emphatic participial construction) and the very different viewpoint of Hermione (142–6):

> φόβωι δ'
> ἡσυχίαν ἄγομεν
> (τὸ δὲ σὸν οἴκτωι φέρουσα τυγχάνω)
> μὴ παῖς τᾶς Διὸς κόρας
> σοί μ' εὖ φρονοῦσαν εἰδῆι.

But we keep quiet through fear (though I really do pity your plight), lest the daughter of Zeus' child should know that I wish you well.

Hermione is thus negatively characterized by the chorus just before her unannounced entrance.[37] It is a subtle preparation, which also, by contrasting the chorus's timidity with the defiance that Andromache shows in the next scene, intensifies the persecuted woman's heroism and transcendence.

The brief conciliatory contribution of the chorus in the first episode (232–3) has little impact on the adamantly opposed positions of the antagonists. Their attempt to restrain is typical

---

[37] Cf. Kumaniecki (1930) 36: 'Thus the parodos has the same spirit as the prologue: the misery of the innocent Andromache is touched upon, and the hybris of Hermione.' For the thought, compare the old woman's assurance to Menelaus, εὔνους γάρ εἰμ' Ἕλλησιν, οὐχ ὅσον πικροὺς | λόγους ἔδωκα δεσπότην φοβουμένη ('I am in fact well-disposed to Greeks, but I spoke bitter words in fear of my mistress', *Hel.* 481–2).

of choral interjections within *agones*,[38] which are rarely very profound (cf. 642–4), but always clear and important for the chorus's relationship to the speakers. Even when one character is justified in the use of charged language, as Andromache surely is in her *agon* with Menelaus, the chorus-leader deplores speech which breaks conservative convention: ἄγαν ἔλεξας ὡς γυνὴ πρὸς ἄρσενας | καί σου τὸ σῶφρον ἐξετόξευσεν φρενός ('You have spoken too freely as a woman to men, and restraint has shot away from your mind', 364–5).[39] Yet the thought has a specific dramatic function: placed between Andromache's reasoned indictment of Menelaus' claim to glory and his own self-righteous reply, the chorus-leader's conventional remark is called into question. The effect of this rupture extends in both directions; Andromache's heroic defence is enhanced, while Menelaus' claim to τὸ σῶφρον ('restraint') is made to appear all the more dubious. In the face of Hermione's speech of intemperate hostility the chorus-leader offers guarded and generalized criticism: ἐπίφθονόν τι χρῆμα θηλείας φρενὸς | καὶ ξυγγάμοισι δυσμενὲς μάλιστ' ἀεί ('A jealous thing is a woman's mind and always very hostile to rivals in her marriage', 181–2). This is hardly rebellious, but the chorus favour Andromache (πείθου τῇδε συμβῆναι λόγοις 233, 'Be persuaded to come to terms with her'), and their response to the competing arguments of the embattled women in turn influences our own attitude to them.

The first stasimon reflects on the key themes of the first episode and expands them by mythical illustration. Stevens's comment (on 274–308), 'This song has no direct relevance to the dramatic situation', is mistaken.[40] The very opposite is the case: 'this ode has specific and carefully constructed links to the drama; it does more than provide background for the present crisis'.[41] The motif of feminine rivalry and destructive conflict which has generated the action thus far is not left to work in isolation. The play's development from the aftermath of the

[38] Cf. Stevens (1971) 178 on 691–2; 'The Chorus leader's attempt at peace-making is regular, conventional, and, as usual, ignored by both contestants.'

[39] Page posited a lacuna after 364; see Diggle's apparatus. However, Kamerbeek's reading of ἐξετόξευσεν as intransitive ('has fled/shot away') is acceptable: see Stevens (1971) 141.

[40] Stevens (1971) 127.

[41] Halleran (1985) 61.

Trojan War is linked in the first strophe to the war's distant cause, the Judgement of Paris (a mythical paradigm of female competition for the attentions of one man); in the second strophe the temporal continuity is pushed yet further back to the events surrounding Paris' inauspicious birth.[42] Past and present cohere in a lyric evocation of human vulnerability, false beauty, and divine deception.

The first strophe and antistrophe present in pictorial detail the rural home of Paris, and stress his solitude: βοτῆρά τ' ἀμφὶ μονότροπον νεανίαν | ἔρημόν θ' ἑστιοῦχον αὐλάν ('to the solitary young shepherd and his lonely hearth and dwelling', 281–2).[43] The idyllic innocence of the scene contrasts with the frenzy and slaughter that grips Troy in the second strophic pair.[44] The ode's first words ἦ μεγάλων ἀχέων ἄρ' ὑπῆρξεν ('Great were the sorrows he began') echo the opening of Andromache's lament (103 ff.). Both stress that disaster began long ago with Paris; Andromache blames the beautiful Helen, while the chorus go further back to the three lovely goddesses. The opening thus sets a tone of disaster which clouds the rustic setting. The motif of beauty (cf. καλλιζύγες 278, 'beautifully-yoked'), which has played a part in the previous mortal *agon* (cf. 207–8), is given chilling expression in the epicizing ἔριδι στυγερᾶι κεκορυθμένον εὐμορφίας ('equipped for the hateful contest of beauty', 279). The chorus use the same words of the goddesses' and the human protagonists' struggle (ἔριδι στυγερᾶι 122 ~ 279, 'hateful contest'). Yet the differences between the two 'beauty contests' are striking. Whereas the three goddesses are all eager to win, and offer massive bribes to do so (cf. *Tro.* 925–31), the contest

---

[42] Cf. Hose (1990–1) ii. 103 on the ἀρχὴ κακῶν ('beginning of evils') technique of the ode.

[43] Pearson (1917) ii. 157 on Soph. fr. 511 τριολύμπιον ἄρμα ('team of three Olympians', quoted by Σ *Andr.* 277) remarks: 'the contrast between the majesty of the goddesses and the rustic seclusion of Paris was especially attractive to Euripides, who often recurs to the theme'. So *Tro.* 924 ff., *Hec.* 644–6, *Hel.* 357, *IA* 573 ff., etc. But as Barlow (1971) 137 n. 12 notes, 'The austere loneliness of Paris in *Andromache* is a new feature [of the Judgement scene].' The solitary Paris excludes the myth of Oenone, in which Paris is already married when he sets out for Sparta, and his wife's assistance comes tragically too late to cure him from his death-wound.

[44] As Cropp (1988) 98 notes of the *Electra* prologue, 'The rustic "scenery" has ethical significance.'

between Hermione and Andromache is only seen as such by the former. Andromache was Neoptolemus' concubine against her own will (36–8). Hermione's allegation of a plot to supplant her is pure fantasy. None the less the isolation of Paris and his presentation as the innocent victim of a divine conflict over beauty is a significant parallel to the situation of Andromache, who is herself both innocent and defenceless.

The antistrophe presents the scene, character, and consequences of the contest in greater detail. The language of the chorus is elaborately descriptive (284–6):[45]

> ταὶ δ' ἐπεὶ ὑλόκομον νάπος ἤλυθον οὐρειᾶν
> πιδάκων νίψαν αἰ-
> γλᾶντα σώματα ῥοαῖς

When they came to the leafy vale, they washed their shining bodies in the flowing waters of mountain springs.

The juxtaposition of humble mortal labour and divine ease heightens our sense of the young man's vulnerability. What for Aphrodite is a victory of sweet-sounding words (τερπνοῖς μὲν ἀκοῦσαι 290, 'delightful to hear')[46] is in human terms the ruin of a city and its people: πικρὰν δὲ σύγχυσιν βίου Φρυγῶν πόλει | ταλαίναι περγάμοις τε Τροίας ('but a bitter destruction of life for

---

[45] Cf. Stinton (1990) 27: 'The treatment is pictorial; each section forms a separate panel in which a scene is more or less visually realized.' This is a feature shared by all the Euripidean descriptions of the episode: cf. Collard (1991) 164 on *Hec.* 629–57: 'The stasimon is intensely pictorial and its arrangement striking.' Rawson (1972) 164 notes: 'In Euripidean language colour patterns and contrasts are clearest in lyric passages.' For the myth of the Judgement in Greek art, see Raab (1972), Carpenter (1991) 197–8. The description of the goddesses bathing adds texture and colour: ὑλόκομος ('leafy') and αἰγλᾶντα ('shining') connote the rustic ease of the setting and the divine radiance of the figures in the landscape; cf. *IA* 182–4, *Hel.* 676–8. The dangers of glimpsing immortal nakedness are handled in Callimachus' fifth *Hymn*, where Aphrodite's vanity is disparaged (13–32). Sophocles wrote a satyr-play called *The Judgement*, where Aphrodite appeared 'anointed with myrrh and looking at herself in a mirror' (Lloyd-Jones (1996) 194–5).

[46] The repetition of λόγων ~ λόγοις ('words . . . words', 288–9) suggests an empty contest based on flattery of the judge rather than the virtues of the competitors (the scholia to 288 speak of the goddesses ἐριστικοῖς λόγοις διαμαχόμεναι πρὸς ἀλλήλας, 'fighting against one another with captious words'). This foreshadows the empty, amoral rhetoric of Menelaus.

the miserable city of the Phrygians and the citadel of Troy',
291–2; cf. *Hec.* 644–9, *IA* 587–9).[47]

Stinton writes: 'That the ἀρχή has no dramatic significance is
shown by the second strophe, which begins with a different
one.'[48] This is too brusque a rejection of a very subtle and
beautiful temporal movement. As often in lyrics with two
strophes, the second moves to an earlier episode in the causal
chain of the myth, whose distant outcome is the basis for the
play's action.[49] The first strophic pair ended with a brief but
powerful intimation of the disaster facing Troy. Now the
second begins with the earlier cause of that disaster, the birth
of Paris and Cassandra's prophecy that the child would destroy
Troy unless killed first. The tale of Hecuba's dream underlies
the description, though here Euripides chooses to focus on
Cassandra's role as interpreter: she is a potent symbol of Troy's
destruction, and the curse which she labours under (not to be
believed when she prophesies, cf. 299–300) reinforces the idea
of the gods' hostility to Troy. More specifically, it recalls the
vengeful Apollo who punished her, in preparation for his
retaliation against Neoptolemus later in the play (compare
παρὰ θεσπεσίωι δάφναι 296, 'beside the prophetic laurel', with
1115, where Orestes and his men hide themselves δάφνηι
σκιασθείς, 'shaded by laurel').

In Euripides' *Alexandros* of 415 Cassandra alone sees the
disaster which will result from sparing the child.[50] In the first
stasimon of the *Andromache* we are given a Greek view on the
Trojan scene, not untouched by pity, and directed by grief for
the mutual carnage of the war. The deaths could have been
averted by the death of the child (293–4):[51]

---

[47] The Chigi Vase (*c*.650 BC, Rome, Villa Giulia 22679) shows the Judgement scene with Hermes, the three goddesses, and Paris all present, as well as
a lion hunt in the background; Osborne (1996) 164 comments, 'Judging
between exotic goddesses, like hunting exotic animals, is a high-risk matter.'

[48] Stinton (1990) 27. One might compare the dense accumulation of ἀρχή
('beginning') terms, working at different levels, which Herodotus deploys,
creating the impression of manifold historical causation; cf. Derow (1994)
74–9.

[49] A further stage appears in the background to Troy's destruction: Helen
came with Paris (103), the Judgement of Paris (274), the birth of Paris (293).

[50] See Scodel (1980) 35–40. Cf. Pind. *Pae.* 8a. 30–3, where Cassandra
relates Hecuba's correct interpretation of her dream.

[51] Cf. Jouan (1966) 114, Wilamowitz (1921) 550. West (1980) 11–12 sees

εἰ γὰρ ὑπὲρ κεφαλὰν ἔβαλεν κακὸν
ἁ τεκοῦσά νιν μόρον
πρὶν Ἰδαῖον κατοικίσαι λέπας

If only his mother had thrown him over her head to an evil death
before he settled on the ridge of Ida.

The unfulfilled wish is profoundly pathetic in the mouths of
Greek women who have suffered from its consequences. The
failed infanticide of Paris contrasts sharply with the threat to
Andromache's children (Astyanax is already dead, another is
being hunted down).[52] The scene evokes the war's many
doomed children.[53] The chorus's question (299–300):

τίν' οὐκ ἐπῆλθε, ποῖον οὐκ ἐλίσσετο
δαμογερόντων βρέφος φονεύειν;

Whom did she [Cassandra] not approach, which elder did she not beg
to murder the baby?

vividly focuses on Troy as the perceiving subject at the fatal
moment of indecision. The Trojan elders (δημογέροντες, the
word is Homeric)[54] fail to kill the child, but their humanity
destroys their city.[55]

In the *Troades* Cassandra argues with deranged, sophistic
logic that the Trojans are the true victors of the war (365–405):
she envisions the loss of family and homeland, and the
deprivation of proper burial rites, undergone by the Greeks.
The Phthian chorus of the *Andromache* present a more comprehensive picture of suffering that embraces both Greek and
Trojan. The anguish of the Trojans is concentrated in the

the codd. πάριν ('Paris') as a gloss on νιν ('him'), and would prefer simply γυνά
('woman') in place of μόρον ('death'), corresponding to γύναι ('woman') in the
antistrophe (302).

[52] Halleran (1985) 62: 'This juxtaposition of image and action accentuates
the confusion, reversals and injustices that Troy and its aftermath bring.' Cf.
Anacr. fr. 347 *PMG*: ὡς ἂν εὖ πάθοιμι, μῆτερ, | εἴ μ' ἀμείλιχον φέρουσα | πόντον
ἐσβάλοις θυίοντα | πορφυρέοισι κύμασι ('How happy I would be, mother, if you
would carry and throw me into the ungentle sea that rages with its dark
waves').

[53] For the fate of children at a sack, cf. *Sept.* 348–50.

[54] Cf. Garner (1990) 133.

[55] Paris is called the λώβα ('ruin'/'destruction', 298) of his city. Mossman
(1995) 85 notes that it is a strong word. Its use to describe a child is
particularly sinister.

enslavement of its women (ζυγὸν . . . | δούλιον 301–2, 'the yoke of slavery'), and specifically of Andromache, whom the chorus directly address (302). As at the close of the second, third, and fourth stasima (492–3, Hermione; 790 ff., Peleus; 1041 f., Andromache), the chorus relate the ode to a figure in the action who operates as a focus for the song's themes.[56] Here it is particularly poignant that 'this song of the city's destruction is performed around one of its victims'.[57]

The antistrophe is tied closely to what has gone before as a negative hypothesis—οὔτ' ἂν ἐπ' Ἰλιάσι ζυγὸν ἤλυθε | δούλιον ('The yoke of slavery would not have come upon the women of Troy', 301–2)—that is, if Hecuba had listened to Cassandra's prophecy. The plight of Andromache, reduced from royal freedom to slavery in an enemy country (τυράννων ἔσχες ἂν δόμων ἕδρας 303, 'you would have dwelt in a royal house'), is placed on the same level, remarkably, as the bereavement of the Greek women who sing the ode (note the continuity of structure with ἄν, 304–8):

παρέλυσε δ' ἂν Ἑλλάδος ἀλγεινοὺς
†μόχθους οὓς ἀμφὶ Τροίαν†
δεκέτεις ἀλάληντο νέοι λόγχαις,
λέχη τ' ἔρημ' ἂν οὔποτ' ἐξελείπετο
καὶ τεκέων ὀρφανοὶ γέροντες.

And it [the killing of Paris] would have released Greece from the painful †toils in which around Troy† the young men wandered in arms for ten years; marriage-beds would never have been left abandoned and old men bereft of their children.

The inevitability of suffering for both sides is presented explicitly, and Euripides' interest in the 'community of feeling . . . that may grow up between enemies during a long war' recalls the closing cadences of the *Iliad*.[58] By contrast with the *Iliad*, however, the Greek victory emerges here as a Pyrrhic one:[59] the Greek fighters 'wandered for ten years' (306), hardly a rousing martial image.[60] The results of the war which the

[56] For the technique in choral lyric, see Kranz (1933) 197, 206 ff.
[57] Rehm (1988) 303.
[58] Mossman (1995) 28–9.
[59] Of course, there is also the unusual viewpoint of Achilles: cf. *Il.* 9. 337 ff., 24. 540 ff.
[60] Cf. Murray (1946) 65 on the similar tenor of the *Troades* prologue: 'The

chorus present are the waste of youth, the deaths of husbands and sons (307–8; cf. Aesch. *Ag.* 427 ff.). The bereaved old men are represented by Peleus, who since the *Iliad* had been the prototype of the bereaved father, abandoned to the mercy of his enemies (*Il.* 24. 486–9).[61] In the *Andromache* the old man also loses his grandson, and barely rescues his great-grandson from murder.

The song thus ends on a note of suffering which embraces both the victorious and the defeated; it deplores the (not so different) war experience of both sides, which continues to resonate throughout the play. The fall of Troy meant also the death of the finest Greeks and the demoralization of the troops. The ode thus prepares for a negative reaction to the self-interested triumphalism of Menelaus (who promptly enters; the effect is not unlike that at the end of the *parodos*, though less directly expressed).[62] The 'ballast of memory'[63] that the chorus provide recognizes the unmerited suffering of the Trojans; and in so doing it strengthens our sympathy for the suppliant Andromache.

The second episode presents the *agon* of Andromache and Menelaus, during which the Spartan's threats to the life of her child force Andromache from sanctuary. Andromache's despair and self-sacrifice excite the chorus-leader's pity for the foreign slave: ᾤκτιρ' ἀκούσασ'· οἰκτρὰ γὰρ τὰ δυστυχῆ | βροτοῖς ἅπασι, κἂν θυραῖος ὢν κυρῆι ('Her words make me feel pity, since misfortunes are pitiable for all mortals, even if the sufferer is a stranger', 421–2). Their sympathy marks Andromache's superior arguments, the injustice of her oppression, and the treachery of Menelaus. But it shows the chorus's powerlessness, and Menelaus' ruthlessness, that he ignores them completely and has his men seize Andromache (425–6). As she and her son are

unburied corpses lie polluting the air; and the conquering soldiers, home-sick and uneasy, they know not why, roam to and fro waiting for a wind that will take them away from the country they have made horrible.' ἀλάομαι ('I wander') has connotations of perplexity and banishment (LSJ) that are appropriate to the mental and physical deprivations of the Greeks; cf. Aesch. *Ag.* 555 ff.

[61] Cf. *Il.* 24. 503–4, 19. 334–7, *Od.* 11. 494–505.

[62] *Ag.* 367 ff. and 681 ff. create a similar but more complex prelude to the entry of the victorious Agamemnon.

[63] Gould (1996b) 225.

led into the palace, the chorus deliver an ode whose dramatic
relevance is striking, though this has often been overlooked in
favour of emphasis on the song's structure (that of a sententious priamel).[64] Its four strophic units are artfully arranged:
the first states the thesis (one wife is best); the second and third
support and illustrate this from other areas of life; and the final
antistrophe applies the thought to the action of the play
(Hermione's attempt to wipe out her rival).

The ode opens with a rejection of 'shared beds' (464–7):

> οὐδέποτε δίδυμα λέκτρ' ἐπαινέσω βροτῶν
> οὐδ' ἀμφιμάτορας κόρους,
> †ἔριδας† οἴκων δυσμενεῖς τε λύπας·

I shall never praise mortals having two bed-partners, or sons by
different mothers, which cause †strife† and bitter hostility in the
house.

The forceful first-person future (οὐδέποτε . . . ἐπαινέσω 465, 'I
shall never praise') plays up their personal reaction to the crisis
in the royal house (compare μοι 469, 'my [husband]').[65] They
take up the theme of the *parodos* (ἀμφὶ λέκτρων | διδύμων 123–4,
'about two sexual relationships'), and again regret the distress
which follows domestic ἔρις ('strife', 467; cf. 122, 279, 490).[66]
Despite the textual problems of 469–70, concentration on the
husband's choice (to remain content with one sexual partner)
fits the action of the play.[67]

The rare ἀμφιμήτορες (466) is glossed by Stevens as 'sons of
the same father by different mothers, i.e. half-brothers'. He

---

[64] Stevens (1971) 151 cogently rejects Aldrich's theory of the transposition
of this stasimon with the first. If we keep the traditional order, there is a
pattern of the second and third stasima (more obviously motivated by the
events on stage, and not, as Kitto (1961) 264 would have them, 'little more
than a conventional curtain') flanked by the first and fourth, which take a more
wide-ranging look at the history of the war and its aftermath.

[65] The gnomic central stanzas are framed by more personal and concrete
exempla in the first and last.

[66] The OCT text here is accepted by Stinton (1990) 294, and explained by
Diggle (1994) 224 (who notes the attractiveness of Schroeder's δήριας,
'contests').

[67] The scholia take the phrase ἀκοινώνητον ἀνδρὸς (470) to refer to the bed of
the female chorus ('unshared with another man'), thus introducing the
different point of a wife's chastity. But as Stevens (1971) 153 points out, it
is unlikely that they would 'bring in a new point so briefly and ambiguously'.

observes that such a description does not match the situation in the play: Hermione has no son.[68] Yet the chorus may be interpreted as speaking generally and hypothetically of children born of different mothers.[69] No less apt, however, to the events of the play is the meaning, 'children with two rival mothers, i.e. a natural mother and a stepmother'.[70] Andromache's son is being condemned to death by Hermione (cf. 431–2, 444) while the child's relationship to his real mother is strengthened in the lament immediately following this choral ode: 'as the son clings to his mother's bosom the word μήτηρ is heard five times in seventeen short lines [498, 504 bis, 511, 514]'.[71] In fact both definitions may be felt as present; the ambiguity is appropriate.

In the middle section of the ode the chorus develop the basic proposition of contentment with a single controlling figure in a series of analogous contexts: statesmanship, poetry, and navigation.[72] The connection between domestic authority and the execution of aims in political, artistic, and technical spheres is gnomic and sententious; these are common qualities of choral pronouncements. The first part approves monarchy, a sentiment appropriate to the heroic world of the play. The stasimon follows Andromache's tirade against the Spartans, and some have detected covert choral reference to the practice of dual kingship in Sparta.[73] What the chorus reject is 'two rulers' in a city (δίπτυχοι τυραννίδες, 471) and such language, like that of στάσιν πολίταις ('dissension for the citizens', 475),[74] must have had a powerful resonance for Athenians of the 420s, where

[68] Stevens (1971) 153; cf. Sommerstein (1987) 498.

[69] Ogden (1996) 19–21 favours this definition.

[70] LSJ Revised Supplement (1996) s.v. *ἀμφιμήτορες.

[71] Sommerstein (1987) 500.

[72] The analogies are generally thought to be unconnected to the dramatic situation, which Kranz (1933) 218 accounts for by seeing them as topoi of contemporary sophistic debate. But the technique is traditional and the content not so remarkably modern: Alcman fr. 1. 90–5 D compares Hagesichora's leadership of the maiden chorus to the role of a trace-horse and a ship's helmsman.

[73] Most vehemently, Firnhaber (1848) 415–17.

[74] The accusative (emended from the MSS nominative) is defended by Diggle (1994) 224: ' "two rulers are worse to bear than one—the result is burden on burden and dissension for the citizens".' Stinton (1990) 294 reads the nominative in apposition.

internal political rivalries were exacerbated by the war with
Sparta.[75] Nevertheless, if we look for relevance to the world of
the dramatic fiction, it is not hard to find: Peleus' continuing
role as ruler of Phthia has already been mentioned (21–3), and
the respectful ceding of power by Neoptolemus to Peleus
contrasts with the tyrannical interference in foreign affairs
practised by Menelaus (at both state and family level, which
in the heroic world are inextricable). The necessity of one
leader is a familiar epic idea and is bluntly asserted by
Odysseus in *Il.* 2. 203–6.[76]

The chorus's final analogy likens the unstable household of
Neoptolemus to a ship caught in a storm. Competition for the
tiller in such a situation would be fatal (479–82):

> πνοαὶ δ' ὅταν φέρωσι ναυτίλους θοαί,
> κατὰ πηδαλίων διδύμα πραπίδων γνώμα
> σοφῶν τε πλῆθος ἀθρόον ἀσθενέστερον
> φαυλοτέρας φρενὸς αὐτοκρατοῦς.

When rushing winds carry sailors along, in terms of steering, the
judgement of two minds or a dense mass of clever people is weaker
than an inferior mind with complete control.

The language of anti-democratic rhetoric, as Lloyd notes, is
strikingly adapted: commonly 'it is the mob which is stupid
and unruly, while intelligence belongs to the one or to the
few'.[77] The opposition of σοφοί ('wise') and φαῦλοι ('simple')
occurs frequently in Euripides.[78] The contrast is often between
'the clever people and the ordinary laymen'.[79] Hermione displays a superior attitude to barbarian ἀμαθία ('ignorance' 170;
cf. 237, 245), and Menelaus claims that if he had not intervened
in Neoptolemus' household, he would be φαῦλος . . . κοὐ σοφός
('useless and not clever', 379). The language of the choral
analogy undermines their claims to cleverness. The chorus
declare that the search for what is appropriate (καιρόν, 485) in
both house and city requires the dominance (ἄνυσις 483)[80] of

---

[75] Gehrke (1985).

[76] His words are cited by Aristotle to crown his proof of the unmoved
mover: *Met.* Λ 1076ª3–4.   [77] Lloyd (1994) 132 on 479–82.

[78] See Dodds (1960) 129–30 on *Bacch.* 430–3.

[79] Mastronarde (1994) 287 on *Phoen.* 494–6.

[80] An unusual phrase: cf. Diggle (1994) 209 (defending the emendation):

one man, a claim which implicitly criticizes Hermione's independence and Menelaus' interference.

The form and movement of the song thus prepares for the
shift back to Hermione in the second antistrophe as the focus of
its generalizations (486–7):[81]

> ἔδειξεν ἁ Λάκαινα τοῦ στρατηλάτα
> Μενέλα· διὰ γὰρ πυρὸς ἦλθ' ἑτέρωι λέχει,
> κτείνει δὲ τὰν τάλαιναν Ἰλιάδα κόραν
> παῖδά τε δύσφρονος ἔριδος ὕπερ.

The Spartan woman, daughter of the commander Menelaus, has
shown this. For she raged like fire against her rival, and is killing
the miserable Trojan girl and her son because of hateful strife.

The idea of Hermione blazing against another union (literally
'bed') captures both the ferocity of her attack and her primary
motivation for it.[82] Stevens remarks, 'in its present position the
ode follows an epeisodion in which Hermione is not present
and it is Menelaus (barely mentioned in this ode) who does all
the threatening'.[83] But the mention of Hermione is dramatically effective. It functions precisely to keep her in mind despite
her absence, while the closing verses of the ode foreshadow the
reverse that will overcome her (491–3):

> ἄθεος ἄνομος ἄχαρις ὁ φόνος·
> ἔτι σε, πότνια, μετατροπὰ
> τῶνδ' ἔπεισιν ἔργων.

Godless, lawless, thankless is the murder! Some day, mistress, change
of fortune for these actions will come upon you!

The repetition of ἔπεισι ('will come upon') from 133, where it
referred to Spartan force overwhelming Andromache, alerts us

'That the noun is not elsewhere found in tragedy can be no argument against
its restoration here.' Wilamowitz (1921) 427 n. 1 suggested ἑνὶ δὲ δύνασις (for
the codd. ἁ δύνασις), which also confirms power in one person.

---

[81] On choral reference to the action of the play as proof of their thought, see
Kranz (1933) 217; for negative paradigms proving the rule, cf. Griffith (1983)
149, 246 on *PV* 347–72, 894–900. The rare responsion in 482 ~ 490, where
ἔριδος ὕ(περ) ('because of strife') is a resolved dactyl, is discussed by Stinton
(1990) 11.

[82] Denniston (1939) 196 on *El.* 1183 notes: 'The metaphorical use of πῦρ for
a violent, destructive agency, and for the passion of love, is not so common in
Greek as in Latin.'   [83] Stevens (1971) 151.

to the radical reversal about to engulf Hermione. The tricolon of privative adjectives in 491,[84] and the asyndetic and verbless directness of the phrase, compound the chorus's repugnance.[85] Each term has a bearing on the action of the play. Firstly, ἄθεος ('godless') prepares for the chorus's perplexity about Apollo's support for the murder of Neoptolemus. Secondly, ἄνομος ('lawless') undercuts the Spartans' claim to order, intelligence, and superiority to barbarian *nomoi* (cf. 176, 243, 665–7). Finally, Hermione's plan is of benefit to herself alone, while 'The essence of χάρις is that it is reciprocal.'[86] The chorus's moral judgement is remarkably explicit. It is even more marked by the switch to direct address (492). The chorus's 'artificial contact'[87] with Hermione sets her action vividly before their communal judgement.

The product of her plot is immediately embodied in a striking visual proof, as the bound Andromache and her son enter under guard to face execution, heralded by the chorus in anapaests, a metre typically used in tragedy for processional entrances, including 'the entry of those condemned to death'.[88] Both rhythm and assonance express the unity of mother and son in danger and misery: δύστηνε γύναι, τλῆμον δὲ σὺ παῖ ('Unhappy woman, and you, miserable boy!', 497).[89] The balance of 'sound and structure . . . is probably evocative of the traditional style of ritual lamentation'.[90] The brief greeting affirms the innocence of the pair, enhancing the pathos of the entrance: μητρὸς λεχέων ὃς ὑπερθνῄσκεις | οὐδὲν μετέχων | οὐδ' αἴτιος ὢν βασιλεῦσιν ('[miserable boy], who are to die because of your mother's marriage, though you played no part and are not to blame in the rulers' eyes', 498–500).[91] The combination of

[84] For examples of this tragic mode of condemnation, see Kannicht (1969) ii. 299 on *Hel.* 1148 προδότις ἄπιστος ἄδικος ἄθεος ('a trustless, unjust, godless traitress').

[85] Note also the total resolution of the iambic dimeter in 491. Aristophanes parodies Euripidean monody's accumulated adjectives at *Frogs* 1335a f.; but Silk (1993) 483 finds this technique, like that of multiple compounds, 'seemingly as characteristic of Aeschylus as of Euripides'.

[86] Griffith (1983) 186 on *PV* 545–6.

[87] Mastronarde (1979) 99.

[88] Taplin (1977) 73.

[89] For rhyme see Hutchinson (1985) 203 on *Sept.* 962.

[90] Mastronarde (1994) 441 on *Phoen.* 1034–5.

[91] Compare the effect of the chorus's anapaests at *Ant.* 801–5.

the mother and son's simple lyric lament[92] with the pitiless interjections of Menelaus (515–22, 537–44)[93] tightens the suspense surrounding Peleus' arrival. He is heralded by the chorus-leader in words which stress his old age: καὶ μὴν δέδορκα τόνδε Πηλέα πέλας | σπουδῆι τιθέντα δεῦρο γηραιὸν πόδα ('Look, I see Peleus close by, setting his aged steps here in haste', 545–6). His repudiation of Menelaus in the next scene thus appears all the more remarkable.

The chorus's third stasimon is 'a magnificent eulogy of the son of Aeacus'.[94] Its triadic form and dactylo-epitrite rhythm, its passages of moralizing and praise of wealth and nobility, and finally its exemplary use of myth are all reminiscent of epinician poetry.[95] In Pindaric mythology Peleus holds an honoured position as the hero who is εὐσεβέστατος ('most pious', *Isthm.* 8. 40) among mortals, and so worthy of marriage to Thetis. Wealth and noble birth, key elements of Pindar's thought, supply the material for the chorus's encomium in the first strophe.[96] Peleus is an example of what they praise generally as magnificent.[97]

The relevance to the play of such an heroic-aristocratic

---

[92] The lament is glyconic (with pherecrateans); this is 'one of the commonest verse-forms in tragic odes' (Itsumi (1984) 66) but it is not so used by the chorus in the *Andromache*.

[93] Dale (1968) 50 compares Menelaus' 'gloating words' to *Ag.* 1448–1577, where Clytemnestra defies the chorus in recitative anapaests.

[94] Jouan (1966) 59–60.

[95] On the metre as an echo of the heroic past, see Webster (1970) 156–7. Collard (quoted in Mossman (1995) 88 n. 48) locates Euripides' purpose in using dactylo-epitrite in stasima 'which contrast the heroic or tragic past with the unlovely present'. For the frequency of dactylo-epitrite in tragedy see L. P. E. Parker (1997) 88–9.

[96] Both are constructs of an archaic, aristocratic style of thinking that celebrates the superiority of inborn ability (τὸ δὲ φυᾷ κράτιστον ἅπαν: *Ol.* 9. 100, 'All that is inborn is best'), and assumes the intrinsically meritorious character of wealth (*Ol.* 2. 53–6). For such felicitous union, compare Sapph. fr. 148 Voigt: ὁ πλοῦτος ἄνευ ἀρετᾶς οὐκ ἀσίνης πάροικος, | ἁ δ' ἀμφοτέρων κρᾶσις †εὐδαιμονίας ἔχει τὸ ἄκρον† ('Wealth without virtue is no safe neighbour. The mixture of both †brings the peak of happiness†').

[97] For Pindar, Peleus is a supreme exemplar of human ὄλβος ('blessedness') and εὐγένεια ('inborn nobility'). What one misses here is reference to what struck Pindar most: union with a goddess (cf. *Pyth.* 3. 86 ff.). Perhaps Euripides omits it here in order to increase the surprise of Thetis' intervention later in the play.

viewpoint centres on the Spartans' claim to social and moral pre-eminence. The ode combines praise of Peleus with repudiation of Spartan conduct. Their criticism, centred on the antistrophe, is expressed in a series of gnomic phrases. In a manner akin to the victory odes of Pindar, the relevance for the drama of such generalized moral reflection can be deciphered by reference to the details of the myth and the context of the song. In Pindar the myths typically furnish meanings which bolster the prestige of his aristocratic patrons. Peleus benefits from this strategy. By contrast, the chorus's allusive rejection of the Spartans' conduct denies their claim to achievement and fame (concepts that are vital to lyric eulogy). Andromache has already exposed Menelaus' fraudulent reputation: ὦ δόξα δόξα, μυρίοισι δὴ βροτῶν | οὐδὲν γεγῶσι βίοτον ὤγκωσας μέγαν ('Ah, reputation, reputation, for countless mortals indeed, who are nothing in themselves, you have inflated their lives to greatness', 319–20). The chorus reject the (Spartans') overthrowing of justice (779–80); it is a negative exemplum, which simultaneously explodes the Spartans' claim to inherited distinction, and magnifies the praise of Peleus.[98] Their clear moral judgement is placed at the centre of a lyric commentary on the rescue of Andromache in the previous scene.

The strophe pointedly equates wealth and good birth with the only life worth living (766–9):

> ἦ μὴ γενοίμαν ἢ πατέρων ἀγαθῶν
> εἴην πολυκτήτων τε δόμων μέτοχος.

I would rather not be born, if not of noble fathers and sharing in a wealthy house!

The variation on the tragic theme of a wished-for death is remarkable for its directness. The ode, even in the generalizing

---

[98] Interestingly, in his first ode (498), and his only one for a Thessalian victor, Pindar connects Sparta and Thessaly through their common ancestor, Heracles: Ὀλβία Λακεδαίμων, | μάκαιρα Θεσσαλία. πατρὸς δ' ἀμφοτέραις ἐξ ἑνός | ἀριστομάχου γένος Ἡρακλέος βασιλεύει ('Fortunate is Sparta, blessed is Thessaly. The ruling family of each is descended from one father, Heracles, best in battle', *Pyth.* 10. 1–3). Both states retained monarchy and serfdom into the fifth century (see *CAH²* v. 19, 27). Thessaly's aristocratic credentials were most obviously displayed in her cavalry, the strongest in all Greece. It came into its own in the 370s under Jason of Pherae: cf. Sekunda (1994) 183–4. Might the similarity of social stratification underline the moral contrast here?

strophe, has a bearing on the action.[99] The declaration εἴ τι γὰρ
πάσχοι τις ἀμήχανον, ἀλκᾶς | οὐ σπάνις εὐγενέταις ('For if someone
were to suffer something awful, there is no lack of protection
for the well-born', 770–1) throws a revealing light on the
contrasting experience of Andromache and Hermione. When
calamity befalls both women successively, Andromache's
rescue by Peleus (a former enemy) contrasts with Hermione's
sense of abandonment by her own father: her 'lack of defence'
(ἀλκᾶς σπάνις) illustrates the fraudulence of Spartan noble
birth. The chorus go on to identify τιμὰ καὶ κλέος ('honour
and glory', 773) as belonging to those heralded from noble
houses (κηρυσσομένοισι δ'ἀπ'ἐσθλῶν δωμάτων, 772), an evocation
of the occasion for epinician poetry.[100] The idea that time does
not efface what the noble leave behind (οὔτοι λείψανα τῶν
ἀγαθῶν | ἀνδρῶν ἀφαιρεῖται χρόνος, 774–5) is a variation on a
topos of funeral orations and epitaphs. The strophe closes with
another gnomic comment, ἁ δ'ἀρετὰ | καὶ θανοῦσι λάμπει ('their
excellence shines forth even in death', 775–6), which uses a
metaphor of light that is characteristic of Pindar.[101]

The antistrophe moves from noble birth to noble actions in
the context of victory and power (777–80):

> κρεῖσσον δὲ νίκαν μὴ κακόδοξον ἔχειν
> ἢ ξὺν φθόνωι σφάλλειν δυνάμει τε δίκαν.

It is better to win without getting a bad reputation than to make
justice fall odiously and by force.

By distinguishing these two types of success the chorus guide
our contrasting responses to the interventions of Peleus and
Menelaus. Peleus' sense of justice, which prompts him to
defend Andromache and her son, is set against the Spartans'
envy and ill-will. The chorus explain their preference: ἡδὺ μὲν
γὰρ αὐτίκα τοῦτο βροτοῖσιν, | ἐν δὲ χρόνωι τελέθει | ξηρὸν καὶ
ὀνείδεσιν ἔγκειται δόμος ('For this [winning unjustly] is sweet at

---

[99] *Contra* Stevens (1971) 187: 'It has no special significance in relation to
the action but serves rather to mark a pause.' The address to the absent Peleus
rather prepares for the move to his suffering in the final scenes: the chorus's
celebration of the hero's past triumphs magnifies his tragedy.

[100] Compare the insistence on lineage at Soph. *El.* 690, 692–5, where the
epinician context is explicit.

[101] See Stevens (1971) 188.

first for mortals, but in time it ends up withered and the house is involved in disgrace', 781–4). The notion of temporary sweetness reminds us of Menelaus' policy of short-term gratification at any price (368–9, 440). The assurance that such pleasure withers in time prepares us for the sudden collapse of Spartan pride in the next scene. The attempted double murder, it is implied, plunges the house of Menelaus into disgrace (cf. 784).[102] Finally, the chorus's moralizing is enforced by self-reference: ταύταν ἤινεσα ταύταν καὶ †φέρομαι† βιοτάν ('This is the life I praise, this the one †I seek to win for myself†', 785);[103] the repetition and the gnomic aorist are emphatic.[104] The course that they approve (μηδὲν δίκας ἔξω κράτος ἐν θαλάμοις | καὶ πόλει δύνασθαι 786–7, 'to wield no power that goes beyond justice in private and in public [literally, 'in bedrooms and the city']') develops the play's striking analogy of political and domestic conduct, and again implies rejection of Menelaus' interference in either sphere. Their sentiment thus commends the victory of Peleus, and so leads into the encomium of the epode.

The personal tone of the epode (note the focalizing direct address, ὦ γέρον Αἰακίδα 790, 'O aged son of Aeacus') stands apart from the generalizing strophes. The patronymic sets Peleus amidst his heroic ancestry (for a catalogue of Aeacid heroes, see Pind. *Nem.* 4. 25–72); in view of the play's exploration of hereditary nobility, it is an apt opening. The bravery shown by the old man points to a truly heroic prime.[105] There follows a selection of three achievements of Peleus: the defeat of the Centaurs, the voyage of the Argonauts,[106] and,

---

[102] See Diggle (1994) 211–12 for the emendation of δόμων.

[103] Diggle (OCT) obelizes φέρομαι, while Kovacs (Loeb) accepts in its place Herwerden's σέβομαι ('I revere'). However, the manuscript reading is acceptable Greek and notably fits the epinician flavour of the ode.

[104] Cf. Stinton (1990) 253: 'emphatic "I" [in tragic lyrics] often introduces a general maxim or *gnome*.'

[105] Kitto (1961) 263 says of the ode, 'There is surely irony here.' But such a tone would spoil the effect of both the previous scene and Peleus' later misfortune. Perhaps one may speak of irony at *El.* 860 ff., where the chorus's epinician (dactylo-epitrite) celebration of Orestes' victory is followed by Electra's disturbing speech over Aegisthus' corpse.

[106] According to Apollonius, the voyage on the Argo proved Peleus a skilled fighter (1. 1042, 2. 121–2) and a wise counsellor (2. 868–84, 1216–25, 4. 1368–79).

with Heracles, the first sack of Troy.[107] The battle of Lapiths
and Centaurs illustrates both the defeat of lawless violence
('barbarism') and the proper handling of sexual passion; each is
relevant to the action of the *Andromache*. Peleus is here
included (for the first time in extant literature) as an ally of
Pirithous against the drunken rapists.[108] The defeat of violence
and sexual excess in the past has striking parallels in the
dramatic present. The chorus's final reminiscence is no less
relevant to the play's treatment of the second sack of Troy and
its aftermath (797–801):

> [πείθομαι . . . σε]
> Ἰλιάδα τε πόλιν ὅτε ⟨τὸ⟩ πάρος
> εὐδόκιμον ὁ Διὸς ἶνις ἀμφέβαλε φόνωι
> κοινὰν τὰν εὔκλειαν ἔχοντ᾽
> Εὐρώπαν ἀφικέσθαι.

[I do believe that], when previously the son of Zeus beset the city of
Troy with slaughter, [you] returned to Europe sharing the glory.[109]

The chorus's celebration of Peleus' role in the first Trojan
defeat contrasts with the presentation of Menelaus' unheroic
conduct during the second war (cf. 456–7, 703–5). Their song
marks the happy resolution of Andromache's crisis, yet the
enduring presence of Greek pride in the sack of Troy intensifies the incongruity and surprise of the developing alliance
between Troy and the house of Peleus.[110]

The disruption of expectations is intensified in the sudden

[107] See Janko (1992) 191 on *Il.* 14. 250–61 for the prowess of Heracles in the
epic tradition.

[108] Cf. *Il.* 1. 263 ff., where 'Nestor's involvement with the war between
Lapiths and Centaurs . . . may be Homer's own idea' (Kirk (1985) 80). Nestor
stresses the awesome strength of the fighters involved; Peleus' involvement
here magnifies his prowess.

[109] For Peleus' involvement in the earlier attack, we must return to Pindar:
his brother Telamon is the focus at *Nem.* 4. 25–32 and *Isthm.* 6. 26–34, but at
Isthm. 5. 35–8 all the Aeacids are associated as sackers of Troy across two
generations (cf. fr. 172 Snell; also *Ol.* 8. 42–6, where Apollo tells Aeacus of
Troy's fated double fall, first to Telamon, then two generations later to
Neoptolemus).

[110] In the fourth stasimon the chorus's tone is very different, as they
concentrate on the ruinous consequences of the Trojan War for both sides.
Even the first sack of Troy is seen there as an inexplicable manifestation of
divine destruction (1037 ff.).

plot reversal of Hermione's despair and attempted suicide. The Nurse urges the chorus to enter the palace and save Hermione (817–19):

> ὑμεῖς δὲ βᾶσαι τῶνδε δωμάτων ἔσω
> θανάτου νιν ἐκλύσασθε· τῶν γὰρ ἠθάδων
> φίλων νέοι μολόντες εὐπιθέστεροι.

Do you go into this house and save her from death; for new people arriving are more persuasive than old friends.

The suggestion, by threatening to flout the stage convention that the chorus does not normally exit during the play, emphasizes Hermione's plight.[111] The breach is avoided by the entry of Hermione herself. The chorus-leader's entry announcement points to the significance of the coming lyric dialogue: δείξειν δ' ἔοικεν ἡ τάλαιν' ὅσον στένει | πράξασα δεινά ('It seems the poor woman will show how much she laments the terrible things she has done', 822–3). Significantly, the chorus remain silent during the amoebean between Hermione and the Nurse: their lack of sympathy is evident. Hermione's lament is itself derailed when a means of escape is offered by the arrival of Orestes.

The chorus-leader remarks on his hasty approach (880), which 'fosters a sense of urgency and heightens excitement'.[112] The announcement also draws attention to Orestes' foreign appearance (ὅδ' ἀλλόχρως τις ἔκδημος ξένος 879, '[Here comes] some foreign looking stranger from abroad'). The description reminds us that the action takes place in remote Thessaly, where even other Greeks look foreign. As so often in the play, though here with particular subtlety, the opposition of Greek and barbarian is queried. Hermione appeals to Orestes, supporting her petition with an attack on αἱ θύραθεν εἴσοδοι | . . . γυναικῶν ('the visits of women from outside', 952–3). However, the chorus respond in a spirit of female solidarity, insisting that

---

[111] On the function of the rare exits, see Gould (1996b) 242 n. 86. The chorus is not merely drawing attention to a stage convention when they threaten to leave the stage but do not. For example, at *Hec.* 1042–3 the effect is to heighten the power of Hecuba's personal revenge. On the chorus's refusal to join Phaedra at the door (*Hipp.* 575–8), Winnington-Ingram (1969) 131 remarks, 'It seems oddly dragged in.' But it is dramatically effective: Phaedra hears Hippolytus' reaction for herself.

[112] Taplin (1977) 147 on *Sept.* 369 ff.

women should pull together 'to disguise female frailties'
(κοσμεῖν . . . τὰς γυναικείας νόσους, 956). They thus ally
themselves with Andromache: she too recognized female
frailty, but claimed superiority in decent concealment (220–1).

Orestes' plans hinge explictly on the assistance of Apollo
(1002–8), so there is a smooth transition from the departure of
Orestes (bent on revenge) to the chorus's exploration of the
role of a vengeful Apollo in the first fall of Troy.[113] As Hose
observes of the fourth stasimon, 'it broadens the horizon of the
play by presenting earlier events, and . . . prepares for the
questioning of the revenge plot by describing the ambivalent
role of Apollo'.[114] The reasons for Apollo and Poseidon's
period of service with Laomedon are obscure,[115] and there
are differing accounts of their respective activities: either the
gods built the walls together (cf. *Il.* 7. 452–3), or Poseidon
alone undertook the task while Apollo worked as a herdsman
(*Il.* 21. 441–57). The idea of joint divine endeavour is
employed in the *Andromache*.[116] It enhances the chorus's
puzzlement that the gods should later dishonour their own
handiwork.[117]

The structure of the strophe foregrounds the baffling behaviour of Apollo by addressing him first and attaching his name
to the building of the walls (1009–18):

ὦ Φοῖβε πυργώσας τὸν ἐν Ἰλίωι εὐτειχῆ πάγον
καὶ πόντιε κυανέαις ἵπποις διφρεύ-
ων ἅλιον πέλαγος,

---

[113] Stevens (1971) 213 comments that the function of the fourth stasimon
'is not primarily to comment on the preceding epeisodion'. But it does
certainly affect our response to Orestes, and its recollection of his bloody
past alters our view of his declared aims at Delphi. For the relation of
Euripides' more imaginative and distant mythical material to the content
and meaning of his plays, see Padel (1974) 240–1.

[114] Hose (1990–1) ii. 75.

[115] Perhaps to test him: so Hellanicus, *FrGH* 4. 26a.

[116] Cf. *Tro.* 4–6, 814.

[117] ὄργανον χεροτεκτοσύνας ('product of your handiwork', 1014–15): Diggle
adopts Carey's emendation here, but Carey's ((1977) 16) arguments for the
word χεροτεκτοσύνη, which does not occur elsewhere and does not look a likely
Euripidean coinage, are not totally convincing (ὄργανον is at least supported by
Phoen. 115). The language of the conjecture does not seem to fit the emotive
context.

τίνος οὕνεκ' ἄτιμον ὄργα-
νον χεροτεκτοσύνας Ἐ-
νυαλίωι δοριμήστορι προσθέν-
τες τάλαιναν τάλαι-
ναν μεθεῖτε Τροίαν;

Phoebus, who built high the well-walled rock of Troy, and you, Lord of ocean, riding your chariot with dark-blue horses over the salty sea, why did you abandon in dishonour the product of your handiwork to Enyalios, master of the spear, and give up miserable, miserable Troy?

The familiar explanation of the gods' change of heart is suppressed;[118] this gives the chorus's questioning of divine inconstancy and mercilessness greater force. It also prepares for the criticisms of Apollo to come: 1036, 1161–5, 1212. The antistrophe graphically depicts the consequences of the gods' disaffection: the desecration of Troy. The slaughter is portrayed in a sinister reversal of the normally joyful imagery of the sporting contest (1019–21):[119]

πλείστους δ' ἐπ' ἀκταῖσιν Σιμοεντίσιν εὐίππους ὄχους
ἐζεύξατε καὶ φονίους ἀνδρῶν ἀμίλ-
λας ἔθετ' ἀστεφάνους.

You yoked very many chariots with fine horses by the banks of the Simois, and established bloody contests of men with no garland as a prize.

The city's communal rites of sacrifice are negated: οὐδ' ἔτι πῦρ ἐπιβώμιον ἐν Τροί- | αι θεοῖσιν λέλαμ- | πεν καπνῶι θυώδει ('and the altar fire in Troy no longer blazes for the gods with fragrant smoke', 1025–7). It is a powerful symbol of the extinction of a community (and at a cost to the gods themselves).[120]

---

[118] Cf. Hor. *C.* 3. 3. 18–22 *Ilion,* | *Ilion fatalis . . . ex quo destituit deos* | *mercede pacta Laomedon* ('Troy, doomed Troy . . . ever since Laomedon cheated the gods of their settled payment').

[119] Cf. *Il.* 22. 158–61. The metaphor perhaps exploits Apollo's and Poseidon's status as patrons of the Pythian and Isthmian games respectively. On Euripides' fondness for such oxymoronic expressions as ἀστεφάνους ('with no garland as a prize'), see Breitenbach (1934) 236–8.

[120] Compare the bafflement of the Trojan chorus at *Tro.* 1060 ff., οὕτω δὴ τὸν ἐν Ἰλίωι | ναὸν καὶ θυόεντα βω- | μὸν προύδωκας Ἀχαιοῖς, | ὦ Ζεῦ . . .; ('Did you indeed thus betray your temple in Troy and its fragrant altar to the Achaeans, Zeus. . .?'); for the idea of gods deserting a captured city, see Hutchinson (1985) on *Sept.* 216–18, 304.

The first strophe and antistrophe have concentrated on the fall of Troy from a Trojan perspective, a notable extension of the Phthian chorus's sympathies. The second strophic pair turns to the suffering on the Greek side as a result of the war. The two countries are thus handled in different strophic forms but equal space is devoted to each. The fates of both Greek and Trojan leaders, though expressed in separate rhythms and movements, are linked by repetition: ἀπὸ δὲ φθίμενοι βεβᾶσιν | Ἰλιάδαι βασιλῆες ~ βέβακε δ' Ἀτρείδας ἀλόχου παλάμαις ('Dead and gone are the Trojan princes', 'Gone is the son of Atreus through the treachery of his wife', 1022~1028). Yet the victims in each case face a very different end. The Trojan princes die in battle, fighting for their homeland; this is a fitting end for a warrior.[121] By contrast, the chief commander of the Greeks meets an ignoble and shameful death through his wife's treachery. In a play so conscious of inherited character, Clytemnestra's παλάμη ('trickery') presages the deceit and violence of Orestes μηχανορράφος ('the cunning contriver', 1116; cf. 995–7).

The cycle of violence culminates in the horror of the matricide: αὐτά τ' ἐναλλάξασα φόνον θανάτου | πρὸς τέκνων ἐπηῦρεν ('and she, in return for murder, received death from her children', 1029–30). The reciprocity of revenge is emphasized by ἐναλλάξασα ('receiving in return'). Apollo's prompting of Orestes provokes astonishment in the chorus, marked by repetition: θεοῦ θεοῦ νιν κέλευσμ' ἐπεστράφη | μαντόσυνον ('A god's, a god's oracular order turned upon her', 1031–2).[122] Orestes' journey from Apollo's sanctuary in Delphi to the scene of the matricide is then rapidly depicted (1032–5):

> ὅτε νιν Ἄργος ἐμπορευθεὶς
> Ἀγαμεμνόνιος κέλωρ, ἀδύτων ἀποβάς,
> ἔκταν', ὧν ματρὸς φονεύς.

---

[121] Note Hector's final resolution, μὴ μὰν ἀσπουδί γε καὶ ἀκλειῶς ἀπολοίμην, | ἀλλὰ μέγα ῥέξας τι καὶ ἐσσομένοισι πυθέσθαι ('May I not perish without a struggle and without glory, but having wrought something great for later men to hear of!', *Il.* 22. 304–5; cf. 15. 496–9).

[122] Cf. the excited cry of the chorus of satyrs in Sophocles *Ichneutae*: θεὸς θεὸς θεὸς θεὸς ἔα ἔα ('A god, a god, a god, a god! Aha! Aha!', fr. 314. 100 R); and the reaffirmation of theodicy marked by a similar choral repetition at *Her.* 773: θεοὶ θεοὶ τῶν ἀδίκων | μέλουσι καὶ τῶν ὁσίων ἐπάιειν ('The gods, the gods take care to perceive the unjust and the pious!').

when Agamemnon's son made for Argos, having left the sanctuary,
and killed her, becoming his mother's murderer.

The route strikingly prefigures Orestes' murderous return to
Delphi in the next scene.[123] Divine support for the matricide
provokes the chorus's incomprehension, which is vividly
expressed in a direct question to the god (placed emphatically
at the end of the strophe): ὦ δαῖμον, ὦ Φοῖβε, πῶς πείθομαι; ('O
god, O Phoebus, how can I believe?', 1036).

The final antistrophe broadens our view of the consequences
of the war for the Greeks, moving from one notable family's
troubles to the universal bereavement of the nation.[124] It
repeats from the first stasimon (307–8) the image of mourning
parents and widows forced to other beds (1037–41):

> πολλαὶ δ' ἀν' Ἑλλάνων ἀγόρους στοναχαὶ
> μέλποντο δυστάνων τεκέων, ἄλοχοι δ'
> ἐξέλειπον οἴκους
> πρὸς ἄλλον εὐνάτορ'.

Many laments were sung for their unfortunate children in the
gathering places of the Greeks, and wives left their homes for
another's bed.

Yet here the description takes on a more vivid force, in view of
Peleus' imminent bereavement and Hermione's recent departure with Orestes. Her peculiar experience is not that of the
conventional war-widow whose husband has been killed at
Troy: she has left with the self-proclaimed murderer of her
husband, and her remarriage to him is expected (cf. 984 ff.).
She contrasts sharply with the desolate wives pitied by the
chorus.

Their song now makes a shift of focus, whose beauty and
pathos have regularly been obscured by critical controversy. As
in previous stasima (cf. 302, 492, 789), the chorus end their
song with an address to an individual who functions as a
reference for their thoughts.[125] However, there is no agreement

---

[123] Kovacs (1980) 38–41 takes a different view of 1032–5. He prefers the
manuscripts' ἐπιβὰς ('standing in') to Wecklein's ἀποβάς ('having left') at 1034,
and at 1035 he accepts Wilamowitz's conjecture ἵκετ' ὢν ('approached as a
suppliant, being [his mother's murderer]'). He also reads Ἀργόθεν ('from
Argos') at 1032. Thus the chorus are taken to describe the journey of Orestes
from Argos to Delphi *after* the matricide. However, emphasis here on the

here about who the recipient of the consolation might be. Let us consider the rhetorical context of the pronoun. We have just heard of the horrors of bereavement and widowhood endured by the Greeks, and now the chorus console an unnamed character that her and her kin's distress is not unique (1041–2):[126]

οὐχὶ σοὶ μόναι
δύσφρονες ἐνέπεσον, οὐ φίλοισι, λῦπαι·

Not on you alone, not on your loved ones, have cruel griefs fallen!

Clearly it is Andromache, not the barren Hermione, who has endured the death of a son, and was forced to another man's bed by the dislocation of war. Consolation of Hermione would be totally out of place here.[127] Though he rejects the re-entry of Andromache at this point, Mastronarde sums up the case for reference to Andromache most convincingly:

the sympathetic tenor of the description of Troy's sufferings and the losses for which consolation is offered (children and husbands) indicate clearly that Andromache is in the chorus' mind. Indeed the ode takes up Andromache's own topics of lament (cf. 394 ff., 461–463). The chorus is thus deliberately dissociating itself from the bargain struck by Hermione and Orestes in the previous scene and reasserting the importance of Andromache's plight in a part of the play in which the episodes no longer deal with it directly.[128]

god's sanctioning of the murder is more relevant to the dramatic context (Apollo's role in Neoptolemus' death) than is an account of Orestes' appeal for purification. The chorus's horror is better captured by Diggle's text, which emphasizes the murder itself; moreover, the picture of Orestes' deadly resolve and swift execution of Apollo's will is better suited to his character and purpose in the *Andromache*.

[124] Hutchinson (1985) xlii n. 18 states: 'Musgrave's interchange of strophe and antistrophe at E. *Andr.* 1027 ff. looks highly attractive.' The resulting movement from general to particular would fit choral practice, but the existing structure has its own merits, and effectively climaxes with the notion of communal suffering.

[125] Grube (1961) 114 comments: 'Such technical devices, though effective, are not dramatically very important.' However, he underestimates the chorus's capacity to influence our response to the action.

[126] Kannicht (1969) ii. 137 on *Hel.* 464 remarks that the *non tibi hoc soli* formula of consolation is 'as old as Greek literature itself'.

[127] *Pace* Steidle (1968) 118–21, Kovacs (1980) 42–3, Erbse (1984) 135, and Lloyd (1994) 154. Hose (1990–1) ii. 74–5 sits on the fence, finding both referents plausible!

[*See p. 228 for n. 128*]

The chorus's shift of focus to Andromache's past, and their
emotional insistence that she and her loved ones are not alone
in their grief, is notably, though not merely, a recognition of
Trojan suffering. The comparison also intensifes our impression of the sorrow and loss of the Greeks, and so prepares for
the transition to the tragedy of Peleus in the last scene.

The chorus end their recollection of the war with a graphic
and horrifying vision (1044–6):

> νόσον Ἑλλὰς ἔτλα, νόσον· διέβα δὲ Φρυγῶν
> καὶ πρὸς εὐκάρπους γύας
> σκηπτὸς σταλάσσων Δαναΐδαις φόνον.

A plague Greece endured, a plague; even to the fertile lands of the
Trojans the storm crossed, raining slaughter on the Greeks.

The textual problems of the lines have led to two polarized
interpretations of the direction of the 'plague'.[129] The imagery
of sickness which has run through the play climaxes here in the
blight of warfare—even for the victors. The chorus picture a
bloody drizzle falling on the Greek warriors. The image is
powerful and macabre.[130] Whatever the exact text, the whole
antistrophe is clearly asserting that both Greeks and Trojans
have been affected. The polarity of Greek and Trojan is
transcended in suffering.

In a brief exchange before the entry of the messenger, the
chorus-leader answers Peleus' inquiries about the departure of
Hermione (1047 ff.). They elucidate the οὐ σαφῆ λόγον ('unclear
report', 1048) relating to Hermione's flight. While Peleus,

---

[128] Mastronarde (1979) 99.

[129] Campbell's Δαναΐδαις ('on the Greeks') is accepted by Diggle; cf. Hel.
238–9. Stevens (1971) 218 and Kovacs (1980) 43 understand Φρυγῶν ('of the
Trojans') as dependent on εὐκάρπους γύας ('fertile lands'): the storm passes
from Greece to Troy. This seems more natural than the reading of Lloyd
(1994) 154, who follows Campbell in seeing the storm moving from Troy to
Greece. He thus interprets Φρυγῶν as a genitive of motion from: 'the storm
crossed from Troy'. He also believes (with Kovacs) that one cannot accept 'on
the Greeks' if the storm passes from Greece to Troy. But it makes perfect
sense if the chorus vividly picture the sufferings of the Greek warriors at
Troy.

[130] Compare the poignant image of Zeus' sorrowful rain at Il. 16. 459–61;
and 11. 53–5, where the bloody rain sent by Zeus is more ominous for the
Greeks.

concerned for his descendants, thinks of the plot against Neoptolemus' son as a reason for Hermione's anxiety, the chorus-
leader stresses the role of Hermione's attempt on Andromache's life (1058–9). Peleus asks about Orestes' motivation
in taking Hermione with him. This prompts the chorus-leader
to summarize the essentials of the previous scene: Orestes'
desire to marry Hermione, his plot against Neoptolemus and
its location. Interestingly, he does not answer Peleus' question
about Orestes' attack unambiguously (1064–5):

> Πη. κρυπτὸς καταστὰς ἢ κατ' ὄμμ' ἐλθὼν μάχηι;
> Χο. ἁγνοῖς ἐν ἱεροῖς Λοξίου Δελφῶν μέτα.

PELEUS: Lying in ambush or meeting him in face to face combat?
CHORUS-LEADER: In Loxias' holy shrine with the men of Delphi.

The effect of the chorus-leader's reply is to stress the troubling
complicity of the god and his servants, while not defusing the
shock of the messenger's imminent narrative, in which the
duplicity and cowardice of Orestes' act are underlined.

The return of Neoptolemus' corpse from Delphi is accompanied by an anapaestic announcement from the chorus, the
metre matching the marching bier. Their balancing direct
address unites grandfather and grandson in suffering: τλήμων
ὁ παθών, τλήμων δέ, γέρον, | καὶ σύ ('Miserable is the one who
has suffered, and miserable too, old man, are you', 1168–9).
The corpse is called τὸν Ἀχίλλειον | σκύμνον ('Achilles' cub',
1169–70): the chorus imply Neoptolemus' wasted youth.[131]
Their *kommos* with Peleus (1173–1225) is a common tragic
extension of the funerary laments of ritual practice, delivered
by close relatives of the dead hero and the women of his
community (the three laments for Hector at *Il.* 24. 718–76
are the epic's most moving and most formal example). The
characteristic stress of ritual laments on the sorrow and
desolation of the survivors is adapted to the circumstances of
the play.[132]

---

[131] Contrast *Or.* 1213: σκύμνον ἀνοσίου πατρός ('whelp of an unholy father'),
where the word is used pejoratively by Orestes of Hermione. Wilkins (1993)
186 on *Hcld.* 1006 notes the metaphor of cubs as avenging sons: Neoptolemus
had asked for reparations from Apollo, who helped kill his father, and is killed
by the same god in turn (cf. 1194–6).

[132] Cf. *Il.* 22. 416–28 (Priam mourns Hector above all his sons), 24. 725–45
(Andromache's widowhood, the fate of their child).

Peleus' lament begins almost entirely in dactylic tetrameters (1173 ff. = 1186 ff.),[133] while the chorus echo his grief, first in spoken trimeters (1184–5) and then in lyric iambics as they take up the funeral song: ὀττοτοτοτοῖ, θανόντα δεσπόταν γόοις | νόμωι τῶι νερτέρων κατάρξω ('Ottotototoi, I shall begin the lament for my dead master in the strain consecrated to the dead', 1197–9). Their participation in the 'spontaneous γόος [lament] of relatives or friends'[134] expresses their close involvement with the action: they are no mere bystanders but concerned (and judging) witnesses of events through whose emotional response that of the audience is guided or adjusted. This is the chorus's last significant part in the action. Their responses throw Peleus' personal tragedy into relief, while their communal grief conveys a sympathetic, yet more distanced and exemplary, reaction to the terrible events before them.

The chorus's role in the *Andromache* is integral to the tragic shape of the play. The dramatist has taken great care to tie the content of the poetry to the movement of the action. (We would surely feel a major dislocation of tone and frustration of dramatic development if this were otherwise.) The *parodos* introduces the theme of Greek sympathy for Trojan suffering, while the chorus's insistence on the necessity of surrender to superior force magnifies the resistance and heroism of Andromache. The *agon* of Hermione and Andromache is followed by a choral song which takes us back to the earliest origins of the Trojan War. The baby Paris was not killed: the consequences of Hecuba's maternal love contrast with the beneficent effects of Andromache's struggle to save her son's life. The goddesses' competition for the favour of a man reflects the strife among the mortal women. Both Greek and Trojan pain are paid equal respect in the chorus's estimation of the war's impact. The *agon* of Menelaus and Andromache ends on her departure with her son for execution; the second choral ode criticizes the wayward independence of Hermione which has led to the crisis of 'two leaders' in the home of Neoptolemus. The murder is unreservedly condemned, and retribution predicted.

---

[133] L. P. E. Parker (1997) 51–2 discusses Euripides' (and Sophocles') fondness for dactyls in passages of lamentation: cf. 103 ff.

[134] Richardson (1993) 352 on *Il.* 24. 719–22, who contrasts 'the θρῆνοι ['dirges'] sung by outsiders or professionals'.

Peleus' defeat of Spartan interference inspires the chorus to an encomiastic ode which rejects unjust violence. At this point the play takes a new turn: Hermione's collapse motivates a second, but expressively contrasting, rescue action from Orestes. He promises a further stage to his murderous career, now involving another death in the Aeacid line. The following ode begins in bafflement about the gods' earlier abandonment of Troy, then recalls Apollo's role in the matricide and questions its justice. The chorus end with a graphic description of the effects of the war; yet here too there is acknowledgement of shared distress. In context the ode complicates and questions the polar opposition between Greek and barbarian.

From even such a brief summary of the place of the various odes in the *Andromache*, it will be clear that they are fundamental to the development and impact of the drama.[135] The form and content of the choral songs are richly varied and they take up the action from many different angles; their wider temporal perspective enhances the intellectual depth of their reflections.[136] The aesthetic pleasure of the poetry, often in contrast to the brutality of the action,[137] heightens the impact of its content. Impressive generalizations and tones of wisdom are part of the tradition derived from choral lyric.[138] This is interestingly combined in tragedy with a character for the chorus which is often limited in perspective. Since choruses have no less subjectivity than the protagonists, and can even be openly prejudiced, the Phthian women's humane concern for Andromache and their respect for Trojan experience are all the

---

[135] To treat any Euripidean ode as a pretty, allusive interlude which articulates neither the questions nor the passions of the play is to undervalue it. Gould (1996a) 573 rightly argues that the so-called 'decline of the chorus' in Euripides must be seen in the context of the 'changing nature of late Euripidean theatre', especially his increased interest in actors' song. Easterling (1997a) 155–6 argues persuasively that although choral performance in tragedy never ceased to change, it continued to play a vital and popular theatrical role in the late fifth century and beyond.

[136] Cf. Segal (1986) 348–9: 'In most of Greek tragedy the strong emotional reactions produced by the events are always pulled into the orbit of moral questioning and raised to a level of poetical and sometimes philosophical reformulation by the choral odes.'

[137] See Mossman (1995) 93.

[138] Even, for example, from Alcman's maidens: ἔστι τις σιῶν τίσις ('There is such a thing as punishment from the gods', fr. 1. 36 D).

more striking. Thay call into question the traditional ethnic divisions and the unsophisticated moral evaluations that are often drawn from them.

The flexibility of the chorus is well illustrated by the way it fits the developing play; each ode conveys a particular atmosphere, from the joyous and hymnic to the perplexed and shocked, and the mood affects our response to the surrounding action. Moreover, the musical and choreographic patterning of the stasima introduces a different energy to the drama. The chorus's response to the changing events before them is shifting but coherent. In their songs, and in the remarks of the coryphaeus, they reveal a malleable, but also intelligible and consistent identity. The Phthian women's increasing alienation from the methods of Menelaus and Hermione, and their criticisms of Orestes and Apollo, are not those of a static bystander. On the contrary, they are a central element of the fictional world and its dramatic workings. We readjust our view of events in response to theirs, supporting or questioning their stance. The chorus thus encourage engaged and critical interest in the moral issues of the play. In the *Andromache*, as always, they are a fundamental source of the polyphony and the questioning spirit of Greek tragedy.

8

Gods

In particular, the reader may regret the absence of a satisfactory
account of the religion of the tragedians, but this question is too
subtle to be treated within the space of a few pages.

W. Burkert[1]

I hope philosophy and poetry will not neutralize each other, and leave
me an inert mass.

Coleridge

The *Andromache* is an interesting text with which to explore
Euripides' handling of the gods. Such plays as the *Hippolytus*
or *Heracles* are more commonly used sources for this discussion, yet the *Andromache* raises questions about divine vengeance and justice which are no less searching and no less
profound. Study of a less obvious text, one of Euripides'
'problem' plays,[2] may be of value in so far as it addresses the
issues from a less familiar perspective. This chapter will contribute to our overall argument that Euripidean tragedy is
multifarious, and that each play is distinctive.[3] By considering
how Apollo and Thetis behave in the *Andromache*, we shall
illuminate Euripides' complex use of the gods, both as characters in the plays and as unseen, enigmatic agents shaping the
action from outside. It is important for such a study that we
should see the gods of tragedy both in the context of fifth-
century speculative thought and as part of the tradition of
Greek mythological poetry.

---

[1] Burkert (1985) 7.

[2] For this description of the *Andromache*, see Kovacs (1987) 22.

[3] This is particularly imperative here because scholars continue to make
blanket statements about Euripides' use of the gods, for example, Ewans
(1996) 455 n. 31: 'quite simply, Euripides' extant dramas . . . are not written
on the assumption that mankind lives in, and interacts with, an animate
universe. The divine is treated, ironically, cynically, or sceptically in most of
Euripides.'

In recent years there has been a strong scholarly reaction against the notion that Euripides was a sophistic and atheistic iconoclast. The critical school of 'Euripides the rationalist' often interpreted his plays as intellectual pamphlets written to expose the gods of tragic myth as all too human.[4] The step back from this picture was justified.[5] But the reactionary interpretations of 'Euripides the traditionalist' which now so abound in the critical literature are as faulty and one-sided as their revolutionary predecessors. It has recently been argued that Euripidean characters only express philosophical notions of theological scepticism in desperate situations, but that the gods are ultimately vindicated as still retaining their traditional powers.[6] Thus one critic can even declare 'the morality of the gods is something of a side issue in his plays'.[7] By contrast, it will be argued here that the behaviour and morality of the gods (rather than doubts about their existence) are fundamental to Greek tragedy and its metaphysical meaning.[8] Euripides pushes traditional poetic criticism of the gods to new extremes, but this must be seen as part of his broader dramatic (and typically tragic) purpose of exploring humanity's inability to understand or control its entire world.[9] Recent treatments of the *Andromache* have advanced a 'pious' reading of the action which is part of a general trend against the excesses of the

[4] For the critical alignments *pro* and *contra* Nestle's picture of Euripides the rationalist, see Rohdich (1968) 13–14.

[5] Contrast, for example, Gould's ((1985) 29) reading of *Hippolytus*, where mortals 'confront the utterly, destructively alien; impossible, uncanny, sickening, yet undeniably "there" and beyond us to will away'.

[6] Lefkowitz (1989) 72, Mikalson (1991) 156, in reaction against such formulations as Rosenmeyer (1982) 283: 'in Euripides, the gods are posted on a grid of Sophistic antinomies'.

[7] Gregory (1991) 188.

[8] Cf. R. Parker (1997) 158: 'If critics of Greek tragedy constantly find themselves discussing the justice or injustice of the gods, this is not because they import anachronistic theological preoccupations, or not merely so: the plays themselves raise these issues with a notable insistence.' Griffin (1998) 55, 60 locates the problems posed by the gods' involvement in tragedy in the modern 'collectivist school of criticism'.

[9] Cf. Segal (1982) 339: 'In the poetry of Euripides the myths of the gods, more often than not, are a source of disorder.' Aristotle's omission of the gods from his study of tragedy is severely criticized by Stinton (1990) 170 ff., who observes (p. 172) 'to ignore divine motivation in Greek tragedy must lead to distortion'.

atheistic paradigm.[10] Yet Neoptolemus' second, apologetic visit to Delphi (probably a Euripidean innovation), combined with Orestes' negative role as the god's agent in a cowardly ambush, suggest that to justify this divine punishment is fundamentally mistaken.[11]

Caricatures of Euripides as hostile to the gods have a long history. In their simplest form, they verge on the absurd, as illustrated by Coleridge's *Table Talk* for 29 December 1822: 'Euripides was like a modern Frenchman, never so happy, as when giving a slap at the Gods altogether.' Ultimately such views go back to the portrayal of Euripides by Aristophanes, who shows him undermining conventional beliefs (*Thesm.* 450–1) and worshipping a private and idiosyncratic pantheon (*Frogs* 888–94).[12] Many critics have produced readings of Euripides' religious thought which are bleakly, and blandly, ironic, because they equated it with that of contemporary avant-garde philosophy. Like Aristophanes, modern critics occasionally disregard dramatic context when citing passages that attack the gods or seem to espouse atheism.[13] When characters comment on the gods (regardless of author), we must take into account both speaker and context. Their attitudes are 'elements in a dramatic situation, not factors in

[10] Burnett (1971) 156, Kovacs (1980) 78–80, (1987) 19–21; cf. Lefkowitz (1987), (1989), Heath (1987) 49–64: 'Euripides the traditionalist'.

[11] The 'something to do with Dionysus' debate has tended to distract attention from other tragic gods. Seaford (1994) 344 ff. has elaborated a sophisticated theory which sees Dionysus as *the* destroyer of the tragic household. But what of Peleus' household? We should look carefully at each god. Apollo's role in many plays is problematic to say the least. Hartigan (1991) remarkably makes no reference to the *Andromache* in her discussion of Euripides' complex presentation of the god.

[12] See Parker (1996) 205 for Aristophanes' hostility to 'atheism' (and rhetoric) as subversive of morality.

[13] Cf. *Bell.* fr. 286. 1–3 K, a notorious denial of the existence of the gods which is refuted by the action of the play itself. Drachmann (1922) argues that an atheist in the ancient world was someone who held unconventional beliefs about the gods, not necessarily denying their existence. Yunis (1988) 60 n. 2 comments on the rarity of outright statements of disbelief in the gods' existence. Obbink (1996) 1–4 with n. 1 succinctly presents the various definitions, and notes (p. 1): 'Atheism in the ancient world was never a well-defined or ideologically fixed position.' It cannot be stressed too much that the religious context of Athens is much more complicated than any believers-versus-atheists model could comprise.

a theological diatribe'.[14] Tragedy remains essentially interrogatory, asking questions rather than supplying dogmatic
answers.

If the crude question is asked 'Was Euripides an atheist?', no
categorical solution is likely to be forthcoming.[15] Similarly,
critics often assume an easy process of inference from drama, a
mythical fiction, to general beliefs about the gods. But the
question that should be asked is far from simple: How justified
is the critical urge to extort from the texts 'religious beliefs',
whether in author or in audience? There is a range of
approaches available to us in appraising the gods within the
dramatic fiction. One reading (particularly frequent with
regard to *Hipp.* and *Bacch.*) asserts that the gods are not
meant to be perceived as real; they are merely symbols of
repressed passions. Here the gods are locked inside the text and
function chiefly as narrative devices or tools of psychological
explanation. Secondly, there is the approach which perceives
the gods as the very deities which the author and audience
believe in. Thirdly, and, I would argue, most persuasively, we
might state that the gods, without necessarily being the gods
that the audience believe in, are to be taken seriously as agents
within the play, acting with both power and personality.[16]
However, this does not limit them to being mere 'literary'
figures.[17] The spectators will have been challenged, particu-

[14] Ireland (1986) 11. Feeney (1998) 7 rightly criticizes the notion that the
Greeks went to tragic festivals 'to learn profound truths about theology'.

[15] One may be forgiven for stating the obvious, but regularly neglected, fact
that Euripides' personal religious beliefs are unattainable: that his works are
fictional plays for the stage in which the author does not speak. Yet scholars
persist in attributing to him irrelevant (and unprovable) descriptions: for
example, Knox (1985) 317 regards it as 'not likely' that Euripides believed in
the gods; see Lefkowitz (1989) 71 n. 4 for a bibliography of like-minded
scholars. In the case of Sophocles, by contrast, it is the poet's alleged piety
which has obscured his plays' questioning of divine justice.

[16] Discussing Burkert's approach to the gods as persons and Vernant's view
of them as powers, Bremmer (1994) 22–3 points out that it is misguided to
prefer one model over the other absolutely, since each aspect is prominent in
different contexts. Poets and artists generally stress the personal side of the
gods, but they are drawing on (and reshaping) a broad cultural system of
divine powers.

[17] Sourvinou-Inwood (1997) 163–70 makes many excellent criticisms of
Mikalson's (1991) strong disjunction between the fictive gods of tragedy and
the actual recipients of sacrifice and cult (cf. Feeney (1998) 24). She also

larly by the plays of Euripides, to reflect on their own attitudes
to the gods in the light of the tragic figures' experience of the
divine.

The relationship between poetic representation and everyday religious attitudes is complex.[18] We simply do not know
how far ordinary people thought in terms of gods rather than of
human motives when interpreting the behaviour of others and
of themselves.[19] Scholars rightly insist that Greek religion was
free of the dogmatism that comes with a holy text or creed,[20]
yet there clearly was a metaphysical world-constructing element to Greek religion, and it is this background which tragedy
explores and challenges.[21] The variety of Greek religion from
polis to *polis* at the level of everyday worship[22] was in some
measure transcended by the powerful poetic model of the
ordered pantheon, common to all Hellas (cf. Hdt. 2. 53. 2).[23]

stresses that the audience would make sense of the deities on stage using
assumptions developed in religious practice: 'it was an interactive process'
(p. 171).

[18] Cf. Gale (1994) 20. The intricate and fertile relationship between
contemporary religious practice and the world of the plays is particularly
evident in Euripides' fondness for ritual aetia.

[19] Discussing the moral implications of anthropomorphic gods, Winnington-Ingram (1948) 14 observes that it is hard to gauge how much authority the
divine myths held for everyday belief and conduct.

[20] But Sourvinou-Inwood (1990) has stressed the important role of the *polis*
as a religious authority. Nock (1972) 545 notes *Sept*. 253, where the gods are
addressed as citizens, and comments: 'their cults were part of the fabric of
civic life, and the upkeep of these cults was a civic obligation'. Isocr. 7. 30
defines piety as changing nothing of what one's forefathers have handed
down. For the piety of adhering to ancestral tradition instead of being *sophos*,
cf. *Bacch*. 200–3 (deleted by Diggle; but Seaford (1996) 169 f. makes a strong
case against interpolation), 395–401. Resistance to foreign cults in Euripides'
own time is perhaps reflected in the *Bacchae*: see Versnel (1990) 100 ff.,
Seaford (1996) 51–2.

[21] Cf. Burkert (1987) 30: 'for moderns, poised between nihilism and
linguistics, it [religion] has become "constructing worlds of meaning"'.
Vernant (1991) 285 f. discusses the ability of divine myth to reach out to a
'certain type of knowledge of the real'. Nussbaum (1986) 49 has some
excellent remarks on how the conflicting gods of Greek polytheism and
myth vividly articulate the contrary pull of ethical obligations.

[22] Cf. Bremmer (1994) 1: 'No Greek city . . . was a religious clone.'

[23] Homer and Hesiod are of course heirs to a long tradition of divine
conflation which shows deep influence from Indo-European and Asiatic
elements: Burkert (1992), ch. 3. This is traced in detail for individual gods

Most striking is the sudden increase in the number of divine
scenes in the visual arts from the mid-seventh century onwards
which show the gods behaving in the roles characteristic of the
epic.[24] The poetry of Homer and Hesiod gives the gods a wider
imaginative context, 'a "history" which makes identifiable and
describable beings out of the recipients of sacrifice and
prayer'.[25] At the same time, the theological framework, based
on the divine family, was extremely flexible, allowing peculiar
skills and spheres of interest to be allotted to specific gods. The
underlying genealogical network meant that the separate beings
(and their domains) could form a cosmos, satisfyingly holistic,
and impressively interconnected.[26] However, the deities of
myth, and especially of tragic myth, were also turbulent
forces that were able to disrupt and complicate the conventional pieties of civic theology.[27]

The gods of myth, shaped by the epic tradition, had a
powerful influence on Greek religious awareness.[28] The epics
were the foundation of literate education throughout the fifth
century, and the epic gods articulated a world-view in which
mankind 'has an insignificant and yet paramount role'.[29] And
they were of course fundamental for the gods of later literature.
In epic the gods are portrayed as 'subject to rage, spite and

by Burkert (1985) 125–189. The Greek trend was to 'elevate and humanize the
Mesopotamian beliefs which they largely adopted' (Janko (1992) 1); the poetic
gods' pan-Hellenic impact is well set out by Nagy (1990) 36 ff. Heitsch (1993)
4 ff. underestimates the shaping role of the poets. Rutherford (1996) 47 is
more accurate: 'Some at least of Homer's conception of the gods is "poetic" in
the sense that it probably lacks any basis in cult. Homeric religion is both
selective and creative.' His words apply equally well to the tragedians.

[24] Burkert (1985) 123–4. Cf. Osborne (1996) 161 ff., esp. 166–7: 'the visual
arts of the seventh century BC grapple with human relationships and relations
between human, animal, and divine worlds in a way not familiar in geometric
art'. The relevance of such representations to the precise dating of Homeric
epic is disputed by Seaford (1994) 145–6 and Snodgrass (1998), esp. 12–13.

[25] Gould (1994) 105.

[26] For the 'plurality and richness' of Greek polytheism, see Nussbaum
(1986) 279.

[27] Cf. R. Parker (1997), who highlights the *Troades* as particularly damaging to 'civic optimism' (p. 155).

[28] Redfield (1975) 76 is a forceful proponent of the 'literary gods' model for
epic; it is effectively rebutted by Griffin (1980) 145–72.

[29] Janko (1992) 7.

lust'.[30] The potential for human suffering in such a context, and the conflict it generates between human and divine conceptions of justice, lie very close to the centre of Euripides' exploration of divine government. As in epic the gods are represented as acting for reasons which men can both appraise and criticize. Medea asserts that Zeus knows all about Jason's behaviour (*Med.* 1352–3), and she implies that the gods approve of her revenge. But if Jason's punishment is sanctioned by the gods, that does not make the infanticide less heinous. In fact, Medea's actions are made more distressing and horrific if the gods are involved. Their support does not settle the problem of the revenge; on the contrary, it becomes more problematic, and that makes the human action all the more disturbing. It is no less disconcerting when in the *Andromache* Apollo colludes in Orestes' murder of Neoptolemus; that also makes us reappraise the divine justice. The perplexing and problematic actions of the gods complicate the texture of the tragic world and illuminate new aspects of human situation and character.

The gulf between the gods and their human worshippers is an important aspect of much post-epic poetry.[31] Pindar poignantly expresses the closeness, but also the crucial boundary, between mortal and immortal, in the opening strophe of *Nemean* 6:[32]

> Ἕν ἀνδρῶν, ἓν θεῶν γένος· ἐκ μιᾶς δὲ πνέομεν
> ματρὸς ἀμφότεροι· διείργει δὲ πᾶσα κεκριμένα
> δύναμις, ὡς τὸ μὲν οὐδέν, ὁ δὲ χάλκεος ἀσφαλὲς
>   αἰὲν ἕδος
> μένει οὐρανός. ἀλλά τι προσφέρομεν ἔμπαν ἢ
>   μέγαν
> νόον ἤτοι φύσιν ἀθανάτοις,
> καίπερ ἐφαμερίαν οὐκ εἰδότες οὐδὲ μετὰ νύκτας
>   ἄμμε πότμος
> ἅντιν' ἔγραψε δραμεῖν ποτὶ στάθμαν.

---

[30] Dover (1974) 76.

[31] The gap is stressed in epic by the separate narrative perspectives of mortals and immortals: see Taplin (1992) 143, who notes the poignant effect of the gods' ignorance of 'the pressures and agonies of human life'.

[32] Finley (1955) 54–5 notes that the passage 'is full of jerks and hesitations because at every suggested likeness of men to gods some reservation seems necessary'. For a related thought, and similar zig-zagging structure, cf. Soph. fr. 591 R.

There is one race of men, one of gods. But from one mother we both take our breath. However, all allotted power separates us, since one is nothing, while the bronze sky remains forever, a secure seat. But we somehow resemble the immortals either in our great mind or nature, although we do not know towards what goal by day or by night destiny has written that we shall run.

Yet while for Pindar human life is uncertain and ephemeral, he also constantly insists on the wisdom of the gods. In his epinician poems he likes to defuse problems about the morality of the gods—even though many of the mythical stories resist such treatment—so that the sense of mortal fragility is over-whelmed by that of the gods' support, which is manifest at high moments of human success. Euripides pushes the idea of human frailty much further. Although the human world is precarious, Pindar handles the divine positively. When confronted, for example, by episodes in the life of Heracles which are difficult to praise, Pindar's reaction is magisterially dismissive. Thus, in the ninth *Olympian*, after partly narrating Heracles' *theomachia* with Poseidon, Apollo and Hades, Pindar says:

> ἀπό μοι λόγον
> τοῦτον, στόμα, ῥῖψον·
> ἐπεὶ τό γε λοιδορῆσαι θεοὺς
> ἐχθρὰ σοφία, καὶ τὸ καυχᾶσθαι παρὰ καιρόν
> μανίαισιν ὑποκρέκει.
>
> (*Ol.* 9. 35–9)

Mouth, throw this story far from me! Since it is a hateful skill to insult the gods, and to blab out of turn sounds in harmony with madness.

There could be no stronger contrast than that between Pindar's abrupt gesture of pious distaste and Euripides' exploration in the *Heracles* of the hero's mortality, pain, and undeserved suffering.[33]

In Euripides there often seems to be no correlation in specific situations between divine and human approaches to justice;[34] this is a disturbing feature of the tragic pathos which

[33] Cf. Stinton (1990) 264.

[34] Gods occasionally try to draw analogies between humans' wishes, e.g. for honour, and their own (cf. *Hipp.* 7–8); it is rather the application of justice that differs: for example, the gods' entitlement to respect rather than Heracles' entitlement to a reward, at least according to Hera.

arrests the attention of the audience and stimulates it to reconsider the moral implications of the gods' role in many heroic myths. By dramatizing a world of divine reasoning and action which is precarious and dangerous, Euripides can arouse natural feelings of fear and uncertainty. He can also show us that the human response to the unpredictable, uncanny, and sometimes horrendous actions of the gods can possess nobility. The *Hippolytus* explores the motives and morality of divine behaviour. The violence of the action, set in motion by a goddess's vengeance, triggers a cycle of retribution which will continue beyond the play: Artemis promises at the earliest opportunity to destroy one of Aphrodite's favourites (*Hipp.* 1420–2). As has been said of Aphrodite in the *Hippolytus*, 'one cannot understand the tragedy without retaining the personified goddess, in the strongest sense of "personified"'.[35] Hippolytus' relationship to Artemis is put in proportion when she leaves him to die; he says, μακρὰν δὲ λείπεις ῥαιδίως ὁμιλίαν ('but how easily you leave our long companionship', 1441), and her easy departure makes all the more emphatic the gulf between divine and human concerns.[36] Hippolytus' relationship to his father, though tragically a factor in his death, is at least more symmetrical: the two unite in grief, and the son forgives the father for his unwitting action (1449–52).[37] The tragic movement of the *Hippolytus* (like Hera's vindictive pursuit of the hero in the *Heracles*) calls into question a fundamental feature of the epic portrayal of the gods: their insistence on the universal human recognition of their τιμή ('honour', cf. 48–50).[38] In a similar way in the *Andromache* Apollo is criticized for acting on a long-held grudge.

[35] Heath (1987) 54. Cf. Burkert (1985) 125: 'The poetic language . . . creates a world of its own, a world in which the gods lead their lives.'

[36] See Griffin (1980) 189 with n. 29, who compares *Ion* 905; Yunis (1988) 121 n. 38 counters Barrett (1964) 414, who sees 'No word of rebuke in this'. Hippolytus' impossible wish φεῦ· | εἴθ' ἦν ἀραῖον δαίμοσιν βροτῶν γένος ('Ah, if only mortals could curse gods!', 1415) stresses the gods' sublimity, but does so critically.

[37] Compare the sympathy between the two heroes at the end of the *Heracles*.

[38] The Homeric gods' concern with honour and their anger when it is slighted are well discussed by Yamagata (1994) 93–101. The consequences of not giving the gods their due are exacted by Aphrodite on Tyndareus through

Tragedy loves to show humans baffled by the reactions of gods. And even when gods do seek to communicate with mortals, their message can be riddling or indistinct: 'The voice of a god needs translating, and translators can be wrong.'[39] Nine of the extant tragedies of Euripides (excluding the Muse of *Rhesus*) are resolved with a speech by a god squaring off the action,[40] and five begin with a god as the speaker of the prologue.[41] This observation shows how vital divine figures are to the structure and atmosphere of Euripides' work.[42] The identity of the speaker may also illuminate the structure and impact of the play, as with the symmetrical appearances of Aphrodite and Artemis in the *Hippolytus*,[43] and the dominance of Dionysus, marked by his framing presence at the beginning and end of the *Bacchae*.[44]

Each play is an entity in itself, and the *Andromache* is as important as any other to our estimation of Euripides' use and representation of the gods. The play possesses a divine frame, opening and closing with Thetis, first with her altar as the site of asylum, and finally with the goddess herself consoling the bereaved and rewarding the virtuous. Of course, there is more to her appearance than that: a Euripidean theophany is never quite so benign and unproblematic.[45] The statue of Thetis is the wayward marriages of his daughters, Clytemnestra and Helen, whose repercussions continue to be felt in the *Andromache* (cf. Stes. fr. 223 D).

[39] Buxton (1996) 41, commenting on *OT* 978–9. Sophocles is particularly fascinated by obscure oracles and their dramatic flexibility. His gods are more in the background than Euripides'. While his characters often act in an atmosphere of divine foreboding, Euripides' are more outspoken in their confrontation with the gods' plans.

[40] Artemis (*Hipp.*), Thetis (*Andr.*), Athena (*Suppl.*, *IT*, *Ion* (cf. also *Erechth.*)), Castor (*El.*, *Hel.*), Apollo (*Or.*), Dionysus (*Bacch.*).

[41] Apollo (*Alc.*), Aphrodite (*Hipp.*), Poseidon and Athena in dialogue (*Tro.*), Hermes (*Ion*), Dionysus (*Bacch.*).

[42] Compare the in-between status of Polydorus' ghost in *Hec.*, and Medea's semi-divine exit. On the latter Easterling (1977) 190 notes how the unconventional *dea ex machina* 'offers no relief whatever from the horror of the situation'.

[43] Artemis too is jealous and destructive, but more generous in her recognition of Phaedra's 'kind of nobility' (τρόπον τινὰ | γενναιότητα, 1300–1).

[44] The parallels between the *absence* of Apollo at the end of *Andr.* and *Ion* will be discussed below.

[45] Complicating Storey (1993) 184: 'Thetis may just be that rare creature, a truly benevolent Euripidean deity.'

mentioned at various points; the goddess's presence in it is suggested by Andromache's appeal to Hermione, ὁρᾷς ἄγαλμα Θέτιδος ἐς σ' ἀποβλέπον; ('Do you see the statue of Thetis looking closely at you?', 246; cf. 260).[46] The chorus sing two odes that are largely concerned with the divine background to the present post-war crisis (274 ff., 1010 ff.), while the action culminates horribly when a hero is murdered on sacred ground, and the murder is sanctioned by Apollo himself.[47] The divine role in events, both at Thetideion and Delphi, is thus important for our response to the play.

The play opens with a prologue spoken by a mortal, which describes the religiously coloured setting (16–20). The monument to Thetis is Andromache's space, and she leaves it only under duress (411–12).[48] The first part of the play revolves around the shrine, and not merely spatially.[49] The very fact that Andromache has sought refuge at the altar of the mother of her husband's killer is in itself 'the first intimation of the restructuring of the conflict of the Trojan war'.[50] The location is also significant because the way characters treat the rules of asylum guides the audience's response to them.[51] The intrinsic emotional tension of the suppliant scene made it an ideal focus for tragic conflict.[52] Moreover, the violation of asylum was an

---

[46] Wiles (1997) 201 remarks: '[it] is not a decorative addendum, but a crucial determinant of how the audience will respond.'

[47] Compare the Erinyes' reaction to the god's acceptance of the matricide Orestes at Delphi: *Eum.* 164–70, 204, 716.

[48] The idea of physical contact with the sacred site is important: Helen rushes back to the protection of Proteus when Menelaus approaches (*Hel.* 541–8), and Andromache embraces the statue of Thetis (115).

[49] Cf. Croally (1994) 196–7 on ἑρμήνευμα ('memorial', 46): 'it has the connotation of a reminder, something concrete (present) in case you forget (the important absence)'.

[50] Kuntz (1993) 71.

[51] Repeatedly in tragedy, the violation of sanctuary is treated as an act of violence against the gods themselves. See the extensive lists of Mikalson (1991) 258 nn. 10–16. Technically, Hermione only threatens but does not violate the laws of asylum (161–2, cf. Theoclymenus' pressure, *Hel.* 61–5). Ion argues strongly against the inviolable rights of sanctuary (*Ion* 1312–19); ironically, since he does not know the suppliant is his own mother. Cf. Eur. *Oed.* fr. 98 Austin. These strictures demand that asylum be granted only to those who are unjustly treated, of whom Andromache is a paradigm instance.

[52] Cf. Aesch. *Suppl.*, *Eum.*, Soph. *OC*; to judge from the extant plays, Euripides had a special liking for it: *Hcld.*, *Andr.*, *Suppl.*, *Her.*, *Ion*, *Hel.*

emotive event outside the plays, as the historians' reactions to it show.[53] Ulrich Sinn has catalogued numerous instances in Greek history where sanctuary was violently or deceitfully undermined, many of them during the Peloponnesian War.[54] What is unique and especially harrowing about the situation in the *Andromache* is the use of the suppliant's son to force her departure from sanctuary. Exploiting a child as bait characterizes Menelaus as particularly brutal and cowardly.

Significantly, on his entry with Andromache's son, Menelaus denigrates the statue of Thetis ($\sigma\grave{\epsilon}$ $\mu\grave{\epsilon}\nu$ $\gamma\grave{\alpha}\rho$ $\eta\check{\upsilon}\chi\epsilon\iota\varsigma$ $\theta\epsilon\hat{\alpha}\varsigma$ $\beta\rho\acute{\epsilon}\tau\alpha\varsigma$ $\sigma\acute{\omega}\sigma\epsilon\iota\nu$ $\tau\acute{o}\delta\epsilon$ 311, 'You were sure that this statue of the goddess would save you') before he presents the suppliant's dilemma: she must choose between her own life and her son's (314–18).[55] There were historical circumstances in the fifth century where aggressors promised not to kill or punish suppliants if they left their place of asylum, and then broke their promise.[56] However, such breaches of the sacred rights of sanctuary were condemned, even in times of war. The situation in Thetideion is far from being one of combat or siege, yet Menelaus' offer covers only the life of mother *or* child, and he reneges even on that promise.[57] Menelaus unambiguously violates the rights of the suppliant. The poet thus uses a basic concern of religious custom to criticize a character and his actions.[58]

Menelaus shamelessly admits his deception ($\kappa\acute{\eta}\rho\upsilon\sigma\sigma$' $\acute{\alpha}\pi\alpha\sigma\iota\nu$· $o\grave{\upsilon}$ $\gamma\grave{\alpha}\rho$ $\grave{\epsilon}\xi\alpha\rho\nu o\acute{\upsilon}\mu\epsilon\theta\alpha$, 'Proclaim it to all, for I do not deny it',

[53] Griffin (1998) 57 sees in such terrible crimes 'one of the most important links between tragedy and history'.

[54] Sinn (1990), Anhang II, esp. pp. 109–11.

[55] In keeping with her nobility and endurance, Andromache does not threaten suicide in the sanctuary; cf. Aesch. *Supp.* 457–67, *Hel.* 980–7. These tragic threats are uniformly successful; real life could be very different: cf. Thuc. 3. 81 (Corcyra, 427), 1. 126–8, 134.

[56] Cf. Gould (1973) 82–3, Sinn (1993) 92: 'Many a suppliant was the victim of malicious deception.'

[57] Gould (1973) 78 notes that there was a 'variety of methods to circumvent the protection of the god by finding some "non-violent" means of breaking the physical contact of supplication'. Menelaus never even contemplates a 'non-violent' solution.

[58] Menelaus disregards the religious sanction of $\mu\iota\alpha\phi\acute{o}\nu o\nu$ $\mu\acute{\upsilon}\sigma o\varsigma$ ('the pollution of murder', 335), invoked by Andromache. Orestes claims his pollution meant he could only marry from among his *philoi*; Menelaus ignored this too (966 ff.). Cf. Parker (1983) 205.

436), but Andromache still hopes that traditional religious sanctions may have some force, and appeals to divine justice (439–40):

> Αν. τὰ θεῖα δ' οὐ θεῖ' οὐδ' ἔχειν ἡγῆι δίκην;
> Με. ὅταν τάδ' ἦι, τότ' οἴσομεν· σὲ δὲ κτενῶ.[59]

ANDROMACHE: Do you think that the gods are not gods and have no sense of justice?
MENELAUS: Whenever these things will be, then I will bear them. But you I will kill.

Menelaus in his reply juxtaposes an off-hand defiance of divine punishment with a promise to kill.[60] During Andromache's lyric lament with her son she calls their death a 'pitiful sacrifice' (θῦμα δάιον, 506). They now stand near the altar of Thetis where Andromache had been suppliant (cf. 411); the imposing shrine enhances the idea of perverted sacrifice.[61] Peleus makes clear in his opening words the barbarity of the imminent executions (547–9):

> ὑμᾶς ἐρωτῶ τόν τ' ἐφεστῶτα σφαγῆι,
> τί ταῦτα, πῶς ταῦτ'; ἐκ τίνος λόγου νοσεῖ
> δόμος;

You men, and the one in charge of the slaughter, I am asking you, what is this, how has it come about? For what reason is the house sick?

The sacrificial connotations of σφαγή ('slaughter') are underlined by Andromache's being bound like an animal victim.[62] Neoptolemus' death is also represented in such terms, as he is killed and mutilated βωμοῦ πέλας ('beside the altar', 1156). Both

---

[59] The text here is Diggle's OCT, although he detects difficulties in each line: see Diggle (1994) 13–14. His suggested improvements to 439 deliver τὰ θεῖα δ' οὐ θεῖ', οὐ Δίκην ἡγῆι Δίκην; ('Do you think the gods are not gods, and justice not justice?'), which retain the connection of divinity with the administration of justice.

[60] Cf. Soph. *OC* 881–3, where Creon acknowledges the omniscience of Zeus and the hybris of his act, but presses on with his removal of Oedipus.

[61] On this motif in tragedy, see Foley (1985) 40–6, 155–62.

[62] Note Peleus' sarcastic question, βοῦν ἢ λέοντ' ἤλπιζες ἐντείνειν βρόχοις; ('Was it a bull or a lion you thought you were tying with knots?', 720). The image is particularly grisly at *Eum.* 305 (the Furies to Orestes): καὶ ζῶν με δαίσεις οὐδὲ πρὸς βωμῶι σφαγείς ('You shall feed me even while you live, without being slaughtered at the altar').

the potential murderers of Andromache and the successful
killer of Neoptolemus (along with his Delphian allies and
divine sponsor) are condemned by the disruption of sacrificial
custom.[63]

As Andromache tells Peleus of the Spartans' plot, she again
invokes the altar of Thetis (565–7). The appeal to reverence of
philoi is appropriate to the familial concerns of the play, and it
also recalls the scene of supplication between Priam and
Achilles in the *Iliad* (24. 486 ff.). Here the generations are
reversed, although the appeal of suffering Trojan to powerful
Greek remains and is equally successful: the daughter-in-law
of the Iliadic petitioner now beseeches the father of the epic
hero. Menelaus tries with characteristic slipperiness to evade
responsibility for the war: Ἑλένη δ' ἐμόχθησ' οὐχ ἑκοῦσ' ἀλλ' ἐκ
θεῶν ('Helen did not get into trouble willingly but because of
the gods', 680; cf. Gorg. *Hel.* 6, 19). He reduces the human
participants in the Trojan War to puppets of divine will, but no
more convincingly than Helen herself in the *Troades* (946–50).
The reality of human motivation must be recognized if moral
evaluation is to have any force. The Spartans' devolution of
responsibility, whether from one human to another, or to the
gods, is an indication of their moral shallowness.

Hermione's despair at her calamity evokes consolation from
the Nurse (851–2):

> τί ταῦτα μοχθεῖς; συμφοραὶ θεήλατοι
> πᾶσιν βροτοῖσιν ἢ τότ' ἦλθον ἢ τότε.

Why distress yourself in this way? Disasters sent by the gods come to
all mortals sooner or later.

Here, however, the conventional sentiment rings hollow:
Hermione's anguish is not a product of divine intervention or
malice. When Orestes arrives, she again disowns responsibility
for her actions, attributing her difficulties only partially to
herself (902–3):

> τὰ μὲν πρὸς ἡμῶν, τὰ δὲ πρὸς ἀνδρὸς ὅς μ' ἔχει,
> τὰ δ' ἐκ θεῶν του· πανταχῆι δ' ὀλώλαμεν.

---

[63] Justified killings at religious occasions did take place (see Parker (1983)
159–60), but the conditions which characterize them (generally, to depose a
tyrant or to exact vengeance on behalf of one's kin) do not apply to the murder
of Andromache and her son or of Neoptolemus.

It is partly myself, partly the man who is my husband, and partly some god. I am ruined on all sides.

Although Hermione's vagueness is meant to diminish her part in the plot, the mention of 'some god' reminds us of Andromache's earlier appeals to Thetis, whose saving appearance at the end of the play complements Peleus' intervention and completes the unlikely turn of events mentioned earlier by Hermione: ἢν δ' οὖν βροτῶν τίς σ' ἢ θεῶν σῶσαι θέληι ('But if some mortal or god should want to save you', 163). By contrast, Orestes' first reference to a god is precise: ὦ Φοῖβ' ἀκέστορ, πημάτων δοίης λύσιν ('Phoebus, Healer, grant us release from our troubles!', 900).[64]

Orestes is of course inextricably linked to Apollo in myth through the god's support for the matricide;[65] the event itself is recalled by Orestes' self-description (884–5).[66] His prediction of Apollo's role as accomplice in the murder of Neoptolemus (1002–8) recalls, and maliciously transforms, Andromache's earlier description of Neoptolemus' purpose in Delphi (50–5). She terms his earlier demand for reparation 'madness' (μανία, 52), but recognizes that his second visit is intended to gain pardon from Apollo for 'his earlier mistakes' (τὰ πρόσθε σφάλματα, 54). Orestes, however, explicitly denies the success of Neoptolemus' mission (1002–6):

[64] The invocation of Apollo the Healer is a regular apotropaic expression, but here, spoken by the matricide, the words have a sinister edge. His wish for a 'release from troubles' points to a solution that is very different from the one envisaged by Hermione (simple flight from Thetideion).

[65] Orestes' killing of his mother to avenge his father was known to Homer, though he normally stresses the murder of Aegisthus: see West *et al.* (1988) 180 f. on *Od.* 3. 309–10, where the matricide is subtly underplayed. The event was treated by Stesichorus in his *Oresteia* (frr. 210–19 D), who is said to be adapting an earlier poem of the same title by Xanthus (fr. 229 D). It is in Aeschylus, however, that we find the first explicit account of Apollo commanding the matricide through his oracle: a version that became canonical for fifth-century tragedy (e.g. *Cho.* 269–96, 900–3, 953; *Eum.* 465–7, Soph. *El.* 32–7; Eur. *El.* 980; *Or.* 164 f., 329–32).

[66] In addition, when Orestes says he is on his way to consult the oracle of Zeus at Dodona (885–6), the lie colours his relation to the gods. Parke (1967) 80 comments on the use of Dodona as a foil to Delphi in tragedy (cf. *Pho.* 982, *Erechth.* frr. 367–8 K). Dodona was sacred to Zeus, god of suppliants; it is ironic that Orestes uses it while manipulating the suppliant Hermione.

πικρῶς δὲ πατρὸς φόνιον αἰτήσει δίκην
ἄνακτα Φοῖβον· οὐδέ νιν μετάστασις
γνώμης ὀνήσει θεῶι διδόντα νῦν δίκας,
ἀλλ' ἔκ τ' ἐκείνου διαβολαῖς τε ταῖς ἐμαῖς
κακῶς ὀλεῖται·

He will regret asking for satisfaction for his father's death from Lord
Phoebus. Nor will his change of mind help him as he makes amends
to the god, but because of Apollo and my slanders he will die
wretchedly.

The crucial role of Phoebus in Neoptolemus' death, and
Orestes' passionate desire for it, are strongly marked by the
enjambment of 'Lord Phoebus' and 'he will die wretchedly'
(1003, 1006). Orestes presents Apollo as proud, insulted, and
unappeasable.[67] However, we must take into account the
identity of the speaker. Orestes has a stake in justifying the
god's collaboration in his revenge. Without it his selfish
personal reasons for wishing Neoptolemus dead would not
justify the murder. But we are led to reject his view of a
hybristic Neoptolemus: the hero is unique in extant tragedy
as a mortal who offends a god, recognizes his mistake, and seeks
pardon. In a broad cultural sense it is true, as is often said, that
Greek religious thought had no place for the Christian notion
of a forgiving god;[68] but that does not mean that Apollo's
refusal to be reconciled, in the context of this play, is anything
but disturbing in its vindictiveness.

Orestes' triumphant prediction that the god will help him is
also negatively coloured by the chorus's following ode, where
they criticize Apollo for his role in the first destruction of
Troy (1010 ff.). The lack of proportion between insult and
penalty in the Trojan past reflects critically on Apollo's
imminent punishment of Neoptolemus. Particularly shocking
to the chorus is the god's support for matricide: they can
scarcely believe that such an order was issued from Delphi: ὦ
δαῖμον, ὦ Φοῖβε, πῶς πείθομαι; ('O god, O Phoebus, how can I
believe it?', 1036).[69] Euripides handles the motif of disbelief in

[67] Only in comedy can a mortal successfully call the gods to task for their
unwelcome actions. In tragedy this leads invariably to disaster.

[68] Cf. Mikalson (1991) 136–9, Kovacs (1987) 18–21.

[69] In the previous ode the chorus expressed their joyful acceptance of
Peleus' heroic past. Now they use the same word (πείθομαι 791 ~ 1036, 'I

mythical tradition, as was noted earlier, in a different way from Pindar. Whereas Pindar asserts his poetic power to mould the story, and does so in a way which is complimentary to divine behaviour, Euripides does not seek to disguise the disturbing amorality or ambiguity of divine purpose communicated by the myths.

Divine motivation is often presented as opaque in tragedy, and Apollo's support for Orestes' matricide is an instance that the Greek tragedians found peculiarly compelling. Before we proceed further with Apollo's role in the play, something should be said on the role of this god in some other plays by Euripides. This will provide important and revealing background, and show the wider bearing of the treatment in the *Andromache*. Euripides develops in a more overt and questioning manner the moral and theological tensions implicit in the myth. In the *Electra* Castor tells Orestes (1244–6):

> δίκαια μέν νυν ἥδ' ἔχει, σὺ δ' οὐχὶ δρᾶις.
> Φοῖβος δέ, Φοῖβος - ἀλλ' ἄναξ γάρ ἐστ' ἐμός,
> σιγῶ· σοφὸς δ' ὢν οὐκ ἔχρησέ σοι σοφά.

She [Clytemnestra] now has just punishment, but your deed is not just. And Phoebus, Phoebus—but he is my lord, I say no more. But wise though he is, his command to you was not wise.

His aposiopesis (rare in Euripides) underlines the criticism of Apollo's decision.[70] Castor announces that Apollo will accept legal responsibility for the matricide (1265–7; cf. *Eum.* 198–200, 465, 579–80), but the response is too detached to make any difference to the experience of exile, mourning, and family dissolution which the human protagonists face at the end of the play: 'the command was not just, nor, if we understand human nature, is its outcome truly happy'.[71]

believe') to express anguished perplexity. The repetition contrasts the behaviour of mortal and god, and forcefully questions the conduct of Apollo.

[70] Compare Electra and the chorus in *Orestes* (194): XO. δίκαι μέν. HΛ. καλῶς δ' οὔ ('CHORUS: It [the murder of his mother] was justly done. ELECTRA: But not well done.'). The line's bold antithesis (emphasized by the metrical repetition of the divided bacchiac dimeter) exposes the problematic morality of Apollo's command.

[71] Roberts (1984) 102. Spira (1960) 105–11 claims unconvincingly that Orestes is at fault for appraising Apollo's command by purely human standards.

In the *Orestes* the 'deceptive movement of the plot towards "calamity"'[72] allows for the surprise of Apollo's appearance, yet the narrowly averted disaster has disturbing implications on the human level. Defenders of Apollo have stressed the gap between divine knowledge and human limitations.[73] Spira's interpretation of the *deus ex machina* ending in Sophocles' *Philoctetes* and in Euripides has been particularly influential. He claims that the gap in understanding is beneficently closed by the divine epiphany. The gods' late appearance makes more vivid their superior perspective.[74] This approach is not without value, but it risks draining the plays of their challenging power. The speeches do indeed assert humans' limited understanding, but they do not secure a *carte blanche* for divine action.

In *Ion* the presence of Athena as *dea ex machina* reminds us that the play, despite its Delphic setting, is also about Athens.[75] However, Athena's positive intervention does not efface the disturbing effects of Apollo's previous conduct.[76] Athena speaks of Apollo's intention ($\H{\epsilon}\mu\epsilon\lambda\lambda\epsilon$, 1566) to sort things out eventually in Athens; an intention that was, one imagines, derailed by the chorus's revelation of Xuthus' good fortune and Creusa's vengeful reaction (774 ff.). Apollo, god of prophecy, seems to have a poor knowledge of the future! To blame human ignorance or Creusa's violent response is to be false to our sympathy for her and our disapproval of the god's deceptions. Athena's closing reflection that the power of the gods is delayed but certain (1614–15), a cliché of popular religion, does not annul the play's unsettling events.[77] The radical discon-

---

[72] Willink (1986) xxxvii.

[73] E.g. Steidle (1968) 110 ff.

[74] Spira (1960) 156: 'The words of the god make the scales fall from the human eyes. They understand . . . in sudden transport to the god's level.'

[75] Influential statement in Loraux (1993) ch. 5; Owen (1939) xxii: 'the scene is Delphi but in a sense it is Athens'.

[76] Yunis (1988) 136–7 argues that 'Ion's relationship with Apollo spends itself' and so overstresses the reassuring aspects of Athena's appearance. Athena explictly justifies her presence by mentioning Apollo's reluctance to come in person to clear matters up (1557–8). The wording of her explanation (indeed the very fact that she feels she must give one) alerts us to the ambiguous 'happy ending' before us. As Owen (1939) 178 remarks, 'Athena makes the best of a bad case.'

[77] Compare Orestes' ironic remark about Apollo: $\mu\acute{\epsilon}\lambda\lambda\epsilon\iota$· $\tau\grave{o}$ $\theta\epsilon\hat{\iota}o\nu$ δ' $\grave{\epsilon}\sigma\tau\grave{\iota}$ $\tauo\iotao\hat{\upsilon}\tauo\nu$ $\phi\acute{\upsilon}\sigma\epsilon\iota$ ('He is biding his time. The divine is like that by nature', *Or.*

tinuity of the plot creates an ending which raises as many questions concerning divine behaviour and human knowledge as it purports to resolve. Human understanding of divine purpose emerges as defective, but it is not so clear that this is a purely mortal failing.

In the *Andromache* Delphi fully enters the play in the words of the messenger. Apollo himself is absent, but his voice is heard, and it brings about a crucial turn in events (the mob rallies and kills Neoptolemus, 1147 ff.). Both here and in the *Bacchae* (1078–9) the divine voice is malevolent (contrast Soph. *OC* 1623–6). Although in the *Andromache* the indefinite τις is used ('someone', 1147), its function is not to make uncertain the identity of the god responsible.[78] In the messenger's narrative we cannot discount the bias inherent in the relationship of slave to master. As de Jong well remarks,

the Euripidean messenger is firmly anchored in the play, taking two roles at a time: within his own narrative he is servant, soldier, sailor, etc., while on stage he is the messenger who reports to other characters the events he has witnessed. The first role influences the second, in that it entails involvement and engagement in the way the story is told.[79]

Yet the reporter's engagement does not deprive his account of authority. The poet regularly gives the messenger a role which is crucial to our experience of the tragic pathos. The murder of Neoptolemus is explicitly linked by the messenger to the intervention of Apollo, who calls into question the justice of the god's action.[80]

420). Willink (1986) 155 notes that the sentiment is consonant with traditional piety, but here 'has a sophistic flavour (bitterly toned)'.

[78] *Pace* de Jong (1991) 15–16. Her account of the play is rather confused: (p. 16) 'thus Apollo's complicity as suggested by the Messenger of *Andr.* is not confirmed by the *deus ex machina* Athena [*sic*], and neither Orestes' words in 1005–8 nor Peleus' lamentation in 1212 can be quoted as reliable evidence'. But since we have no reason to believe that Orestes, Peleus, or the messenger has any motive for giving the audience false information, the responsibility of Apollo is incontrovertibly evident in the text.

[79] de Jong (1991) 72.

[80] From such works as *Iliad* 1, Pind. *Pyth.* 3, and Soph. *OT*, the impression is well established that Apollo can be a destructive god. In the *Agamemnon* Cassandra expresses the destructiveness of Apollo with a novel *nomen omen*: ὤπολλον ὤπολλον, | ἀγυιᾶτ᾽, ἀπόλλων ἐμός· | ἀπώλεσας γὰρ οὐ μόλις τὸ δεύτερον

Although Delphi is a site of great religious holiness, Euripides depicts the situation there as rather sordid, with rumours and worries about money in the air (1092–9). There was an alternative version of the myth which told that Neoptolemus intended to plunder the temple (cf. Paus. 10. 7. 1). Euripides is aware of this and has Orestes allege it as the motive both for Neoptolemus' first *and* second visit (1094–5). We know, however, that Neoptolemus wishes to make amends for a former error. We see how sincere he is from his orderly preparations for sacrifice and for contact with the god through his priests (1100–3):

ἡμεῖς δὲ μῆλα, φυλλάδος Παρνασίας
παιδεύματ', οὐδὲν τῶνδέ πω πεπυσμένοι,
λαβόντες ᾖμεν ἐσχάραις τ' ἐφέσταμεν
σὺν προξένοισι μάντεσίν τε Πυθικοῖς.

And we, knowing nothing yet of these things [the effects of Orestes' rumours on the Delphians], took sheep, reared on the grass of Parnassus, and came and stood at the altar with our hosts and Pythian prophets.[81]

The messenger's quotation of an anonymous Delphian's question (1104–5) and Neoptolemus' response makes more vivid the motif of apology (1106–8):

ὁ δ' εἶπε· Φοίβωι τῆς πάροιθ' ἁμαρτίας
δίκας παρασχεῖν βουλόμεσθ'· ᾔτησα γὰρ
πατρός ποτ' αὐτὸν αἵματος δοῦναι δίκην.

And Neoptolemus replied, 'I want to make amends to Phoebus for my earlier mistake. For I asked him once to make reparation for the shedding of my father's blood.'

('Apollo, Apollo, god of ways, my destroyer! For once again you have destroyed me easily!', 1080–2). Contrast Call. fr. 114 Pf. On Apollo as the target of Euripides' most trenchant criticism see Collard (1981) 35 n. 16. Pindar's attitude to Apollo makes for a striking contrast: 'No other deity is portrayed so vividly and sympathetically in his poetry' (Richardson (1992) 226).

[81] Rutherford (1998) 148 observes that the messenger is at pains 'to represent Neoptolemus as a genuine pilgrim, engaging for three days in sacred contemplation' (*Andr.* 1086–7). Neoptolemus is killed while praying and sacrificing; on Euripides' use of this motif in other plays see Langholf (1971) 104.

But the Delphians choose to believe Orestes' μῦθος ('tale', 1109) and Neoptolemus is ambushed while sacrificing before the inner shrine.

One might be tempted to see a political angle to Euripides' criticism of the Delphians. Roberts comments: 'the best case that can be made is for the impact of such a political issue on the *Andromache*',[82] and she ties this reading to the play's anti-Spartan tone. Thucydides relates that the Spartans got a favourable response from the oracle at the start of the Peloponnesian War: καὶ αὐτὸς ἔφη [note the personal response (and responsibility) of the god] ξυλλήψεσθαι καὶ παρακαλούμενος καὶ ἄκλητος ('and he himself said he would help them whether he was called upon or not', 1. 118. 3).[83] But as Roberts is right to stress, 'even if the political situation did encourage a negative portrayal of the Delphic Apollo, this fact does not account in any detailed way for the literary form of that portrayal in Greek tragedy'.[84]

While political factors cannot be ruled out of consideration, it is more rewarding to approach the god's behaviour as part of the tragic fiction. This method helps us appreciate the theologically provocative impact of Apollo's role. In separate plays we see different gods as the centre of interest. Why Apollo in the *Andromache*? As he is a god associated particularly with truth and authority (both religious and poetic), his behaviour is of especial interest to the tragedians. Davies traces Apollo's role in literature as 'the patron, or direct author, of laws and of a moral order'; he notes, however, that by the fifth century 'his imputed role as "prophet of right" virtually evaporates', and that his profile in extant tragedy is 'less than admirable'.[85]

---

[82] Roberts (1984) 83.

[83] Osborne (1996) 204–7 details the growth of Delphi as a political centre, and observes (p. 206): 'Men consult oracles not in order to discover the future, nor in order to get ideas, but in order to get their own way.' Burkert (*CAH*² v. 263) succinctly details Delphi's changing attitude to Athens from the deposition of the tyrants to the outbreak of the Peloponnesian War. Cf. Parke & Wormell (1956) i. 180 ff. Free access to the oracle for all states was among the terms of the Peace of Nicias in 421 (Thuc. 5. 18. 2). It seems that Athenians still wanted to make dedications and consultations at Delphi (cf. Vogt (1998) 35–6). Davies (1997) 57 warns against exaggerating the decline of Delphi as a major Greek shrine.

[84] Roberts (1984) 83.

[*See p. 254 for n. 85*]

The messenger's closing reflection repudiates Apollo's traditional claim to be an arbiter of justice (1161–5):

> τοιαῦθ' ὁ τοῖς ἄλλοισι θεσπίζων ἄναξ,
> ὁ τῶν δικαίων πᾶσιν ἀνθρώποις κριτής,
> δίκας διδόντα παῖδ' ἔδρασ' Ἀχιλλέως.
> ἐμνημόνευσε δ' ὥσπερ ἄνθρωπος κακὸς
> παλαιὰ νείκη· πῶς ἂν οὖν εἴη σοφός;

That is what the god who prophesies to others, the judge of what is right for all men, did to the son of Achilles as he offered amends. He remembered past grievances like a bad man. How then can he be wise?

As has already been suggested, the messenger's emotional reaction to his master's death does not make his criticisms less effective. Rather, the passionate rhetoric of the narrative persuasively guides our response. We are clearly meant to take seriously and to sympathize with the messenger's evaluation.[86] The god is assimilated to his grudge-bearing mortal accomplice, behaving 'like a bad man' (1164). The gap between human expectation and divine action is disturbing.[87]

Scholars have significantly misinterpreted the use of the temple setting and its furnishings. Neoptolemus is caught without armour on (ἀτευχῆ, 1119), and so to defend himself he seizes some equipment that had been dedicated in the temple (1121–3):

> ἐξέλκει δὲ καὶ παραστάδος
> κρεμαστὰ τεύχη πασσάλων καθαρπάσας
> ἔστη 'πὶ βωμοῦ γοργὸς ὁπλίτης ἰδεῖν

---

[85] Davies (1997) 47, 49. Remarkably, his list of passages in tragedy that deal with Apollo (p. 60) lacks any reference to the *Andromache*.

[86] Burnett (1971) 152 does not recognize the impact of Neoptolemus' second visit, which is heavily stressed in the *Andromache*; hence it is certainly simplifying things to say 'the poet leads his audience to accept and almost to comprehend the catastrophe'. Even Apollo's naïve enthusiast Ion sees the unwelcome implications of a world ruled by such wayward gods: ἀλλ', ἐπεὶ κρατεῖς, | ἀρετὰς δίωκε ('But, since you have power, pursue goodness', *Ion* 439–40).

[87] Kovacs (1987) 20 is too dismissive: 'The messenger's protest . . . could not be the considered opinion of anyone but a philosopher.' Yunis (1988) 93 rightly argues that it is wrong to reject the messenger's standards of behaviour for Apollo as too exalted, since the god's conduct is 'presented in the play as a real dilemma'.

He drew his sword, and, grabbing from its pegs some armour which hung on the side-wall, he stood upon the altar, a warrior terrible to behold.

Burnett reads this as further impiety on Neoptolemus' part:

This very prowess serves to remind us of the Neoptolemus who outraged both Priam and Astyanax, and once again it involves him in acts of desecration. In his most superb moment the hero unwittingly gives truth to Orestes' slanders, actually 'sacking' Apollo's shrine (note καθαρπάσας, 1121–2; cf. 1095), seizing the arms that had been dedicated to the god and using them in a battle with Apollo's priests.[88]

This is not at all convincing. Firstly, Neoptolemus' atrocities at Troy are notably absent from the play. The ruthless murder of the defenceless old Priam and baby Astyanax bears no significant relation to Neoptolemus' spirited repulse of Orestes' attack. Secondly, Neoptolemus does not 'sack' the temple any more than Hermione's slaves 'sack' her, ἔκ τε δεξιᾶς | ξίφη καθαρπά- ζουσιν ἐξαιρούμενοι ('and they snatched a sword from her right hand and removed it', 812–13). In both cases the sense is 'snatch down'.[89] Yet there is also a meaningful opposition between the two scenes: Hermione makes exaggerated suicide attempts, while Neoptolemus doggedly fights for his life.[90]

Finally, a reading of the scene in terms of Neoptolemus' desecration of the shrine is ruled out: his heroism is presented too positively.[91] The mutilation of Neoptolemus' corpse is both

---

[88] Burnett (1971) 152.

[89] Cf. Luc. i. 239–40: *rupta quies populi, stratisque excita iuventus* | *deripuit sacris adfixa penatibus arma* ('The people's sleep was broken, and the young men, summoned from their beds, *snatched down* weapons hanging by the holy household gods').

[90] Iolaus' borrowing of weapons from the temple of Zeus (*Hcld.* 695–701) makes for an interesting contrast to this scene. Whereas Iolaus promises to return the armour (κἀποδώσομεν | ζῶντες, θανόντας δ' οὐκ ἀπαιτήσει θεός, 696–7, 'I will give it back if I live, but if I die, the god will not ask for it back'), Neoptolemus is forced to use Apollo's weapons against his human agents.

[91] Kovacs (1980) 106 n. 71 sees the murder as a divine 'cure' for Phthian and Trojan troubles: 'It may not be too fanciful to see the death of Neoptolemus as a φάρμακον ('cure') precisely because he is in some way a φαρμακός ('scapegoat'). There is a ritual quality to his death that suggests magical efficacy. He is pelted—like the pharmakos at the Thargelia—and after his death he is cast out of the precinct. The silence of his attackers suggests ritual too.' Bremmer (1983) has distinguished between scapegoating in ritual, typically involving banishment of 'the poor, the ugly and criminals' (p. 304),

a symbol of the Delphians' wild anger and also serves to elevate the heroic representation of Neoptolemus.[92] The echo in 1123 (above) of Andromache's sarcastic description of Menelaus (νῦν δ' ἐς γυναῖκα γοργὸς ὁπλίτης φανείς 458, 'And now you appear against a woman as a dazzling warrior') could hardly be more pointed. Moreover, Neoptolemus leaps upon his attackers from the altar's δεξίμηλον ἐσχάραν ('sheep-receiving hearth', 1138).[93] The rare adjective pointedly recalls the chorus's description of Thetis' shrine earlier in the play: λεῖπε δεξίμηλον | δόμον τᾶς ποντίας θεοῦ ('Leave the sea goddess's sheep-receiving shrine', 129–30). The contrast between the temples' functions, one offering succour, the other destruction, extends to the dramatic role of Thetis and Apollo themselves.[94]

The precarious relationship between god and hero is a feature of epic, and, as we shall see, this tension is reflected in cult ritual as well as myth. Humans are free to criticize and its presentation in myth, where 'attractive, aristocratic, and royal figures' are killed. Here a noble Neoptolemus is killed, but if we see his death in terms of human sacrifice, one should take into account this theme's wider treatment in tragedy as a perversion of normal practice: see Burkert (1966) and Foley (1985) 38, 58. Hall (1989) 146–7 notes its barbaric character in Greek eyes (cf. the harmless simulation decreed by Athena in IT 1458–61). The silence of the Delphians (1127–8) rather indicates their lack of a just response to Neoptolemus' demand. And when his corpse is expelled like a polluted object from the holy site (1156–7), the distorted ritual imagery contrasts significantly with the pious concern of his companions for proper burial rites (1158–60). Such sacrificial overtones as are present (Seaford (1994) 48 n. 77 notes the main ones) would thus tend to condemn Neoptolemus' murderers, not the hero himself (cf. 506). This is the point of the strong clash at 1144–5: κραυγὴ δ' ἐν εὐφήμοισι δύσφημος δόμοις | πέτραισιν ἀντέκλαγξ' ('An unholy din in the holy temple echoed from the cliffs').

[92] Cf. Griffin (1980) 47 on Il. 22. 371 and scholia; also Vernant (1991), ch. 2, esp. p. 74: 'Epic uses the theme of the disfigurement of the corpse to underscore the exceptional position and status of heroic honour, of a beautiful death, of imperishable glory: they far surpass ordinary honor, death, and renown.' However, this heroization does not diminish the Delphians' brutality or Apollo's vindictiveness. Kovacs's argument 'that the touch of heaven, whether in love or anger, confers beauty' (Kovacs (1987) 21, paraphrasing Burnett (1971) 156) is too little discriminating.

[93] Rutherford (1998) 147 notes that Neoptolemus' defence of the altar is surprising, given his earlier antipathy to Apollo.

[94] Wiles (1997) 201 remarks perceptively: 'The sanctuary and altar of Thetis provide a visual focus for the long description of that sanctuary and altar at Delphi where Neoptolemus is sacrilegiously murdered.'

divine behaviour, but they have to reckon with the consequences of the gods' superior (and unpredictable) power. The
words of Neoptolemus' apology quoted above let us see how
the play makes a connection between Apollo's punishment of
Neoptolemus and the death of Achilles. Apollo is often referred
to as the killer of Achilles: 50–5, 1002–3, 1194–6, 1212. The
Iliad presents Achilles' defiance of Apollo in terms which stress
both his rage for revenge and the unbridgeable gap between
man and god, whose injury Achilles is powerless to pay back
(*Il.* 22. 20). For it is really Apollo who seals Patroclus' death,
smiting him effortlessly 'with the flat of his hand',[95] leaving
him dazed and stripped of his armour (*Il.* 16. 791–804). In the
Andromache the persistence of divine hostility, which is a
familiar motif of religious thought, is turned into a critical
reflection on the brooding vengeance of the gods. A goddess's
slighted honour had been the basis a few years before for the
action of *Hippolytus*. Phaedra is innocent, but she is swept into
the plan of Aphrodite to punish Hippolytus. In the *Andromache* the god's enemy attempts to make amends for his former
arrogance, but he is killed all the same.

Our response to Neoptolemus' death has been prepared by
the messenger's narrative, and it is heightened by the moving
lament of Peleus. We see an innocent and noble man suffer for
a god's spitefulness. It is natural that the grieving Peleus
should wish Neoptolemus had never married Hermione or
blamed Apollo for Achilles' death (1189–96). It is understandable that those who lament should wish some parts of the past
had been different so that the victim might have avoided
death.[96] It would be wrong to read this as Peleus attaching
blame to Neoptolemus. Apollo is not exonerated. The chorus's
resigned talk, and the general language of fate, still make
Apollo's role clear (θεοῦ γὰρ αἶσα, θεὸς ἔκρανε συμφοράν 1204,
'It is the god's fate, the god brought disaster about'). Peleus
identifies Apollo as responsible, and invokes the wider Phthian
polis as his witness, ὦ πόλις, | διπλῶν τέκνων μ' ἐστέρησε Φοῖβος
('My city, Phoebus has deprived me of both my children',
1211–12). The loss of both son and grandson leaves Peleus

[95] See Griffin (1980) 136.
[96] Lloyd (1994) 160 on 1189–92; on 1205–7 Lloyd also notes the common
lamentatory motif of blaming the dead for abandoning the living.

alone in Phthia: μόνος μόνοισιν ἐν δόμοις ἀναστρέφηι ('Alone you dwell in a lonely house', 1221). The pity of the chorus prompts Peleus to invoke the absent Thetis (1224–5):

σύ τ᾽, ὦ κατ᾽ ἄντρα νύχια Νηρέως κόρα,
πανώλεθρόν μ᾽ ὄψεαι πίτνοντα.

And you, daughter of Nereus in your dark cave, you will see me falling in utter ruin!

Peleus' despairing prediction is immediately answered by the epiphany of Thetis. The question of endings has become a major theme in criticism of tragedy. The responsive *threnos* of Peleus and the chorus shares some features with the funeral processions which conclude other tragedies. Oliver Taplin has said that singling out such plays is the 'best strategy for a critic who wanted to maintain that tragedy normally approached a closed resolution'.[97] However, as he points out (citing the end of *Trach.*), 'a simply redemptive ending' is a rare thing. Charles Segal offers an interpretation of the *Andromache* in terms of 'the collective lamentation for a tragic loss' which expresses 'resolution in a spirit of community and continuity'.[98] He argues: 'Collective lament gives way to individual miracle', as Thetis arrives; and further, 'the contrast between the mortal sufferer and the goddess defines the appropriate human response . . . Thetis' last words point back to, and reaffirm, the larger community of mortals (1268–72)'.[99] The focus on human community is enlightening, but more needs to be said about the troubling picture of the gods which lies behind it. Without such awareness, the *Andromache* loses its interrogatory edge. We risk reducing its final impact, along with that of many other plays, to the affirmation of a 'civically reassuring aetiology'.[100] At the same time, however, we must beware of the common modern trick of finding some devious points to make a cheering passage gloomy.

The divinity who appears to close the tragedy is always one appropriate to the action.[101] The choice of Thetis functions

[97] Taplin (1996) 197.   [98] Segal (1996) 159.
[99] Segal (1996) 159–60.   [100] Taplin (1996) 201 n. 32.
[101] It is Athena, not Apollo and Artemis, who appears at the end of *Ion* and *IT* because these plays are centred on Athens: Ion will become king there, while Artemis' cult statue will be transferred to Brauron in Attica (it was said

both visually and thematically. Her statue, significantly visible throughout the action (cf. 115, 246), is now joined by the goddess herself.[102] She is both goddess and wife of the mortal Peleus. Her altar has been the focus of Andromache's supplication, and her personal involvement underlines the themes of marriage and continuity of descent (cf. 20, 1231, 1253). In the *Iliad* Thetis is portrayed as 'the god who mourns as a mortal mourns'[103] because of her entry into human life (and death) by marriage, an unequal union forced on her by Zeus (*Il.* 18. 429–34). The theme of enforced marriage reverberates throughout the *Andromache*, in the form of the Trojan concubine's unwilling sexual servitude, and in Hermione's dynastic marriage to Neoptolemus at her father's behest. Thetis' pain is repeatedly stressed in Homer (cf. *Il.* 18. 54–62, 24. 83–102). Her epic background of grief makes her a particularly appropriate choice as comforter of the mortal Peleus.[104] Thetis' maternal concern, familiar from the *Iliad*, is augmented in the *Andromache* by her care for Peleus. The survival of Andromache's son marks the continuity of the Aeacid line: it is a powerful and positive reversal of epic alignments. However, it is central to our response to the play as a whole that we do not simply forget Apollo.

We are bound to compare and contrast the two deities. In general, the appearance of a specific deity directs our attention to distinct divine identities, and polytheism is often brought

to have been removed by the Persians: see Dunn (1996) 63). Divine intervention is not limited to the end of the play: cf. Athena in Soph. *Aj.* (beginning), *Aj. Locr.* fr. 10c R (middle?), *Niobe* fr. 441a (Apollo and Artemis; middle), Eur. *Her.* 822 ff. (Iris and Lyssa), *Tro.* 1 ff. (Poseidon and Athena). Thetis may have appeared as *dea ex machina* in Sophocles' *Peleus* and *Sundeipnoi* (fr. 562 R). In the final scenes of *Hcld.* and *Hec.* the gift of prophecy is given to mortals, but their predictions contain less universalizing or aetiological material. Mossman (1995) 67–8 observes that the stichomythic structure of Polymestor's prophecy lacks the calm dignity of a full *deus* speech.

[102] So too with Artemis' statue in the *Hippolytus*, though she cannot save her favourite.

[103] Griffin (1980) 190.

[104] On Thetis' grief in the *Iliad*, see Slatkin (1991) 17–52. Like all Greek deities, however, Thetis enjoys a multiplicity of roles. Her cosmogonic role in Alcman fr. 5 D may point to a cult in Sparta; cf. Sorel (1994) 49–54, West (1997) 525.

out explicitly in these speeches (as with Athena at 1251–2).
Here, what immediately precedes Thetis' appearance forcefully
juxtaposes the deities: Apollo ends the strophe (1211–12),
Thetis the antistrophe (1224–5; note the despairing direct
address just before we see the goddess herself). We are thereby
enouraged to relate (and soon to contrast) the gods' impact.
One may add that mythology, and earlier tragedy, brought
these two gods into interesting relation.[105]

Our critical response to Apollo's actions is sharpened by the
beneficent arrangements made by Thetis. Before we consider
Peleus' fate, it will be useful to look at the impact of Thetis'
plans for Neoptolemus' corpse. We saw in Chapter 1 that
Euripides has probably altered the myth of Neoptolemus'
murder by a Delphian, Machaereus, so as to implicate Orestes
in the deed, and that he has underscored the crucial intervention of the god within his own shrine. Most strikingly,
Pindar insists in *Nemean* 7 that Neoptolemus' death is
honourable for the hero, since he will now enjoy for ever
(thanks to Apollo's election) the glory of a hero-cult.[106] In the
Andromache, however, this compensatory honour, familiar to
the audience from the fifth-century cult of Neoptolemus at
Delphi, has a provocatively critical impact. Thetis' words
declare her dead grandson a hero, but at the same time they
insist on his tomb's function as a reproach to his cowardly
attackers (1239–42):

> τὸν μὲν θανόντα τόνδ᾽ Ἀχιλλέως γόνον
> θάψον πορεύσας Πυθικὴν πρὸς ἐσχάραν,
> Δελφοῖς ὄνειδος, ὡς ἀπαγγέλληι τάφος
> φόνον βίαιον τῆς Ὀρεστείας χερός.

Take this dead man, Achilles' son, to the Pythian hearth and bury
him, a reproach to the Delphians, so that his grave may proclaim the
violent murder by Orestes' hand.

---

[105] The enmity between Thetis and Apollo derives from his part in the
death of Achilles. Apollo's treachery is castigated by Thetis in Aesch. fr. 350
R, and by Hera in *Il.* 24. 62–3. Cf. Cat. 64. 301–2, who has Apollo shun the
wedding celebrations of Peleus and Thetis.

[106] See Howie (1998) 106. Parker (1998) 114 observes that the demise of
Croesus at the hands of Apollo compelled Bacchylides and Herodotus—and
indeed Delphi—to 'great feats of apologetic ingenuity'.

The violence of Neoptolemus' death is not forgotten, nor is the moral turpitude of Orestes and the Delphians in any way underplayed.[107]

The relationship between god and hero in both myth and cult is extremely complex. Neoptolemus' role as the ritual antagonist of Apollo relates to a pattern that is familiar in Greek hero-cult. Nagy goes so far as to call it 'a fundamental principle in Hellenic religion: antagonism between hero and god in myth corresponds to the ritual requirements of symbiosis between hero and god in cult'.[108] The polarity of god and hero is a common motif.[109] However, such ritual antagonism or 'symbiosis' does not entirely entail or explain the treatment of their relationship in any particular play or other creative work.[110] Euripides was very much interested in hero-cult, but he was also free to develop new versions of events around basic details such as the site of the hero's tomb. In the *Andromache* Euripides has shaped the polarity of Apollo and Neoptolemus into a 'heroic myth that reconstructs the action as a human tragedy'.[111] One should also stress that the particular details of Pindar's and Euripides' treatments of Apollo and Neoptolemus, for example, were not necessarily reflected in actual cult practice at Delphi.[112] The peculiar pathos of Neoptolemus'

[107] Contrast Spira (1960) 96, who speaks solely of 'honour and satisfaction' in the burial. For a cult which is certainly not consolatory, cf. *Med.* 1378–83.

[108] Nagy (1979) 121. Burkert (1983) 119–20 discusses the paradox of Neoptolemus' destruction by Apollo as an honour. Cf. Fontenrose (1959) 418–26.

[109] Cf. Burkert (1983) 96–8 on Zeus and Pelops at Olympia, and p. 157 on Poseidon and Erechtheus at Athens. Apollo was opposed to Hyacinthus at Amyclae near Sparta; cf. Kannicht (1969) ii. 383 on *Hel.* 1469–75.

[110] Seaford (1994) 130 n. 121 notes that such associations of god and hero 'may involve *reconciliation* with the deity', an aspect that is notably missing from the portrayal of Neoptolemus' death in the *Andromache*.

[111] Burkert (1983) 119.

[112] On Neoptolemus as the hero of a Delphic cult, see Farnell (1921) 311–21; further bibliography in Most (1985) 163 n. 135. Fontenrose (1960) 191–266 argues most ingeniously that Neoptolemus and Orestes are (in disguise) an ancient pair of divinities continually struggling for control of Delphi (Neoptolemus has 'become confused with the old enemy Python-Dionysus' (1959) 400). The coincidence of the legends of Achilles and Neoptolemus in 21 respects lead him to identify them as a single numinous entity (Fontenrose (1960) 209–10): 'The original Achilles-Neoptolemus . . . was an ancient

death as presented by Euripides was hardly easy material for religious worship in Delphi,[113] just as Heracles' harrowing murder of his children in his name play was unlikely to feature in his cult at Thebes.

Thetis' silence over the role of Apollo in the murder is significant, but it should not be read as justifying his action.[114] His very aloofness, his presence just as a voice, is both enigmatic and sinister. Gods rarely criticize one another openly on the tragic stage (cf. *Hipp.* 1400). Their speeches *ex machina* usually bid mortals desist from some course of action: παῦσαι δὲ λύπης τῶν τεθνηκότων ὕπερ ('Stop grieving for the dead', 1270; cf. 1234).[115] Thetis, despite her close personal interest in the fate of Peleus and his descendants, is a minor deity, and not likely in such a context to condemn Apollo outright.[116] But we have already seen humans fail to understand the vindictiveness of the god. His retaliations bring disaster on Trojan and Greek alike: the chorus cannot comprehend his destruction of Troy, nor his oracular support for Orestes' matricide (1010 ff.). The god's apologists argue that the sympathetic characters (Andromache and Peleus) are rewarded, while Neoptolemus, the brutal murderer of Priam, deserves to die.[117] But not only has Euripides suppressed the negative side of Neoptolemus' war record; he has also presented a second visit to Delphi with an honourable motive for the hero.[118] According to the familiar versions of Neoptolemus'

Thessalian deity, a god or *daimôn*, that in terms of classical Greek religion had both celestial and chthonian characteristics'.

[113] Either in Delphi or in Molossia, where Neoptolemus was no doubt also honoured in cult; cf. Kearns (1989) 3: 'heroes could be worshipped even when their bones were thought to be elsewhere'.   [114] So Erbse (1984) 135–6.

[115] Cf. *Hipp.* 1286–9, *IT* 1435–6, *Ion* 1553, *Hel.* 1641–2, *Or.* 1625.

[116] See Cropp (1988) 182 on Castor's guarded criticism of Apollo in *Electra* (1245–6); Dunn (1996) 32 sees here 'an obvious hierarchy of power'. Cf. *Il.* 20. 105–7: Apollo encourages Aeneas to confront Achilles by asserting that his mother, Aphrodite, a child of Zeus, is superior to Thetis. But at 21. 187–9 Achilles himself claims descent from Zeus through his grandfather Aeacus.

[117] So Erbse (1984) 136: 'The sufferings of humans come from their transgressions.'

[118] Missed by Spira (1960) 95 and Kovacs (1980) 78–80. For Neoptolemus' grief, cf. Soph. fr. 557. 6–7 R: κἀμοὶ γὰρ ἂν χάριν γε δακρύων πατὴρ | ἀνῆκτ' ἂν εἰς φῶς ('For if tears could have helped, my father would have been brought back up to the light!').

death and cult at Delphi, it was standard to have him killed there on the first visit.[119] There must be some expressive point to the mythical revisions and innovation. As we have seen, the circumstances of his victim's death and burial call the god's revenge into question.

Nevertheless, our critical response to Apollo is distinct from the impact made by Thetis' welcome news for the sympathetic Peleus and Andromache. The cheering revelations of Thetis make Apollo look all the more petty, but it is also appropriate to view her arrangements in their own right. What strikes us immediately is the space given in Thetis' speech to Peleus and his surprising fate (1253–68). This responds in part to the shape of the drama, which in its latter part has concentrated on Peleus' grief over his dead family. Thetis laments that her line is almost extinct. That gives added weight to the explicit connection made between the future of Phthia and that of Troy (1249–51):[120]

οὐ γὰρ ὧδ' ἀνάστατον
γένος γενέσθαι δεῖ τὸ σὸν κἀμόν, γέρον,
Τροίας τε.

For your race and mine, old man, is not fated to be so rooted out, nor that of Troy.

The postponement of the Trojan link marks its unexpectedness. And most remarkably, Thetis invokes the survival of Andromache's son as evidence that the gods do after all care about Troy (1251–2):

καὶ γὰρ θεοῖσι κἀκείνης [Τροίας] μέλει,
καίπερ πεσούσης Παλλάδος προθυμίαι.

For the gods are concerned about Troy as well, although it fell through the determination of Athena.

Thetis' claim touches on a disturbing feature of polytheism—the colliding wills of the gods—as embodied in Athena's desire for Troy's destruction, but it overrides it with a positive

[119] The dangers of accusing Apollo in his own temple are insisted on by Ion (*Ion* 369 ff.).

[120] One should also note that the basic pattern of crisis and rescue (Peleus saving Andromache, then both being aided by Thetis) itself connects the fortunes of Troy and Phthia.

assertion of divine concern. The ironist's desire to see Thetis' consolation as poor recompense for both Andromache and Peleus is contradicted by the explicitly exalted status awarded Peleus (1255–6):

κακῶν ἀπαλλάξασα τῶν βροτησίων
ἀθάνατον ἄφθιτόν τε ποιήσω θεόν.

Releasing you from mortal evils, I shall make you a deathless and imperishable god.

Moreover, the gift of immortality to Peleus is accompanied by the no less unexpected news that Achilles, the son he presumed to be dead, has in fact been made an immortal hero, and that Peleus may visit him on the White Island (1259–62). Her predictions are ratified by the highest authority: τὸ γὰρ πεπρωμένον | δεῖ σ' ἐκκομίζειν, Ζηνὶ γὰρ δοκεῖ τάδε ('You must carry out what is fated, for this is Zeus' will', 1268–9).[121]

It has been claimed that particularly in his late plays Euripides 'tends to tie up loose ends with an exaggerated completeness . . . to give us endings that are so firmly but oddly concluded that we feel them as arbitrary'.[122] The most glaring example is generally taken to be Apollo's intervention in the *Orestes*, which by its very arbitrariness 'only serves to intensify the general impression of senselessness and futility'.[123] Put very baldly, the dramatic technique of having the gods sort things out at the end draws attention to what they have been up to in the rest of the play! The *Andromache* is significantly different, in so far as Thetis' consolation rewards the sympathetic figures of the drama but does not make it any easier to explain the actions of Apollo in a way that is humanly satisfying. The tensions thus reverberate behind the *deus ex machina* speech and create a closure which is partially 'open, cracked, unhealed'.[124] For all the saving power of Thetis' intervention, the play remains interrogatory: a benign deity set against a malign one does not remove our questions.

Throughout his work Euripides explores the concept of

---

[121] Stevens (1971) 245 sees the phrase as 'probably conventional' but the agreement of Zeus elevates Peleus' reward.

[122] Roberts (1988) 192.

[123] Seidensticker (1996) 392.

[124] Cf. Taplin (1996) 199.

theodicy and its problematic relation to the anthropomorphic gods of myth.[125] Euripides is aware of philosophical speculation about the nature of the gods and their morality, and his plays reflect upon it and respond variously to it, thereby enriching the intellectual provocation of his tragic world.[126] Protagorean uncertainty whether the gods can be known (DK B4) is a frequent theme: e.g. *Her.* 1263, *Tro.* 884–9, *Hel.* 711–12, 1137–8, *Or.* 418, *Bacch.* 894. However, no less challenging effects are obtained by the portrayal of religious fervour.[127] Euripides achieved a creative *transformation* of contemporary thought about the gods.[128] That is, he 'created his theology, as he created his poetry, for imaginative ends'.[129] In this way his tragedies explore, but do not endorse, various aspects of Greek theology.

In Euripides' *œuvre* the traditional idea of the mystery of divine will (e.g. Aesch. *Suppl.* 87–90) is overridden by a more disturbing uncertainty about what the gods will do.[130] In the *Andromache* the dangerous unpredictability of the gods is augmented by a chilling atmosphere of divine pettiness.[131]

---

[125] In his tragedies the power of the gods is indubitable, but their wisdom is not. They appear no more rational or impartial in their reactions than the humans they destroy: cf. *Hipp.* 120; *Her.* 1345–6; *Bacch.* 1249–50, 1348.

[126] Critias *TrGF* ii. 43 fr. 19 was attributed to Euripides in antiquity. Regardless of whether it comes from him (adjudged unlikely on stylistic grounds by Sutton (1981) 34, though Davies (1989b) 28 thinks the evidence for authorship indecisive; see Obbink (1996) 353–5 for fuller discussion), it is a provocative example of contemporary speculation about religion and morality. Sisyphus argues that the gods are the invention of some clever man. Fear of their omniscience and punishment deters secret wrongdoing; the law by itself is too weak. (For a related Calliclean view of religion, see *Bellerophon* fr. 286 K: small pious cities are overrun by impious ones with big armies!) Comic criticism or parody suggests that such anthropological hypotheses about the origins of belief in the gods were both topical and controversial in late fifth-century Athens.

[127] In the *Bacchae* the chorus's praise of religious bliss creates a disturbing dissonance with the savage violence and dismemberment of Pentheus. Burkert (1974) 109 illuminates the extreme emotions which Euripides explores here.

[128] See Wilamowitz (1959) 22–31.

[129] Said of John Donne, in J. Carey (1981) 209–10.

[130] At *Tro.* 59–60 even Poseidon is taken aback by Athena's desire to destroy the Greeks.

[131] Divine punishment or revenge in tragedy is typically complex and contentious. R. Parker (1997) 152 f. outlines the contrast with oratory.

Apollo displays a typically divine 'fixity of purpose . . . [and] certainty of accomplishment',[132] but Euripides focuses on the tragic disparity between mortal and divine approaches to justice.[133] His plays repeatedly explore in a provocative way the differences in moral behaviour between the gods.[134] In the *Andromache* the entry of Thetis responds to the nobility of the survivors and bridges the gap between human and divine perspectives, but even here the result is not simply to annul the disturbing event we had been immersed in.

[132] Gredley (1996) 205, contrasting the ruthless Dionysus of the *Bacchae* with his indecisive counterpart in the *Frogs*.

[133] Cf. Vernant and Vidal-Naquet (1988) 14: 'divine justice may frequently appear as opaque and arbitrary as violence done by a tyrant'.

[134] Here he is continuing a theme of Homeric epic; one thinks in particular of the opposition of Athena and Poseidon in the *Odyssey* (cf. *Erechth*.). These differences are often manifested in competing divine projects. Yet even when the gods do agree on a plan, as in the prologue to the *Troades*, it may be to mortal ruin.

Conclusion

There is always an exception to any statement about Euripides.

B. M. W. Knox[1]

It has been the thesis of this book that every play represents a distinct thematic and dramatic complex which merits individual attention. We have now considered the *Andromache* from many different angles, and I hope that a richer conception and a keener appreciation of this absorbing play have resulted. More boldly, I hope that some central areas of Euripidean study may now look a little different. Debate has too often concentrated on some well-known plays; too often the *Andromache* has been neglected. This is unfortunate. Close confrontation with a play in detail, especially a less widely known one, may help us to challenge and to complicate our all too familiar images of Euripidean tragedy.

The *Andromache* has been long disparaged, but it is a brilliant piece of theatre. It is neither a loosely dramatized political pamphlet nor a tawdry melodrama of women and sex. Politics, war, nationality, sexuality, power: each of these topics is vital to the workings of the play, but scholars have tended to concentrate on one element, and so to obscure the originality and the effect of the larger design. It has often been assumed that Euripides writes so-called set-scenes (e.g. self-sacrifice, *agon*) because he is poor in creative power; this is the very reverse of the truth. The variety of his plays shows Euripides tirelessly experimenting with a range of dramatic forms for multiple tragic effects, while in doing so he creates in each work an individual tragic world.[2]

By looking closely at the play's structure we have discovered a meaningful pattern of diversion, delay, surprise, and suspense. The action is neither episodic nor rambling; it is

---

[1] Knox (1985) 338.

[2] Contrast Burnett (1971) 155, who sees the first part of the play as making the audience doubt 'the validity of tragedy itself' by its 'wrenching of traditional forms and an irrational assignment of roles'.

structured by verbal and scenic similarities and contrasts (for example, the motifs of supplication and rescue) which point up the moral differences between the characters. Euripides is a great and controlled writer. He certainly knew what he was doing when he combined the suppliant tragedy of Andromache (the one part of the play that has consistently received critical praise) with the calamity of Hermione and the revenge of Orestes. The emotional impact of each action is formally distinct: the play is constructed according to an aesthetics of surprise; but that underlies a broadly philosophical reflection on the instability of the world in which the characters live.

Euripides is a restless innovator, constantly exploring new structural effects. That is bound up with his equally innovative approach to the literary and dramatic tradition of myth. From his various sources—Homeric and cyclic epic, Pindaric lyric, the Orestes-myths of earlier tragedy and lyric poetry, and perhaps Sophocles' *Hermione*—Euripides inherited a range of mythical figures with their more or less definitive histories. These traditional story-patterns are not a constraint. On the contrary, they are the generically essential raw material that the poet is free to adapt to his dramatic purpose. Aristophanes accuses Euripides of subverting tragic tradition by his innovations of form and substance. But in the *Andromache* the mythical innovations and adaptations are wholly geared to forming an original, eventful, and moving tragedy.

The play has no unifying theme: it presents a variety of issues. It works through a plurality of action and a shifting of focus. These qualities, viewed by many earlier critics as a fault, in fact possess their own distinctive theatrical excellence. The combination and expansion of mythical data (the concubinage of Andromache, the conflict of Neoptolemus and Orestes over Hermione, the quarrel between Neoptolemus and Apollo, and so on) enable Euripides to expand his exploration of the destructive impact of war, sex, and revenge, in new and interesting directions.[3] The *Troades* (415) is in every sense a war-play; the *Hecuba* (*c*.424) is scenically removed from the

---

[3] Friedrich (1953) 59 suggests that the death of Neoptolemus (familiar from cult) is appended to the Andromache tragedy because Euripides was afraid to furnish a play entirely from his own invention; however, this misses the significant connections between the various 'movements' of the drama.

burning ruins of Troy but dramatizes the after-effects of the struggle. In the *Andromache* the action is further from the war in both time and place, yet it is still intimately marked by war's aftermath.[4] Andromache is a war-captive and slave. Hermione too was a 'prize' of war, promised to Neoptolemus by Menelaus, if he should capture Troy. Most strikingly, the enmities of the Trojan War live on in Menelaus, but are undermined by his own brutal conduct. Despite the loss of Achilles, Peleus is able to see through Menelaus' spurious anti-barbarian rhetoric. His noble response to Andromache's plight points up the inadequacy, indeed the self-regarding hypocrisy, of the Spartans' claim to *eugeneia* and *sophrosyne*.

Andromache is a victim of war like no other. Her Iliadic past defines her as the archetypal mourning wife.[5] The *Iliad* also looked forward to the hardships and indignities of her enslavement after the fall of Troy. Euripides has taken her familiar role as loyal wife and mother and pointedly reconstructed it in Greece. The dramatic situation of a woman as victim appears in several other plays (e.g. *Med.*, *El.*, *Tro.*, *Ion*, *Hel.*, *IA*); often it is coupled with the woman taking revenge (*Med.*, *Hipp.*, *Hec.*, *El.*). In the *Andromache* the victim herself does not exact revenge. Not only does Andromache lack the status and support to make that possible; she also has none of the vengefulness displayed by Hecuba in the *Iliad*. Andromache's heroism is expressed instead by solitary defiance of her enemies and by the decision to die for her son. It is her opponents who present themselves as acting to avenge wrongs. Yet Hermione's attack is in fact powered by sexual jealousy and by her frustration at being unable to exercise full power in the *oikos* because of her childlessness. The play reverses the traditional roles of wife and concubine: that is thought-provoking. It is another bitter twist to the perverted *nostos* of Neoptolemus that he returns to a faithful concubine and an errant wife. The extravagant claims to submissiveness made by Andromache in her *agon* with Hermione complicate the scene, and so prevent it

---

[4] The power of the Trojan War as a metaphor for human cruelty and suffering underlies its continuing fascination: cf. Steiner (1996) 538: 'Massacre, rape, enslavement, infanticide, and a chain of sadistic retribution converge towards an essential nightmare and dehumanization.'

[5] Compare Hecuba the supreme mourning mother, *Hec.* 421, 580–2.

from becoming a monotone contrast of right and wrong conceptions of marriage and womanhood; the polarization of views stimulates critical reflection on both positions. The play dramatizes a crisis of marriage in heroic times, and thus reflects challengingly on contemporary sexual mores.

The nature of *philia* and its ties lies at the heart of the play's reflections on human relationships. Hermione is the wife of Neoptolemus and a member of the house of Peleus; that means that the conflicts of the drama are intrafamilial as well as interfamilial. She is rescued by Orestes, her cousin, who is himself bent on a vendetta against her husband. Menelaus claims—selfishly—to be concerned for his kin, and he bolsters his claim by declaiming on hackneyed themes: barbarians are inferior, and enemies should be injured. The polar opposition of friend and enemy, Greek and barbarian, gives way to a more humane reciprocity based on noble *physis* proved in action. Peleus rescues Andromache and her son, and thereby shows a sense of justice and a generosity which connect with the arguments and the self-sacrifice of Andromache herself. The contrast with Hermione is evident: she cannot rely even on her own father when her plans fall apart. The moral unity of Trojan and Phthian, embodied physically in the son of Andromache and Neoptolemus, is sealed by the child's survival. It is finally rewarded when Thetis prophesies a flourishing Molossian dynasty.

I have set out to show how densely the different aspects of Euripides' work are interwoven, and how greatly, in terms of the individual dramatic text, the various elements combine and interact, so as to create a unique work of art. Thus rhetoric, for example, is not an autonomous impulse at odds with effective characterization, nor are the choral songs merely peripheral to the action of the play. At the same time my argument has been that the *Andromache*, like any other Euripidean play, should not be seen as simply a sealed-off artistic experience: the plays provoke thought about large issues beyond the confines of the drama. They offer stimulation and interest rather than theories and ultimate views.

Our enquiry has, above all, sought to display the *Andromache* as a play which poses questions. The polarity of Greek and barbarian is undermined; two deities are provocatively opposed, one destructive and one benign; we see reason to question revenge as a motive for action; the role of women is explored: as wives, mothers and, most incisively, as victims of war, be they Greek or Trojan, victorious or defeated. These are among the central concerns that make the *Andromache* a moving and thought-provoking tragedy, full of suffering, suspense, and moral interest. I cannot claim to offer a truly comprehensive vision of this work, since, like all tragic texts, the *Andromache* is not only complex but inexhaustible. Nevertheless, I hope to have shown that this neglected play deserves its share of the attention and the praise lavished on the other masterpieces of Euripides.

REFERENCES

AÉLION, R. (1986), *Quelques grands mythes héroïques dans l'œuvre d'Euripide* (Paris).

AICHELÉ, K. (1971), 'Das Epeisodion', in W. Jens (ed.), *Die Bauformen der griechischen Tragödie* (Munich), 47–83.

ALBINI, U. (1974), 'Un dramma d'avanguardia: l'*Andromaca* di Euripide', *Maia*, 26: 83–95.

AMOROSO, F. (1994), 'Una lettura progressista dell'*Andromaca* di Euripide', in A. Bierl and P. von Möllendorff (eds.), *Orchestra: Drama, Mythos, Bühne* (Stuttgart), 139–50.

ANZAI, M. (1994), 'First-Person Forms in Pindar: A Re-examination', *BICS* 39: 141–50.

ARTHUR, M. B. (1981), 'The Divided World of *Iliad* VI', in H. Foley (ed.), *Reflections on Women in Antiquity* (New York), 19–44.

AUSTIN, N. (1994), *Helen of Troy and her Shameless Phantom* (Ithaca).

BACON, H. H. (1995), 'The Chorus in Greek Life and Drama', *Arion*, 3. 1: 6–24.

BAIN, D. (1975), 'Audience Address in Greek Tragedy', *CQ* 25: 13–25.

—— (1987), 'Some Reflections on the Illusion in Greek Tragedy', *BICS* 34: 1–14.

BARLOW, S. A. (1971), *The Imagery of Euripides* (London).

BARNER, W. (1971), 'Die Monodie', in W. Jens (ed.), *Die Bauformen der griechischen Tragödie* (Munich), 277–320.

BARRETT, W. S. (ed.) (1964), *Euripides: Hippolytos* (Oxford).

BARTHES, R. (1972), *Mythologies*, tr. A. Lavers (London).

BATES, W. N. (1930), *Euripides: A Student of Human Nature* (New York).

BEARD, M. (1991), 'Adopting an Approach', in T. Rasmussen and N. Spivey (eds.), *Looking at Greek Vases* (Cambridge), 12–35.

BEAUVOIR, S. DE (1949), *Le Deuxième Sexe* (Paris).

BERS, V. (1994), 'Tragedy and Rhetoric', in I. Worthington (ed.), *Persuasion: Greek Rhetoric in Action* (London), 176–95.

BEVIS, R. W. (1988), *English Drama: Restoration and Eighteenth Century, 1600–1789* (London).

BLUNDELL, S. (1995), *Women in Ancient Greece* (London).

BOAS, F. S. (1953), *An Introduction to Eighteenth-Century Drama 1700–1780* (Oxford).

BOEDEKER, D. and SIDER, D. (eds.) (1996), *The New Simonides*, *Arethusa*, 29. 2.

BOND, G. W. (ed.) (1963), *Euripides:* Hypsipyle (Oxford).

——(ed.) (1981), *Euripides:* Heracles (Oxford).

BORNMANN, F. (ed.) (1962), *Euripidis Andromacha* (Florence).

BORTHWICK, E. K. (1967), 'Trojan Leap and Pyrrhic Dance in Euripides' *Andromache*', *JHS* 87: 18–23.

BOULTER, P. N. (1966), 'Sophia and Sophrosyne in *Andromache*', *Phoenix*, 20: 51–8.

BOUVRIE, S. DES (1990), *Women in Greek Tragedy: An Anthropological Approach* (Oslo).

BOWIE, A. M. (1993), *Aristophanes: Myth, Ritual and Comedy* (Cambridge).

——(1997), 'Tragic Filters for History: Euripides' *Supplices* and Sophocles' *Philoctetes*', in C. Pelling (ed.), *Greek Tragedy and the Historian* (Oxford), 39–62.

BOWIE, E. L. (1986), 'Early Greek Elegy, Symposium and Public Festival', *JHS* 106: 13–35.

BOWRA, C. M. (1961), *Greek Lyric Poetry* (2nd edn., Oxford).

BRADFORD, A. S. (1994), 'The Duplicitous Spartan', in A. Powell and S. Hodkinson (eds.), *The Shadow of Sparta* (London), 59–85.

BREITENBACH, W. (1934), *Untersuchungen zur Sprache der euripideischen Lyrik* (Stuttgart).

BREMMER, J. N. (1983), 'Scapegoat Rituals in Ancient Greece', *HSCP* 87: 299–320.

——(ed.) (1987), *Interpretations of Greek Mythology* (London).

——(1994), *Greek Religion* (Oxford).

BROOKS, C. and WIMSATT, W. K. (1957), *Literary Criticism: A Short History* (New York).

BULLOCH, A. W. (ed.) (1985), *Callimachus: The Fifth Hymn* (Cambridge).

BURIAN, P. (1997), 'Myth into *Muthos*: The Shaping of Tragic Plot', in P. Easterling (ed.), *The Cambridge Companion to Greek Tragedy* (Cambridge), 178–208.

BURKERT, W. (1966), 'Greek Tragedy and Sacrificial Ritual', *GRBS* 7: 87–121.

——(1974), 'Die Absurdität der Gewalt und das Ende der Tragödie: Euripides' *Orestes*', *A&A* 20: 97–109.

——(1979a), 'Griechische Mythologie und die Geistesgeschichte der Moderne', in W. den Boer (ed.), *Les Études classiques aux XIXe et XXe siècles*, Entretiens Hardt, 26 (Geneva), 159–99.

——(1979b), 'Mythisches Denken', in H. Poser (ed.), *Philosophie und Mythos* (Berlin), 16–39.

—— (1979c), *Structure and History in Greek Mythology and Ritual* (Berkeley).

—— (1983), *Home Necans*, tr. P. Bing (Berkeley).

—— (1985), *Greek Religion*, tr. J. Raffan (Oxford).

—— (1987), *Ancient Mystery Cults* (Cambridge, Mass.).

—— (1992), *The Orientalizing Revolution: Near Eastern Influence on Greek Cult in the Early Archaic Age* (Cambridge, Mass.).

—— (1996), *Creation of the Sacred: Tracks of Biology in Early Religions* (Cambridge, Mass.).

BURNETT, A. P. (1971), *Catastrophe Survived. Euripides' Plays of Mixed Reversal* (Oxford).

—— (1985), '*Rhesus*: Are Similes Allowed?', in P. Burian (ed.), *Directions in Euripidean Criticism: A Collection of Essays* (Durham), 13–51.

BURTON, R. W. B. (1980), *The Chorus in Sophocles' Tragedies* (Oxford).

BUXTON, R. G. A. (1982), *Persuasion in Greek Tragedy: A Study of Peitho* (Cambridge).

—— (1994), *Imaginary Greece. The Contexts of Mythology* (Cambridge).

—— (1996), 'What Can You Rely on in *Oedipus Rex*? Response to Calamé', in M. Silk (ed.), *Tragedy and the Tragic: The Greek Theatre and Beyond* (Oxford), 38–48.

CAIRNS, D. L. (1993), *Aidos* (Oxford).

CALAME, C. (1987), 'Spartan Genealogies: The Mythical Representation of a Spatial Organisation', in J. Bremmer (ed.), *Interpretations of Greek Mythology* (London), 153–86.

—— (1995), 'From Choral Poetry to Tragic Stasimon: The Enactment of Women's Song', *Arion*, 3. 1: 136–54.

CAMERON, A. (1995), *Callimachus and his Critics* (Princeton).

CANTARELLA, E. (1987), *Pandora's Daughters*, tr. M. B. Fant (Baltimore).

CAREY, C. (1977), 'Euripides, *Andromache* 1014–15', *PCPS* 23: 16.

—— (1981), *Commentary on Five Odes of Pindar: Pythian 2, Pythian 9, Nemean 1, Nemean 7, Isthmian 8* (New York).

—— (1994), 'Rhetorical Means of Persuasion', in I. Worthington (ed.), *Persuasion: Greek Rhetoric in Action* (London), 26–45.

CAREY, J. (1981), *John Donne: Life, Mind and Art* (London).

CARPENTER, T. H. (1991), *Art and Myth in Ancient Greece* (London).

CARTLEDGE, P. (1997), ' "Deep plays": Theatre as Process in Greek Civic Life', in P. Easterling (ed.), *The Cambridge Companion to Greek Tragedy* (Cambridge), 3–35.

CASTELLANI, V. (1989), 'The Value of a Kindly Chorus: Female

Choruses in Attic Tragedy', in J. Redmond (ed.), *Women in Theatre* (Cambridge), 1–18.

CAVE, T. (1988), *Recognitions: A Study in Poetics* (Oxford).

CAWKWELL, G. (1997), *Thucydides and the Peloponnesian War* (London).

CLARK, G. (1993), *Women in Late Antiquity: Pagan and Christian Life-Styles* (Oxford).

COHEN, D. (1991), *Law, Sexuality, and Society: The Enforcement of Morals in Classical Athens* (Cambridge).

COLDSTREAM, J. N. (1976), 'Hero-Cults in the Age of Homer', *JHS* 96: 8–17.

COLE, T. (1988), *Epiploke: Rhythmical Continuity and Poetic Structure in Greek Lyric* (Cambridge, Mass.).

——(1991), *The Origins of Rhetoric in Ancient Greece* (Baltimore).

COLLARD, C. (ed.) (1975), *Euripides: Supplices*, 2 vols. (Gröningen).

——(1981), *Euripides* (Oxford).

——(ed.) (1991), *Euripides:* Hecuba (Warminster).

——(1993), 'Formal Debates in Euripides' Drama', in I. McAuslan and P. Walcot (eds.), *Greek Tragedy* (Oxford), 153–66.

COLLARD, C., CROPP, M. J. and LEE, K. H. (eds.) (1995), *Euripides: Selected Fragmentary Plays, Volume I* (Warminster).

CONACHER, D. J. (1967), *Euripidean Drama: Myth, Theme and Structure.* (Toronto).

——(1981), 'Rhetoric and Relevance in Euripidean Drama', *AJP* 102: 3–25.

——(ed.) (1988), *Euripides:* Alcestis (Warminster).

CRAIK, E. (1990), 'Sexual Imagery and Innuendo in *Troades*', in A. Powell (ed.), *Euripides, Women, and Sexuality* (London), 1–15.

CREED, J. L. (1973), 'Moral Values in the Age of Thucydides', *CQ* 23: 213–31.

CROALLY, N. T. (1994), *Euripidean Polemic: The Trojan Women and the Function of Tragedy* (Cambridge).

CROPP, M. J. (ed.) (1988), *Euripides: Electra* (Warminster).

CROPP, M. and FICK, G. (1985), *Resolutions and Chronology in Euripides* (London).

——(1995), 'Cresphontes', in C. Collard, M. J. Cropp, and K. H. Lee (eds.), Euripides: Selected Fragmentary Plays, Vol. 1 (Warminster), 121–47.

CSAPO, E. and SLATER, W. J. (1995), *The Context of Ancient Drama* (Ann Arbor).

DAKARIS, S. I. (1964), Οἱ γεννεαλογικοὶ μῦθοι τῶν Μολοσσῶν (Athens).

D'ALESSIO, G. B. (1994), 'First-Person Problems in Pindar', *BICS* 39: 117–39.

DALE, A. M. (ed.) (1954), *Euripides:* Alcestis (Oxford).
——(1968), *The Lyric Metres of Greek Drama* (2nd edn., Cambridge).
——(1969), 'The Chorus in the Action of Greek Tragedy', in *Collected Papers* (Cambridge), 210–20.
DANGEL, J. (1995), *Accius: Œuvres (fragments)* (Paris).
D'ANNA, J. (1967), *M. Pacuvii Fragmenta* (Rome).
DAVIDSON, J. N. (1997), *Courtesans and Fishcakes: The Consuming Passions of Classical Athens* (London).
DAVIES, J. K. (1977–8). 'Athenian Citizenship: The Descent Group and the Alternatives', *CJ* 73: 105–21.
——(1997), 'The Moral Dimension of Pythian Apollo', in A. B. Lloyd (ed.), *What is a God? Studies in the Nature of Greek Divinity* (London), 43–64.
DAVIES, M. (1989a), *The Epic Cycle* (Bristol).
——(1989b), 'Sisyphus and the Invention of Religion', *BICS* 36: 16–32.
——(ed.) (1991), *Sophocles:* Trachiniae (Oxford).
Dawe, R. D. (1963), 'Inconsistency of Plot and Character in Aeschylus', *PCPS* 9: 21–62.
DEAN-JONES, L. (1994), *Women's Bodies in Classical Greek Science* (Oxford).
DECOURT, J.-CL. (1990), *La Vallée de l'Énipeus en Thessalie* (Athens and Paris).
DEFRADAS, J. (1972), *Les Thèmes de la propagande Delphique* (2nd edn., Paris).
DELCOURT, M. (1959), *Oreste et Alcméon: Étude sur la projection légendaire du matricide en Grèce* (Paris).
DEMAND, N. (1994), *Birth, Death, and Motherhood in Classical Greece* (Baltimore).
DENNISTON, J. D. (ed.) (1939), *Euripides:* Electra (Oxford).
DEROW, P. (1994), 'Historical Explanation: Polybius and his Predecessors', in S. Hornblower (ed.), *Greek Historiography*, (Oxford), 73–90.
DETIENNE, M. (1981), *L' invention de la mythologie* (Paris).
DEVEREUX, G. (1985), *The Character of the Euripidean Hippolytos: An Ethno-Psychoanalytical Study* (Chico).
DI BENEDETTO, V. (1971), *Euripide: teatro e società* (Turin).
DIGGLE, J. (1994), *Euripidea: Collected Essays* (Oxford).
DILLER, H. (1960), 'Umwelt und Masse als dramatische Faktoren bei Euripides', in O. Reverdin (ed.), *Euripide*, Entretiens Hardt 6 (Geneva), 89–105.
DOCHERTY, T. (1983), *Reading (Absent) Character: Towards a Theory of Characterization in Fiction* (Oxford).

DODDS, E. R. (ed.) (1960), *Euripides:* Bacchae (2nd edn., Oxford).

DOVER, K. J. (1974), *Greek Popular Morality in the Time of Plato and Aristotle* (Oxford).

——(1987), *Greek and the Greeks. Collected Papers*, i (Oxford).

——(1989), *The Greeks and their Legacy: Collected Papers*, ii (Oxford).

——(ed.) (1993), *Aristophanes:* Frogs (Oxford).

DOWDEN, K. (1992), *The Uses of Greek Mythology* (London).

DRACHMANN, A. B. (1922), *Atheism in Pagan Antiquity* (London).

——(1927), *Scholia Vetera in Pindari Carmina*, 3 vols. (Leipzig).

DUCHEMIN, J. (1968), *L'ΑΓΩΝ dans la tragédie grecque* (2nd edn., Paris).

DUNBAR, N. (ed.) (1995), *Aristophanes:* Birds (Oxford).

DUNN, F. (1989), 'Comic and Tragic Licence in Euripides' *Orestes*', *CA* 8: 238–51.

——(1996), *Tragedy's End: Closure and Innovation in Euripidean Drama* (Oxford).

EAGLETON, T. (1976), *Marxism And Literary Criticism* (London).

EASTERLING, P. E. (1977), 'The Infanticide in Euripides' *Medea*', *YCS* 25: 177–91.

——(ed.) (1982), *Sophocles:* Trachiniae (Cambridge).

——(1984), 'The Tragic Homer', *BICS* 31: 1–8.

——(1985), 'Anachronism in Greek Tragedy', *JHS* 105: 1–10.

——(1987), 'Women in Tragic Space', *BICS* 34: 15–26.

——(1990), 'Constructing Character in Greek Tragedy', in C. Pelling (ed.), *Characterization and Individuality in Greek Literature* (Oxford), 83–99.

——(1993), 'The End of an Era? Tragedy in the Early Fourth Century', in A. Sommerstein *et al.* (eds.), *Tragedy, Comedy and the Polis* (Bari), 559–69.

——(1994), 'Euripides outside Athens: A Speculative Note', *ICS* 19: 73–80.

——(ed.) (1997a), 'Form and Performance', in *The Cambridge Companion to Greek Tragedy* (Cambridge), 151–77.

——(1997b). 'Constructing the Heroic', in C. Pelling (ed.), *Greek Tragedy and the Historian* (Oxford), 21–37.

EDMUNDS, L. (1997), 'Myth in Homer', in I. Morris and B. Powell (eds.), *A New Companion to Homer* (Leiden), 415–41.

ELAM, K. (1980), *The Semiotics of Theatre and Drama* (London).

ERBSE, H. (1968), 'Euripides' *Andromache*', in E.-R. Schwinge (ed.), *Euripides*, 275–304 [= *Hermes*, 94 (1966): 276–97].

——(1984), *Studien zum Prolog der euripideischen Tragödie* (Berlin).

EUBEN, J. P. (ed.) (1986), *Greek Tragedy and Political Theory* (Berkeley).

EWANS, M. (1996), 'Patterns of Tragedy in Sophokles and Shakespeare', in M. Silk (ed.), *Tragedy and the Tragic: The Greek Theatre and Beyond* (Oxford), 438–57.

FANTHAM, E. (1986), 'Andromache's Child in Euripides and Seneca', in M. Cropp, E. Fantham, and S. Scully (eds.), *Greek Tragedy and its Legacy* (Calgary), 267–80.

FARNELL, L. (1921), *Greek Hero Cults and Ideas of Immortality* (Oxford).

FEENEY, D. C. (1991), *The Gods in Epic* (Oxford).

——(1998), *Literature and Religion at Rome: Cultures, Contexts, and Beliefs* (Cambridge).

FINKELBERG, M. (1998), *The Birth of Literary Fiction in Ancient Greece* (Oxford).

FINLEY, J. H., JR. (1951), 'The Date of Paean 6 and Nemean 7', *HSCP* 60: 61–80.

——(1955), *Pindar and Aeschylus* (Cambridge, Mass.).

FIRNHABER, C. G. (1848), 'Über die Zeit und politischen Tendenzen der euripideischen Andromache', *Philologus*, 3: 408–35.

FOLEY, H. P. (ed.) (1985), *Ritual Irony: Poetry and Sacrifice in Euripides* (Ithaca).

——(1993), 'The Politics of Tragic Lamentation', in A. Sommerstein *et al.* (eds.), *Tragedy, Comedy and the Polis* (Bari), 101–43.

——(1996), 'Antigone as Moral Agent', in M. S. Silk (ed.), *Greek Tragedy and the Tragic: The Greek Theatre and Beyond* (Oxford), 49–73.

FONTENROSE, J. (1959), *Python: A Study of Delphic Myth and its Origins* (Berkeley).

——(1960), 'The Cult and Myth of Pyrrhos at Delphi', *Univ. of Cal. Publ. in Class. Archaeology*, 4, 3: 191–261.

FORBES IRVING, P. M. C. (1990), *Metamorphosis in Greek Myths* (Oxford).

FOUCAULT, M. (1986), *The Use of Pleasure*, tr. R. Hurley (New York).

FOWLER, D. (1994), 'Postmodernism, Romantic Irony, and Classical Closure', in I. J. F. de Jong and J. P. Sullivan (eds.), *Modern Critical Theory and Classical Literature* (Leiden), 231–56.

FOXHALL, L. (1989), 'Household, Gender and Property in Classical Athens', *CQ* 39: 22–44.

——(1996), 'The Law and the Lady: Women and Legal Proceedings in Classical Athens', in L. Foxhall and A. D. E. Lewis (eds.), *Greek Law in its Political Setting* (Oxford), 133–52.

FOXHALL, L. and SALMON, J. (eds.) (1998), *Thinking Men: Masculinity and its Self-Representation in the Classical Tradition* (London).

FRAENKEL, E. (1931), 'Livius Andronicus', *RE* Suppl. V. 598–607.

——(ed.) (1950), *Aeschylus:* Agamemnon, 3 vols. (Oxford).

——(1964), 'Lyrische Daktylen', in id., *Kleine Beiträge zur klassischen Philologie*, vol. 1 (Rome), 165–233.

FRIEDLÄNDER, P. (1926), 'Die griechische Tragödie und das Tragische', *Die Antike*, 2: 79–112.

FRIEDRICH, R. (1996), 'Everything to Do with Dionysos? Ritualism, the Dionysiac, and the Tragic', in M. S. Silk (ed.), *Tragedy and the Tragic: The Greek Theatre and Beyond* (Oxford), 257–83.

FRIEDRICH, W. H. (1953), *Euripides und Diphilos: zur Dramaturgie der Spätformen* (Munich).

FRIIS JOHANSEN, H. (1959), *General Reflection in Tragic Rhesis* (Copenhagen).

FUQUA, C. (1976), 'Studies in the Use of Myth in Sophocles' *Philoctetes* and the *Orestes* of Euripides', *Traditio*, 32: 29–95.

GADAMER, H.-G. (1986), *The Relevance of the Beautiful and Other Essays* (Cambridge).

GAGARIN, M. (ed.) (1997), *Antiphon: The Speeches* (Cambridge).

GALE, M. (1994), *Myth and Poetry in Lucretius* (Cambridge).

GANTZ, T. (1993), *Early Greek Myth: A Guide to Literary and Artistic Sources* (Baltimore).

GARNER, R. (1990), *From Homer to Tragedy. The Art of Allusion in Greek Poetry* (London).

GARRISON, E. P. (1995), *Groaning Tears: Ethical and Dramatic Aspects of Suicide in Greek Tragedy* (Leiden).

GARVIE, A. F. (1978), 'Aeschylus' Simple Plots', in R. D. Dawe, J. Diggle, and P. E. Easterling (eds.), *Dionysiaca* (Cambridge), 63–86.

GARZYA, A. (1951), 'Interpretazione dell' Andromaca di Euripide', *Dionisio* 14: 109–38.

——(ed.) (1963), *Euripides:* Andromaca (2nd edn., Naples).

GEHRKE, H. J. (1985), *Stasis: Untersuchungen zu den inneren Kriegen in den griechischen Staaten des 5. und 4. Jahrhunderts v. Chr.* (Munich).

GENTILI, B. (1979), *Theatrical Performance in the Ancient World: Hellenistic and Early Roman Theatre* (Amsterdam).

GIBERT, J. (1995), *Change of Mind in Greek Tragedy* (Göttingen).

GILL, C. (1995), *Greek Thought* (Oxford).

——(1996), *Personality in Greek Epic, Tragedy and Philosophy* (Oxford).

GLOVER, J. (1988), *I. The Philosophy and Psychology of Personal Identity* (London).

GOEBEL, G. H. (1989), '*Andromache* 192–204: The Pattern of Argument', *CPh* 84: 32–5.

GOFF, B. (1990), *The Noose of Words: Readings of Desire, Violence and Language in Euripides' Hippolytos* (Cambridge).

GOLDER, H. (1983), 'The Mute Andromache', *TAPA* 103: 123–33.

——(1996), 'Making a Scene: Gesture, Tableau, and the Tragic Chorus', *Arion*, 4. 1: 1–19.

GOLDHILL, S. (1986), *Reading Greek Tragedy* (Cambridge).

——(1990a), 'Character and Action, Representation and Reading: Greek Tragedy and its Critics', in C. Pelling (ed.), *Characterization and Individuality in Greek Literature* (Oxford), 100–27.

——(1990b), 'The Great Dionysia and Civic Ideology', in J. J. Winkler and F. I. Zeitlin (eds.), *Nothing to Do with Dionysos?* (Princeton), 97–129.

——(1994), 'The Failure of Exemplarity', in I. J. F. de Jong and J. P. Sullivan (eds.), *Modern Critical Theory and Classical Literature* (Leiden), 51–73.

——(1995), *Foucault's Virginity: Ancient Erotic Fiction and the History of Sexuality* (Cambridge).

——(1996), 'Collectivity and Otherness—The Authority of the Tragic Chorus: Response to Gould', in M. S. Silk (ed.), *Tragedy and the Tragic: The Greek Theatre and Beyond* (Oxford), 244–56.

——(1997a), 'The Audience of Athenian Tragedy', in P. E. Easterling (ed.), *The Cambridge Companion to Greek Tragedy* (Cambridge), 54–68.

——(1997b), 'The Language of Tragedy: Rhetoric and Communication', in P. E. Easterling (ed.), *The Cambridge Companion to Greek Tragedy* (Cambridge), 127–50.

GOMME, A. W. (1925), 'The Position of Women in Athens in the Fifth and Fourth Centuries', *CPh* 20: 1–25.

GOOSSENS, R. (1962), *Euripide et Athènes* (Brussels).

GOULD, J. (1973), 'Hiketeia', *JHS* 93: 74–103.

——(1978), 'Dramatic Character and "Human Intelligibility" in Greek Tragedy', *PCPS* 24: 43–67.

——(1980), 'Law, Custom and Myth: Aspects of the Social Position of Women in Classical Athens', *JHS* 100: 38–59.

——(1983), 'Homeric Epic and the Tragic Moment', in K. W. Gransden *et al.* (eds.), *Aspects of the Epic* (London), 32–45.

——(1985), 'On Making Sense of Greek Religion', in P. E. Easterling and J. V. Muir (eds.), *Greek Religion and Society* (Cambridge), 1–33.

GOULD, J. (1989), *Herodotus* (London).

—— (1994), 'Herodotus and Religion', in S. Hornblower (ed.), *Greek Historiography* (Oxford), 91–106.

—— (1996a), 'Euripides', in *OCD*³ (Oxford), 571–4.

—— (1996b), 'Tragedy and Collective Experience', in M. S. Silk (ed.), *Tragedy and the Tragic: The Greek Theatre and Beyond* (Oxford), 217–43.

GRAF, F. (1993), *Greek Mythology*, tr. T. Marier (Baltimore).

GREDLEY, B. (1996), 'Comedy and Tragedy—Inevitable Distinctions: Response to Taplin', in M. Silk (ed.), *Tragedy and the Tragic: The Greek Theatre and Beyond* (Oxford), 203–16.

GREGORY, J. (1991), *Euripides and the Instruction of the Athenians* (Ann Arbor).

—— (1995), 'Genealogy and Intertextuality in *Hecuba*', *AJP* 116: 389–97.

GRIFFIN, J. (1980), *Homer on Life and Death* (Oxford).

—— (1990), 'Characterization in Euripides: *Hippolytus* and *Iphigeneia in Aulis*', in C. Pelling (ed.), *Characterization and Individuality in Greek Literature* (Oxford), 128–49.

—— (ed.) (1995), *Homer:* Iliad IX (Oxford).

—— (1998), 'The Social Function of Attic Tragedy', *CQ* 48: 39–61.

GRIFFITH, M. (ed.) (1983), *Aeschylus:* Prometheus Bound (Cambridge).

—— (1995), 'Brilliant Dynasts: Power and Politics in the *Oresteia*', *CA* 14, 1: 62–129.

GRUBE, G. M. A. (1961), *The Drama of Euripides* (2nd edn., London).

GUTHRIE, W. K. C. (1969), *The History of Greek Philosophy*, iii (Cambridge).

HAINSWORTH, J. B. (ed.) (1993), *The Iliad: A Commentary. Vol. III: Books 9–12* (Cambridge).

HALL, E. (1989), *Inventing the Barbarian* (Oxford).

—— (1995), 'Lawcourt Dramas: The Power of Performance in Greek Forensic Oratory', *BICS* 40: 39–58.

—— (ed.) (1996a), *Aeschylus:* Persians (Warminster).

—— (1996b), 'Is there a *Polis* in Aristotle's *Poetics*?', in M. Silk (ed.), *Tragedy and the Tragic: The Greek Theatre and Beyond* (Oxford), 295–309.

—— (1997a), 'Electra's Baby in Euripides', *Omnibus* 33: 17–20.

—— (1997b), 'The Sociology of Athenian Tragedy', in P. E. Easterling (ed.), *The Cambridge Companion to Greek Tragedy* (Cambridge), 93–126.

HALLERAN, M. R. (1985), *Stagecraft in Euripides* (London).

—— (ed.) (1995), *Euripides:* Hippolytus (Warminster).

HALLIWELL, S. (1997), 'Between Public and Private: Tragedy and Athenian Experience of Rhetoric', in C. Pelling (ed.), *Greek Tragedy and the Historian* (Oxford), 121–41.

HALPORN, J. W. (1983), 'The Skeptical Electra', *HSCP* 87: 101–18.

HAMEL, D. (1998), *Athenian Generals: Military Authority in the Classical Period* (Leiden).

HAMMOND, N. G. L. (1967), *Epirus* (Oxford).

——(1988), 'The Campaign and Battle of Cynoscephalae in 197 BC', *JHS* 108: 60–82.

——(1997), 'Ancient Epirus', in M. B. Sakellariou (ed.), *Epirus: 4000 Years of Greek History and Civilization* (Athens), 34–62.

HARDER, A. (ed.) (1985), *Euripides' Kresphontes and Archelaos* (Leiden).

HARRISON, A. R. W. (1968), *The Law of Athens: Family and Property*, 2 vols. (Oxford).

HARRISON, J. E. (1922), *Prolegomena to the Study of Greek Religion* (Cambridge).

HARTIGAN, K. V. (1991), *Ambiguity and Self-Deception: The Apollo and Artemis Plays of Euripides* (Frankfurt am Main).

HARTUNG, J. A. (1844), *Euripides Restitutus, sive scriptorum Euripidis ingeniique censura*, 2 vols. (Hamburg).

HARVEY, A. E. (1955), 'The Classification of Greek Lyric Poetry', *CQ* 5: 157–75.

HARVEY, F. D. (1966), 'Literacy in the Athenian Democracy', *REG* 79: 585–635.

HAVEL, V. (1986), *Living in Truth* (London).

HAWCROFT, M. (1992), *Word as Action: Racine, Rhetoric, and Theatrical Language* (Oxford).

HEATH, M. (1987), *The Poetics of Greek Tragedy* (London).

——(1989), *Unity in Greek Poetics* (Oxford).

——(1993), 'Ancient Interpretations of Pindar's *Nemean* 7', *PLLS* 7: 169–99.

HEDREEN, G. (1991), 'The Cult of Achilles in the Euxine', *Hesperia*, 60: 313–30.

HEITSCH, E. (1993), *Die Welt als Schauspiel: Bemerkungen zu einer Theologie der Ilias* (Stuttgart).

HELLY, B. (1995), *L'État thessalien* (Lyons).

HENRICHS, A. (1986), 'The Last of the Detractors: Friedrich Nietzsche's Condemnation of Euripides', *GRBS* 27: 369–97.

——(1995), ' "Why Should I Dance?": Choral Self-Referentiality in Greek Tragedy', *Arion*, 3: 56–111.

HERINGTON, J. (1985), *Poetry into Drama* (Berkeley).

HERRNSTEIN SMITH, B. (1968), *Poetic Closure: A Study of How Poems End* (Chicago).

HEUBECK, A. and HOEKSTRA, A. (eds.) (1989), *A Commentary on Homer's Odyssey. Vol. II: Books IX-XVI* (Oxford).

HOEKSTRA, A. (1962), 'The Absence of the Aeginetans (On the Interpretation of Pindar's Sixth Paean)', *Mnem.* Suppl. 15: 1–14.

HOMEYER, H. (1977), *Die spartansiche Helena und der trojanische Krieg* (Wiesbaden).

HOMMEL, H. (1980), 'Der Gott Achilleus', *Sitzungsberichte der Heidelberger Akademie der Wissenschaften, Philos.-Hist. Klasse.* Vol. 1.

HOOKER, J. T. (1988), 'The Cults of Achilles', *RhM* 131: 1–7.

HOPE SIMPSON, R. and LAZENBY, J. F. (1959), 'The Kingdom of Peleus and Achilles', *Antiquity*, 33: 102–5.

—— (1970), *The Catalogue of Ships in Homer's Iliad* (Oxford).

HORNBLOWER, S. (1987), *Thucydides* (London).

—— (1991a), *A Commentary on Thucydides, Volume I: Books I–III* (Oxford).

—— (1991b), *The Greek World 479–323 BC* (2nd edn., London).

—— (1992), 'The Religious Dimension to the Peloponnesian War, or, What Thucydides Does not Tell Us', *HSCP* 94: 169–97.

Hose, M. (1990–1), *Studien zum Chor bei Euripides.* 2 vols. (Stuttgart).

—— (1995), *Drama und Gesellschaft. Studien zur dramatischen Produktion in Athen am Ende des 5. Jahrhunderts* (Stuttgart).

HOURMOUZIADES, N. C. (1965), *Production and Imagination in Euripides* (Athens).

HOWIE, J. G. (1998), 'Thucydides and Pindar: The *Archaeology* and *Nemean* 7', *PLLS* 10: 75–130.

HUBBARD, M. (1974), *Propertius* (London).

HUNGER, H. (1952), 'Euripides' *Andromache* 147–53 und die Auftrittszenen in der attischen Tragödie', *RhM* 95: 369–73.

HUNTER, R. (1993), *Apollonius of Rhodes: Jason and The Golden Fleece* (Oxford).

HUNTER, V. J. (1994), *Policing Athens: Social Control in the Attic Lawsuits, 420–320 B.C.* (Princeton).

HUTCHINSON, G. O. (ed.) (1985), *Aeschylus: Septem contra Thebas* (Oxford).

—— (1988), *Hellenistic Poetry* (Oxford).

IRELAND, S. (1986), *Aeschylus* (Oxford).

ITSUMI, K. (1984), 'The Glyconic in Tragedy', *CQ* 34: 66–82.

JACOBY, F. (1956), *Griechische Historiker* (Stuttgart).

JAEGER, W. (1947), *Paideia: The Ideals of Greek Culture*, i, tr. G. Highet (Oxford).

JANKO, R. (ed.) (1992), *The Iliad: A Commentary. Vol. IV: Books 13–16* (Cambridge).

JENS, W. (ed.) (1971), *Die Bauformen der griechischen Tragödie* (Munich).

JOCELYN, H. D. (ed.) (1967), *The Tragedies of Ennius* (Cambridge).

JONG, I. J. F. DE (1990), 'Three Off-Stage Characters in Euripides', *Mnem.* 43: 1–21.

——(1991), *Narrative in Drama: The Art of the Euripidean Messenger-Speech* (Leiden).

JOUAN, F. (1966), *Euripide et les légendes des chants cypriens* (Paris).

KAIMIO, M. (1988), *Physical Contact in Greek Tragedy: A Study of Stage Conventions* (Helsinki).

KAMERBEEK, J. C. (1943), 'L'*Andromaque* d'Euripide', *Mnem.* 11: 47–67.

KANNICHT, R. (ed.) (1969), *Euripides:* Helena, 2 vols. (Heidelberg).

KASSEL, R. (1954), *Quomodo quibus locis apud veteres scriptores Graecos infantes atque parvuli pueri inducantur describantur commemorentur* (Meisenheim am Glan).

KEARNS, E. (1989), *The Heroes of Attica* (London).

KERFERD, G. B. (1981), *The Sophistic Movement* (Cambridge).

KERMODE, F. (1966), *The Sense of an Ending* (Oxford).

KEULS, E. C. (1985), *The Reign of the Phallus: Sexual Politics in Ancient Athens* (New York).

KIRK, G. S. (ed.) (1985), *The Iliad: A Commentary. Vol. I: Books 1–4* (Cambridge).

KITTO, H. D. F. (1961), *Greek Tragedy: A Literary Study* (3rd edn., London).

KNOX, B. M. W. (1979), 'Myth and Attic Tragedy', in *Word and Action: Essays on the Ancient Theater* (Baltimore), 3–24.

——(1985), 'Euripides', in B. M. W. Knox and P. E. Easterling (eds.), *Cambridge History of Classical Literature, Vol. 1, Greek Literature* (Cambridge), 316–39.

KNOX, P. E. (ed.) (1995), *Ovid Heroides: Select Epistles* (Cambridge).

KONSTAN, D. (1993), 'Aristophanes' Lysistrata: Women and the Body Politic', in A. Sommerstein *et al.* (eds.), *Tragedy, Comedy and the Polis* (Bari), 431–44.

KOPPERSCHMIDT, J. (1971), 'Hikesie als dramatische Form' in W. Jens (ed.), *Die Bauformen der griechischen Tragödie* (Munich), 321–46.

KOSTER, W. J. W. (1962), *Traité de métrique grecque* (Leiden).

KOVACS, P. D. (1980), *The Andromache of Euripides: An Interpretation* (Chico).

KOVACS, P. D. (1986), 'On Medea's Great Monologue (Eur. *Medea* 1021–80)', *CQ* 36: 343–52.

——(1987), *The Heroic Muse* (Baltimore).

——(1989), 'Euripides, *Electra* 518–44: Further Doubts about Genuineness', *BICS* 36: 67–78.

——(1994), *Euripidea* (Leiden).

——(1995), *Euripides: Children of Heracles, Hippolytus, Andromache, Hecuba*, Loeb translation, Vol. 2 (Cambridge, Mass.).

——(1996), *Euripidea Altera* (Leiden).

——(1998), *Euripides: Suppliant Women, Electra, Heracles*, Loeb translation, Vol. 3 (Cambridge, Mass.).

KRANZ, W. (1933), *Stasimon: Untersuchungen zu Form und Gehalt der griechischen Tragödie* (Berlin).

KRIEGER, X. (1973), *Der Kampf zwischen Peleus und Thetis in der griechischen Vasenmalerei. Eine typologische Untersuchung* (Diss. Münster).

KRON, U. (1996), 'Priesthoods, Dedications and Euergetism: What Part Did Religion Play in the Political and Social Status of Women', in P. Hellström and B. Alroth (eds.), *Religion and Power in the Ancient Greek World* (Uppsala), 139–82.

KUMANIECKI, C. F. (1930), *De consiliis personarum apud Euripidem agentium* (Kraków).

KUNTZ, M. (1993), *Narrative Setting and Dramatic Poetry* (Leiden).

LADA, I. (1996), 'Emotion and Meaning in Tragic Performance', in M. S. Silk (ed.), *Tragedy and the Tragic: The Greek Theatre and Beyond* (Oxford), 397–413.

LANGHOLF, V. (1971), *Die Gebete bei Euripides und die zeitliche Folge der Tragödien* (Göttingen).

LATTIMORE, R. (1958), *The Poetry of Greek Tragedy* (Baltimore).

LEE, K. H. (1975), 'Euripides' *Andromache*: Observations on Form and Meaning', *Antichthon*, 9: 4–16.

LEFKOWITZ, M. R. (1981), *The Lives of the Greek Poets* (London).

——(1987), 'Was Euripides an Atheist?', *SIFC* 5. 2: 149–66.

——(1989), ' "Impiety" and "Atheism" in Euripides' Dramas', *CQ* 39: 70–82.

——(1991), *First-Person Fictions: Pindar's Poetic 'I'* (Oxford).

LEO, F. (1912), *Plautinische Forschungen* (2nd edn., Berlin).

LESKY, A. (1947), 'Der Ablauf der Handlung in der *Andromache* des Euripides', *Anzeiger der österreichischen Akademie der Wissenschaften, Philos.-Hist. Klasse*, 84: 99–115.

——(1972), *Die Tragische Dichtung der Hellenen* (3rd edn., Göttingen).

——(1983). *Greek Tragic Poetry*, tr. M. Dillon (Yale).

LLOYD, M. (1986), 'Realism and Character in Euripides' *Electra*', *Phoenix*, 40: 1–19.

——(1992), *The Agon in Euripides* (Oxford).

——(ed.) (1994), *Euripides:* Andromache (Warminster).

LLOYD-JONES, H. (1971), *The Justice of Zeus* (Berkeley).

——(1973), 'Modern Interpretation of Pindar: The Second Pythian and Seventh Nemean Odes', *JHS* 93: 109–37 [= *Academic Papers*, 2 vols. (Oxford, 1990), i. 110–53].

——(ed.) (1996), *Sophocles: Fragments* (Cambridge, Mass.).

LORAUX, N. (1987), *Tragic Ways of Killing a Woman*, tr. A. Forster (Cambridge, Mass.).

——(1993), *The Children of Athena*, tr. C. Levine (Princeton).

——(1995), *The Experiences of Tiresias: The Feminine and the Greek Man*, tr. P. Wissing (Princeton).

LUCAS, D. W. (1959), *The Greek Tragic Poets* (2nd edn., London).

LUSCHNIG, C. A. E. (1988a), *Time Holds the Mirror: A Study of Knowledge in Euripides' Hippolytus* (Leiden).

——(1988b), *Tragic Aporia: A Study of Euripides' Iphigenia at Aulis* (Melbourne).

McDERMOTT, E. A. (1989), *Euripides' Medea: The Incarnation of Disorder* (Pennsylvania).

——(1991), 'Double Meaning and Mythic Novelty in Euripides' Plays', *TAPA* 121: 123–32.

MacDOWELL, D. M. (1976), 'Bastards as Athenian Citizens', *CQ* 70: 88–91.

——(1978), *The Law in Classical Athens* (London).

——(1982), *Gorgias: Encomium of Helen* (Bristol).

——(1995), *Aristophanes and Athens: An Introduction to the Plays* (Oxford).

MACLEOD, C. W. (1983), *Collected Essays* (Oxford).

MARCH, J. R. (1987), *The Creative Poet: Studies in the Treatment of Myths in Greek Poetry* (London).

——(1990), 'Euripides the Misogynist?', in A. Powell (ed.), *Euripides, Women, and Sexuality* (London), 32–75.

MARTIN, R. P. (1989), *The Language of Heroes: Speech and Performance in the Iliad* (Ithaca).

MASTRONARDE, D. J. (1979), *Contact and Discontinuity. Some Conventions of Speech and Action on the Greek Tragic Stage* (Berkeley).

——(1990), 'Actors on High: The Skene Roof, the Crane, and the Gods in Attic Drama', *CA* 9. 2: 247–94.

——(ed.) (1994), *Euripides:* Phoenissae (Cambridge).

MELLERT-HOFFMANN, G. (1969), *Untersuchungen zur Iphigenie in Aulis des Euripides* (Heidelberg).

MENU, M. (1992), 'L'Enfant chez Euripide: affectivité et dramaturgie', *Pallas*, 38: 239–58.

MÉRIDIER, L. (1927), *Euripide: Hippolyte, Andromaque, Hécube* (Paris).

MICHELINI, A. N. (1987), *Euripides and the Tragic Tradition* (Madison).

MIKALSON, J. D. (1991), *Honor Thy Gods* (Chapel Hill).

MILLS, S. (1997), *Theseus, Tragedy and the Athenian Empire* (Oxford).

MITCHELL-BOYASK, R.N. (1996), 'Dramatic Scapegoating: On the Uses and Abuses of Girard and Shakespearean Criticism', in M. Silk (ed.), *Tragedy and the Tragic: The Greek Theatre and Beyond* (Oxford), 426–37.

MOGYORÓDI, E. (1996), 'Tragic Freedom and Fate in Sophocles' *Antigone*: Notes on the Role of the "Ancient Evils" in "the Tragic"', in M. Silk (ed.), *Tragedy and the Tragic: The Greek Theatre and Beyond* (Oxford), 358–76.

MOSSMAN, J. (1995), *Wild Justice: A Study of Euripides' Hecuba* (Oxford).

——(1996a), 'Chains of Imagery in *Prometheus Bound*', *CQ* 46: 58–67.

——(1996b), 'Waiting for Neoptolemus: The Unity of Euripides' *Andromache*', *G&R* 43: 143–56.

MOST, G. W. (1985), *The Measures of Praise* (Göttingen).

MURRAY, G. (1946), *Euripides and His Age* (2nd edn., London).

NAGY, G. (1979), *The Best of the Achaeans* (Baltimore).

——(1990), *Greek Mythology and Poetics* (Ithaca).

NESSELRATH, H.-G. (1992), *Ungeschehenes Geschehen. 'Beinahe-Episoden' im griechischen und römischen Epos von Homer bis zur Spätantike* (Stuttgart).

NESTLE, W. (1901), *Euripides, der Dichter der griechischen Aufklärung* (Stuttgart).

NILSSON, M. P. (1951), *Cults, Myths, Oracles and Politics in Ancient Greece* (Lund).

NOCK, A. D. (1972), 'Religious Attitudes of the Ancient Greeks', in Z. Stewart (ed.), *Essays on Religion and the Ancient World* (Oxford), ii. 534–50.

NORDHEIDER, H. W. (1980), *Chorlieder des Euripides in ihrer dramatischen Funktion* (Frankfurt am Main).

NORTH, H. (1966), *Sophrosyne: Self-Knowledge and Self-Restraint in Greek Literature* (Ithaca).

——(1979), *From Myth to Icon: Reflections of Greek Ethical Doctrine in Literature and Art* (Ithaca).

NORWOOD, G. (ed.) (1906), *Euripides: Andromache* (London).

——(1954), *Essays on Euripidean Drama* (Berkeley).

NUSSBAUM, M. C. (1986), *The Fragility of Goodness* (Cambridge).

OBBINK, D. (ed.) (1996), *Philodemus: On Piety. Part I* (Oxford).

OBER, J. and STRAUSS, B. (1990), 'Drama, Political Rhetoric, and the Discourse of Athenian Democracy', in J. J. Winkler and F. I. Zeitlin (eds.), *Nothing to Do with Dionysos?* (Princeton), 237–70.

OGDEN, D. (1995), 'Women and Bastardy in Ancient Greece and the Hellenistic World', in A. Powell (ed.), *The Greek World* (London), 219–44.

——(1996), *Greek Bastardy in the Classical and Hellenistic Periods* (Oxford).

OSBORNE, M. J. (1983), *Naturalization in Athens. Vols. iii–iv* (Brussels).

OSBORNE, R. G. (1996), *Greece in the Making, 1200–479 B.C.* (London).

——(1997), 'Law, the Democratic Citizen and the Representation of Women in Classical Athens', *Past and Present*, 155: 3–33.

OWEN, A. S. (ed.) (1939), *Euripides: Ion* (Oxford).

PADEL, R. (1974), 'Imagery of the Elsewhere: Two Choral Odes of Euripides', *CQ* 24: 227–41.

——(1992), *In and Out of the Mind: Greek Images of the Tragic Self* (Princeton).

PAGANI, G. (1968), 'La figura di Ermione nell'Andromaca euripidea', *Dioniso*, 42: 200–10.

PAGE, D. L. (1934), *Actors' Interpolations in Greek Tragedy* (Oxford).

——(1936), 'The Elegiacs in Euripides' *Andromache*', in *Greek Poetry and Life* (Oxford), 206–23.

——(ed.) (1938), *Euripides:* Medea (Oxford).

PARKE, H. W. (1967), *The Oracles of Zeus: Dodona, Olympia, Ammon* (Oxford).

PARKE, H. W. and WORMELL, D. E. W. (1956), *The Delphic Oracle*, 2 vols. (Oxford).

PARKER, L. P. E. (1997), *The Songs of Aristophanes* (Oxford).

PARKER, R. (1983), *Miasma: Pollution and Purification in Early Greek Religion* (Oxford).

——(1996), *Athenian Religion: A History* (Oxford).

——(1997), 'Gods Cruel and Kind: Tragic and Civic Theology', in C. Pelling (ed.), *Greek Tragedy and the Historian* (Oxford), 206–23.

——(1998), 'Pleasing Thighs: Reciprocity in Greek Religion', in C. Gill *et al.* (eds.), *Reciprocity in Ancient Greece* (Oxford), 105–25.

PARSONS, P. J. (ed.) (1992), 'Simonides, *Elegies*', *The Oxyrhynchus Papyri*, 59: 4–50.

PATTERSON, C. B. (1991), 'Marriage and the Married Woman in

Athenian Law', S. B. Pomeroy (ed.), *Women's History and Ancient History* (Chapel Hill), 48–72.

PEARSON, A. C. (ed.) (1917), *The Fragments of Sophocles*, 3 vols. (Cambridge).

PEASE, A. S. (ed.) (1967), *Vergili Aeneidos Liber Quartus* (Darmstadt).

PELLICCIA, H. (1992), 'Sappho 16, Gorgias' *Helen*, and the Preface to Herodotus' *Histories*', *YCS* 29: 63–84.

PELLING, C. B. R. (ed.) (1990), *Characterization and Individuality in Greek Literature* (Oxford).

——(1997a), 'Aeschylus' *Persae* and History', in Pelling (ed.), *Greek Tragedy and the Historian* (Oxford), 1–19.

——(1997b), 'Conclusion', in Pelling (ed.), *Greek Tragedy and the Historian* (Oxford),213–35.

PFEIFFER, R. (1968), *History of Classical Scholarship from the Beginnings to the End of the Hellenistic Age* (Oxford).

PFISTER, M. (1988), *The Theory and Analysis of Drama*, tr. J. Halliday (Cambridge).

PHILLIPPO, S. (1995), 'Family Ties: Significant Patronymics in Euripides' *Andromache*', *CQ* 45: 355–71.

PICKARD-CAMBRIDGE, A. W. (1968), *The Dramatic Festivals of Athens* (2nd edn., revised by J. Gould and D. M. Lewis; Oxford).

POHLENZ, M. (1954), *Die griechische Tragödie*, 2 vols. (2nd edn., Göttingen).

POMEROY, S. B. (1975), *Goddesses, Whores, Wives, and Slaves: Women in Classical Antiquity* (New York).

——(1994), *Xenophon: Oeconomicus. A Social and Historical Commentary* (Oxford).

POOLE, W. (1994), 'Euripides and Sparta', in A. Powell and S. Hodkinson (eds.), *The Shadow of Sparta* (London), 1–33.

PORTER, J. R. (1994), *Studies in Euripides' Orestes* (Leiden).

PÒRTULAS, J. (1988), 'L'*Andromaque* d'Euripide: Entre le mythe et la vie quotidienne', *Metis*, 3: 283–304.

PRATT, L. H. (1993), *Lying and Poetry from Homer to Pindar: Falsehood and Deception in Archaic Greek Poetics* (Ann Arbor).

PRITCHETT, W. K. (1969), *Studies in Ancient Greek Topography. Part II (Battlefields)* (Berkeley).

RAAB, I. (1972), *Zu den Darstellungen des Parisurteils in der griechischen Kunst* (Berne).

RABINOWITZ, N. S. (1993), *Anxiety Veiled: Euripides and the Traffic in Women* (Ithaca).

RADERMACHER, L. (1951), *Artium Scriptores: Reste der voraristotelischen Rhetorik* (Vienna).

RADT, S. L. (1958), *Pindars Zweiter und Sechster Paian* (Amsterdam).

RANKIN, H. D. (1983), *Sophists, Socratics and Cynics* (London).

RAWSON, E. (1972), 'Aspects of Euripides' *Orestes*', *Arethusa*, 5: 155–67.

REDFIELD, J. M. (1975), *Nature and Culture in the Iliad* (Chicago).

——(1995), 'Homo Domesticus', in J.-P. Vernant (ed.), *The Greeks*, tr. C. Lambert and T. L. Fagan (Chicago), 153–83.

REHM, R. (1988), 'The Staging of Suppliant Plays', *GRBS* 29: 263–307.

——(1992), *Greek Tragic Theatre* (London).

——(1994), *Marriage to Death: The Conflation of Wedding and Funeral Rituals in Greek Tragedy* (Princeton).

REID, J. D. (ed.) (1993), *The Oxford Guide to Classical Mythology in the Arts, 1300–1990s*, 2 vols. (Oxford).

RHODES, P. J. (with D. M. Lewis) (1997), *The Decrees of the Greek States* (Oxford).

RICHARDSON, N. J. (1992), 'Panhellenic Cults and Panhellenic Poets', in *CAH²*, v. 223–44.

——(ed.) (1993), *The Iliad: A Commentary. Vol. VI: Books 21–24* (Cambridge).

RIVIER, A. (1975), *Essai sur le tragique d'Euripide* (2nd edn., Paris).

ROBERTS, D. H. (1984), *Apollo and his Oracle in the Oresteia* (Göttingen).

——(1988), 'Sophoclean Endings: Another Story', *Arethusa*, 21. 2: 177–94.

ROBERTSON, D. S. (1923), 'Euripides and Tharyps', *CR* 37: 58–60.

RODE, J. (1971), 'Das Chorlied', in W. Jens (ed.), *Die Bauformen der griechischen Tragödie* (Munich), 85–115.

ROHDICH, H. (1968), *Die Euripideische Tragödie: Untersuchungen zu ihrer Tragik* (Heidelberg).

ROMILLY, J. DE (1961), *L'Évolution du pathétique d'Eschyle à Euripide* (Paris).

——(1992), *The Great Sophists in Periclean Athens*, tr. J. Lloyd (Oxford).

——(1995), *Tragedies grecques au fil des ans* (Paris).

ROSENMEYER, T. G. (1982), *The Art of Aeschylus* (Berkeley).

ROSSETTO, P. C. and SARTORI, G. P. (eds.) (1994), *Teatri greci e romani*, 3 vols. (Rome).

ROSSUM-STEENBEEK, M. VAN (1998), *Greek Readers' Digests? Studies on a Selection of Subliterary Papyri* (Leiden).

ROY, J. (1997), 'An Alternative Sexual Morality for Classical Athens', *G&R* 44: 11–22.

RUSCHENBUSCH, E. (1966), *ΣΟΛΩΝΟΣ ΝΟΜΟΙ* (Wiesbaden).

RUTHERFORD, I. (1998), 'Theoria as Theatre: Pilgrimage in Greek Drama', *PLLS* 10: 131–56.

RUTHERFORD, R. B. (1982), 'Tragic Form and Feeling in the *Iliad*', *JHS* 102: 145–60.

——(1986), 'The Philosophy of the *Odyssey*', *JHS* 106: 145–62.

——(ed.) (1992), *Homer: Odyssey XIX–XX* (Cambridge).

——(1995), *The Art of Plato* (London).

——(1996), *Homer* (Oxford).

——(1998), 'General Introduction', in J. Davie, *Euripides: Electra and Other Plays* (London), pp. vii–xl.

SAUNDERS, T. J. (1995), 'Plato on Women in the *Laws*', in A. Powell (ed.), *The Greek World* (London), 591–609.

SCHAPER, E. (1968), *Prelude to Aesthetics* (London).

Schmid, W. and STÄHLIN, O. (1940), *Geschichte der griechischen Literatur*, Vol. 1/3 (Munich).

SCHMIDT, H. W. (1971), 'Die Struktur des Eingangs', in W. Jens (ed.), *Die Bauformen der griechischen Tragödie* (Munich), 1–46.

SCHWINGE, E.-R. (1968), *Die Verwendung der Stichomythie in den Dramen des Euripides* (Heidelberg).

SCODEL, R. (1980), *The Trojan Trilogy of Euripides* (Göttingen).

SEAFORD, R. (1987), 'The Tragic Wedding', *JHS* 107: 106–30.

——(1990), 'The Structural Problems of Marriage in Euripides', in A. Powell (ed.), *Euripides, Women, and Sexuality* (London), 151–76.

——(1994), *Reciprocity and Ritual: Homer and Tragedy in the Developing City State* (Oxford).

——(ed.) (1996), *Euripides: Bacchae* (Warminster).

SEALEY, R. (1984), 'On Lawful Concubinage in Athens', *CA* 3: 111–33.

SEGAL, C. (1971a), 'Andromache's *Anagnorisis*: Formulaic Artistry in *Iliad* 22. 437–76', *HSCP* 75: 33–57.

——(1971b), *The Theme of the Mutilation of the Corpse in the Iliad* (Leiden).

——(1982), *Dionysiac Poetics and Euripides' Bacchae* (Princeton).

——(1986), *Interpreting Greek Tragedy: Myth, Poetry, Text* (Ithaca).

——(1992), 'Tragic Beginnings: Narration, Voice, and Authority in the Prologues of Greek Drama', *YCS* 29: 85–112.

——(1993), *Euripides and the Poetics of Sorrow* (Durham).

——(1994), *Singers, Heroes, and Gods in the Odyssey* (Ithaca).

——(1996), 'Catharsis, Audience, and Closure in Greek Tragedy', in M. S. Silk (ed.), *Tragedy and the Tragic: The Greek Theatre and Beyond* (Oxford), 149–72.

SEIDENSTICKER, B. (1982), *Palintonos Harmonia* (Göttingen).

—— (1995), 'Women on the Tragic Stage', in B. Goff (ed.), *History, Tragedy, Theory: Dialogues on Athenian Drama* (Austin, Tex.), 151–73.

—— (1996), '*Peripeteia* and Tragic Dialectic in Euripidean Tragedy', in M. S. Silk (ed.), *Tragedy and the Tragic: The Greek Theatre and Beyond* (Oxford), 377–96.

SEKUNDA, N. V. (1994), 'Classical Warfare', in J. Boardman (ed.), *CAH²*, Plates to Volumes V and VI (Cambridge), 167–94.

SHAPIRO, H. A. (1994), *Myth into Art: Poet and Painter in Classical Greece* (London).

SILK, M. S. (1993), 'Aristophanic Paratragedy', in A. Sommerstein *et al.* (eds.), *Tragedy, Comedy and the Polis* (Bari), 477–504.

—— (1996), 'Tragic Language: The Greek Tragedians and Shakespeare', in M. S. Silk (ed.), *Tragedy and the Tragic: The Greek Theatre and Beyond* (Oxford), 458–96.

SINN, U. (1990), 'Das Heraion von Perachora: Eine sakrale Schutzzone in der korinthischen Peraia', *AM* 105: 53–116.

—— (1993), 'Greek Sanctuaries as Places of Refuge', in N. Marinatos and R. Hägg (eds.), *Greek Sanctuaries: New Approaches* (London), 88–109.

SLATKIN, L. M. (1991), *The Power of Thetis: Allusion and Interpretation in the Iliad* (Berkeley).

SLUGA, H. (1996), ' "Whose House is That?" Wittgenstein on the Self', in H. Sluga and D. G. Stern (eds.), *The Cambridge Companion to Wittgenstein* (Cambridge), 320–53.

SNODGRASS, A. (1980), *Archaic Greece: The Age of Experiment* (London).

—— (1998), *Homer and the Artists: Text and Picture in Early Greek Art* (Cambridge).

SOLMSEN, F. (1975), *Intellectual Experiments of the Greek Enlightenment* (Princeton).

SOMMERSTEIN, A. H. (1987), '*ΑΜΦΙΜΗΤΩΡ*', *CQ* 37: 498–500.

—— (1988), 'The End of Euripides' *Andromache*', *CQ* 38: 243–6.

—— (ed.) (1989), *Aeschylus: Eumenides* (Cambridge).

SOREL, R. (1994), *Les Cosmogonies grecques* (Paris).

SORUM, C. E. (1995), 'Euripides' Judgement: Literary Creation in *Andromache*', *AJP* 116: 371–88.

SOURVINOU-INWOOD, C. (1990), 'What is Polis Religion?', in O. Murray and S. Price (eds.), *The Greek City: From Homer to Alexander* (Oxford), 295–322.

—— (1997), 'Tragedy and Religion: Constructs and Readings', in C. Pelling (ed.), *Greek Tragedy and the Historian* (Oxford), 160–86.

SPIRA, A. (1960), *Untersuchungen zum Deus ex machina bei Sophokles und Euripides* (Kallmünz).

STÄHLIN, F. (1924), *Das hellenische Thessalien* (Stuttgart).

STEIDLE, W. (1968), *Studien zum antiken Drama unter besonderer Berücksichtigung des Bühnenspiels* (Munich).

STEINER, G. (1967), *Language and Silence* (London).

——(1996), 'Tragedy, Pure and Simple', in M. S. Silk (ed.), *Tragedy and the Tragic: The Greek Theatre and Beyond* (Oxford), 534–46.

STEPHANOPOULOS, T. K. (1980), *Umgestaltung des Mythos durch Euripides* (Athens).

STEVENS, P. T. (ed.) (1971), *Euripides:* Andromache (Oxford).

——(1976), *Colloquial Expressions in Euripides* (Wiesbaden).

STINTON, T. C. W. (1990), *Collected Papers on Greek Tragedy* (Oxford).

STOREY, I. C. (1993), 'Domestic Disharmony in Euripides' *Andromache*', in I. McAuslan and P. Walcot (eds.), *Greek Tragedy* (Oxford), 180–192.

STROHM, H. (1957), *Euripides: Interpretationen zur dramatischen Form* (Munich).

——(1977), 'Zur Gestaltung euripideischer Prologreden', *Grazer Beiträge*, 6: 113–32.

SUTTON, D. F. (1981), 'Critias and Atheism', *CQ* 31: 33–8.

——(1984), *The Lost Sophocles* (New York).

SZONDI, P. (1978), *Versuch über das Tragische* (Frankfurt am Main).

TAPLIN, O. P. (1977), *The Stagecraft of Aeschylus* (Oxford).

——(1986), 'Fifth-Century Tragedy and Comedy: A *Synkrisis*', *JHS* 106: 163–74.

——(1992), *Homeric Soundings: The Shaping of the* Iliad (Oxford).

——(1993), *Comic Angels and Other Approaches to Greek Drama through Vase-Paintings* (Oxford).

——(1996), 'Comedy and the Tragic', in M. S. Silk (ed.), *Tragedy and the Tragic: The Greek Theatre and Beyond* (Oxford), 188–202.

——(1999), 'Spreading the Word through Performance', in R. Osborne and S. Goldhill (eds.), *Performance Culture and Athenian Democracy* (Cambridge), 33–57.

TAPLIN, O. and WILSON, P. (1993), 'The Aetiology of Tragedy in the *Oresteia*', *PCPS* 39: 169–80.

THIEL, R. (1993), *Chor und tragische Handlung im 'Agamemnon' des Aischylos* (Stuttgart).

THOMAS, R. (1989), *Oral Tradition and Written Record in Classical Athens* (Cambridge).

——(1994), 'Literacy and the City-State in Archaic and Classical

Greece', in A. K. Bowman and G. Woolf (eds.), *Literacy and Power in the Ancient World* (Cambridge), 33–50.

TIGERSTEDT, E. N. (1965), *The Legend of Sparta in Classical Antiquity. Vol. 1* (Stockholm).

TODD, S. C. (1993), *The Shape of Athenian Law* (Oxford).

TRENDELL, A. D. (1991), 'Farce and Tragedy in South Italian Vase-Painting', in T. Rasmussen and N. Spivey (eds.), *Looking at Greek Vases* (Cambridge), 151–82.

USHER, S. (1999), *Greek Oratory: Tradition and Originality* (Oxford).

VAN ERP TAALMAN KIP, A. M. (1996), 'The Unity of the Oresteia', in M. Silk (ed.), *Tragedy and the Tragic: The Greek Theatre and Beyond* (Oxford), 119–38.

VELLACOTT, P. (1975), *Ironic Drama: A Study of Euripides' Method and Meaning* (Cambridge).

VERNANT, J.-P. (1980), *Myth and Society in Ancient Greece*, tr. J. Lloyd (Brighton).

——(1991), *Mortals and Immortals: Collected Essays*, ed. F. Zeitlin (Princeton).

VERNANT, J.-P. and VIDAL-NAQUET, P. (1988), *Myth and Tragedy in Ancient Greece*, tr. J. Lloyd (2nd edn., New York).

VERRALL, A. W. (1905), *Essays on Four Plays of Euripides* (Cambridge).

VERSNEL, H. S. (1990), *Inconsistencies in Greek and Roman Religion. Vol. 1 Ter Unus* (Leiden).

VEYNE, P. (1988), *Did the Greeks Believe in their Myths?*, tr. P. Wissing (Chicago).

VICKERS, B. (1973), *Towards Greek Tragedy: Drama, Myth, Society* (London).

VOGT, S. (1998), 'Delphi in der attischen Tragödie', *A&A* 44: 30–48.

WALBANK, F. W. (1967), *A Historical Commentary on Polybius, Volume II, Books VII–XVIII* (Oxford).

WALCOTT, D. (1987), *The Arkansas Testament* (London).

WALKER, H. J. (1995), *Theseus and Athens* (Oxford).

WARDY, R. (1996), *The Birth of Rhetoric: Gorgias, Plato and their Successors* (London).

WARMINGTON, E. H. (1936), *Remains of Old Latin, Vol. 2* (Cambridge, Mass.).

WEBSTER, T. B. L. (1967), *The Tragedies of Euripides* (London).

——(1970), *The Greek Chorus* (London).

——(1971), *Greek Tragedy* (Oxford).

WEST, M. L. (1974), *Studies in Greek Elegy and Iambus* (Berlin).

——(1980), 'Tragica IV', *BICS* 27: 9–22.

——(1982), *Greek Metre* (Oxford).

WEST, M. L. (1990), 'Colloquialism and Naïve Style in Aeschylus', in E. Craik (ed.), *'Owls to Athens'* (Oxford), 3–12.

——(1992), *Ancient Greek Music* (Oxford).

——(1996), *Die griechische Dichterin: Bild und Rolle* (Stuttgart).

——(1997), *The East Face of Helicon: West Asiatic Elements in Greek Poetry and Myth* (Oxford).

WEST, S., HEUBECK, A., and HAINSWORTH, J. B. (eds.) (1988), *A Commentary on Homer's Odyssey. Vol. I: Books I–VIII* (Oxford).

WESTLAKE, H. D. (1968), *Individuals in Thucydides* (Cambridge).

——(1969), *Thessaly in the Fourth Century* B.C. (Gröningen).

WHITEHEAD, D. (1986), *The Demes of Attica 508/7–ca. 250 B.C.* (Princeton).

WHITMAN, C. H. (1974), *Euripides and the Full Circle of Myth* (Oxford).

WILAMOWITZ-MOELLENDORFF, U. VON (1875), *Analecta Euripidea* (Berlin).

——(1921), *Griechische Verskunst* (Berlin).

——(1959), *Euripides Herakles. Erster Band: Einleitung in die griechische Tragödie* (4th edn., Darmstadt).

——(1962), 'Lesefrüchte 193–202', in *Kleine Schriften. Vol. IV* (Berlin), 368–403 [= *Hermes* (1925) 60: 280–316].

——(1970), 'Pindars siebentes nemeisches Gedicht', in W. M. Calder and J. Stern (eds.), *Pindaros und Bakchylides* (Darmstadt), 127–58.

WILES, D. (1997), *Tragedy in Athens: Performance Space and Theatrical Meaning* (Cambridge).

WILKINS, J. (ed.) (1993), *Euripides:* Heraclidae (Oxford).

WILLCOCK, M. M. (ed.) (1995), *Pindar: Victory Odes* (Cambridge).

WILLIAMS, B. (1993), *Shame and Necessity* (Berkeley).

WILLINK, C. W. (ed.) (1986), *Euripides:* Orestes (Oxford).

WILSON, P. J. (1996), 'Tragic Rhetoric: The Use of Tragedy and the Tragic in the Fourth Century', in M. S. Silk (ed.), *Tragedy and the Tragic: The Greek Theatre and Beyond* (Oxford), 310–31.

WINKLER, J. (1990), *The Constraints of Desire: The Anthropology of Sex and Gender in Ancient Greece* (New York).

WINNINGTON-INGRAM, R. P. (1948), *Euripides and Dionysus: An Interpretation of the Bacchae* (Cambridge).

——(1969), 'Euripides: *Poietes Sophos*', *Arethusa*, 2: 127–42.

——(1980), *Sophocles: An Interpretation* (Cambridge).

WITTGENSTEIN, L. (1984), *Über Gewißheit*, ed. G. H. von Wright, Suhrkamp Werkausgabe Band 8 (Frankfurt am Main).

WOODBURY, L. (1979), 'Neoptolemus at Delphi: Pindar, *Nem.* 7.30 ff.', *Phoenix* 33: 95–133.

XANTHAKIS-KARAMANOS, G. (1980). *Studies in Fourth-Century Tragedy* (Athens).

——(1986), '*P. Oxy.* 3317: Euripides' *Antigone* (?)', *BICS* 33: 107–11.

YAMAGATA, N. (1994), *Homeric Morality* (Leiden).

YUNIS, H. (1988), *A New Creed: Fundamental Religious Beliefs in the Athenian Polis and Euripidean Drama* (Göttingen).

ZAGAGI, N. (1994), *The Comedy of Menander: Convention, Variation and Originality* (London).

ZEITLIN, F. I. (1980), 'The Closet of Masks: Role-Playing and Myth-Making in the *Orestes* of Euripides', *Ramus*, 9: 51–77.

——(1990), 'Playing the Other: Theater, Theatricality, and the Feminine in Greek Drama', in J. J. Winkler and F. I. Zeitlin (eds.), *Nothing to Do with Dionysos?* (Princeton), 63–96.

ZIMMERMANN, B. (1992), *Die griechische Tragödie: Eine Einführung* (2nd edn., Munich).

ZUNTZ, G. (1965), *An Inquiry into the Transmission of the Plays of Euripides* (Cambridge).

ZÜRCHER, W. (1947), *Die Darstellung des Menschen im Drama des Euripides* (Basle).

INDEX OF *ANDROMACHE* PASSAGES

GENERAL INDEX